The Struggle for Power in Early Modern Europe

PRINCETON STUDIES IN INTERNATIONAL
HISTORY AND POLITICS

SERIES EDITORS

G. John Ikenberry and Marc Trachtenberg

RECENT TITLES

The Struggle for Power in Early Modern Europe: Religious Conflict, Dynastic Empires, and International Change by Daniel H. Nexon

Strong Borders, Secure Nation: Cooperation and Conflict in China's Territorial Disputes by M. Taylor Fravel

The Sino-Soviet Split by Lorenz M. Lüthi

Nuclear Logics: Contrasting Paths in East Asia and the Middle East by Etel Solingen

Social States: China in International Institutions, 1980–2000 by Alastair Iain Johnston

Appeasing Bankers by Jonathan Kirshner

The Politics of Secularism in International Relations by Elizabeth Shakman Hurd

Unanswered Threats: Political Constraints on the Balance of Power by Randall L. Schweller

Producing Security: Multinational Corporations, Globalization, and the Changing Calculus of Conflict by Stephen G. Brooks

Driving the Soviets up the Wall: Soviet-East German Relations, 1953–1961 by Hope M. Harrison

Legitimacy and Power Politics: The American and French Revolutions in International-political Culture by Mlada Bukovansky

Rhetoric and Reality in Air Warfare: The Evolution of British and American Ideas about Strategic Bombing, 1914–1945 by Tami Davis Biddle

Revolutions in Sovereignty: How Ideas Shaped Modern International Relations by Daniel Philpott

The Struggle for Power in Early Modern Europe

RELIGIOUS CONFLICT,
DYNASTIC EMPIRES,
AND INTERNATIONAL CHANGE

Daniel H. Nexon

PRINCETON UNIVERSITY PRESS
PRINCETON AND OXFORD

Copyright 2009 © by Princeton University Press
Published by Princeton University Press, 41 William Street, Princeton: New Jersey 08540
In the United Kingdom: Princeton University Press, 6 Oxford Street,
Woodstock, Oxfordshire OX20 1TW

All Rights Reserved

Library of Congress Cataloging-in-Publication Data

Nexon, Daniel H.
  The struggle for power in early modern Europe : religious conflict, dynastic empires, and international change / Daniel H. Nexon.
    p. cm. — (Princeton studies in international history and politics)
  Includes bibliographical references and index.
  ISBN 978-0-691-13792-6 (alk. paper) — ISBN 978-0-691-13793-3 (alk. paper)
  1. Europe—Politics and government—1517–1648. I. Title.
  D217.N49 2009
  940.2′32—dc22   2008042219

British Library Cataloging-in-Publication Data is available

This book has been composed in Sabon

Printed on acid-free paper. ∞

press.princeton.edu

Printed in the United States of America

10 9 8 7 6 5 4 3 2 1

*This book is dedicated to
the memory of Charles Tilly*

Contents

List of Figures and Tables	ix
Preface	xi
CHAPTER 1 Introduction	1
CHAPTER 2 Theorizing International Change	20
CHAPTER 3 The Dynastic-Imperial Pathway	67
CHAPTER 4 Religious Contention and the Dynamics of Composite States	99
CHAPTER 5 The Rise and Decline of Charles of Habsburg	135
CHAPTER 6 The Dynamics of Spanish Hegemony in the Sixteenth and Early Seventeenth Centuries	185
CHAPTER 7 The French Wars of Religion	235
CHAPTER 8 Westphalia Reframed	265
CHAPTER 9 Looking Forward, Looking Back	289
References	301
Index	333

Figures and Tables

Figures

1.1	Anarchy and Hierarchy as Relational Structures	15
2.1	Simple Patron-Client Network	43
2.2	Network Density	44
2.3	Variation in Relational Contexts and Collective Mobilization	49
2.4	The States-under-Anarchy Framework as a Nested Relational Configuration	54
2.5	Hypothetical Relational Configuration of "Weak States"	59
2.6	Stylized Representation of the French and the Spanish Domains during the Dutch Revolt and the French Wars of Religion	60
3.1	Contracting, Rule, and State Forms	73
3.2	Europe Prior to the Ascension of Charles of Habsburg	74
4.1	Ideal-Typical Structure of Imperial Composite States	102
4.2	"Firewalls" Limit the Spread of Resistance	107
4.3	Trans-Segment Ties Lead to Coordinated Resistance	110
4.4	Uncoordinated Resistance in Multiple Segments	112
5.1	The Domains of Charles V	136
5.2	Iberia at the Time of Charles V	139
5.3	The German Empire at the Election of Charles V	151
5.4	The German Empire on the Eve of the War of Schmalkald	174
6.1	The Domains of Philip II	187
6.2	The Netherlands Prior to the Dutch Revolt	195
6.3	Disposition of the Provinces of the Low Countries during the Later Phases of the Dutch Revolt	217
7.1	France at the Middle of the Sixteenth Century	237

7.2 Religious Divisions after the St. Bartholomew's
     Day Massacre   252
8.1a The 1648 Peace of Westphalia: Europe   274
8.1b The 1648 Peace of Westphalia: The German Empire   275

Table

7.1 Chronology of the French Wars of Religion   238

Preface

I BEGAN THIS PROJECT with the aim of demonstrating the significance of the Reformations in the development of the sovereign-territorial state and system. But as I pushed further into history and theory, its focus changed dramatically. I realized that the historical evidence, in fact, undermined the contention that the Reformations played an expansive role in the emergence of sovereign territoriality. I also discovered that, for all the energy expended by international-relations scholars on this issue, few had even scratched the surface of an important puzzle: why the Reformations produced a crisis in the European political order. I could make sense of this puzzle, furthermore, by treating the Reformations era as a case of translocal and trans-state religious contention interacting with the dynamics of resistance and rule in composite polities that, in turn, had more in common with empires than with nation-states.

Although I always thought this insight important, it took on added significance in the aftermath of the September 11, 2001, terrorist attacks on Washington, D.C., and New York City. Scholars, pundits, and policymakers developed a renewed interest in the nexus between international relations and religion. The American-led invasions of Afghanistan and Iraq placed the concept of "empire" back on the agenda. While I argue against attempts to unproblematically generalize from past experiences to contemporary concerns, I cannot deny that the events of the last few years profoundly inflected the final form of this study. At the very least, my findings challenge some important assumptions about both of these issues in the policy and international-relations literatures.

This book also engages with international-relations theory, particularly as it relates to the analysis of international change. Many of my specific arguments about the impact of the Protestant Reformations on European politics, appropriate forms of comparative-historical generalization, and the entire question of whether the period under study comprises a case of international change derive from a theoretical approach I term "relational institutionalism." I have some doubts about introducing such a neologism into the vocabulary of the discipline. Not a few among those who have commented upon—or even served as reviewers of—earlier drafts, have questioned why I do not simply use the existing terms "relationalism" or "historical institutionalism" to describe my approach.

The fact that some see my approach as fundamentally relationalist while others see it as ultimately historical institutionalist provides at least some justification for concluding that neither existing body of work, on its own, captures its analytic sensibilities. I offer other reasons for this conclusion, at least implicitly, in the body of the book. But the conjunction also provides a constant reminder, at least for me, of my profound debts to my two primary graduate-school advisors: Ira Katznelson and the late Chuck Tilly. From the former I learned to think as an historical institutionalist, from the latter as a relationalist. I see both scholars as the intellectual parents of this book, and although Ira may not care for the motley offspring found within its pages, Chuck almost certainly wouldn't have. But it represents a mimetic hybrid of the ideas and sensibilities I absorbed from both of them.

I will have more to say about both Ira and Chuck later. For now, let me note that the earliest stages of this project began roughly eleven years ago. Such a long gestation carries with it a mixed blessing. On the one hand, it has benefited from the support of a great many people and institutions. On the other hand, so many debts make omissions in my list of acknowledgments inevitable. To those of you whom I should have acknowledged but forgot to, I apologize in advance.

I completed important parts of this project while a residential fellow at the Center for International Security and Cooperation (CISAC) at Stanford University and at the Mershon Center for International Studies at Ohio State University. The Berkley Center for Religion, Peace, and World Affairs at Georgetown University provided me with crucial intellectual and financial support. I also extend my gratitude to participants in seminars at CISAC, Mershon, the University of Minnesota's Department of Political Science, the Norwegian Institute of International Affairs, the Center for International Studies at the University of Southern California, the Mortara Center for International Studies at Georgetown University, the Lansing Lee Seminar at the University of Virginia, and the Workshop on Contentious Politics and the Harriman Institute at Columbia University.

For support, comments, and advice on various components of this project, I would also like to thank my colleagues at Georgetown University, as well as Fiona Adamson, Matthias Albert, David Auerswald, Tarak Barkarwi, Karin Barkey, Peter Bearman, Mark Blyth, Mlada Bukovansky, Jane Burbank, Barry Buzan, Benjamin de Carvalho, Jeffrey Checkel, Fred Chernoff, Alex Cooley, Frederick Cooper, Dale Copeland, Consuelo Cruz, Jack Donnelly, Raymond Duvall, David Edelstein, Lyn Eden, James Fearon, Yale Ferguson, Martha Finnemore, Rodney Bruce Hall, John Haslam, Ron Hassner, Michael Hechter, Emile Hafner-Burton, Richard Herrmann, Ted Hopf, Peter Katzenstein, Robert Keohane, Charles King, Markus Kornprobst, Fritz Kratochwil, Ronald Krebs, Mark Laffey, David Lake, Jospeh Lapid, George Lawson, Adrienne LeBas, Richard Ned Lebow, Jeffrey Legro, Halvard Leira, David Leon, Charles Lipson,

Paul MacDonald, Alex Macleod, Richard Mansbach, Janice Bially Mattern, David McBride, Kate McNamara, Jennifer Mitzen, Alex Montgomery, John Mueller, Iver Neumann, Geoffrey Parker, Vincent Pouliot, Richard Price, Chris Reus-Smit, Scott Sagan, Herman Schwartz, Randall Schweller, Vivek Sharma, Lee Sigelman, Hendrik Spruyt, Jennifer Sterling-Folker, Sherrill Stroschein, George Thomas, Alex Thompson, Kenneth Waltz, Jutta Weldes, Alexander Wendt, Colin Wight, and William Wohlforth. In truth, all of these individuals deserve special words of gratitude. Each of them showed tremendous generosity toward me, sometimes in spite of the fact that my work often, directly or indirectly, criticized their own scholarship. I hope, not least in this respect, to treat others with the same kindness and openness that they have shown to me.

I have also benefited enormously from the comments of anonymous reviewers and those who have subsequently disclosed their identities to me, including Edward Keene, Richard Little, and Daniel Philpott. I admit that I did not always follow their recommendations, and I recognize that the manuscript likely suffers from my failure to do so. Edward Keene, in particular, suggested that I engage directly with the new wave of Marxist-inspired work on international change. In a perfect world, I would have done so, as the work of Justin Rosenberg, Benno Teschke, and their intellectual compatriots deserves extended discussion.

I thank my editors at Princeton University Press, G. John Ikenberry and Chuck Myers, for their efforts on behalf of this book. They both provided, at every stage of this manuscript, invaluable assistance. I am also grateful to Heath Renfroe and the other members of the production team at Princeton: as well as to Jon Munk for the arduous task of copyediting the manuscript.

A version of chapter 4 first appeared as "What's at Stake in the American Empire Debate" in the *American Political Science Review*. I extend special appreciation to its coauthor, Thomas Wright, who deserves much credit and none of the blame for the arguments contained within it.

Stacie Goddard and Patrick Thaddeus Jackson have been my friends and collaborators since graduate school. Through our discussions, discoveries of articles and books to share with one another, exercises in coauthorship, and reading of one another's work we have often reached a point at which none of us can assign sole credit for even the origination of particular ideas and insights. My friends in the field like to joke, in particular, that Patrick and I "share a brain." While aspects of this book should lay that notion to rest, my intellectual debts to both Stacie and Patrick remain enormous.

The same is true of my wife, Maia Gemmill. I have been blessed with a spouse who not only reads, edits, and comments upon my work, but also serves as a genuine intellectual collaborator. My obligations to Maia, of course, extend well beyond the realm of ideas, as they do to my parents, David and Philaine Nexon. I am very lucky to have parents even willing to attempt to read their son's academic work.

I find it difficult to express the scope of my gratitude to Ira Katznelson, Jack Snyder, Wayne te Brake, and Chuck Tilly. Each, as the phrase goes, is a real mensch, as was Chuck. Everyone who has enjoyed the privilege of working with Jack already knows of his generosity toward graduate students, and that his support extends to those who share neither his interests nor his theoretical orientations. Wayne offered me his friendship and mentorship despite having no stake in my success or failure. He provided crucial assistance in the matters of historical accuracy and interpretation, and whatever mistakes I have made occur despite his best efforts. In many ways I view this book as a footnote to his terrific *Shaping History: Ordinary People in European Politics, 1500–1700*.

Ira exemplifies what it means to be both a scholar and an intellectual, a combination increasingly rare in the academy. He never loses sight of what really matters, including the ethical dimension of scholarship. While many of us fall prey to the petty divisions of methodological camps, Ira seeks to build intellectual bridges and preserve the social sciences as a joint enterprise of knowledge production for the greater good. Ira's attitude toward scholarship finds reflection in his style of mentorship. He is always supportive, but never shrinks from reminding his students to cultivate their better natures. Despite his powerful intellect and stature in the field, Ira has little interest in producing a cadre of graduate students to advance his particular way of parsing the world. He lets his students figure things out for themselves; if we come to similar conclusions as he, we do so through our own critical reasoning.

What can I possibly say about Chuck Tilly that an endless number of his students and peers have not already written in their prefaces? I hope the others I thank will take no offense if I describe his as the most powerful intellect I have ever encountered in the social sciences. I expect that people will still be reading and debating his enormous and varied corpus of work for decades to come. Yet Chuck treated all of his students as members of an intellectual community of equals. He sought out their opinions; he discussed his own views with humility and an open mind. Chuck carefully and quickly read everything I sent him—his rapid turnaround of others' work, like Jack's, was legendary—and never imposed his views upon me. Instead, Chuck would make subtle suggestions that, once I worked through them, had profound implications for my research. If he sensed a contradiction or tension in my arguments, he would never tell me how to resolve it. Instead, he would alert me and explain that I needed to make a decision about which interpretation I wanted to pursue. I know that my penchant for endless discussion—of ideas, of personal challenges, and just about everything else—must have repeatedly strained his tolerance, but he never turned me away. I could not have hoped for a better mentor.

I also offer many thanks to Darcy Kern and Lindsay Pettingill for compiling an excellent glossary that, unfortunately, had to be cut from the final manuscript. Darcy also copyedited the manuscript and checked for historical errors. Andrew Rolfson, operating under the auspices of Georgetown University's Office of Scholarly and Literary Publications, produced the many fine maps found in the book.

Finally, I want to extend a different kind of acknowledgment. To my daughter, Lyra, I write the following: you cannot possibly understand right now how much you have inspired me and enriched my life over the last four years. Perhaps one day you will read the preface to your father's first academic monograph and appreciate these words.

The Struggle for Power in Early Modern Europe

CHAPTER 1

Introduction

IN JUNE 1546 Charles V, Holy Roman Emperor and ruler of a vast realm stretching from the New World to Central Europe, began preparations for war against the rebellious towns and princes of the Protestant Schmalkaldic League. He explained to his sister, Mary of Hungary, that

> if we failed to intervene now, all the Estates of Germany would be in danger of breaking with the faith . . . After considering this and considering it again, I decided to embark on war against Hesse and Saxony as transgressors of the peace against the Duke of Brunswick and his territory. And although the pretext will not long disguise the fact that this is a matter of religion, yet it serves for the present to divide the renegades.[1]

Charles's gambit inverts one of the standard stories found in political-science scholarship: that elites use the rhetoric of identity—whether religious, ethnic, or nationalist—as a way of generating support for policies that, in truth, serve their own power-political or material ends. Critics often challenge such stories, of course. They argue that a particular set of claims about identity reveal the genuine interests of elites. Or they suggest that even if elites deploy identity claims cynically, we still need to understand why such claims succeed or fail in generating popular support for particular policies.[2] We seldom, however, envision the reverse: that a head of state might seek to fragment the opposition by hiding his *religious* objectives behind a cloak of *political* rhetoric.

It is even more striking, then, that Charles's divide-and-rule tactics met with initial success; his forces scored a decisive victory in the Schmalkaldic War. But at the 1547–1548 Diet of Augsburg, he overplayed his hand. The 1548 Interim of Augsburg sought to reconcile religious schism in Germany, but instead prompted a new Protestant alliance against Charles.

---

[1] Quoted in Bonney 1991, 118. Cf. Repgen's interpretation, which argues that Charles does not, in this letter, "expressly concede . . . that his public justification of the Schmalkaldic War is only a pretense and a pretext." See Repgen 1987, 319–20.

[2] Fearon and Laitin 2000; Gagnon 1994–1995; Van Evera 1994, 30–33. For critical views, see Barnett 1999 and Kaufman 1996. For an overview and discussion of "instrumentalist" approaches to the relationship between religion and conflict, see Hasenclever and Rittberger 2000, 644–50.

With the support of the French king, Henry II of Valois, it seized the offensive against Charles and his supporters. Charles's brother, Ferdinand, opened negotiations with the rebels. Ferdinand ultimately concluded the 1555 Peace of Augsburg. Charles abdicated his titles and divided his domain between Ferdinand and Charles's son, Philip II of Spain.[3]

This chain of events represents only one puzzling part of a much larger story: *how the Protestant Reformations led to a profound crisis in the European political order.*[4] Over the course of the sixteenth and seventeenth centuries, the emergence of new forms of religious heterodoxy catapulted much of the European continent into violent conflict, caused political authority in entire states and regions to implode, and destroyed the Habsburg bid for European hegemony. Despite significant attention to early modern Europe among international-relations scholars, few treat these events as an explanatory puzzle. Some look to the period merely for evidence of the enduring struggle for security and domination among great powers. Others expend a great deal of energy arguing over whether or not the Protestant Reformations, and the 1648 Peace of Westphalia, which supposedly put an end to inter-state religious conflict in Europe, marked the origins of the modern, sovereign-territorial state system.[5]

Contemporary developments render our comparative lack of interest in the dynamics of religious struggles in early modern Europe all the more puzzling. We live, many tell us, in an age of religious revival. Anxieties about violent religious movements now exercise a strong influence over foreign and domestic policy in the United States, Europe, and many other political communities. Most existing attempts to draw "lessons" from the European experience, unfortunately, suffer from extraordinary superficiality or a terminal infatuation with stylized stories about European political development. Thus, serious policy analysts inform their readers that "Islam's problem" is that it never had a "Westphalian moment." Some suggest, similarly, that Islam needs a "reformation" that will break the hold of its clerics and usher in an era of tolerant religious pluralism and secularism.[6] Henry C. K. Liu, writing in the *Asia Times Online*, draws an even more breathtaking set of analogies:

> The Peace of Westphalia ended the Thirty Years' War, a secular war with religious dimensions. Subsequent wars were not about spiritual issues of religion, but rather revolved around secular issues of state.

---

[3] For a detailed account of these events, see chapter 5.

[4] Most historical and social-scientific texts refer to "the Reformation." I write of "the Reformations" to stress the temporal, spatial, and doctrinal heterogeneity of reformation movements during the early modern period.

[5] See Gross 1948, Krasner 1993, Osiander 2001, Philpott 2000 and 2001, and Teschke 2003.

[6] Miles 2003, Wilson 2002.

The "war on terrorism" today is the first religious war in almost four centuries, also fought mainly by secular institutions with religious affiliations. The peace that eventually follows today's "war on terrorism" will also end the war between faith-based Christian evangelicals and Islamic fundamentalists. Westphalia allowed Catholic and Protestant powers to become allies, leading to a number of major secular geopolitical realignments. The "war on terrorism" will also produce major geopolitical realignments in world international politics, although it is too early to discern its final shape . . . . [It] will eventually lay to rest U.S. hegemony and end the age of superpower, possibly through a new balance of power by sovereign states otherwise not particularly hostile to the United States as a peaceful nation.[7]

Whatever the merits of these claims, the fact remains that international-relations theorists have been staring directly into the face of a rich and consequential case of the impact of transregional and transnational religious movements on conflict, resistance, political authority, and international change for decades. Yet we have mounted few sustained investigations into its causal processes and mechanisms.[8]

This book addresses, first and foremost, this oversight: *I provide an explanation for why the Protestant Reformations produced a crisis of sufficient magnitude to alter the European balance of power, both within and among even its most powerful political communities.* I argue that the key to understanding this impact lies in the analysis of the dynamics of resistance and rule in the composite political communities that dominated the European landscape. Many of the most important political ramifications of the Protestant Reformations did not stem from any sui generis features of religious contention; they resulted from the intersection of heterogeneous religious movements with ongoing patterns of collective mobilization.

Religious contention, given particular formal properties and specific ideational content, triggered up to five processes extremely dangerous to the stability of early modern rule:

- It overcame the institutional barriers that tended to localize resistance against the rulers of composite states, thereby making widespread mobilization against dynastic rulers more likely.

---

[7] Liu 2005.
[8] Clark 1998, 1268. For exceptions, see Owen 2005, Philpott 2000 and 2001. Philpott's theory, as I argue below, fails to adequately capture these processes precisely because of his focus on religion as a source of ideas about political order that produced the sovereign state system. Owen's account dovetails with my own, but his decision to view religion as one source of inter-state ideological alignment misses other important dynamics set in motion by the Protestant Reformations.

- It undermined the ability of rulers to signal discrete identities to their heterogeneous subjects, thereby eroding their ability to legitimate their policies on a range of issues, from religion to taxation.
- It provided opportunities for intermediaries to enhance their own autonomy vis-à-vis dynastic rulers; religious contention complicated the tradeoffs inherent in the systems of indirect rule found in composite polities.
- It exacerbated cross-pressures on rulers—by injecting religious differentiation into the equation, by increasing the likelihood of significant resistance to central demands, and by creating often intense tradeoffs between political and religious objectives.
- It expanded already existing channels, as well as generated new vectors, for the "internationalization" of "domestic" disputes and the "domestication" of inter-state conflicts.

Given the right circumstances—a transnational, cross-class network surrounding religious beliefs and identities—the spread of the Protestant Reformations therefore activated many of the existing vulnerabilities in early modern European rule. Not every instance of religious contention, of course, produced all of these dynamics. Variation in institutional forms, the choices made by agents, and other contextual factors also influenced how these mechanisms and processes played out in particular times and places. And nonreligious contention sometimes triggered similar processes. On balance, however, the injection of religious identities and interests into ongoing patterns of resistance and rule made cascading political crises more likely than they might otherwise have been.

This explanation contributes to this book's secondary task: *to assess the status of the early modern period as a case of international change.* Was the early modern period, as Daniel Philpott suggests, a "revolution in sovereignty" or otherwise, as traditionally understood in international-relations theory, a key moment in the emergence of the modern state system?[9] My answer involves two claims. On the one hand, the Protestant Reformations shaped the development of the sovereign-territorial order, but in far more modest ways than many international-relations scholars assume. On the other hand, a better analytic approach to the concepts of "continuity and change" in world politics allows us to see what *kind* of a case of change the Reformations era represents: one of the rapid emergence of new actors—transnational religious movements—altering the structural opportunities and constraints of power-political competition.

The third, and final, goal of this book is *to specify precisely such an analytic framework for the study of international continuity and change.*

---

[9] Philpott 2000 and 2001.

I develop an approach to this problem, called "relational institutionalism," in the second chapter. It combines key aspects of sociological-relational analysis with historical-institutionalist sensibilities. This framework provides the theoretical infrastructure for my explanation of the book's primary puzzle, as well as for how we should understand early modern Europe as an instance of international change. But I also intend it to serve as a novel way of approaching inquiry into continuity and transformation in world politics. Relational institutionalism, I argue, incorporates insights from the major prevailing approaches to the study of international relations; it also provides a way of reconciling some of their apparently very different claims about the fundamental dynamics that drive international relations.

The next three sections of this chapter offer a more comprehensive introduction to these facets of the book. I provide greater detail with respect to my central argument about the impact of the Protestant Reformations on early modern European politics, and I briefly elaborate on my claims about the Reformations' role in the emergence of the sovereign-territorial state system. The second section situates the subject matter of this book within the broader debate about international change; the third section provides an overview of the analytic wagers and key claims associated with a relational-institutionalist approach to international change. In the final section, I discuss the organization of the rest of the book.

THE ARGUMENT

My argument begins with the most banal of claims: we cannot understand the political impact of the Protestant Reformations without reference to the institutional structures and dynamics of early modern European states. How, the reader might ask, could it be otherwise? Some of the most influential international-relations literature on international change in early modern Europe, I answer, pays very little attention to patterns of resistance and rule. Scholars too often content themselves with taking a "before" and "after" picture and then explaining the changes in between primarily through an assessment of the content of new religious beliefs and identities. This kind of analysis provides us with a great many insights, but it spends too much time in the realm of the spirit—of ideas, doctrines, and what constructivists call "constitutive norms"—and not enough in the profane world of political disputes over taxation and governance.[10]

---

[10] For an elaboration of this point, see Nexon 2005.

Princes, magnates, urban leaders, and ordinary people in early modern Europe pursued wealth, power, security, and status through the medium of existing authority relations and well-rehearsed forms of political contention. Their political struggles, within the confines of existing political communities, almost invariably involved disputes over the extent of local rights and privileges, the scope and distribution of taxation, and the relative power of different social classes.[11] Such conflicts often included what we would now call an "international" dimension. Princes, magnates, and even urban leaders sometimes negotiated, conspired, or allied with outside powers. Rulers exploited internal conflicts to advance their power-political interests and make good their territorial claims.[12]

Early modern European polities were neither radically decentralized "feudal" entities nor modern nation-states. Many historians now use the term "composite state" to describe the heterogeneous political communities that dominated the early modern European landscape. Whether confederative or imperial, ruled by hereditary or elected princes, or operating as autonomous republics, most early modern European states were composed of numerous subordinate political communities linked to central authorities through *distinctive contracts* specifying rights and obligations. These subordinate political communities often had their own social organizations, identities, languages, and institutions. Local actors jealously guarded whatever autonomy they enjoyed. Subjects expected rulers to uphold their contractual relationships: to guarantee what they perceived as "customary" rights and immunities in matters of taxation and local control.[13]

By the end of the fifteenth century, dynastic norms and practices almost completely dominated European high politics.[14] Rulers and would-be rulers competed to extend not only their own honor, prestige, and territory, but also that of their dynastic line. They did so through principles—marriage, conquest, inheritance, and succession—that, as Vivek Sharma argues, "were the primary organizing principles of European government for over six centuries."[15] As Richard Mackenney notes, for "those who governed, the interests of the family were all important" and that, in consequence, "the survival or extinction of the dynasty was the difference between peace and war, and the accidents of inheritance shaped the power blocs of Europe as a whole."[16]

---

[11] See te Brake 1998.

[12] See, generally, Bonney 1991 and Koenigsberger 1987.

[13] Elliott 1992; Koenigsberger 1986, 1–26; Oresko, Gibbs et al. 1997; te Brake 1998, 14–17.

[14] Mattingly 1988, 140.

[15] Sharma 2005, 8. Sharma's magisterial study constitutes the most thorough international-relations analysis of dynasticism yet written. For a Marxist variant, see Teschke 2003.

[16] Mackenney 1993, 219.

Dynastic rulers enjoyed important advantages over other political leaders, including superior access to the means of warfare and greater political legitimacy in the context of political expansion and consolidation. Such advantages meant that the most significant pathway of state formation in the late medieval and early modern periods was dynastic and agglomerative. In Wayne te Brake's words, "Most Europeans lived within composite states that had been cobbled together from pre-existing political units by a variety of aggressive 'princes' employing a standard repertoire of techniques including marriage, dynastic inheritance, and direct conquest."[17]

Charles of Habsburg's expansive monarchy presents the most spectacular case of dynastic agglomeration. Between 1515 and 1519, Charles acquired—as a result of contingencies of dynastic marriage, death, insanity, and political maneuvering—a realm including present-day Spain, the Netherlands and Belgium, parts of what is now Italy, Germany, and Austria, as well as Spain's New World possessions. He became king of the Romans and, later, emperor, which placed him in charge of the unwieldy Holy Roman Empire.[18] His wealth, territories, and his status as emperor "raised the spectre of a Habsburg universal monarchy in Europe, fuelled by the bullion of the Indies and the trade of Seville."[19]

Martin Luther began his public call for reformation of the Catholic Church in 1517. Historians and social scientists continue to debate why, and to what extent, Luther's actions sparked an explosion of heterodox challenges to the institutional structure and theological principles of the Catholic Church.[20] But his influence, and that of other religious leaders and movements, led to over a century and a half of tumult across Latin Christendom. The Reformations did so, as I have suggested, because of the ways they intersected with the underlying dynamics of early modern European politics.

Early modern European composite states suffered from chronic instabilities. They were, as we have seen, agglomerations of different peoples and territories divided by distinctive interests and identities. They enjoyed comparatively weak coercive and extractive capacity and relied largely on indirect rule through magnates, urban oligarchs, and other elites who often pursued their own interests and agendas. Endemic dynastic conflicts, for their part, outstripped the extractive capacities of early modern states, engendering resistance and rebellion among their subjects. Dynastic composite states, moreover, experienced recurrent succession crises.

[17] te Brake 1998, 14.
[18] Bonney 1991, 109.
[19] Armitage 1998a, xix.
[20] See Elton 1964, Fernández-Armesto and Wilson 1996, Kittelson 1986, Lambert 1977, Matheson 1998, McGrath 2004, Ozment 1975, and Tracy 1999.

Dynastic succession only functioned smoothly if a ruler lived long enough to produce a competent male heir old enough to assume the reins of power. In an era of high infant mortality and minimally effective medical care, disputed successions occurred with great frequency.[21]

Many of these sources of instability, however, also conferred specific benefits to dynastic rulers. First, the composite quality of early modern states created strong firewalls against the spread of resistance and rebellion. Because subjects in different holdings had different identities and interests, and because they were ruled via distinctive contractual relations, they had little motivation or capacity to coordinate their resistance against the centralizing impulses of their rulers.

Second, the underlying bargains of composite states reflected and exacerbated the stratification of early modern European society along divisions of class and status. Composite states distributed rights and privileges among urban centers, aristocrats, and rural society in such a way that for one group to gain an advantage meant a diminishment in the position of another. Rulers exploited these fault lines through strategies of extending differential privileges, such as granting exemptions to nobles to secure their loyalty during periods of urban unrest.

Subjects riven by class and regional differences could not easily join together to oppose their rulers. Dynastic agglomerations, therefore, usually only suffered widespread internal conflict under three conditions: when exogenous shocks, such as famines, led to generalized unrest; when rulers severely overreached in their demands and thus provoked simultaneous uprisings; or when a succession crisis drew in contending elites from across the dynastic agglomeration in the high stakes struggle over who would control the center.[22]

Early modern struggles over central and local control, taxation, and the distribution of rights and privileges were often contentious; they usually ended in blood and tears. But only under specific circumstances did they spiral out of control and risk collapsing central authority. The spread of heterodox religious movements intersected with sources of chronic instability in early modern Europe and made them more dangerous. At the most basic level, once a dispute over tax collection took on religious dimensions, the stakes became even higher: the ultimate fate of one's immortal soul. The interjection of religious disputes into routine political disagreements rendered them much more difficult to resolve.

The spread of heterodox religious movements also produced new social ties centering around common religious identities and grievances. These

---

[21] Sharma 2005, 16.

[22] te Brake 1998, 14–21. For a general discussion of these factors, see Zagorin 1982a and 1982b.

ties often crossed regional, class, and even state boundaries. In doing so, they created the potential for the most dangerous kinds of resistance to rulers—insurrections that were well funded, militarily capable, highly motivated, and that mobilized diverse peoples and interests against their rulers.

Religious disagreements were neither necessary nor sufficient to produce such rebellions. Religious conflict played, at best, an indirect part in the Catalan (1640–1652) and Portuguese (1640–1668) revolts against the Habsburgs and the French *Fronde* (1648–1653). All of the major "wars of religion," in fact, involved disputes over some combination of taxation, local autonomy, succession, and factional control of the court. Religious movements, particularly if they had limited class or regional appeal, might actually hinder individuals and groups from forming effective alliances against their ruler's demands. The Dutch Revolt (1572–1609), the Schmalkaldic Wars (1546–1547), the French Wars of Religion (1562–1629), and other religious-political conflicts in early modern Europe all displayed aspects of this complex relationship, in which the spread of reformation interacted with the structural dynamics of resistance and rule to produce both a variety of different specific outcomes and an overall crisis in the European political order.

What, then, were the ultimate implications of the Protestant Reformations on international change in early modern Europe? Not, I argue, the emergence of a sovereign-territorial state system in 1648. The Reformations stretched early modern states to their limits. They nearly collapsed the French composite state and produced an independent Dutch polity locked in conflict with its erstwhile Habsburg overlords. The Reformations directly undermined the Habsburg bid for hegemony and weakened the dynastic agglomerative path of state formation. They expanded the conditions of possibility for the future construction of national, sovereign states by linking religious differences to territory.[23] As J. H. Elliott writes of Castile and England, "As strong core states of composite monarchies," both "sharpened their own distinctive identities during the religious upheavals of the sixteenth century, developing an acute, and aggressive, sense of their unique place in God's providential design."[24]

As many international-relations theorists note, the sixteenth and seventeenth centuries marked the rise of new theories of sovereignty, of notions of "reason of state," and of the balance of power.[25] The Reformations contributed to these developments. Most of the important theories of sovereignty developed in the period were reactions to the turmoil produced

---

[23] Gorski 1993, 1999, 2000, Schilling 1992.
[24] Elliott 1992, 59. See also Marx 2005.
[25] Armitage 1998a, xx.

by religious conflict.[26] Conflicts between dynastic and religious interests forced statesmen and scholars to justify their policies through doctrines of "necessity" and other conceptual innovations that held, in essence, that long-term religious goals should be made subservient, in the short-term, to security and power.[27] We cannot fully appreciate such conceptual changes in the absence of an understanding of the practical political consequences of the Reformations.

State institutions, if not the specific contours of dynastic agglomerations, weathered the storm of the Reformations. This fact suggests that we need to be extremely careful about overplaying the broad impact of religious contention on the emergence of the modern state.[28] Shifts in the nature of warfare and economic relations ultimately contributed more to the emergence of a Europe composed of sovereign-territorial and nation-states than did the introduction of new religious ideas.[29] But recognizing the more subtle impact of the Reformations on European state formation should not blind us to their importance in the study of international relations and international change.

Early Modern Europe as a Case of Political Change

The field of international relations has a strong "presentist" bias. Colin and Miriam Elman argue that "social scientists have an explicit mandate to seek out policy-relevant knowledge, and to answer the 'so what' question."[30] I believe that international-relations scholars study world politics, whether in its historical or contemporary manifestations, and that this "explicit mandate" justifies, on its own, analysis of the political impact of the Protestant Reformations. The study of early modern Europe, however, has important implications for the debate about continuity and change in international-relations scholarship.

One of the most enduring questions in international-relations theory—even before there was such a distinct field of inquiry—concerns whether the nature and conduct of world politics undergoes significant alterations over the course of time. Realists argue that their basic parameters are constant: world politics has been, and will always be, marked by a struggle for power between political communities. Cultural practices, norms,

---

[26] See Bodin 1992 and Hobbes 1951.
[27] Elliott 1984, Mackenney 1993.
[28] Glete 2002.
[29] Nexon 2005, 715–16.
[30] Elman and Elman 1997, 8.

beliefs, and identities may alter, but they themselves will never change the underlying texture of international relations.[31]

In this view they echo one of their canonical theorists, Niccolò Machiavelli, who chastised those who read history as if "the heavens, the sun, the elements, human beings had changed in their movement, organization, and capacities, and were quite different from what they were in days gone by."[32] Or, as Kenneth Waltz notes in his seminal but much-maligned *Theory of International Politics*, "State behavior varies more with differences of power than with differences in ideology, in internal structure of property relations, or in governmental form."[33]

A variety of other schools disagree. English-school scholars adopt a strongly historicist approach to world politics; they trace mutations in international society as a way of understanding the "primary institutions" that govern contemporary world politics.[34] A more recent approach, known as "constructivism," articulates a view of international relations as socially and historically contingent: as cultural and social relations alter, so, too, does the basic texture of international politics. "Anarchy," as the title of one of Alexander Wendt's well-known articles claims, "is what states make of it."[35]

Nonrealist scholars, in general, study international change with two objectives. They seek to demonstrate that the basic processes of international politics are far more malleable than realists suggest. But they also hope to discover from past instances of international change how present developments might alter the parameters of international relations in the not-so-distant future.[36] In this latter task, they are joined by those in the realist tradition who, while stressing the basic continuity of power-political competition—whether in the form of the rise and decline of hegemonic states or the workings of the balance-of-power mechanism— also want to understand how shifts in military technology, economic relations, and other factors might shape future struggles for power.[37] We need more, not fewer, inquiries into the two crucial questions of international-relations theory: how plastic the texture of international-relations really is and under what kinds of circumstances that texture undergoes significant alterations.

---

[31] See Mearsheimer 2001.
[32] Machiavelli 1994, 83.
[33] Waltz 1986, 329.
[34] Bull 1977, Bull and Watson 1984, Buzan 2004, Buzan and Little 2000, Watson 1992.
[35] Wendt 1992. See also Dessler 1989, Hobden and Hobson 2002, Onuf 1989, Ruggie 1998, and Wendt 1987, 1994, 1996.
[36] E.g., Bukovansky 2002, Hall 1999, Holsti 2004, Philpott 2001, Spruyt 1994.
[37] E.g., Gilpin 1981, Van Evera 1998

But all of this is merely prelude. No one can accuse international-relations scholarship of *lacking* interest in the development of the European state system. If anything, "eurocentrism" might be a more pressing problem for international-relations theory than its presentist bias.[38] So what, after all, does another study of early modern Europe contribute to our understanding of international continuity and change and the pressing problems of the day?

First, most international-relations scholars approach the period with the wrong set of questions. Many, as I noted at the outset, understand its significance primarily in terms of sovereignty, rather than as a case of the impact of religious contention on resistance, rule, and international conflict. They treat the most important question—why the Reformations led to a profound crisis in European politics—as, at best, subordinate to the debate over the relative importance of ideas, warfare, or economic change in the emergence of the modern state system. Realists, on the other hand, tend to see the fate of the Spanish monarchy as either an archetypal case of hegemonic overextension or the workings of the balance-of-power mechanism.[39] Both processes operated in the period, but their theoretical framework overlooks not only the role of religious contention in the defeat of the Habsburgs, but also the underlying mechanisms of resistance and rule that account for Habsburg overextension. As I argue in later chapters, Habsburg overextension stemmed less from an iron law of the rise and decline of great powers than from the politics of imperial management—problems exacerbated by religious politics.

Second, as Colin and Miriam Fendius Elman note, "the stakes are high" in matters of historical analogies "because once constructed, historical understandings have an important effect on political behavior."[40] The standard accounts of the period, as a key moment in the development of state sovereignty or as a straightforward process of hegemonic overexpansion and counterbalancing, inform not only international-relations theory but, at least indirectly, policymaking. We have already seen, moreover, that pundits and analysts struggling to make sense of the current era draw upon the early modern European experience. This study demonstrates the strengths and weaknesses of those analogies by providing a theoretically informed account of the consequences of the intersection of religious movements with hegemony, empire, and composite states in early modern Europe.

---

[38] Hui 2004 and 2005; Wong 1997.
[39] Gilpin 1981, 120–21, 164–65, 176–77; Kennedy 1987, 112; Kupchan 1996, 35; Walt 1985, 15.
[40] Elman and Elman 1997, 9–10.

Theorizing International Change

Many of the processes found in early modern Europe resonate with pressing concerns in the study of world politics: the rise of transregional and transnational religious movement; the fate of hegemonic powers, empires, and composite states; and the role of such processes in shaping (or not shaping) the fate of sovereign modes of authority. This book also advances a broader theoretical and analytical agenda: how we should approach questions of continuity and change in world politics.

International-relations scholars deploy a wide variety of analytical and theoretical frameworks in their studies of change. Realists focus on shifts in the relative power of states, the changing sources of military and economic power, and alterations in variables such as the relative efficacy of offensive and defensive operations. Their approach captures important features of political change in early modern Europe, but it comes up short in at least two crucial respects. It presupposes that the structure of early modern European politics approximates the states-under-anarchy framework deployed in realist theory. The composite character of early modern European states, as well as the structure of identity and authority relations generated by dynasticism, disappears from our purview.[41] Contemporary realist theory, furthermore, simply cannot make sense of the power-political dimensions of nonstate movements, let alone of how their dynamics might interface with different forms of state organization.[42]

The predominant constructivist and English-school accounts of international change focus on, variously, the autonomous role of beliefs and ideas, alterations in the constitutive norms of international politics, or the workings of international cultural systems. This allows them to treat practices and norms, such as dynasticism, as changing and alterable. It also creates far greater room to consider the role of nonstate actors in world politics. Yet it also leads to problematic accounts of international change. Some argue, for example, that change results from contradictions between various norms, beliefs, and practices that produce "legitimation crises" or, less usefully, from the alteration of norms, beliefs, and practices.[43]

Indeed, between predominant realist and social-constructivist accounts we face a set of unpalatable alternatives. Realists provide straightforward ways to generalize across time and space about processes of continuity and change. International systems, they argue, are characterized by anarchy—the lack of a common authority—and vary in terms of their distribu-

---
[41] See Osiander 2001, Sharma 2005, and Teschke 1998.
[42] See Keck and Sikkink 1998, Sikkink 1999.
[43] E.g., Hall 1999, Holsti 2004.

tion of power. Hegemonic, bipolar, and multipolar systems, they claim, involve broadly similar dynamics no matter where or when we find them. Constructivist scholarship makes clear the problem with this view: it obscures important differences in the structure and texture of international politics across time and space.[44] Yet because constructivists often render international structure in terms of a catalogue of unique norms, identities, and rules, they both make it difficult to generalize in useful ways about processes of change and they have difficulty "explaining the astonishingly similar types of . . . behavior evident across many different types of different polities, cultures, and historical eras."[45]

This book puts forward an alternative framework for understanding international continuity and change that I call "relational institutionalism." I elaborate this approach in the next chapter; here, I put forth some of its core principles. Relational institutionalism combines the historical-institutionalist insight that "institutions" operate as "ligatures fastening social sites, relationships, and large-scale processes to each other to produce historically variable outcomes"[46] with a sociological-relationalist understanding of structures as patterns of social interaction (social ties) that take on particular network properties.[47]

This approach provides us with a way to cut into what constructivists refer to as the "co-constitutive" relationship between agents and structures. Once we treat structures as networks composed of social transactions, it follows that structures exist by virtue of ongoing processes of interaction but simultaneously position actors in various structurally consequential positions relative to one another. This applies across different levels of aggregation: states themselves are network configurations, but they are also social sites—or collections of social sites—within the broader network-structure of the international system.[48] For example, we can say that the relationship between two actors is "anarchical" in the absence of relevant authoritative ties, either between one another or with a third social site (see Figure 1.1).[49] But these relations are a far cry from the full-blown states-under-anarchy conception of the international system found in realist theory.

---

[44] E.g., Biersteker and Weber 1996, Bukovansky 2002, Hall 1999, Hobson 2002, Hobson and Sharman 2005, Onuf 1989.
[45] Cooley 2005, 12.
[46] Katznelson 1997, 103.
[47] E.g., Emirbayer 1997, Jackson and Nexon 1999, Tilly 1995, 1997b, 1998.
[48] On agent-structure co-constitution, see Bhaskar 1989, Dessler 1989, Giddens 1984, 1995, Wendt 1987, Wight 1999. For elaborations on this point, see Jackson and Nexon 1999, 2001, and 2002. My argument here draws inspiration from Ferguson and Mansbach's conception of "nested" polities. See Ferguson and Mansbach 1996, 48ff.
[49] Hobson and Sharman 2005, Lake 1996, 2001, 2003.

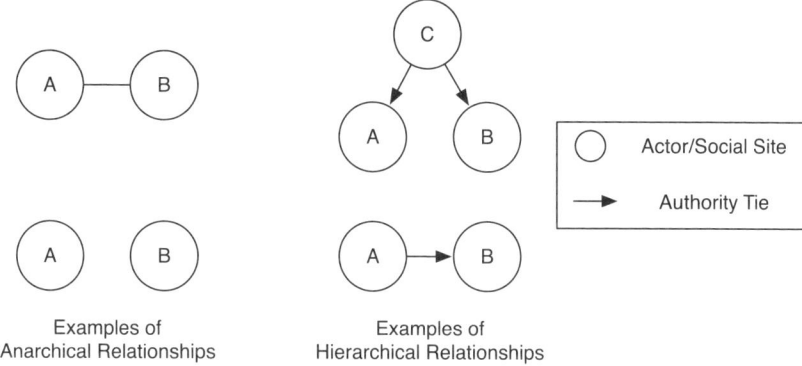

Figure 1.1 Anarchy and Hierarchy as Relational Structures

When realists refer to the international system as "anarchical," they implicitly describe a nested network-structure in which (1) ties *between* states are relatively sparse and contain no significant vectors of authority, (2) collective identification *between* states is, at best, weak, (3) ties *within* states are relatively dense and involve significant patterns of legitimate domination, and (4) collective identification *within* states is comparatively strong. The realist world is one of billiard-ball like nation-states; in relational terms, the network-structure of inter-state anarchy is co-constitutive with the network-structure of states themselves: each produces the other.[50]

Relational institutionalism, therefore, helps make sense of why realists and constructivists see such different things when they examine early modern Europe. Early modern Europe contained elements of anarchy. The relations between dynastic heads of state did sometimes involve asymmetric authority ties but such ties seldom rendered their relations nonanarchical. But in other ways the relational structure of early modern Europe departed significantly from realist descriptions of anarchy: authoritative ties crisscrossed composite states, collective identification frequently shared little relationship with the boundaries of dynastic agglomerations, and ties within segments of dynastic agglomerations might be stronger than ties between them.[51] Thus, even without considering the effects of the spread of heterodox religious movements, it should be clear that a system composed of composite states generates a different

---

[50] I develop this argument in chapter 2. On these assumptions, see Keohane and Nye 1989, 24–25; Lapid and Kratochwil 1996; Waltz 1979, 88, 104–5; Wendt 1994; Zacher 1992.

[51] Greengrass 1991.

kind of international structure than that associated with realist descriptions of international anarchy. Such an international structure, as I argue in this study, produces distinctive patterns of collective action and collective mobilization from those associated with the states-under-anarchy framework.[52]

A relational-institutionalist approach, in fact, resolves at least two problems found in international-relations accounts of state formation and international change. First, it enables scholars to persuasively link variation in the organization of political communities to variation in international structure. Second, it provides a reasonable compromise between, on the one hand, the social-scientific goal of nontrivial generalization and, on the other, a recognition of historical particularity and contingency.

Recall my central arguments for why the Protestant Reformations led to a crisis of European politics and state formation: the spread of religious heterodoxy intersected with ongoing dynamics of resistance and rule in ways that, given the right circumstances, made resistance far more dangerous to central authorities. These arguments, as such, apply only to a form of political organization—dynastic agglomerations—that existed in a particular period of European history. They also invoke a host of historical contingencies to account for the particular impact of the Reformations in specific times and places. Some readers might rightly wonder, therefore, how we could possibly construct generalizations with any applicability outside of the confines of sixteenth- and seventeenth-century Europe. We can, I submit, generalize about the *mechanisms and processes associated with the formal network-structures of composite states.*

In chapter 4 I construct an idealized account of the structure and dynamics of composite political communities based on an analysis of their network properties. These network characteristics make sense of many aspects of the dynamics of resistance and rule in early modern Europe. But they also suggest that we can generalize about those dynamics, such that when we find similar institutional network-structures in other times and places we should also expect to see broadly similar mechanisms and processes at work.[53] The ideal-typical network-structure of composite states, in fact, shares important similarities with that found in many formal and informal empires, as well as in hegemonic systems that involve informal imperial characteristics.[54] In consequence, as I argue in chapter 9, we can make a number of limited and provisional generalizations about contemporary processes of international change.

[52] Hall 1999, 28–46.
[53] Cooley 2005, 2–7, 12–13; Simmel 1971, 25–26.
[54] See chapter 3. This claim receives further elaboration in Nexon 2006.

How these structural dynamics resolve in any particular setting will, as in the early modern European cases, depend on a variety of historically specific factors, such as prevailing norms, the ideological content of institutional legitimacy, adjacent macro- and microlevel processes, and how the structural relationship is embedded in other network configurations. No single theory will ever encompass the complex causal configurations that produce unique historical outcomes, but that should not prevent us from generalizing about how specific institutional structures act as ligatures in the translation of events and processes into political outcomes.[55]

Plan of the Book

This book adheres to a rather conventional structure. Chapters 2–4 deal primarily with questions of broad theory and the character of early modern European political relations, chapters 5–7 with the theoretical analysis of cases from early modern Europe, and the remaining chapters with conclusions about European state formation and the general problem of international-political change.

Chapter 2 lays the analytical and theoretical groundwork for the rest of the book. It elaborates the relational-institutionalist framework through a critical engagement with, on the one hand, major schools of international-relations theory such as realism, liberalism, and constructivism and, on the other hand, a number of important studies of international change. I discuss the specific problems generated by, in particular, attempts to apply mainstream realist and constructivist frameworks to early modern Europe. But I also illustrate my conceptual and theoretical claims by drawing on a wide variety of examples, including the 2006 military conflict between Hezbollah and Israel, the American-led invasion of Afghanistan, and the problem posed by "weak states" for conventional international-relations analysis. This reflects my attempt to develop relational-institutional analysis as a general way of parsing international continuity and change.

I make, in this respect, a number of important arguments. First, one of the fundamental debates between contemporary varieties of realism, liberalism, and constructivism concerns the pathways of and proclivities for change in the international system. Second, relational institutionalism provides a way of conceptually unifying many of the most important claims found in these approaches, specifically in their systemic variants. Third, we should approach social-scientific generalization about continuity and change not by identifying invariant relations between causes and

---

[55] On configurational and singular causal analysis, see Jackson and Nexon 2002, Katznelson 1997, Tilly 1997b.

effects, but by specifying recurrent dynamics associated with similar social-structural conditions.

Chapter 3 supplies the crucial empirical infrastructure for this last task. I show how dynastic agglomerations constituted the ascendant form of political organization in early modern Europe, and that the dynastic-imperial pathway of state formation remained a vibrant trajectory of political change. Alterations in the mode of warfare and economic relations, as well as the inherent logic of dynasticism, contributed to the predominance of the dynastic-imperial pathway. A sovereign-territorial system was not the inevitable outcome of underlying processes of political transformation; the European state system we take for granted in international-relations theorizing remained only a contingent possibility well into the early modern period.

Once we recognize the composite nature of early modern European states, in fact, the problems with many accounts of the emergence of sovereignty fall into place. While some early modern European polities—both before and immediately after the Peace of Westphalia—had many of the attributes of modern states, they did not combine these attributes in ways that justify identifying them as inexorably "on their way" to becoming modern states.

Chapter 4 brings together my theoretical architecture with the empirical infrastructure elaborated in the preceding chapter. I construct an ideal-typical account of the network-structures of composite states, which provides a deductive basis for explaining observed patterns of resistance and rule in early modern Europe. This, in turn, allows us to identify the mechanisms and processes triggered by the spread of religious heterodoxy. Throughout the chapter I draw not only upon cases from early modern Europe, but also from other composite polities with imperial, or empire-like, structural characteristics. I provide a sustained evaluation of these mechanisms and processes through a comparison of three uprisings in the Low Countries between 1477 and 1540.

The next section of this book applies this framework to developments in early modern Europe. Chapter 5 explores the rise and fall of Charles V. Chapter 6 traces the Spanish bid for hegemony from Charles's abdication through the start of the so-called Thirty Years' War. Chapter 7 deals with the French Wars of Religion—the decades-long political struggles in France marked by the emergence of the Huguenot movement and culminating in its political isolation and defeat. Within these cases I examine dynamics of resistance and rule, shifting political coalitions, and interdynastic conflict with a focus on a number of subcases. In some, such as the *Comuneros* revolt (1520–1521), religious difference played only the most peripheral of roles. In others, such as the Schmalkaldic War (1546–1547) and the Dutch Revolt (1572–1609), religious differences decisively shaped the onset and direction of the conflict.

Each of these chapters also focuses on one or two competing explanatory frameworks. Chapters 5 and 6 highlight the problems with balance-of-power and hegemonic-order explanations for the rise and decline of the Habsburg bid for European preeminence. Ideationalist accounts provide the major foil for my analysis of the French Wars of Religion in chapter 7. In none of these chapters do I dismiss competing accounts outright, but instead show how relational analysis both corrects and modifies the arguments advanced by their proponents. My argument, I contend, identifies the key mechanisms and processes that translated power-political and ideational developments into historically specific outcomes.

The final section of the book contains two different kinds of conclusions. Chapter 8 opens with a discussion of the Thirty Years' War, the Peace of Westphalia, and its aftermath. After dispensing with arguments that the Peace of Westphalia marked the origins of the sovereign-territorial state system, I expand my purview beyond the empirical ground covered in the second section and reflect broadly on the often subtle ways in which the Reformations shaped European state formation. Chapter 9 returns us to the general theme of international change and what "lessons" we can extract from early modern Europe for the present. I focus on three major points.

First, not only did composite states never disappear from the world, but they may be back with a vengeance. The last century has seen developing fissures, in Europe and in many other areas of the world, along the fault lines produced through state building via territorial agglomeration.[56] Supernational and regional formations, such as the European Union, reflect, in some ways but not in others, a movement "back to the future" in world politics.

Second, broader processes of globalization are shifting the "opportunity structure" for collective action in world politics in ways that favor the emergence of transnational and transregional movements. Some of these movements have, to put it mildly, a religious dimension. Although many, but far from all, contemporary states enjoy greater capacity than early modern polities, these movements do, as well.

Third, contemporary developments are leading many scholars and pundits to rethink the widespread assumption that the dynamics of empires and imperial formations matter little in the era of nation-states. The conjunction of these developments suggests that the material studied and theorized in this book has at least some, however qualified, relevance for the analysis of contemporary and future international change.

[56] Roeder 2007.

CHAPTER 2

Theorizing International Change

IN JULY 2006 Hezbollah, a nonstate Shiite political-military movement based in Lebanon, captured two Israeli soldiers from the disputed Shebaa Farms region. Israel responded with air strikes and ground incursions into Lebanon; Hezbollah responded in turn with thousands of rockets launched into Israeli territory. The Israeli government declared Hezbollah's actions an "act of war" and demanded that the Lebanese government—which included members of Hezbollah—take action against the movement. Hundreds of combatants and noncombatants died during the month-long conflict, which weakened the Lebanese government but failed to destroy Hezbollah or effectuate the return of the kidnapped Israeli soldiers.[1]

A few weeks into the conflict, British academic and public intellectual Timothy Garton Ash wrote an op-ed entitled "Lebanon, North Korea, Russia . . . here is the world's new multipolar disorder." He noted that "the state of Israel is now at war with Hizbullah, but not with the state of Lebanon. The Lebanese state does not control its own territory. Iran heavily influences, but does not control, Hizbullah." The implications of these and other developments, for Garton Ash, suggest a future world disorder transcending traditional great-power rivalry:

> [I]t could be worse. It could be that kind of great-power rivalry on a world scale, plus terrorists. And corporations. And transnational religious communities. And international NGOs. No moral equivalence is suggested between these very different kinds of actor, but what they all have in common is that they don't fit neatly into a world order of states.[2]

All of this brings into focus two of the issues in theorizing international change that I raised in the previous chapter. First, consider how Garton Ash's analysis, and the events that motivated it, resonates with aspects of the early modern European experience. The Spanish Habsburgs embarked on repeated attempts—of which the 1588 Armada presents the

---

[1] Hardy 2006, Salem 2006.
[2] Garton Ash 2006.

best-known example—to invade the British Isles in the hope that doing so would cut the legs out from under the predominantly Calvinist rebels in the Low Countries. But how much weight should we place on this kind of analogy? The world of sixteenth- and seventeenth-century Europe was very different from that of our current era. Whatever continuities we may find between international processes in these two periods, we also have to recognize the many significant changes in the centuries between them. Given such concerns, then, how do we construct plausible generalizations that shed light on international processes?

Second, how do we make sense of the texture of international relations when it involves actors that "don't fit nearly into a world order of states"? Realists might view the Israel-Hezbollah conflict as relatively unproblematic. Hezbollah and Israel confront one another under more-or-less anarchical conditions; Hezbollah, with its organized military and provision of public goods to its constituents, is sufficiently state-like to trigger realist modes of analysis. At the very least, Israel and Hezbollah meet the criteria for "conflict groups," and hence face realist dynamics.[3]

A number of issues caution against this assessment. Israel, after all, pursued a strategy designed, in part, not only to cripple Hezbollah's military capabilities but also to sever its ties with the Lebanese state and to discredit Hezbollah's claim that it brought security to Lebanon. Indeed, Hezbollah's ties to the Lebanese state included participation in its cabinet; Lebanese factional struggles involved, and continue to involve, third parties—Iran and Syria—seeking greater influence over Lebanese politics through, among other things, patronage of Hezbollah. Hezbollah, some believe, initiated the conflict to improve its own standing in Lebanon and to deflect international pressure from Iran's nuclear program; Israel responded with a major campaign, backed by the United States, not only to greatly damage Hezbollah but also to weaken Iran's influence in the region.[4]

These factors clearly involved realpolitik considerations; some of them reflect very traditional power-political games. But actors pursue power and influence under a variety of different conditions. The conditions of the Israel-Hezbollah conflict involve far more complicated structural opportunities and constraints than those found in the realist states-under-anarchy model, such as patron-client relations, governments linked in patterns of cooperation and conflict with violence-wielding nonstate actors within their own territories, and categorical religious and ethnic

[3] Gilpin 1986, 325. See also Brenner 2006, 516–17; Schweller and Wohlforth 2000, 70–72.
[4] Blanford 2007a and b, Haas 2006, Salem 2006.

cleavages that fail to track with the boundaries of states.[5] Such structural arrangements blur the distinction between "international" and "domestic" arenas and therefore make a hash of international-relations theory's "levels of analysis."[6]

Overview

In this chapter I develop one way to cut into both of these critical issues in the study of international continuity and change. The approach involves applying relational modes of analysis and historical-institutionalist sensibilities to international-relations theory.[7] But before proceeding, I should address a basic question: what do I mean by "international change?" The study of international change, I argue, focuses on *transformations in the structure* of international relations. These transformations involve alterations in *the pathways of and proclivities for collective mobilization* in the international arena.

International Change

The debate over international continuity and change might strike some as puzzling. International politics, after all, involves constant change. Alli-

---

[5] We could, of course, model the strategic interactions between the various actors implicated in the conflict or debate about the relative salience of any number of domestic and international interests in their decision-making processes. But that would also sidestep the basic questions posed here.

[6] See, e.g., Jervis 1976, 13–31.

[7] A small, but growing, number of scholars deploy relational analytics to make sense of specific puzzles in world politics. Self-consciously relationalist studies do exist in international-relations scholarship, but they occupy a relatively marginal position in the field. See, e.g. Cederman and Daase 2003, Goddard 2006, Jackson 2003 and 2006a, Jackson and Nexon 2001, Krebs and Jackson 2007, and Montgomery 2005. Relational sociological principles have, in contrast, made significant inroads into cognate areas of study in comparative politics, such as the study of social movements and other forms of "contentious politics." See McAdam, Tarrow et al. 2001. Some international-relations scholars use insights from this field to make sense of the dynamics of transnational-advocacy networks. See, e.g., Carpenter 2007, Keck and Sikkink 1998, and Risse-Kappen 1995b. Fiona Adamson argues, in fact, that the role of violent transnational movements in contemporary world politics implies a relational turn in how we conceptualize actors and international structure. See Adamson 2005a and b. A still limited, but increasing, number of scholars deploy quantitative network analysis to study the impact of membership in international organization, alliances ties, and other transactional patterns on state behavior. See Hafner-Burton, and Montgomery 2006. Relationalist sensibilities, moreover, operate in a variety of other approaches to international politics, such as those associated with poststructuralism and other linguistic-turn frameworks. See, e.g., Fierke and Jørgensen 2001 and Mattern 2004.

ances rise and fall. States initiate wars and make peace. Markets grow, retreat, and collapse. Most international-relations scholars, however, mean something more specific by continuity and change; their interest lies in alterations in the basic texture of international politics.[8] They disagree, of course, about what constitutes such alterations, but they generally agree that international-political change involves shifts in the fundamental opportunities and constraints faced by actors in world politics: the "more or less embedded" structural patterns that confront "decision-making agents" as they pursue their objectives.[9]

It follows that collective action—the processes whereby the behavior of actors converges on common aims—occupies a central place in analysis of international continuity and change.[10] As Norbert Elias notes, "It is not hard to grasp the idea that what we attempt to conceptualize as social forces are in fact forces exerted by people over one another and over themselves."[11] The basic parameters of international politics are a collective achievement, sustained—both intentionally and unintentionally—by the joint-action of many individuals and corporate actors. Some forms of collective action reproduce international structures. Others concatenate to fundamentally alter international-political relations, and thus give rise to new dominant pathways of collective mobilization. Within structures lies the potential for both their reproduction and transformation. Theories of international-political change center around what kinds of choices made by agents, and what kinds of adjacent processes, are likely to activate those transformative dispositions and generate new structural arrangements.[12]

Consider the debate between realists, liberals, and constructivists. Why do structural realists believe that international politics undergoes few fundamental transformations? The states-under-anarchy model posits a fundamental asymmetry in the opportunity structures for collective action in world politics: collective mobilization within states faces fewer barriers then collective action among them. This asymmetry greatly reduces the likelihood that actors in international politics will engage in the kinds of joint-action necessary to transform international structure.

Hegemonic-order realists, for their part, root international change in shifts in collective mobilization capacities among polities. They argue,

[8] See, e.g., Holsti 2004, 6–27; Waltz 1979, 66.
[9] Cerny 1995, 596–97.
[10] This represents a broad definition of "collective action," in that it does not require self-identification of relevant actors as members of the same group. My reason for doing so will become clear later, as I treat collective identification as a distinct process.
[11] Elias 1978, 17.
[12] This argument echoes those found in historical-institutionalist modes of analysis. I elaborate on this point later in the chapter.

among other things, that a political community sometimes experiences innovations in its ability to collectively mobilize resources. These innovations, in turn, may provide it with a significant advantage over other actors in international politics and allow it to achieve a position of international primacy. Furthermore, this process often involves a domination-seeker exploiting collective-action problems among its rivals to preclude the formation of effective countervailing coalitions. Once a polity achieves a hegemonic position, it then uses its superior capabilities to establish patterns of international collective action—"rules of the game"—consistent with its own interests and values.[13]

Contemporary liberal theorists, however, argue that realists overestimate the barriers to international collective action. Actors deploy a number of strategies to realize their preferences that, given the right conditions, enable and sustain durable collective mobilization in world politics. They create international institutions, legal agreements, and other phenomena that in turn change the nature of international relations by shifting the opportunities and constraints for subsequent collective action.[14] A number of constructivists, in contrast, criticize realist claims by stressing processes of joint-action involving norm-governed behavior, collective identification, and nonstate actors. These processes, they contend, account for durable forms of collective action embodied, for example, in international institutions.[15] But because identities and norms themselves shape patterns of collective action, changes in their content also amount to transformations in the structure of world politics.

Relationalism

Although most international-relations scholars would agree that "structure" refers to durable patterns of interaction, they cash out this insight in different ways. Many think of international relations as a "system" composed of overarching structures: the condition of anarchy, the distribution of power, sets of regulative and constitutive norms, primary and secondary institutions, and so forth. This mode of analysis treats, at least implicitly, structures as entities defined by their categorical attributes.[16]

Relationalists focus on patterns of transaction themselves. For relationalists the "stuff of social reality—of action no less than structure, and their intersection in history—lies in relations."[17] Individuals derive many

---

[13] See Gilpin 1981, Hui 2004 and 2005, and Wohlforth, Little et al. 2007.
[14] See Axelrod and Keohane 1993, Keohane 1984, and Weber 1997.
[15] See Adler and Barnett 1998a and Wendt 1994.
[16] White 1992, 9.
[17] Bourdieu and Wacquant 1992, 15.

of their politically significant impulses and attributes—their identities, norms, values, interests, and influence—from their participation in ongoing processes of social interaction. As they pursue goals, such as resources and status, they reproduce, modify, create, and sever relatively durable material and symbolic exchange relationships. These relatively durable, but fundamentally dynamic, interactions constitute the structural contexts in which individuals operate.[18]

Relationalist operationalize this position in a number of different ways. The approach developed here relies heavily on concepts and analytics familiar to relational sociologists and social-network analysts, but less so to international-relations scholars. It seems, therefore, appropriate to highlight three key concepts. I will return to these concepts later, but they form an integral part of the remaining comments that frame this chapter.[19]

- *Social ties*: routine transactions "to which participants attach shared understandings, memories, forecasts, rights, and obligations."[20]
- *Categories*: generalized roles embedded in routine transactions—such as "burgher," "Castilian," "Catholic," and "dynast"—that provide, among other things, potentially salient forms of collective identification.[21]
- *Networks*: patterns of ties produce networks with varying properties, such as the density and distribution of social interactions, the location and direction of super- and subordinate relationships, and so forth.[22]

We can think about any corporate actor in international politics—whether a nation-state, an empire, a multinational firm, or a transnational religious movement—in terms of its constituent social ties and categorical identities. This structure of such actors, of course, varies tremendously. Ideal-typical nation-states involve transactional structures very different from those found in ideal-typical empires. Real states and empires vary tremendously in terms of their structures of informal and formal rule.[23] In this way, relationalism provides a means of not only parsing international structure, but of interrogating the structure and dynamics of political institutions in ways suggested by historical institutionalists.

---

[18] Emirbayer 1997, 287–88; Tilly 2003, 5–6. See also Sommers 1998.
[19] For key statements of this kind of argument, see Bearman 1993, Tilly 1978 and 2002, and White 1972 and 1992.
[20] Tilly 2002, 80.
[21] Ibid., 48–49, 80, 155–56, 199.
[22] In general, see Emirbayer and Goodwin 1994, 1481; Tilly 1998, 399; Wellman 1983, 156–62; and White, Boorman et al. 1976, 733–34.
[23] Jackson 1990, Motyl 1997, Sørensen 1998.

We often, moreover, take for granted that such variations shape the dynamics of collective action within political communities.[24] But many of the scholars who advance these claims operate within the traditional levels-of-analysis framework. Variation in the "internal" institutional structures of political communities, therefore, serves mainly to explain variation in "external" behavior or outcomes of inter-state competition.[25] These distinctions quickly break down, however, once we recognize that domestic institutional structures impact opportunities and constraints for collective action not only within, but between and across, political communities. Important patterns of collective action generated by the informal and formal institutions of the Lebanese state, for example, differ significantly from those in Israel and Syria with, as we have seen, crucial consequences for conflict, violence, and cooperation in the Middle East.

Instead of approaching international politics through pre-given levels of analysis, therefore, we should think about international structures as "network[s] of networks" co-constituted by the network-structures of the actors that populate it,[26] and also by the structure of social ties across and between them.[27] Levels of analysis, in turn, simply refer to the different levels of aggregation through which we examine the relational contexts of individual and collective political action.[28] Anarchy constitutes not an overarching structural condition of a system, but a particular network-structure in which actors—whether human or corporate—lack authoritative ties with one another or to a common third party. In "international politics," however, we find a variety of embedded relationships involving different relational forms, such as patron-client ties, semisovereign arrangements in which actors invest international institutions with the right to make authoritative claims over their citizens in specific domains, and joint decision-making arrangements in alliances.[29]

---

[24] For examples, see Barkey 1991 and 1994; Beissinger 2002; Bin Wong 1997; Cooley 2005; David 1991a and b; Hall 1999; Hui 2005, 26–34; Nathan 2006; Schweller 2004 and 2006; Tilly 2003; Togan 1998; and Wohlforth, Little et al. 2007.

[25] Hui provides a partial exception to this rule. She argues that "international politics should be seen as processes of strategic interaction between domination-seekers and targets of domination." For her, mechanisms involved in these struggles operate at both the structural and domestic level, hence a "dynamic theory" focuses on "the mutual constitution of systems and states and the interaction of structural pressures and agential strategies." See Hui 2004, 33, 23.

[26] See Craven and Wellman 1973.

[27] See Hafner-Burton and Montgomery 2006, Montgomery 2005, and Nexon and Wright 2007.

[28] See Alexander 1988, 257; and Wight 2006, 90–120.

[29] Cooley 2000/2001 and 2005, Hobson and Sharman 2005, Krasner 1999, Lake 1996, Lake 2003.

A relational approach seeks to analyze the structural opportunities and constraints created by these various embedded social formations and the way that they interact with one another. This requires us to abandon attempts to describe overarching international structures in spare terms, such as "anarchy" or "intersubjective norms." We might, of course, map—as some international-relations scholars using social-network analysis do—the network-structure of international trade, membership in international organizations, or alliances.[30] These snapshots provide one way to identify the actual structure of social ties—as well as other relational factors such as the structural positions of specific sites—in some specific domain. They help us to correlate behaviors with structural locations or other network-properties. But they neither provide a totality of the structure of international politics, nor adequately capture the dynamic interplay of "negotiation and creativity" often at stake in specific processes of transformative and reproductive collective action.[31]

This humility extends to how we approach causal generalization. Recall from the preceding chapter another important wager of relational modes of analysis: significant aspects of causation in social and political life inhere in transactions themselves. Many important causal mechanisms and processes, in particular, stem from the *formal* properties of specific relational structures in which actors operate. In patron-client networks, composite political communities, and polarized networks, we find general dynamics that operate across time and space. How these dynamics resolve into specific outcomes, however, depends upon a number of contextual factors: their cultural content, how they intersect with adjacent processes and relational contexts, and the specific decisions of relevant actors.[32] The approach I develop here thus allows us to construct generalizations of the following form: when we identify similar embedded relational structures in different times and places, we should expect to see similar dynamics.

Roadmap

I develop these conceptual and analytic claims in the remainder of this chapter. I begin by revisiting realism and constructivism. I focus on the application of realist and constructivist principles to early modern Europe, and discuss how the limitations of these accounts reflect broader

---

[30] See, e.g., Hafner-Burton and Montgomery 2006; Hammarström and Birger 2002; Ingram, Robinson et al. 2005; and Ward 2006.
[31] Tilly 2003, 6. For a variation of this argument, see McAdam 2003, 296–98.
[32] See Jackson and Nexon 2002, Tilly 1997b.

problems of the kind noted above. I then expand upon the relational-institutionalist approach to international continuity and change. I elaborate the three key concepts mentioned above and discuss how viewing international politics as nested configurations of categorical identities and social networks allows us to link variation in the structure of political communities to variation in international structure. I then show how recoding international structures as nested relational configurations provides a way of making sense of what is really at stake in the debate about international change. I conclude with a discussion of how relational analysis can be conjoined to historical-institutionalist principles to theorize specific aspects of international continuity and change. In brief, I argue that the dynamics of institutions can be understood by interrogating their relational organization—that is, their network architecture, their distributions of identities, and the structural locations actors within them occupy.[33]

Continuity and Change in International-Relations Theory

The question of international change lies at the heart of the so-called paradigmatic debate that dominated international-relations theory in the 1990s. Realism, liberalism, constructivism, and other broad schools of thought disagree with one another about a number of key issues related to international continuity and change. They debate the relative frequency of major changes in the basic texture of international relations and the causes of those alterations. Moreover, their disagreements concern both different ways of conceptualizing international structure and claims about the processes of collective action involved in international change.[34] We can tackle these issues by considering how prominent international-relations theories of continuity and change understand, or might be deployed to understand, political dynamics in early modern Europe. Here I focus on realism and constructivism, although I consider other approaches both inter alia and later in this chapter.

---

[33] See Burt 1992, Lange 2003, Stevenson and Greenberg 2000. Despite the growing influence of social-network analysis in international-relations theory, many scholars still instinctively think of "institutions" and "networks" as different kinds of phenomena; they associate networks with informal ties that operate outside of institutional contexts. The relevant distinction here, however, is not between "networks" and "institutions," but between different classes of networks: informal and formal, institutional and societal, and so forth.

[34] See, e.g., Bukovansky 2002, Copeland 2000, Hall 1999, Holsti 2004, Krasner 1993, Nexon 2005, and Philpott 2001.

Realism

Realists, as I have already suggested, contend that the basic parameters of international politics are marked by fundamental continuity rather than change: a struggle for security and power among—and, often, within—well-bounded political communities. As E. H. Carr argues, "Politics are, then, in one sense always power politics. . . . While politics cannot be satisfactorily defined exclusively in terms of power, it is safe to say that power is always an essential element of politics."[35] For realists, military capabilities provide the primary—and economic influence the secondary—currency of international relations. Carr explains the basic logic: "The supreme importance of the military instrument lies in the fact that the *ultima ratio* of power in international relations is war. . . . War lurks in the background of international politics just as revolution lurks in the background of domestic politics."[36]

The distribution of power in world politics exercises a decisive influence over states, because "the foreign policy of a country is limited not only by its aims, but also by its military strength or, more accurately, by the ratio of its military strength to that of other countries."[37] Ethical codes and successful propaganda, according to realists, both track with military and economic power; they reflect the interests of powerful groups and those who struggle against them.[38] Indeed, most realists agree, as Randall L. Schweller and William C. Wohlforth argue, that "necessity and reason of state trump morality and ethics when those values conflict."[39] Religious beliefs, dynastic norms, and other ideational factors matter, but not to the extent that they conflict with power-political concerns. Actors in international politics pursue "logics of consequences" rather than "logics of appropriateness."[40] They make decisions, including about whether and when to engage in joint-action, based upon calculations of whether doing so will improve or undermine core interests in security, wealth, and power.[41]

ANARCHY AND THE BALANCE OF POWER

Most contemporary realists claim that these dynamics stem from the anarchical structure of international relations. As Kenneth Waltz argues, "The

---

[35] Carr 1946, 102. See also Schweller and Wohlforth 2000, 69–71; and Waltz 1979, 88–89.
[36] Carr 1946, 109.
[37] Ibid., 110.
[38] Ibid., 1946, 79, 132–41.
[39] Schweller and Wohlforth 2000, 69.
[40] On this distinction, see Finnemore and Sikkink 1998, 891–92; and March and Olsen 1998.
[41] Krasner 1999, 5–6, 10, 41, 72, 237–38.

parts of the domestic system stand in relations of super- and subordination. Some are entitled to command; others are required to obey." In the international-political system, however, each actor "is the equal of all the others. None is entitled to command; none is required to obey. International systems are decentralized and anarchic."[42] Anarchical orders are governed by principles of self-help: "Units in the condition of anarchy—be they people, corporations, states or whatever—must rely on the means they can make for themselves."[43] Since self-help systems require states to place power-political concerns before other considerations, anarchy primes states to pay attention to changes in relative capabilities. Those that fail to respond to this imperative will fall to the wayside through conquest, informal subordination, or by becoming weak and insignificant actors on the global stage.[44]

In structural-realist theory, the result of all this is what many term the "balance-of-power mechanism." Anarchy inclines states to respond to shifts in the distribution of power between them either by developing their own capabilities (internal balancing) or by forming alliances of convenience to check potential threats (external balancing).[45] All international systems tend, over time, to develop recurrent balances of power regardless of the specific composition of states, their governing ideologies, or their regime type.

HEGEMONIC ORDERS

Hegemonic-order theorists, in contrast, view the rise and fall of pre-eminent powers as the primary vector of international continuity and change.[46] Over time, hegemonic-order theorists argue, some political communities develop political, economic, or technological innovations that give them a decisive advantage over their rivals. If such advantages in social technologies of collective mobilization magnify a domination-seeker's power in comparison to the rate at which it diffuses to—and can be adopted by—other actors in the system, then that state will be able to achieve control over them.[47]

This process may culminate in the establishment of formal empire, informal empire, or hegemony.[48] The pre-eminent power, in any of these

[42] Waltz 1979, 88.

[43] Ibid., 1979, 88. See also Mearsheimer 2001, 32–33; and Schweller 2004, 103.

[44] Gilpin 1981, 85–87; Waltz 1979, 116–22.

[45] Waltz 1979, 102–28.

[46] For discussions, see Gilpin 1981, Ikenberry 2001, Lake 1993, and Lemke 2002. On the importance of "state mobilization capacity" to balance-of-power dynamics, see Schweller 2006, 13–15.

[47] See Gilpin 1981, 29; and Ikenberry 2001, 23–26.

[48] For a similar argument applied to sovereignty norms, see Krasner 1999. For discussions of the structural differences between these forms of primacy, see Mastanduno 2005 and Nexon and Wright 2007.

configurations of authority, establishes and enforces "rules and rights" that govern international economic and political relations, as well as sets standards of relative prestige among states. As G. John Ikenberry argues, "Compliance and participation within the order is ultimately ensured by the range of power capacities available to the hegemon—military power, financial capital, market access, technology, and so forth."[49] The fate of hegemonic powers, in turn, hinges on the interaction of three factors: the ability of a pre-eminent power to sustain its economic, military, and technological leadership; the propensity for hegemonic overextension; and the degree to which potential challengers believe they benefit from the existing international order.

First, economic, political, or military innovations may provide a non-pre-eminent political community with an innovation in collective mobilization that shifts relative power in its favor. It extracts wealth, employs labor and resources for economic production, raises and organizes military forces, or otherwise engages in forms of joint-action more effectively than the existing hegemon. The gradual effects of relative economic growth may also, less dramatically but no less consequentially, undermine the preeminence of the dominant power over time. Hegemonic-order theorists identify specific processes of internal decay that exacerbate these trends, including domestic economic stagnation and the growth of factional struggles within domestic society.[50]

Second, pre-eminent powers that establish hegemonic orders—rules of military and economic conduct, as well as other aspects of the prevailing normative order—have to actively preserve that order. Such activities involve the use of costly carrots and sticks, including military action designed to maintain both rules of conduct and the overall distribution of power. These conditions invest the pre-eminent power with wide-ranging interests and responsibilities; hegemonic and imperial powers often face difficulties in efficiently prioritizing their interests. They therefore frequently overexpand: they make more military and political commitments than they can support and otherwise cross the limits of the "loss-of-strength gradient." This process accelerates their loss of relative power, particularly because many of the states that benefit from the public goods the hegemon provides also avoid paying the costs of maintaining them.[51]

Third, both of these sources of relative decline produce potential challengers: a state or states with sufficient relative power to challenge the

[49] Ikenberry 2001, 27.
[50] Gilpin 1981, 159–68 and 175–85. See also; Kennedy, 1987; Lemke 2002, 21–47; and Organski 1958 #1051.
[51] Gilpin 1981, 168–75; Kupchan 1996, 1–104. For a critique of this logic, see Grunberg 1990. These kinds of issues motivated, at least in part, American policymakers to call for greater "burden sharing" among American allies during the 1980s. On overextension more generally, see also Mearsheimer 2001, 209–24; and Snyder 1991 and 2003.

pre-eminent power's leadership. If these states believe that they derive significant benefits from the current order—in terms of wealth, territory, prestige, and other goods—then they will retain a status-quo orientation. Pre-eminent powers may therefore accommodate potential challengers or otherwise provide an attractive order to those potential rivals. In either case the order persists either because the hegemon retains its position or because rising states become part of a cartel that works to maintain the rules of the game. Challengers that seek an alteration in the order that the pre-eminent power refuses to make, however, develop strongly revisionist orientations. Both power-transition and hegemonic-order theorists argue that the result may be a "hegemonic war." If the hegemon emerges victorious, it either retains or recasts the order from its newfound position of strength. If its rivals emerge victorious, they will construct a new order and the cycle begins anew.[52]

REALISM AND THE CASE OF EARLY MODERN EUROPE

Realist accounts of the early modern period, therefore, stress dynamics associated with balance-of-power politics and the rise and decline of hegemonic orders. Realist stories of the period focus, in particular, on two primary explanations for the decline and eventual collapse of Habsburg hegemony. First, increasing Habsburg power threatened other actors in Europe, such as the rulers of France and those German princes seeking to consolidate and expand their political autonomy. Second, Charles V and his Spanish Habsburg successors suffered from conventional problems of hegemonic overextension and decline in the face of strategic commitments that exceeded their underlying resources.[53]

Very few realists would reject the proposition that religious differences, religious movements, and dynastic practices influenced the specific ways in which these processes unfolded. Rather, they might highlight how early modern European rulers frequently lent support to religious rivals when doing so advanced their strategic interests. Realists might also point to the specific features of the period—polarized religious identities, transnational religious movements, dynastic norms, and so forth—as evidence for the basic truth of realist theory. Despite these factors, they might note, balance-of-power and hegemonic-order logics still predominantd in early modern Europe.

Europe in the sixteenth and seventeenth centuries thus demonstrates how, as Waltz puts it, through "all of the changes in boundaries, of social, economic, and political form, of military and economic activity the sub-

---

[52] Gilpin 1981, 186–210. See also Ikenberry 2001, Kennedy 1987, Lemke 2002, Lemke and Werner 1996, and Organski 1958.
[53] Gilpin 1981, 120–21.

stance and style of international politics remains strikingly constant."[54] The Habsburg experience reflects, in Robert Gilpin's terms, how the "fundamental problem of international relations in the contemporary world is the problem of peaceful adjustment to the consequences of uneven growth or power among states, just as it was in the past."[55]

Realist accounts of early modern European politics cannot, however, make sense of the role of nonstate actors, the implications of norms and identities for patterns of collective action, and state forms that deviate in significant ways from the hierarchic, centralized, sovereign, and national logics of organization associated with the states-under-anarchy approach to world politics. These difficulties apply to realist analysis of continuity and change in other eras; they stem from basic limitations of realist theory.

Consider the problem of transnational, identity-based movements. William Brenner notes that even "within the realist research program there is a grudging acknowledgement of the increasing importance of nonstate actors."[56] John Mearsheimer, a leading realist scholar, supplies a thoughtful realist take on this difficulty: "My theory and realist theories don't have much to say about transnational actors," but argues that their activities "will be played out in the state arena and, therefore, all of the Realist logic about state behavior will have a significant effect on," for example, "how the war on terrorism is fought."[57] Such a response reaffirms the basic assumptions of the states-under-anarchy framework: as long as states (or statelike entities) remain the primary sites of collective action, they will also remain the conversion points through which the activities of substate and transnational actors translate into outcomes relevant to the basic parameters of world politics.[58]

But the empirical proposition that states are the primary sites of collective action supplies an insufficient warrant for realist accounts of continuity and change. It describes scope conditions for the salience of realist logics; a robust analytic account of international structure and its relationship to various dynamics of collective action would allow for variation in these conditions. When the influence of transnational movements on international politics increases, let alone that of coercion-wielding trans- and substate actors, it follows that we are looking at a different interna-

---

[54] Waltz 1986, 329. See also Mearsheimer 2001, 365. Although Mearsheimer believes that anarchy inclines states to maximize power, and thus sees regional hegemony rather than balances of power as the norm in world politics, his theoretical architecture tracks closely to that found in conventional structural-realist approaches.

[55] Gilpin 1981, 230.

[56] Brenner 2006, 504.

[57] Mearsheimer 2002.

[58] Glaser 2003, 408; Waltz 1979, 88.

tional opportunity structure for collective action than that assumed in realist theory.[59]

These assumptions, moreover, get us into real trouble when we look at cases such as that of early modern Europe. In these circumstances the impact of trans- and substate movements depend a great deal on the specific structural characteristics—and consequent collective-action dynamics—of states themselves. The composite character of early modern states accounts for why the spread of religious heterogeneity triggered a crisis in the European order. If they had been organized differently, the development of heterogeneous transnational religious movements would not have produced such a crisis.

Constructivism

Constructivists argue that the basic character of international politics is socially and historically contingent. The dynamics of international relations, such as those described by realists, "need not have existed, or need not be at all as [they are]." International relations, "as it is present, is not determined by the nature of things; it is not inevitable."[60] In Alexander Wendt's well-known phrase, "anarchy is what states make of it" rather than a parametric constraint that imposes some form of natural necessity on the behavior of actors.[61]

Most constructivists argue that the structural arrangements in political, social, and economic life—including anarchy—should be thought of as "intersubjective": that is, as products of the shared meanings actors attach to their interactions and to the wider world. Structures, in this sense, are "social facts." They appear to individual actors "as if" they are objective features of their environment, but actually represent relative stabilities in the patterns of interactions among agents—including norms, collective beliefs, identities, and social knowledge.[62] Agents and structures exist in relations of "co-constitution." Actors produce, reproduce, and transform structures at the same time that structural patterns give rise to opportunities, constraints, and conditions of possibility for agents and agency.[63]

Realist accounts of anarchy, therefore, mistakenly treat its implications as if they were effectively objective. Realist anarchy, instead, reflects one particular configuration of authority, norms, identities, and beliefs. If we adopt this view it makes little sense to argue that ideologies, norms, and

---

[59] Adamson 2005a and b, Keohane and Nye 1989.
[60] Hacking 1999, 6.
[61] Wendt 1992. See also Adler 1997, Jackson and Nexon 2004, Onuf 1989, and Wendt 1987, 1994, and 1996.
[62] Berger and Luckmann 1966, Pouliot 2004.
[63] Elias 1989, Giddens 1984 and 1995, Wendt 1987 and 1992, Wight 1999.

other aspects of social meaning are somehow "secondary" to the dynamics of international politics, or to give causal priority to distributions of military or economic capabilities and interests.

Consider two related versions of this argument. One holds that variations in identities profoundly shape collective mobilization dynamics. When actors view one another as members of a common "in group," the argument goes, they will be more likely to trust one another and even sacrifice parochial interests for the good of the larger community. Thus, states that share common identities—religious, ethnic, national, and so forth—both will be more likely to share common interests and will also have an easier time credibly committing to engage in joint-action.[64] It follows that realist accounts of anarchy as a "self-help" environment presuppose heterogeneity in actor identities; for example, that each state has a distinctive national identity that trumps other forms of interstate collective identification.[65] As Rodney Bruce Hall argues, "The self-understandings, or collective identities, of collective actors, do have causal significance for the interaction of 'units' and thus must be included as an element of structure."[66]

Another form of this argument focuses on variations in intersubjective norms, or "collective understandings for the proper behavior of actors within a given identity."[67] Many constructivists claim that alterations in pathways and proclivities for collective mobilization in world politics result from changing norms about appropriate conduct. In this view actors do not simply seek to maximize their material welfare. They make determinations about what kinds of goals to pursue and how to pursue those goals with reference to predominant norms. Some constructivists argue that, for example, changes in dominant social understandings of the legitimate purposes of warfare and intervention create new conditions of possibility for intervention and war making.[68] Others explain successful or unsuccessful instances of international joint-action—such as whether or not states use chemical, biological, or nuclear weapons in warfare—with reference to changing international norms.[69] In this reckoning, then, the impact of anarchy on collective action depends on the character of prevailing norms in world politics, rather than the innate properties (if any) of anarchical structures. Alterations in that normative environment are both cause and consequence of transformative collective mobilization in international relations.[70]

[64] See Abdelal, Herrara et al. 2006, 699; Mercer 1995; Tajfel 1978 and 1981.
[65] Lapid and Kratochwil 1996.
[66] Hall 1999, 73.
[67] Katzenstein 1996, 5.
[68] Finnemore 2004.
[69] Legro 1997, Price 1995, Price 1998, Tannenwald 2005.
[70] Finnemore and Sikkink 1998, Keck and Sikkink 1998.

TRANSNATIONAL AND SUBSTATE ACTORS

Constructivists also contend that realists underestimate the role of transnational and substate actors in processes of international continuity and transformation. Such criticisms extend beyond constructivism—they predate the emergence of constructivism as a self-identified intellectual movement in international-relations theory—but they have intensified of late. The debate centers on the basic question of whether or not nonstate actors operate as sufficiently robust sites of collective action that, even if they cannot match the influence of most states, they cannot be ignored in any account of the basic dynamics of world politics.[71]

A major branch of constructivist theory, in fact, focuses on the putative role of transnational actors in shaping social identities and norms in world politics. They stress "the ability of nontraditional international actors to mobilize information strategically to help create new issues and categories and to persuade, pressure, and gain leverage over much more powerful organizations and governments."[72] Many constructivist studies show how contemporary transnational movements—in the domains of human rights, environmental activism, arms control, and so forth—change the normative environment of international politics and lead to "shifts in interstate relations that are not driven either by national interests or by 'self-help' as traditionally understood."[73]

Much of this literature rests on the claim that contemporary changes in communications, travel, and economic relations increase the effectiveness of "transnational networks" as sites of collective action.[74] While the states-under-anarchy framework may capture certain moments of world politics, the argument goes, realist theory generally underestimates the transformative potential of nonstate and transnational actors. The rise of such actors not only testifies to a shift in the basic parameters of international politics, but such actors now operate as agents of change themselves.[75] Much the same might be argued of trans-state and -regional religious movements in early modern Europe.

STATE FORMS AND INTERNATIONAL STRUCTURES

Some variants of the above arguments put forth a relatively limited critique of realist accounts of continuity and change: that realist theory neglects the important role of nonstate actors. Attention to those actors might, therefore, enrich realist theory by, for example, providing better

---

[71] Adamson 2005a and b, Brenner 2006, Philpott 2002.
[72] Keck and Sikkink 1998, 2.
[73] Ibid., 1998, 216. For examples see Busby 2007, Checkel 1999, and Joachim 2003.
[74] Keck and Sikkink 1998, Risse 2000, Risse-Kappen 1995a.
[75] Slaughter 2004.

accounts of the specific processes that lead states to adopt particular foreign policies. Other variants launch a more comprehensive criticism: that realist accounts of international structure, and hence the dynamics isolated by realist theory, presuppose international systems populated largely by sovereign-territorial nation-states. Changes in the character of actors, according to this line of reasoning, also involve alterations in the fundamental opportunities and constraints for both reproductive and transformative collective mobilization in world politics.

John Ruggie, in his seminal critique of structural realism, argues that the "modern [international] system is distinguished from the medieval . . . by *the principles on the basis of which the constituent units are separated* from one another [original emphasis]." The "feudal state . . . consisted of chains of lord-vassal relationships" and therefore produced an "international" system lacking a clear distinction between " 'internal' and 'external' political realms": princes, lords, ecclesiastical officeholders, and the papacy engaged in what we would now consider international politics. Each constituted important focal points for collective mobilization, including collective violence.[76]

A number of scholars extend these claims; they argue that empires, city-states, and other kinds of actors not only exhibit different domestic processes than sovereign states, but that the basic structural characteristics of international politics depend upon the structure of the units that populate international politics. "Changes in unit type," argues Hendrik Spruyt, "are simultaneously changes in domestic and external politics. . . . [T]he agents that make up the state system . . . create a particular structure of interunit behavior."[77] We should expect different patterns of interaction—as well as reproductive and transformative collective mobilization—in systems dominated by empires, city-states, sovereign states, or mixtures of various kinds of actors.[78]

CONSTRUCTIVISM AND THE EARLY MODERN EUROPEAN CASE

Constructivists view the case of sixteenth- and seventeenth-century Europe as proof of the basic mutability of international politics. The main story of the period, for at least some constructivists, concerns how the Protestant Reformations produced new ideas and identities that thrust Europe into a legitimation crisis—involving deadly struggles over religion

---

[76] Ruggie 1983, 274–75. See also Spruyt 1994, 36–51; and Teschke 1998.
[77] Spruyt 1994, 17.
[78] Ferguson and Mansbach 1996, 10–21; Hall 1999, 14; Spruyt 1994, 15–17. For an attempt to reconstruct structural realism in light of, among other things, variation in unit type, see Buzan, Jones et al. 1993. Spruyt would probably not identify as a constructivist—many of his arguments reflect liberal and Marxist mechanisms—but he nicely summarizes a position shared by constructivists.

and authority—that, in turn, actors resolved by developing new norms and practices of international politics. In some renderings, the Protestant Reformations resulted in a system of sovereign states.[79] In others, they marked the emergence of first a "dynastic-sovereign" and then a "territorial-sovereign" order.[80]

Although others contest these precise claims, most constructivist scholars—and other critics of realism—would probably agree that developments in sixteenth- and seventeenth-century Europe cast doubt upon key aspects of realist theory. First, dynastic practices, religious identities, and the influence of religious movements shaped early modern European politics in ways that belie realist claims about the fundamental continuity of international relations. Second, variation in the structure of political communities altered the structure and dynamics of inter-state relations. The period demonstrates how realist accounts of anarchy depend on principles of unit differentiation specific to sovereign-territorial nation-states.[81]

Realist theory, however, sensitizes us to the importance of providing transposable accounts of international structure. Waltz correctly argues that part of our explanation for patterns of collective mobilization should reference the formal properties of structures, because doing so allows us to account for the existence of similar aggregate mechanisms and processes across time and space. The central problem with predominate alternatives, particularly those found in constructivist theory, is that they render such generalizations difficult.

Constructivists, as we have seen, often conceptualize international structures as collections of intersubjective norms, rules, principles, identities, and roles. Hall, for example, identifies important shifts in European political relations over the last few centuries, which he labels as transitions between the "dynastic-sovereign" (c. 1555–1648), "territorial-sovereign" (c. 1648–1800) and "national-sovereign" (c. 1800–present) systems.[82] Philpott adopts a similar position. He argues that the fundamental structure of international politics rests in "constitutions of international society." These, he writes, "are sets of norms. . . . What makes constitutional norms unique is that they constitute polities and endow them with their basic prerogatives."[83] Philpott analyzes two "revolutions in sovereignty": the 1648 Peace of Westphalia and the 1960 UN Declaration that marked the end of colonial empires as a legitimate form of politi-

---

[79] Philpott 2000 and 2001
[80] Hall 1999 and 2002.
[81] For aspects of these claims, see Bukovansky 2002, Osiander 2001, Sharma 2005, and Spruyt 1994.
[82] Hall 1999, 28–46.
[83] Philpott 2001, 21–22.

cal organization. In both cases, he argues, ideational shifts—the Reformations and the spread of ideas of national self-determination—led states to negotiate new governing norms for international politics.[84]

Many English-School scholars, for their part, define international systems in terms of their "primary institutions" and "secondary institutions." The former involve constitutive rules and norms, such as sovereignty. The latter involve specific practices, such as the balance of power.[85] These approaches provide a wealth of insights. They do capture important political differences between international relations in various times and places. One cannot, as realists suggest, simply exclude intersubjective meanings as elements of political structure. But if we conceptualize international structures—and related pathways and proclivities of collective mobilization—primarily in terms of norms, rules, and principles, then we cannot easily generalize *across* time and space. Each international system has a unique structure—composed of different norms, rules, and principles—and is therefore, in some fundamental sense, sui generis.[86]

Many existing constructivist accounts suffer from an additional difficulty. Realist accounts of early modern European politics rightly call attention to the importance of balance-of-power politics, the dynamics of hegemonic overextension and decline, and actors who often sacrificed short-term religious concerns at the altar of power-political considerations. Constructivists not infrequently respond to these kinds of observations through a kind of rearguard action: they stress that they do not deny the importance of material power, relative capabilities, or even realist dynamics. They argue, instead, that constructivist processes play—on balance—a more important role than those identified by realists, that their studies explain residual variation not accounted for by nonconstructivist studies, or that intersubjective structures enjoy logical priority with respect to dynamics of power politics.[87] Some of these arguments actually place constructivism quite close to realism, while others reassert constructivist principles. None, I submit, provide a satisfactory way of resolving these debates.

Relationalism

A turn to relational analysis resolves many of the difficulties found in realist and constructivist approaches to international continuity and change. Recall the claim I advanced at the outset: international structures

---

[84] Ibid., 2001, 30–36ff. See also Philpott 2000 and 2001/2002.
[85] Bull 1977, Buzan 1993 and 2004, Holsti 2004, Watson 1992.
[86] Cooley 2005, 12.
[87] For a discussion, see Nexon 2005.

resolve as "networks of networks."[88] The relational structures of the actors that populate international politics, in conjunction with the patterns of interaction among them, translate into international structures at higher levels of aggregation. As historical-institutionalists suggest, the formal and informal structures of institutions take on particular significance. They provide not only some of the most fundamental opportunities and constraints for collective action, but also allow us to identify transformative and reproductive mechanisms at various levels of aggregation.

The next two sections expand upon the three key concepts introduced earlier: social ties, categories, and networks. Any relatively durable transaction—whether economic or political, coercive or voluntary—constitutes a social tie. Patterns of social ties resolve into networks, which we can describe in terms of a variety of formal properties. Networks, in this framework, are crucial elements of what we mean by "social structure." Generalized social roles comprise categorical identities, or categories. The relationship between categories and networks gives rise to varying collective mobilization dynamics. Conceptualizing relational structures in this way provides important insights into the relationship between actors, structures, and collective action in international politics. Structural-realist accounts of the implications of anarchy, for example, reflect a particular ideal-typical nested relational configuration.[89] Many of the specific claims made by proponents of various other schools of international relations, for example, about the way transnational collective identification might alter international politics, also fit comfortably within this framework.[90]

SOCIAL TIES AND NETWORKS

Predominant forms of structural analysis in international-relations theory tend to treat political and social structures as abstract qualities of systems or otherwise in terms greatly removed from the very practices that constitute them.[91] Relational approaches, in contrast, view structures as ongoing, dynamic patterns of transaction between actors and other social sites. In this sense they embrace a strong notion of agent-structure co-constitution. How does this cash out with respect to the concepts of "social ties" and "networks"? I illustrate with a story about patron-client structures, one that will turn out to matter a great deal to the political dynamics of early modern European polities and the impact of the Protestant Reformations on dynamics of resistance and rule.

[88] See Craven and Wellman 1973.
[89] Nexon and Wright 2007. See also Keohane and Nye 1989, 24–25.
[90] See Adler and Barnett 1998b, Wendt 1992, 1994, and 1996.
[91] Jackson and Nexon 2001.

Not long into the American-led invasion of Afghanistan in the autumn of 2001, a colleague of my wife's asked her an important question: why did so many individuals previously aligned with the Taliban regime suddenly abandon it in favor of the United States? All the United States had done, after all, was offer carrots and sticks to Afghani warlords. American "paramilitary teams . . . spread out through the country and won the campaign for the U.S.-led coalition. By distributing [seventy-million dollars] to the traditionally mercenary Afghan warlords during the last three months of 2001, they ensured the swift collapse of the Taliban militia."[92] Why would their followers suddenly take up arms against their erstwhile allies?[93]

We find a major part of our answer in the general structure of social ties associated with clientelism. Most of the actors we designate as "warlords" are violence-wielding patrons. A warlord operates in what Jeremy Boissevain describes as an "asymmetrical, quasi-moral relation" in which he "directly provides protection and assistance (patronage) and/or influences persons who can provide these services (brokers), to persons (clients) who depend upon him for such assistance."[94] Such patterns of social ties not only define general structural locations (patron, broker, and client) but account for such apparent radical shifts in the orientation of collective mobilization. "Patronage," notes Sharon Kettering, "encourages cooperation and is effective in moving people to action."[95] Because clients are tied to their patrons in material and affective relationships of dependency, they have, all things being equal, few structural opportunities (or incentives) to break from their patrons. Clients, therefore, often follow where their patrons lead.

Note here that we need not rely on "logics of appropriateness" or "logics of consequence" to understand, at least in a general sense, the political implications that follow when patrons shift their allegiances. Their clients may act out of logics of appropriateness, such as their loyalty to their patron, their sense of honor, or whatever. They may also act out of logics of consequence, such as a recognition that breaking from the patron will result in an immediate loss of status, security, and economic resources. Both decision-making processes may often be at work.

Thus, an understanding of the kinds of social ties involved in patron-client relations provides significant explanatory power independent of specific microfoundations. Analysis of the relational structure of patron-

[92] Burke and Vuliamy 2002.
[93] As Burke and Vuliamy note, at least one warlord's followers killed him after he cut a deal with the Americans. Yet this was an extremely rare outcome of the bribery campaign. See ibid.
[94] Quoted in Walston 1988, 3.
[95] Kettering 1986b, 3.

client relations tells us a great deal even before we analyze the meanings attached to those ties in a specific time and place: how cultural practices of superiority and deference, honor and loyalty, and so forth shape the workings of clientele systems in Afghanistan, Hezbollah, the Italian Mafia, early modern France, or the Roman Empire.[96] As we will see in subsequent chapters, clientele networks mattered tremendously in early modern Europe; their dynamics help explain, in part, patterns of mass conversion from Catholicism to the Reformed Church among the nobility of France and how actors mobilized significant military resources for and against their dynastic rulers. But let us continue with our conceptual exploration of the notion of "social ties" and "networks."

In any given clientele network, a patron may be *directly* tied to a client, such as in the relationship between a warlord and his trusted lieutenant or a noble and his immediate retainer. A patron may also be *indirectly* tied to a client, such as in a relationship heavily mediated by multiple levels of *brokerage*. A patron-client relationship may, furthermore, involve restricted dimensions. Or it may involve many multiple vectors, as when a patron marries his youngest daughter to a client and therefore establishes a kinship tie with him. The material, affective, and dimensional intensity of interactions factor in the *strength* and *weakness* of social ties.[97]

Any relatively durable transaction, such as economic exchange, ongoing communication, coercion, and alliance, produces social ties. The overall pattern of social ties—including their strength, weakness, and valence—gives rise to a network. In this sense, the notion of patron-client networks is more than metaphor: when we characterize patterns of relationships as patron-client (or patron-broker-client) we claim that they approximate a particular kind of analytic or ideal-typical kind of network structure (figure 2.1). In social-network analysis the networks produced by arrangement of ties are, in essence, social structures.[98] Any social structure, whether decentralized or centralized, heterogeneous or homogenous, can be represented in terms of a network of ties.[99] It follows that,

---

[96] For discussion of the last examples, see Lendon 1997.

[97] For example, Gould 1993, 190; and Granovetter 1973, 1361. One way of conceptualizing this variable is what White calls the "multiplexity" of ties: "a concrete tie can better be visualized as multiplex, e.g., a vector quantity of different amounts of several components." See White 1972, 9.

[98] See Wellman and Berkowitz 1998.

[99] Some distinguish "networks" from "hierarchies." Such attempts to limit the concept of network to decentralized structural relations, or even to associate networks with nonhierarchical scale-free networks, are common not only in popular and political-science discussions of terrorism, but also in work on transnationalism. See, e.g., Arquilla, Ronfeldt et al. 1999, and Keck and Sikkink 1998. While this may be heuristically useful for certain pur-

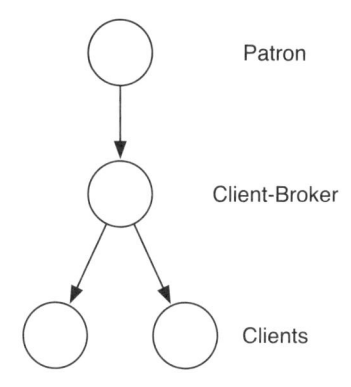

Figure 2.1 Simple Patron-Client Network

in relational and network approaches to social structure, structures emerge from patterns of transaction.[100] This view is broadly consistent with the constructivist emphasis on agent-structure co-constitution, since social ties—ongoing processes and practices of interaction—simultaneously produce the terms of agency and structure.[101]

Indeed, through identifying and mapping—whether qualitatively or quantitatively—the form and content of social networks we observe social structures.[102] Patterns of strong and weak ties give rise to specific attributes of networks. Networks, for example, vary in terms of their *sparseness* and *density*. A standard definition of network density is the "ratio of existing ties to possible ties."[103] A network is completely sparse when no actor is connected to any other actor. A network is maximally dense when every actor is directly linked to every other actor. In sparse networks most actors are linked indirectly to one another through a small number of other actors in the network. Sparse networks contain a great many "structural holes": that is, network gaps (figure 2.2.)[104]

The structural location of any actor, whether an individual, interest group, or state, depends on how she is positioned within one or more networks. Actors within various networks, for instance, exhibit various

---

poses, hierarchies are also networks, although ones characterized by various relations of super- and subordination. See Chase 1980.

[100] Emirbayer and Goodwin 1994, 1481; Mardsen 1990, 435–36[Daniel: "Mardsen" correct? "Marsden"?]; Tilly 1998, 399; and Wellman 1983, 156–62.

[101] Dessler 1989, Doty 1999, Jackson and Nexon 1999 and 2001, Wendt 1987 and 1992, Wight 1999.

[102] Wasserman and Faust 1994, White and Boorman 1976, White, Boorman et al. 1976.

[103] Gould 1993, 190.

[104] Burt 1992.

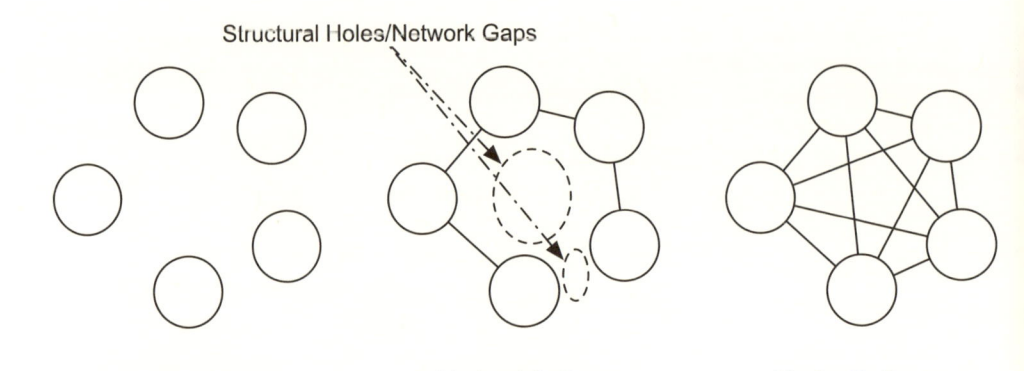

Figure 2.2 Network Density

degrees of *centrality*—in other words, the degree to which they are connected to other actors in the network.[105] *Brokers*, as previously noted, occupy central positions between segmented social relations; a "broker," as Mario Diani explains, "may be defined as an actor connecting other actors [whom] are not directly related to one another" either because of a lack of opportunities or because of "some specific political or social barrier" that precludes direct interaction (for example, the "client-broker" position in figure 2.1).[106]

Actors are frequently positioned within multiple networks, which gives rise to sometimes complimentary and sometimes contradictory structural forces.[107] An actor may be central to a particular political network, but peripheral with respect to a different network. In addition, the content—the meanings and symbols—of the social relations that make up a network have important influences on its structural dynamics.[108] In a general sense, networks of enmity do not have the same basic dynamics as networks of friendship. A given political network, however, is likely to contain multiple kinds of ties, which influence the structural opportunities of and constraints upon actors located at particular points in the network.

CATEGORIES

Meanings and identities play a constitutive role in social ties and networks. Both ties and network structures involve not simply material ex-

[105] Wellman and Berkowitz 1998
[106] Diani 2003, 107. See also chapter 4 in the present volume.
[107] Mische 2003, 261, 274–75.
[108] Ibid., Tilly 2002.

changes, but also communication and symbolic transactions. Many forms of social-network analysis, nevertheless, contain strong elements of structural determinism. Cultural factors and agency drop out of analysis.[109] But identities can be parsed in relational and positional terms.

Identification involves a process of boundary drawing—manifested in the structure of social ties—implicated in claims making and negotiation. Strongly sedimented relational identities produce *categories*: social positions that constitute the actors located within them: that is, social roles such as "mother," "father," "Catholic," "English," "dynast," "king of France," "banker," and so forth. Norms, similarly, may become attached to these social positions.[110] In general, relational approaches view discourses, frames, norms, and legitimating frameworks in terms of public claims making by social sites—as scripts that diffuse through networks and otherwise embed in the ongoing transactions that constitute social and political life. At the same time, claims making and discourse construct, reproduce, and alter social relations "within the constraints of social settings."[111]

A number of factors render categorical identities particularly important for any analysis of collective mobilization. As constructivism holds, the activation of common categorical identities often facilitates collective mobilization between actors and social sites. It also orients joint-action toward norms associated with relevant categorical identities.[112] But, since multiple categories attach to any actor or social site, identity will rarely provide a self-sufficient explanation for individual and collective action. We need to know something, also and at least, about the arrangement of social ties—the network structures—in which actors are embedded and how these relate to categorical identities.[113]

Corporate actors—whether universities, states, or multinational firms—present, in fact, both a special and highly significant kind of configuration of categories and networks. They result from networks with two crucial characteristics. First, they are bounded such that only a limited number of actors enjoy the right to form specific kinds of exchange relationships with actors outside of the network—to act as brokers between sites within one network and sites outside of it. When "one site" within each network "has the right to establish cross-boundary relations

---

[109] Emirbayer and Goodwin 1994.

[110] For a similar distinction—between "relational" and "categorical" identities—see Brubaker and Cooper 2000, 19–21.

[111] Mische 2003, 264. See also Goddard 2006, Jackson 2006a, Jackson and Nexon 2001, and Tilly 2002 and 2005.

[112] McAdam 2003, 293–96.

[113] Adamson 2005a, 549–57, and 2005b, 33–42; Goddard and Nexon 2005, 37; Tilly 1998, 399–401; Tilly 2003, 31–34; Tilly 2005, 60–67, 131–52.

that bind members of internal ties," then each network constitutes a discrete "organization."[114] In a multinational firm only corporate decision makers have the ultimate right to make contracts with states, suppliers, distributors, and other firms: that is, to act as brokers between networks. Second, every member of the network is distinguished from every actor outside of the network by virtue of a particular marker—a categorical identity. In a multinational firm every employee is a an employee of that firm, and not of any other.[115]

These two characteristics account for how a particular network takes on agentic properties. The firm, state, or whatever can "act" in ways analogous to an individual because of, on the one hand, the ability of certain "brokers" or "gatekeepers" to regulate cross-boundary exchanges and, on the other, the association of a common "corporate" identity with actions originating within the network. When individuals act "on behalf" of the network we speak, sometimes in a juridical and other times in a pragmatic sense, as if the entire network acted. Action "on behalf" of the entity, in fact, sustains and constitutes the corporate agent as such.[116]

Relational analytics, therefore, provide important leverage over an undertheorized dimension of debates over international change: it suggests some of the kinds of processes through which the emergence of new identities and patterns of interaction translate into corporate actors. Two related mechanisms are at stake here: *yoking* and *brokerage*.

As Andrew Abbott argues, "Yoking means connection of two or more proto-boundaries such that one side becomes defined as 'inside' the same entity." Yoking occurs through one of two processes. First, "when a division of social space into entities is already established," he contends, "the only ways to radically change arrangements . . . are to delegitimize old differences or to emphasize new ones. The former strategy yokes entities together, the latter divides them."[117] The spread of heterodox religious ideas and identities in early modern Europe created multiple effects along these lines. In Germany, for example, religious cleavages within the Swabian League helped destroy its ability to act collectively.[118] Princes and

---

[114] Tilly 1999, 413.

[115] Tilly 1998, 399. A note on the example given here: in some instances, a consultant or temporary worker may be contracted to occupy a position in which they are both employee of the firm and employee of another firm. These kinds of relationships complicate patterns of authority, obligation, and structural dynamics, but they do not contradict the basic thrust of my argument.

[116] See Jackson 2004, and Jackson and Nexon 1999. The argument here echoes, in some respects, criticisms of the "state-as-unitary-actor" assumption that stresses the importance of the existence of final decision makers. See Milner 1997.

[117] Abbott 2001, 272–73.

[118] Owen 2005.

Theorizing International Change • 47

towns deployed religious commonalities to yoke together the League of Schmalkald—a Protestant alliance—that rapidly emerged as an international actor treating with foreign princes and influencing developments outside of the empire.[119] Second, "When a social space is empty or, rather, unstructured . . . yoking means literal connection of boundaries." In this process of "the emergence of an entity is the assemblage of various sites of difference . . . into a set of boundaries in the topologically strict sense, boundaries that define an inside and an outside."[120] I do not systematically explore examples of this kind of yoking in this study.[121]

Both of these processes call our attention to mechanisms of brokerage. Yoking creates, of course, new brokerage relations by mapping, and re-mapping, social relations in terms of different categories. But the fate of yoking processes also often involves the activities of brokers. According to Charles Tilly, brokerage that "connects factions on each side of an us-them boundary without establishing new connections across the boundary" polarizes social relations. When a member of an ethnic group, for example, establishes herself as the key broker between her coethnics and members of another ethnic category, then she severs other significant cross-cutting ties. She may do this to "opportunity hoard," to gain power, influence, status, and material resources associated with monopolizing cross-cutting ties. Strategies of ethnic cleansing, for example, involve the use of violence and intimidation to activate and polarize social relations—to, in other words, make it untenable for most individuals to maintain routine social and political relations across categorical differences.[122]

If, however, "brokers compete for control on the same side of a boundary, then fragmentation results—at least until one broker eliminates the other." Competition between brokers within a well-bounded network represents a familiar process in the formation of factions and submovements.[123] Such competition sometimes presents opportunities for external actors to form alternative cross-boundary ties, and even to manipulate emerging cleavages as part of divide-and-rule or divide-and-conquer strategies. If these intragroup brokerage struggles involve claims based upon

---

[119] Elton 1964, 156.
[120] Abbott 2001, 273.
[121] The early phases of the Reformations, however, involved the emergence of a variety of loosely connected and often inchoate theological claims and religious movements. Both opponents and supporters of religious reformation linked together, through concrete social practices and rhetorics, aspects of these doctrinal claims and elements of these movements into many of the sects we now use as shorthand to describe them: Protestantism writ large, Lutheranism, Zwinglianism, Calvinism and the Reformed movement, and so forth.
[122] Tilly 2003, 10, 96.
[123] Ibid., 21.

alternative categorical differences to those that mark existing group boundaries, then they may produce new yoking effects.

We will see these kinds of dynamics throughout subsequent chapters, but they have clear resonance with sectarian conflict after the American-led invasion of Iraq, as well as numerous other examples of violent and nonviolent collective mobilization in international and domestic politics.[124] The key point is as follows: actors may deploy identities and engage in forms of bargaining that, in specific settings, contribute to or fragment collective mobilization among social sites. Some of these activities may even produce, sustain, or decompose corporate actors, including religious movements and states themselves.

INTERNATIONAL STRUCTURE AS NESTED RELATIONAL CONFIGURATIONS

These concepts flesh out my treatment of international structure as "networks of networks." A sole focus on patterns of social ties fails to capture important dimensions of socio-political structures. Pathways and proclivities for collective mobilization, both across and within different levels of analysis, stem from patterns of social ties *and* distributions of categorical identities. Variation in *catness* (the degree of homogeneity of salient identities) and *netness* (the density of salient social ties) gives rise to relational contexts that display, at a general level, different patterns of collective action.[125] International structures, seen in this way, resolve from the ways in which various relational configurations nest within one another and thereby give rise to, in their relation, reproductive and transformative structural tendencies for joint-action.[126]

Consider four different ideal-typical combinations of categorical homogeneity and network density: low-category/low-network, high-category/high-network, high-category/low-network, and low-category/low-network (figure 2.3).[127] Each of these contexts produces different collective-action dynamics. One of the major oversights in contemporary international-relations theory, as I will argue in detail below, involves conflating

---

[124] On the importance of brokerage to the problems in the American occupation of Iraq, see Hulsman and Debat 2006, and MacDonald 2006.

[125] This is one of Tilly's key insights in *From Mobilization to Revolution*. See Tilly 1978. The following discussion also derives from Peter Bearman's extensions of Tilly's argument. See Bearman 1993.

[126] Yale Ferguson and Richard Mansbach articulate this point in the context of the structure of political communities. They argue that many "of the most interesting and consequential aspects of political life flow from the fact that polities share space and can claim the loyalties of all or some of the same constituents." Further, since "some actors occupy the same space, are located entirely within one another or stretch across other actors, what function as 'structures' in some contexts will become 'agents' in other contexts." See Ferguson and Mansbach 1996, 48, 29.

[127] I discuss ideal-typical methodology below.

Theorizing International Change • 49

```
High  ┌─────────────────────────────────────────┐
      │ Ephemeral Collective   Sustained Collective │
      │ Mobilization           Mobilization Relatively │
      │ Stemming from          Easy                │
      │ Identity-Based                             │
      │ Triggers                                   │
      │                                            │
      │                                            │
      │                                            │
      │ Prisoners' Dilemma    Collective Action    │
      │ Collective-Action     through Interest-    │
      │ Problems              Adjudication and     │
      │                       Coalition Formation  │
Low   └─────────────────────────────────────────┘
       Low                                    High
                    Network Density
```
(y-axis: Categorical Homogeneity)

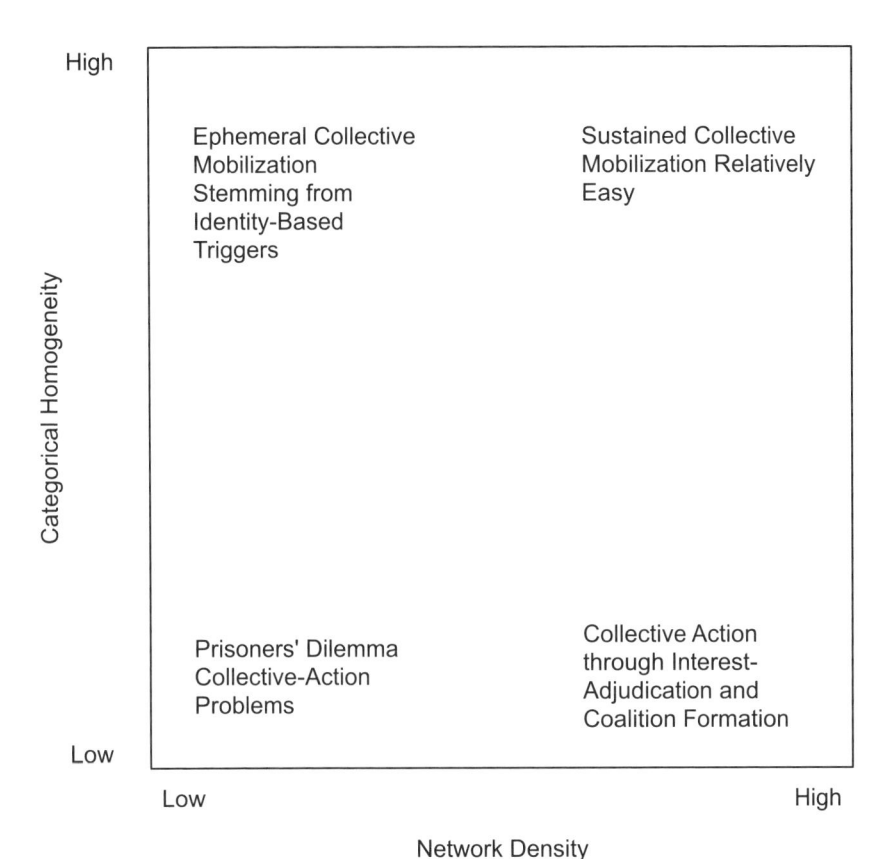

Figure 2.3 Variation in Relational Contexts and Collective Mobilization

collective-action processes in low-network/low-category contexts with something called the "collective-action problem."[128] We then, as Wendt notes, associate that collective-action problem with "anarchy" regardless of the structures of the actors found within it.[129]

Low-Category and Low-Network. Many international-relations scholars take sparse social ties and heterogeneous identities as the baseline condition for collective mobilization. In this environment, collective action faces the barriers associated with the "Prisoner's Dilemma": actors pursue their own interests in the absence of durable interactions through which they can monitor and enforce compliance with collective

---
[128] I thank Chuck Tilly for repeatedly hammering home this point in our discussions.
[129] Wendt 1994.

agreements. They, therefore, worry about the tendency for other actors to exploit the gains that follow from joint-action without paying the costs of collective action; as realists point out, the competitive disadvantages actors face from being "suckered"—from engaging in joint-action when another actor does not participate—may even jeopardize their own survival.

If one actor upholds, for example, an arms-limitation agreement while the other continues to develop its own military capabilities, the results might be disastrous for the actor complying with the collective agreement.[130] The absence of collective identification and routine pathways of interaction presents serious barriers to collective mobilization in the first place, as well as to the capacity of actors to sustain collective mobilization over time.[131] Both realist and neoliberal-institutionalist accounts of anarchy, as most readers will have already recognized, presuppose a low-category/low-network relational context. But the existence of an aggregate low-category/low-network context does not, in fact, produce the full range of anarchical dynamics associated with the states-under-anarchy framework. I will return to this point shortly.

High-Network and High-Category. When actors operate in dense networks and share salient categorical identities, they face few conventional barriers to collective action. In an ideal-typical world, where "network density approaches saturation . . . the 'local' boundary of rationality becomes globalized and no transaction costs accrue to interpersonal interactions, including informational exchange." Collective mobilization "is the norm, not the exception."[132]

In less extreme conditions, the conjunction of shared salient identities and high network density work to render collective action relatively easy. Collective identification increases trust, willingness to incur costs for others, and the likelihood of shared orientations toward collective goods, while dense networks facilitate monitoring and other nuts-and bolts components of joint-action. The primary research questions for analysis of collective mobilization in this configuration include: first, what different kinds of stimuli (events, social agency, and so on) activate collective mobilization; and, second, how processes of collective mobilization may trigger changes—either toward low-network or low-category—that undermine the continued vitality of collective action.

---

[130] See Axelrod 1984; Axelrod and Keohane 1993; Gould 1993, 182; Grieco 1993; and Jervis 1978.

[131] Axelrod 1984, 85; Kim and Bearman 1997, 88.

[132] Kim and Bearman 1997, 88.

I have difficulty imagining an "international" environment that remotely approximates this ideal-typical position. But many international-relations theories, particularly those that deal with systems-level analysis, presuppose that states represent—at least in relative terms—high-category/high-network environments. As Schweller argues,

> This assumption of "constant mobilization capacity" allows balance-of-power and other systemic theories to ignore the politics of extraction, treating responses to threats as if there were no significant variations across time and space in elites' ability to mobilize domestic resources in pursuit of foreign-policy aims. . . . Thus, efforts to create an elegant systemic theory of international politics set aside differences in unit attributes such as state extractive capacity.[133]

High-Category and Low-Network. This configuration describes settings that combine sparse social ties and homogeneous categorical identities. Collective-mobilization dynamics in these structural settings often takes the form of convergence around a highly salient common identity, such as "worker," "co-religionist," or "nation." The standard pathways involve a strong trigger, sometimes exogenous, of the salient categorical identity that leads to rapid joint-action; once that trigger wanes, however, actors have difficulty sustaining continued collective mobilization. The problems for collective action, therefore, involve not the classic "barriers" described above but, first, coordination of action during mobilization and, second, sustaining collective mobilization once the trigger loses its immediate salience.

After the attacks of September 11, 2001, for example, Americans engaged in a large array of joint-actions: flying flags from houses and cars, assembling in hastily arranged gatherings to mourn the victims of the attacks, and otherwise engaging in ritualized displays of common identity and purpose. But, as many American commentators noted (usually with regret), it did not take long for old regional, local, political, and other divisions to resurface; such collective mobilization soon dissipated into the normal routines of social and political life. Collective mobilization in such settings displays "ephemerality—the tendency of the movement to disappear because it is based on one dimension. While this dimension may be powerful for a time, other social cleavages may re-emerge after" or during collective action; these cleavages—lower-level collective identities—often prevent lasting political change through collective action.[134]

[133] Schweller 2006, 13.
[134] Bearman 1993, 113.

52 • Chapter 2

Low-Category and High-Network. Collective mobilization in these settings faces few transaction costs but often founders on heterogeneous identities and interests. Collective action sometimes takes one of two pathways. First, actors maintain collective action through ongoing efforts to convert actors to a common set of identities and norms, or to sever ties between actors with distinctive categorical identities. Thus, salient dynamics of collective mobilization in these contexts run the gamut from those that produce alterations in salient norms and identities to the violent destruction of cross-category social ties exemplified by ethnic cleansing and other strategies of coercive boundary activation.[135]

Second, processes of collective mobilization may involve dynamics familiar to rationalist accounts of bargaining: shifting coalitions between interests with free-rider problems mitigated by dense social networks.[136] Furthermore, low-category/high-network environments may exercise differential influence on collective mobilization depending on the location of initiators of collective action. Roger V. Gould finds that dense networks only facilitate collective action initiated by those at the margins of the network. In contrast, dense networks expose centrally located actors to countervailing pressures from those disinterested or opposed to pursuit of the collective good.[137]

The high-network/low-category relational context, as I will soon discuss, bears an important resemblance to neoliberal-institutionalist "solutions" to the problem of cooperation under anarchy. These accounts focus on how repeated interactions form, in essence, social ties that facilitate cooperation.

INTERNATIONAL STRUCTURES REVISITED

Treating the structure of international interactions in terms of nested relational configurations allows us to link variation in the structure of polities—and other corporate actors—to international structures. Not only does this analytic move capture the co-constituted relationship between agents and structures at different levels of analysis, but it provides a way

---

[135] See variously Keck and Sikkink 1998, Mitzen 2005, Ringmar 1996, Risse 2000, and Tilly 2003.

[136] Dense social networks composed of weak ties—those in which actors interact but do so fleetingly and without likely future interaction—may actually inhibit collective action. As Michael W. Macy argues, "The greater the number of possible interactions, the lower the possibility that any two players will interact again, and if they should, the lower the possibility that the victim will recognize his or her predator." It may also be the case that overly dense social ties in large groups make it difficult for actors to keep track of the behavior of others. See Macy 1991, 828, 832–33. But at the level of abstraction considered here, we need not be overly troubled by these interesting possibilities.

[137] Gould 1993, 194. See also Kim and Bearman 1997, 88.

to think about how transactional patterns give rise to opportunity structures for collective action in world politics.[138] I should note, however, that when we parse large-scale aggregates such as "states" and "international structures" as relational configurations, our claims about network density and categorical homogeneity will always be relative and analytical in character. The key question focuses on asymmetries in network density and categorical homogeneity in relational contexts.

In this light, the states-under-anarchy framework so familiar in realist analysis describes, in these terms, a *particular kind of nested relational configuration*. At the aggregate level, the framework posits a low-category/low-network structure. Ties between social sites—in this case, states—are comparatively weak and sparse. Furthermore, they involve no significant authoritative ties among social sites.[139] The relational structure also exhibits a great deal of categorical heterogeneity: realists assume, at least implicitly, that each state represents a different national or ethnic identity.[140] As Wendt argues, each state is constituted by a distinct "corporate identity"; the standard states-under-anarchy framework (whether realist or neoliberal-institutionalist) presupposes little collective identification between states. Their orientation is self-regarding, rather than other-regarding.[141]

At the next lower level of analysis, however, we confront a very different relational context. States themselves, at least in *relative* terms, comprise high-category/high-network social sites. According to Waltz, "the division of labor across nations . . . is slight in comparison with the highly articulated division of labor within them. Integration draws the parts of a nation closer together."[142] Note that a high-category/high-network structure at the unit-level co-constitutes the low-category/low-network structure at the international level (figure 2.4).

This nested structure, moreover, creates *strong asymmetries in pathways and proclivities for collective mobilization and collective action*.[143] These asymmetries, as we have already seen, underpin realist accounts of international politics. Because categorical identities related to the nation-state congeal closely with dense social relations within each unit, collec-

---

[138] Adamson 2005a, 553.
[139] Waltz 1979, 88.
[140] Lapid and Kratochwil 1996.
[141] Wendt 1994, 1996, 1999.
[142] Waltz 1979, 105.
[143] Cerny notes the importance of these asymmetries when he argues that "in the modern study of international relations, the state has constituted the key unit of collective action, while the interaction of states has been the very object of inquiry; in the domestic arena, the state has both encompassed the political system and constituted a potentially autonomous collective agent within that field." See Cerny 1995, 596.

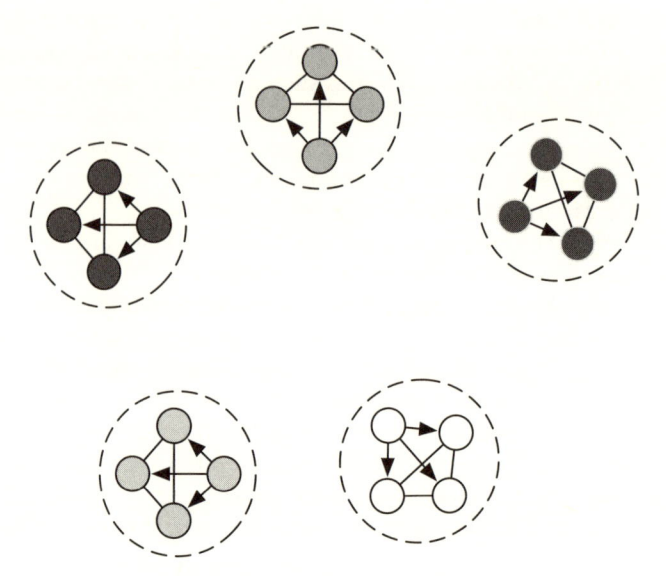

Figure 2.4 The States-under-Anarchy Framework as a Nested Relational Configuration

tive action faces relatively few hurdles. Collective mobilization *between* states, however, faces strong structural barriers. States, therefore, become focal points for the provision of collective goods, while international collective action carries with it a number of risks that disincline the leaders of states—those that act as gatekeepers between "domestic" and "international" transactions—to engage in transformative joint-action.[144]

Recoding the states-under-anarchy framework as a nested relational configuration provides important analytic leverage on a number of important debates about collective action, international structures, and international change. First, recall the constructivist claim that realist accounts of international structure presuppose specific kinds of units and associated intersubjective norms: sovereign-territorial nation-states. Realists disagree. Gilpin argues that realism only requires the existence of "conflict groups" and that the precise nature of conflict groups varies across time and space.[145] Waltz, for his part, maintains that the lack of a common authority is a sufficient condition for structural-realist dynamics. Neither side gets it

---

[144] Indeed, many realists now argue not only that anarchy pressures states to pay careful attention to relative gains, but that the tendency for groups to favor their own at the expense of outsiders—in other words, the overlap between categorical identities and the dense political ties of states—also helps account for state egoism, relative-gains sensitivity, and the failure of international collective action. See Sterling-Folker 2002a and b.

[145] Gilpin 1986, 325. See also Brenner 2006, 516–17; and Schweller and Wohlforth 2000, 70–72.

entirely right. Realist dynamics become increasingly salient as relational contexts approach the structural configuration specified above. A system composed of sovereign-territorial nation-states certainly makes such a configuration more likely to obtain, but other intersubjective norms and kinds of units might also produce such a structural environment.[146]

Thus, realism describes relevant dynamics in many different transactional settings, including some involving nonstate actors. But we should recognize two important caveats. On the one hand, pockets of realist anarchy will involve different consequences depending on how they embed in other relational structures. Security dilemmas between ethnic groups in an occupied territory, for example, will not necessarily unfold the same way as they would between two consolidated nation-states. On the other hand, once we move toward a more dynamic view of structure, we can recognize that processes of collective action may transform such "anarchical" relationships in ways often dismissed by realists.

These observations entail important consequences. John M. Owen IV provides one of the few international-relations treatments of the conflicts in Germany that preceded the 1555 Peace of Augsburg. He insightfully conjoins realist accounts of the security dilemma with ideational dynamics; thus, he argues, the conflict spiral involved an ideational security dilemma that gave rise to increasingly polarized alliances.[147] But, as I argue in chapter 5, the particulars of his account depend on an incorrect coding of the empire as an example of international anarchy. We gain better leverage over these dynamics by recognizing how the institutional structures of the empire contributed to relational contexts for brokerage, including how they shaped attempts at divide-and-rule strategies and processes of yoking together new collective actors.

Realists, in fact, seldom expend much energy in delineating analytical principles for identifying such "conflict groups." They hold, in essence, that if we find groups—states, ethnic movements, and so forth—in conflict, then realist dynamics, such as security dilemmas, also operate.[148] But plenty of intergroup conflict occurs under conditions that deviate from these relational structures. Sometimes categorical identities do not perfectly overlay the boundaries of the groups or we find a more complicated variation in network density across and within the relevant social sites. I develop this theme throughout the rest of the book.[149]

---

[146] Note how this line of argument coheres with my emphasis on generalizing about the *formal* properties of relational structures. Consider, for example, Hui's claim that China during the Warring States period provides an example of realist anarchy. Hui 2005, 5–6. For similar arguments, see Buzan 1996; Buzan, Jones et al. 1993; and Buzan and Little 2000.

[147] Owen 2005.
[148] Glaser 2003, 407–8.
[149] Tilly 2003.

Second, a relational approach provides better purchase on key claims about international change. Major strands of liberal theory, in essence, relax the assumption of extremely weak network density between states. Consider the neoliberal-institutionalist argument that, under the right conditions, repeated interaction between states provides a basis for successful international collective action. Repeated interaction amounts to a change in the relational context for collective action: that is, an increase in the density and strength of ties between actors.[150]

In some respects, this pathway of international collective action presents less of a "solution" to standard Prisoners' Dilemma situations than a different structural condition for collective action altogether, in which free-ridership ceases to be an insurmountable problem in the first place. As Peter Kollack remarks of Robert Axelrod's studies, "The structural property that is doing most of the work in these analyses—the fact that transactions occur repeatedly with the same actions—is fixed by assumption." Indeed, such work raises questions about imputed mechanisms of cooperation because "conditional cooperation occurs only because of iterated transactions with identifiable others; yet there is no explanation of how a longitudinal exchange relationship is established or maintained or what patterns these networks of relations might take."[151]

Complex-interdependence theory, on the other hand, supplies a more relational account of how increasing network density in world politics alters collective-action dynamics. Many of the theory's predictions track with what we should expect to happen as ties increase among states and across their boundaries. As the *relative* network density of states themselves diminishes with respect to that across and among them, their centrality as sites of collective mobilization declines; leaders of states become increasingly subject to cross pressures from transnational forces and thus less able to prioritize traditional power-political concerns over the interests of trans- and substate economic networks—such as multinational firms—and other social sites.[152]

If much of the action in rationalist accounts of inter-state collective mobilization centers on variation in network density, then *constructivist accounts often privilege shifts in categorical identities*. At the most basic level, constructivists simply point out that categorical homogeneity reduces the salience of standard barriers to collective action: when states, through social interaction, come to collectively identify with one another, processes of collectivity shift toward the high-category structural domain.[153]

---

[150] See, e.g., Axelrod 1984, Axelrod and Keohane 1993, and Keohane 1984.
[151] Kollock 1994, 317.
[152] Keohane and Nye 1989.
[153] Wendt 1994, 386.

Thus, Wendt contends that "collective identification is an important condition for the emergence of 'international states,' which would constitute a structural transformation of the Westphalian state system."[154] Constructivist work on security communities echoes this line of argument: collective identification among states, at least in some accounts, allows states to overcome the dilemmas of collective action associated with anarchy. In such security communities, states no longer view military conflict as an appropriate way to resolve disputes, and thus escape security dilemmas and anarchical constraints upon joint-action.[155]

Most constructivists, however, rest their argument not simply on increasing categorical homogeneity but also on increasing network density. Some accounts focus on a process of positive feedback between the two, in which relations between states take on properties of increasing catness and netness.[156] But, of course, the two need not emerge in tandem. Indeed, as we have seen, variation on both dimensions leads to different problems for and processes of collective mobilization. Constructivist arguments about collective identification—as well as neoliberal-institutionalist solutions to collective action—work from the premise that increased categorical homogeneity and/or network density "overcomes" collective-action problems. From a relational perspective, however, the standard articulation of the collective-action problem focuses on a single structural context and therefore neglects how different relational conditions shift the pathways and proclivities for collective action.

Indeed, as constructivists routinely argue, shifts in norms of reciprocity, political networks, and categorical identities may themselves result *from* collective mobilization and processes of interaction. When actors form cooperative agreements, they produce new political ties, which in turn take on autonomous dynamics. In consequence, actors become situated in new network locations or at the intersection of new political ties, both of which may supply new relational, or even categorical, identities and may shift the preferences and interests that neoliberals and relational-contracting theorists treat as exogenously given.

Third, it follows that we should view international structures, at a minimum, as dynamic products of transactions between states and other well-bounded social sites. William C. Wohlforth contends that "alliances are not structural." He argues that, "because alliances are less effective than states in producing and deploying power internationally, most scholars . . . [make] a distinction between the distribution of capabilities among

---

[154] Ibid., 385.
[155] Adler and Barnett 1998b.
[156] Wendt 1994, 388–91. Cf. Pouliot 2006.

states and the alliances states may form."[157] While we should draw such a distinction—the positional effects of relative power are different from the positional effects of alliance ties—we should reject the consequent. Alliances, ties generated by membership in international organizations, patterns of animosity, economic exchange, and so forth *are* structural.[158] They embed states in shifting conditions of possibility for reproductive and transformative collective action.

Fourth, political communities often deviate significantly from the ideal-typical states presupposed in the states-under-anarchy framework. In his analysis of African politics, Robert Jackson refers to most African states of the modern period as "quasi-states" in that they are far more fragmented and subject to overlapping authority-networks than idealized nation-states.[159] Many of the Central Asian states formed from the collapse of the Soviet Union have contracted out "control rights" to Russia that give it authority over assets within their territory.[160] In fact, although "most of our encyclopedias, textbooks, atlases, and almanacs portray states as holistic entities, unified and distinct," linguistic, national, economic, ethnic, and religious affiliations seldom conform to the boundaries of modern states.[161] Michael Mann, for instance, claims that the very pressures embodied in such contradictions gave rise to the First World War.[162]

The structure of political communities matters a great deal for dominant pathways and proclivities of international collective mobilization. As we have seen, during the Israeli-Hezbollah conflict of 2006, the Israeli government demanded that the Lebanese government rein in Hezbollah and conducted some of its military operations with that objective in mind. But Lebanon was a categorically fragmented state in which political ties sometimes linked and sometimes separated movements claiming to represent different factions—such as Sunni, Shia, and Christian—which themselves controlled significant mobilization networks. The Lebanese government simply could not dictate terms to Hezbollah, which enjoyed an advantage in violent collective mobilization over its putative sovereign. Indeed, the government lacked the fundamental ability to police cross-boundary exchanges between Hezbollah, on the one hand, and Iran and Syria, on the other.[163]

---

[157] Wohlforth 1999, 29.

[158] See Cerny 1995; Hafner-Burton and Montgomery 2006; Ingram, Robinson et al. 2005; Jackson and Nexon 1999; and Montgomery 2005

[159] Jackson 1990.

[160] Cooley 2000/2001, 101.

[161] Lewis and Wïgen 1997, 8.

[162] Mann 1993, 87.

[163] Salem 2006.

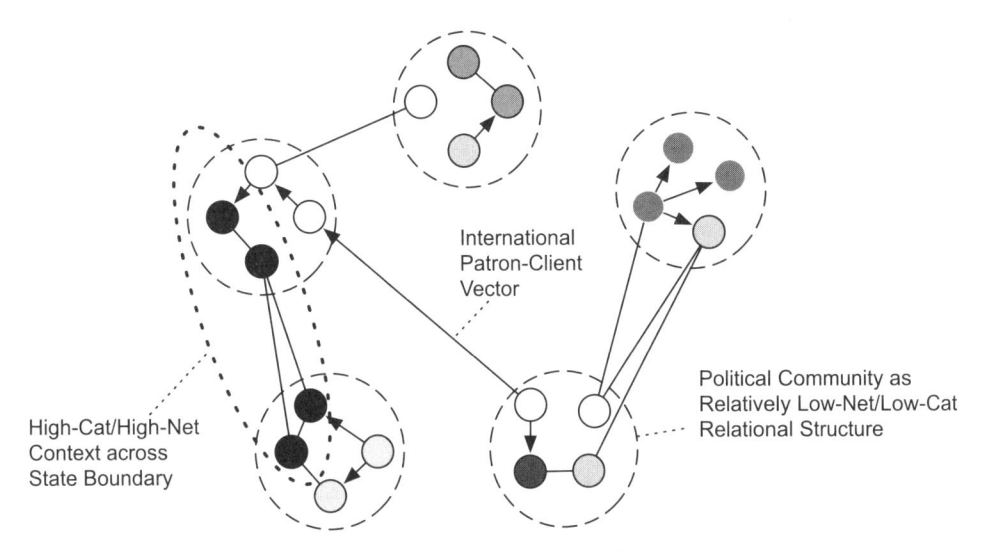

Figure 2.5 Hypothetical Relational Configuration of "Weak States"

Variations in the "domestic structure" of political communities away from the nation-state ideal type thus involve shifts in the "international structures" that shape and shove collective action among relevant actors—governments, nonstate groups, transnational movements, and so forth. We tend to ignore these kinds of nested relations when agents of states enjoy a preponderance of control over cross-boundary exchanges; we consider them only when, as in the case of Lebanon or so-called "failed states," governmental agents lack such practical authority. But states always co-constitute relational structures at the international level.

Recall the semihypothetical example of an international arena composed of "weak states" that I offered in the introduction. Figure 2.5 shows a nested relational structure in which collective mobilization asymmetries do not necessarily correspond to state borders. I have delineated a few significant nested relational structures, such as the existence of an international client-patron relationship between leaders of two polities, a co-identity high-category/high-network context operating across the boundaries of two polities, and so forth. Note the brokerage positions that emerge from this aggregate relational structure compared to those in the ideal-typical states-under-anarchy framework.

Now let's take a look at a simplified—and hence illustrative rather than empirically accurate—nested international structure of the kind found during the French Wars of Religion and the Dutch Revolt (figure 2.6). An international arena composed of imperial composite polities, let alone one

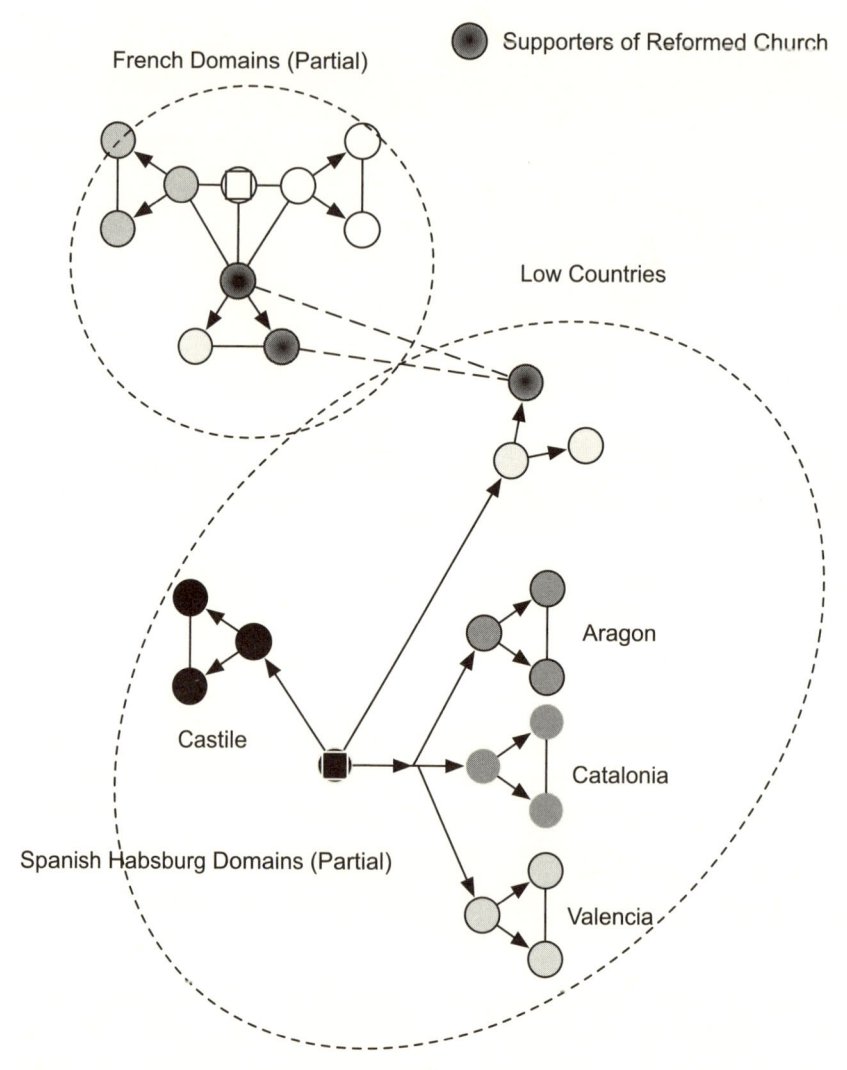

Figure 2.6 Stylized Representation of the French and the Spanish Domains during the Dutch Revolt and the French Wars of Religion

involved in "transnational" religious contention, involves significantly different nested configurations, with different collective-mobilization dynamics at various levels of analysis, than that associated with the states-under-anarchy framework.

All of this, of course, operates at a rather high level of generality. The point is that we can gain better analytical leverage over questions of international continuity and change by thinking in relational and institutionalist terms. Specific theories of continuity and change, for their part, require additional analytic work.

Constructing Specific Theories of Change: Conjoining Relationalism and Historical Institutionalism

By this point, readers should have a pretty good idea about what relationalism entails for how we conceptualize actors, structures, and dynamics of collective action. We should now consider the last task I set for myself at the outset: to explain how we might construct specific theories of international continuity and transformation that balance the goals of *taking historical particulars seriously* with *producing generalizable propositions*. I proceed by conjoining relational concepts to historical-institutionalist sensibilities. I have already alluded to much of what this entails: the development of mechanism- and process-based generalizations that link specific dynamics to the formal properties of relational structures.

The Importance of the Mesolevel

Any given account of international continuity and change aims to explain specific historical phenomena, such as the impact of the Protestant Reformation on European politics or the consequences of the American invasion of Iraq for Middle Eastern power politics. Such accounts involve, at the very least, significant mechanisms and processes that operate between broad overarching macrostructures, such as the aggregate structure of the "international system," and microlevel dynamics, such as those involved in individual decision making.[164]

Relationalist approaches caution against describing very large-scale structures, such as that of the "international system," in terms of singular properties. Recall my discussion of the idea that anarchy operates as some kind of overarching structure in international politics. Even contemporary world politics involves all sorts of hierarchical and governance relations: states exert asymmetric influence over other states, international institutions regulate forms of commerce and criminal activity, alliances engage in various kinds of joint—decision making, and so on.[165] Thus, it

---

[164] In principle, "micro-," "macro-," and "meso-" are relative and analytical terms: they simply refer to levels of aggregation and not to any concrete levels of analysis, such as "states" or "the international system." Here I use them to refer to actor-level processes, broad structures, and embedded relational contexts. For discussions, see Alexander 1988, 257; and Wight 2006, 90–120.

[165] See Buzan, Jones et al. 1993; Mearsheimer 2001; Schweller 2001; and Waltz 1979.

makes little sense to explain dynamics within these relations primarily with reference to the putatively anarchical character of world politics.

Or take the example of constructivist claims about the existence of "systemic norms" or "constitutive rules" of international politics. The problem with such accounts stems not from their identification of a wide range of deeply sedimented practices in international politics, but from their analytical decision to treat them as a catalog of properties of something called "the international system" or "international society." Since we can only posit the existence of such institutions by studying practices—how actors legitimate their actions, how they relate to one another, and so forth—the attempt to elevate them to the level of systemic norms carries with it (unnecessary) additional theoretical baggage. Moreover, it may lead to errors similar to those found in structural-functional analysis, such as the notion that "tensions" or "discrepancies" between reified practices provide a self-sufficient explanation for change.[166]

Once we adopt a suitable humility toward identifying spare properties of international structures, however, we face a difficult question: where should we lodge our analysis of the dynamics of these relational contexts? We confront problems related to the quantity and complexity of the transactional patterns that constitute world politics. The potential for analytical overload increases once we no longer draw rigid demarcations between "international" and "domestic" politics, in that we now admit social ties at multiple levels of analysis into our understanding of "international structure."[167]

Historical-institutionalist modes of analysis provide a way forward by allowing us to identify focal points for the study of continuity and change.[168] Institutions involve routine and relatively bounded networks of social, political, and economic transactions. Their bounded quality enables us to demarcate them, however provisionally, from adjacent patterns of transaction and processes. Their routine quality—the fact that they endure over significant periods of time—implies that they involve

---

[166] Goddard and Nexon 2005.

[167] Practitioners of quantitative and formal social-network analysis, no matter what level of analysis they study, tend to simplify this complexity either by looking at specific types of networks, by using mathematical and statistical techniques that "flatten" social networks, or both. See Wasserman and Faust 1994; White and Boorman 1976; and White, Boorman et al. 1976.

[168] Historical institutionalisms come in many flavors, such as "rational" and "sociological." I offer relational institutionalism as an alternative insofar as it explores institutions through a relational, rather than, say, rational-choice or norms-oriented framework. I should note, however, that the same criticisms I advance of the logics of appropriateness/logics of consequences debate among international-relations scholars apply to many forms of rational- and sociological-institutionalism.

specific "mechanisms of reproduction that sustain them" in the face of typical variations in agent-level choices and the cross-currents generated by broader political, economic, and social circumstances.[169] Institutions, therefore, operate as conversion points for these processes into political outcomes. These processes, at the same time, interact with institutional mechanisms of reproduction. They may reinforce them or disrupt them in such a way as to produce a range of outcomes: from stability, to gradual mutation, to revolutionary reconfigurations.[170]

As I argue in the next chapter, broad shifts in economic relations and modes of warfare profoundly influenced the evolution of the European state system and played a significant role in shaping the emergence, spread, and repercussions of the Protestant Reformations. But how these processes shape the texture of international politics depends on how they interact with—and sometimes even how they are produced by—institutions. Scholars of the influence of modes of warfare on state formation, for example, demonstrate that the impact of shifts in military technologies varies with respect to (among a variety of factors) institutional logics of extraction, the relative power of various social and economic classes, and the kinds of resources available to specific political communities.[171]

We should, therefore, focus our attention on the particular embedded institutional contexts, and their specific network properties, that come into play during episodes of potential international transformation. Asymmetries in proclivities and trajectories for collective mobilization— themselves resulting from differences in embedded relational structures— shape the possibility for the reproduction and transformation of international politics. Actors who are positioned at the intersection of emerging and long-standing ties—who occupy bridging or brokerage positions— often become crucial players in international change. Which ties they commit to, and how other actors respond to these commitments, has the potential to alter the fundamental nature of political communities and institutional forms.[172]

---

[169] Thielen 1999, 398, 399–401.
[170] Bates, Greif et al. 1998; Katznelson 1997; Thielen 1999.
[171] See Ertman 1997, Tilly 1992.
[172] Katznelson 1997, 103–4. This last point recodes, in relational terms, typical claims found in accounts of European state formation. Marxist and Marxist-influenced theories of the origin of the modern state focus, for example, almost entirely on which economic classes commit to alliances with one another, and frequently upon whether monarchs side with the bourgeoisie or the aristocracy. See Anderson 1974, Kiernan 1980. Similarly, war-making accounts of state formation examine how various modes of warfare put differing fiscal pressures on rulers that influence their brokerage relations with social coalitions. These brokerage relations, in turn, shape the contours of state formation. See Hintze 1975, Tilly 1992.

Generalization

According to Georg Simmel, "In any given social phenomenon, content and societal form constitute one reality."[173] Social, political, and economic structures, for example, are relative stabilities in patterns of interaction that scholars code in a variety of ways: as networks, rules and resources, and so forth. Such structures have no existence independent of the specific content—meanings, interests, and the like—of those transactions. The content of a social phenomenon's constitutive social relations, for instance, produces the formal properties of a network. But this claim about the ontological co-dependence of form and content should not preclude us from drawing analytical distinctions between the two.

As I argued both with respect to clientele networks and corporate actors, a focus on the formal properties of network and relational structures allows us generalize about their dynamics. Similarly structured clientele networks will display similar mechanisms and processes regardless of the specific content of those networks. The relationship between network density and the distribution of identities helps us to isolate patterns of collective action without a great deal of knowledge about the specific content of the identities or social ties at play.

Isomorphisms (identical structures) between the formal properties of networks, in other words, generate similar causal logics and dynamics. This should be the case regardless of the particular historical period in which a network structure is found, what level of analysis it operates at, or the specific cultural content of the ties that make up a network. Simmel contends that

> superiority, subordination, competition, division of labor, formation of parties, representation, inner solidarity coupled with exclusiveness towards the outside, and innumerable similar features are found in the state as well as in a religious community, in a band of conspirators as in an economic association, in an art school as in a family. However diverse the interests that give rise to these sociations, the forms in which the interests are realized are identical.[174]

We should be skeptical, however, about the degree to which historical structures display actual isomorphisms. Some international-relations scholars argue, with good reason, against the very existence of isomorphisms in political relations and institutions.[175] Thus, I argue instead for coupling formal and ideal-typical analysis. That is, we can construct ideal-

---

[173] Simmel 1971, 25.
[174] Ibid., 26.
[175] Hobson 2002.

typifications of the formal properties of relational structures. Researchers construct ideal types in order to create an idealization of a phenomenon's characteristics that can then be compared against other, related ideal typifications. A particular ideal type will never accurately or exhaustively describe the concrete manifestations of a specific phenomenon, but it does provide a benchmark for the comparison of real political formations.

This approach enables us to connect explanation of particular outcomes—what Max Weber calls "singular causal analysis"—with more general causal claims.[176] To the extent that specific formal properties of relational contexts endure across time and space, we should expect to see similar mechanisms and processes at work. But these dynamics will concatenate with other factors—differences in content, agent-level decisions, adjacent processes, other nested relational structures—to produce historically variable outcomes.

Setting the Stage

This book provides an example of how one conducts the kind of analysis I have discussed above. We face, in any analysis of early modern Europe, an enormously complex history, in which many outcomes of interest resulted from contingent concatenations of events and decisions. Dynastic rulers, aristocrats, merchants, and religious leaders made difficult decisions in matters of war, trade, religion, resistance, and rule. If they had chosen different courses of action—if, for example, Philip II had returned to the Netherlands instead of staying in Castile or key brokers had remained loyal to the papacy—history would have unfolded in very different ways. The fate of Europe often hinged on the confusion of battle, the temperament of negotiators, or even, as in 1588, the weather. The scope of my analysis, moreover, covers centuries and diverse political terrain. Since I have already ruled out the standard international-relations procedure of treating inter-state politics as being governed by distinctive and timeless principles, how, then, can I discipline my inquiry to construct social-scientific generalizations?

I begin, in the next chapter, by identifying a number of macrolevel and microlevel processes crucial to the development of European states and

---

[176] Ringer 1997, 5–6, 17, 110–16. Max Weber describes his method as "the one-sided *accentuation* of *one* or *more* points of view and . . . the synthesis of a great many diffuse and discrete *individual* phenomena, present sometimes more, sometimes less, and occasionally not at all, which are arranged according to those one-sided emphatic points of view into a unified construction *in thought*. In its conceptual purity, this thought construction can be empirically found nowhere in reality, it is a utopia." See Weber 1999, 170 (emphasis in original). Translation courtesy of Patrick Thaddeus Jackson.

"international" relations prior to the onset of the Protestant Reformations: military-technical change, economic change, and the logic of dynastic practices. These factors helped produce a "Europe of composite states," which I survey in terms of their logics and development. But they do not simply provide us with a "before" snapshot exogenous to the later argument of the book. Rather, they are part of the configuration of processes that account for the intersection of the Protestant Reformations with the dynamics of resistance and rule in early modern Europe.

Chapter 4 operationalizes the central move of a relational-institutionalist approach. I develop an ideal-typical account of the dynamics of imperial composite states that centers on mechanisms and processes generated by their formal network structures. This allows me to specify a set of relatively spare reproductive and transformative mechanisms centering around their collective-mobilization dynamics. Here, I move from the historically specific to the abstract and general; I draw not only upon observations from early modern Europe, but from other cases involving imperial composite polities. These formal structural dynamics should obtain whenever we see similar social forms, although their manifestation will depend on a variety of contextual factors. Thus, I show how my ideal type accounts for why certain kinds of legitimating frameworks, specific political coalitions, and other factors made collective resistance to dynastic authorities more or less dangerous to the stability of early modern states.

In subsequent chapters I show that the mechanisms I associate with resistance and rule in composite states operated *in conjunction with specific contextual factors, interactions, broader processes, and agent-level choices* to account for varying political outcomes during, most notably, the reign of Charles V, those of his Spanish Habsburg successors, and in the French Wars of Religion. Here, the institutional dynamics of composite states act as ligatures that translate events, processes, and decisions into outcomes.[177] I aim to demonstrate that those mechanisms and processes I identify are robust across multiple cases; that the structural dynamics and key social sites I associate with imperial composite states not only explain why the Reformations led to a general European political crisis, but also are plausible enough to travel to other times and places that involve similar social forms embedded in very different contexts.

---

[177] For extended discussions of a mechanism-based and configurational approaches to causal generalization, see Jackson 2006b; Jackson and Nexon 2002; Katznelson 1997; McAdam, Tarrow et al. 2001, 22–27; and Tilly 1995, 1997b, 1999.

CHAPTER 3

The Dynastic-Imperial Pathway

INTERNATIONAL-RELATIONS SCHOLARSHIP often falters in the face of early modern Europe. Most of our accounts of international change aim to explain the emergence of a sovereign-territorial state system out of so-called medieval heteronomy. They take up, in one way or another, John Gerald Ruggie's challenge to explain "the most important contextual change in international politics in this *millennium*: the shift from the medieval to the modern international system [original emphasis]."[1] The decision to begin with medieval Europe and end with the consolidation of "sovereign-territorial" or "nation-states" places early modern Europe in conceptual purgatory; it becomes little more than a way-station in the journey between medieval and modern.[2] Realists, for their part, treat early modern Europe as simply another data point in their ongoing debates over the balance of power and the formation of hegemonic systems.[3] They read out of their historical analysis the distinctive character of early modern European politics.

The sovereign-territorial state did not develop, as Spruyt claims, in late Capetian France. Nor did a sovereign-territorial state system emerge, as Philpott argues, with the 1648 Peace of Westphalia.[4] But realist accounts of the period also misrepresent its political dynamics. Early modern European political relations, before and after the Peace of Westphalia, do not conform to the idealized model of states competing for power and security under anarchy. "Composite states" and "dynastic conglomerations" dominated the early modern European political landscape.[5] By the sixteenth century, in fact, one of the dominant pathways of European state formation was *dynastic-imperial* in character: dynasts cobbled together composite polities through conquest, marriage, and inheritance, but each segment generally retained its identity and many of its distinct institutions. In dynastic agglomerations, rulers occupied titular positions that

---

[1] Ruggie 1983, 273.
[2] Teschke 2003, 30. In this respect, international-relations scholars adopt a set of well-rehearsed assumptions about the European experience, ones inscribed in the very term "early modern" Europe.
[3] Kupchan 1996, 35; Schweller 1994, 73, 89–90; Walt 1985, 15.
[4] Philpott 2001, Spruyt 1994.
[5] Bonney 1991, Koenigsberger 1971a.

linked together their different domains based on explicit and implicit contractual obligations between rulers and subjects. These contractual obligations differed not only across different domains, but between different groups and classes—towns, cities, nobles, magnates, and so forth. Some of these contracts provided for comparatively direct rule but, overall, dynasts controlled their holdings through a variety of local intermediaries. Reason of dynasty, rather than contemporary notions of reason of state, drove international-political competition.

State Formation in Late Medieval and Early Modern Europe

In his seminal *Coercion, Capital and European States, AD 990–1990*, Charles Tilly fired a broadside against the "unilinear" approaches to state formation and international change that inform most contemporary approaches to these subjects. Theories of political change, he argued, must dispense with "any notion of European state formation as a single, unilinear process, or of the national state—which did, indeed, eventually prevail—as an inherently superior form of government."[6] Tilly's insight forms the core of most contemporary theories of political change, yet important scholarly works have yet to fully assimilate its implications into their accounts of European state formation. Many of the fallacies associated with unilinear accounts continue to distort our analysis of late medieval and early modern composite states.

Some of the best accounts of European state formation simply ignore the existence of composite states in early modern Europe and thus miss the significance of the dynastic-agglomerative pathway of state formation. Hendrik Spruyt, for example, locates the origins of the modern state in Capetian France and reduces subsequent centuries to the triumph of that form over city-state and city-league alternatives.[7] Others, such as Daniel Philpott, make much of the significance of the rise of the vast Habsburg composite state, but treat it as a "reversal of momentum" toward sovereignty in which "all political authorities were linked arcanely—medievally—over much of the surface of Europe, yet looked to no common ruler or law."[8] J. H. Elliott puts the problems with such interpretations of the early modern period quite well: "If sixteenth-century Europe was a Europe of composite states, coexisting with a myriad of smaller territorial and jurisdictional units . . . its history needs to be assessed from this

[6] Tilly 1992, 21, 12.
[7] E.g., Spruyt 1994.
[8] Philpott 2001, 80–81.

standpoint rather than from that of the society of unitary national states that it was later to become."[9]

Early modern and late medieval European states contained, of course, many of the elements of later sovereign-territorial and nation-states. Some princes claimed forms of sovereign authority not unrelated to that of the modern state. Political communities involved narratives and experiences of collective identification that would later become the basis of contemporary nationalist ideology. Elements of contemporary bureaucratic rule existed in parts of Europe. Centralizing impulses, particularly in Western Europe, worked to produce political communities more unified than those that preceded them.[10] But none of these features of early modern European states should lead us to treat the period as merely a transition point between medieval heteronomy and the modern state system. If we do so, we cannot appreciate the processes and mechanisms through which the Protestant Reformations produced a crisis of European state formation.

Accounts of the emergence of the modern European states divide roughly into three camps. *Bellocentrists* stress the impact of changing forms of warfare. They argue that processes of war-making played a fundamental role in state formation.[11] *Econocentrists* focus on the role of economic change in altering patterns of rule and the viability of different forms of political organization.[12] *Ideationalists* favor accounts that center on changing norms, ideas, identities, and discourses. They often argue that major shifts in state formation result from the interplay of prevailing ideas with new beliefs about political authority.[13] Most scholars working on state formation and international change recognize the importance of all three factors. They differ largely on matters of emphasis.

These divisions map imperfectly onto the major international-relations theories of continuity of change discussed in the preceding chapter. We might say that, in some respects, realists tend to be bellocentrists, liberals tend to be econocentrists, and that constructivists tend to be ideationalists. Constructivists, as a practical matter, almost always embrace ideationalist accounts of state formation and international change.[14] A great many contemporary liberal theories, when applied to the study of international change, take on an econocentric character.[15] Many realists favor,

[9] Elliott 1992, 51.
[10] Bonney 1991, Downing 1992, Ertman 1997.
[11] E.g., Bean 1973, Downing 1992, Glete 2002, Kiser and Linton 2001, Tilly 1975 and 1992.
[12] E.g., Anderson 1974, Hechter and Brustein 1980, North 1990, North and Thomas 1973.
[13] For an earlier version of this typology, see Nexon 2005.
[14] E.g., Bukovansky 2002, Hall 1999, Philpott 2001.
[15] E.g., Keohane 1984, Keohane and Nye 1989, Moravcsik 1997.

either implicitly or explicitly, bellocentric accounts.[16] Yet other realists openly embrace a combination of bellocentric and econocentric arguments.[17] Some of the most econocentric theories of the emergence of sovereignty can be found in the Marxist international-relations tradition.[18] We therefore need to be cautious about conflating international-relations approaches to continuity and change with the approaches to state formation and the emergence of sovereignty considered here.

For our present purposes, we should focus on three issues involving bellocentric, econocentric, and ideationalist accounts: how they understand the early modern period in relation to the emergence of the modern, sovereign-territorial state; how they interpret the significance—or lack thereof—of the Protestant Reformations; and, finally, the extent to which warfare, economic changes, and ideational developments shaped the contours of the early modern European states and state formation. Because many accounts of state formation in political science and sociology neglect the significance of the composite-state form and of the dynastic-agglomerative pathway, they either understate or overstate the significance of the Protestant Reformations and the Peace of Westphalia. Those that call our attention to the specific characteristics of early modern European states, for their part, tend to reduce them to economic or normative arrangements and thus fail to adequately address the processes and mechanisms by which the Protestant Reformations created a crisis in European state formation.

Instead of surveying these accounts—many of which I have discussed in the previous chapter—this section analyzes the "state of the state" in early modern Europe. In doing so, I highlight the strengths and weaknesses of representative arguments in the bellocentric, econocentric, and ideationalist traditions. My argument, in turn, borrows from insights found in each approach: changes in the nature of warfare and economic relations intersected with dynastic social institutions to favor dynastic-agglomerative pathways of state formation by the end of the fifteenth century.

A Europe of Composite States

Scholars have used the term "composite state" for quite some time. In the latter part of the nineteenth century, for example, we can find many uses of the term to refer to federative and confederative polities: those that unite several independent political communities without erasing their dis-

---

[16] Scholars working in offense/defense balance theory, for instance, link changes in dominance of offensive or defensive warfare to state and system formation. See Van Evera 1998.
[17] Krasner 1993.
[18] E.g., Anderson 1974, Teschke 2003.

tinctive legal identities.[19] Contemporary historians resurrected the phrase in response to a number of analytic problems raised by the status of early modern European political communities.[20] They contend that commonly used conceptions of "the state", such as that associated with Max Weber's ideal-typical definition of modern states, imply a developmental teleology in which centralization, bureaucratization, sovereignty, territoriality, and national identity emerge in necessary tandem with one another.[21] Recognizing the composite character of early modern political communities allows us to treat them as entities in their own right.

Many historians now use the term to cover many different kinds of early modern political communities. One scholar notes that it has been "used to define apparently very distant systems, like the Republic of Venice and the great European monarchies."[22] Although we should be cautious about treating the variety of early modern forms of political organization as manifestations of any single logic, the notion of "composite states" does capture important aspects of early modern political topography and state formation.

The general pattern of early modern state formation stemmed from the vast number of independent and quasi-independent centers of political power that operated in Europe during the Middle Ages.[23] European state formation—whether through dynastic inheritance, conquest, or voluntary unification—proceeded by linking together these nodes into larger political communities. In this process, state builders often lacked the capacity or opportunity to entirely eliminate the independent character of towns, counties, duchies, and other political units. Instead, they subordinated them, connected local actors to the center through patronage, and otherwise established contractual relations that implicitly or explicitly specified varying rights and obligations between center and periphery.[24]

These features define the range of composite state forms. All composite states involve elements of *indirect rule*, in which superordinate authorities control subordinate political segments through intermediaries who enjoy some significant autonomy over local rule making and enforcement. In consequence, subordinate political communities maintain or develop

---

[19] E.g., Robinson 1894, Smith 1895. Such phrasing extends back at least as far as Pufendorf. See Schroeder 1999.

[20] Muldoon 1999, 7. As Muldoon notes, the phrase was popularized by H. G. Koenigsberger, who argued that it captured the character of early modern polities better than terms such as "state" or "empire."

[21] Oresko, Gibbs et al. 1997, 3. On Weber's definition of the state, see Weber 1946, 55–56.

[22] Guarini 1995, S64.

[23] Tilly 1992.

[24] Elliott 1992, Koenigsberger 1986, Spruyt 1994, Tilly 1992.

their own personality—manifested in their identity, institutions, and so forth—distinct from one another and from the center. The composite quality of these states often extended into subordinate polities themselves; early modern composite monarchies, for example, typically agglomerated underlying composite states.[25]

We can further distinguish between at least two ideal-typical forms of composite states: empires and federations. The main difference between these two forms reflects the character of political contracting. All political systems are based upon implicit and explicit bargains that specify rights and obligations. Such bargains concern the relative authority of different actors, the extent of political obligations, the benefits received by citizens and subjects, and so forth. Some of the parties involved in these contracts may, of course, have a great deal more control over the terms of the relationship than others. Not a few political contracts in human history reflect little more than an agreement of rulers to refrain from using force if their subjects provide regular tribute. But even such highly coercive bargains still represent contractual relations. As David A. Lake notes, "All relationships, whether entered into voluntarily or as a result of coercion, can be considered as based upon some 'contract' between the two parties."[26]

Ideal-typical empires are characterized by *heterogeneous contracting*: the terms of incorporation between the center and each periphery involve different rights and responsibilities. Ideal-typical federations involve *uniform contracting*: the same set of generalized agreements hold between all incorporated political communities (figure 3.1).[27] Actual composite polities, of course, may mix elements of uniform and heterogeneous contracting. Composite states may also vary in terms of their reliance on indirect and direct rule. The Holy Roman Empire, for example, specified different rights and privileges for constituent segments such as imperial towns, principalities, and electoral principalities. But the fact that all of the segments of the empire were governed by the same overarching contract lent it a federative character.[28] Early modern France, for its part, was composed of *pays d'état* and *pays d'élection*. The former maintained their provincial estates and thus not only involved higher levels of indirect rule

---

[25] Muldoon 1999, 119.

[26] Lake 1996, 7. See also Cooley 2000–2001 and 2005; Cooley and Ron 2002; Lake 1996, 1999, 2001, and 2003; and Weber 1997.

[27] Galtung 1971, 89–90; Tilly 1997a, 3. Ideal-typical nation-states involve direct rule and uniform contracting. The remaining parametric combination of indirect rule and heterogeneous contracting involves differential bargains not across segments but across populations in a single segment. Many empires and empire-like entities, including early modern composite states, combine these two types of heterogeneous contracting.

[28] Wilson 1999.

The Dynastic-Imperial Pathway • 73

```
Direct
         ┌─────────────────────────────────────────┐
         │  Nation-States        Class-Divided States │
         │                                         │
         │                                         │
         │                                         │
    Rule │                                         │
         │                                         │
         │                                         │
         │                                         │
         │                                         │
         │  Federations              Empires       │
Indiret  └─────────────────────────────────────────┘
            Uniform                  Heterogeneous

                        Contracting
```

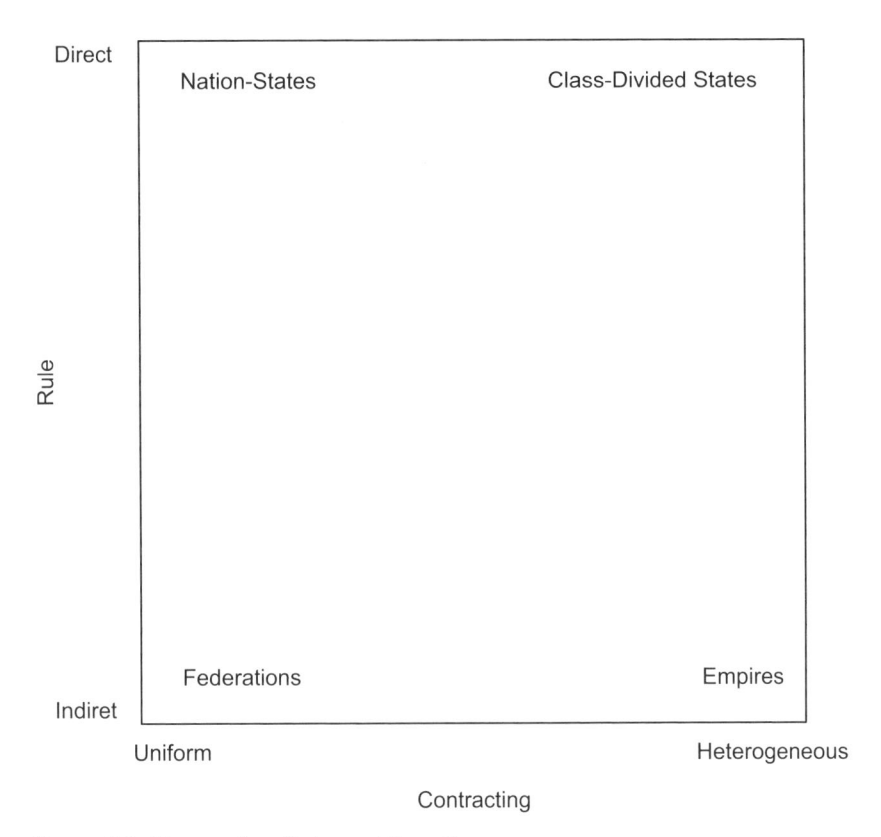

Figure 3.1 Contracting, Rule, and State Forms

within France, but also more heterogeneous bargains with central authorities than those associated with the *pays d'élections*.[29]

This distinction—which generates a continuum between imperial and federative composite states—does not exhaust the differences between early modern European polities. Some, such as France, Castile, and England, were hereditary monarchies. Others, such as the Holy Roman Empire and, from 1572, Poland-Lithuania, were elective. A few composite states, such as the Swiss Confederation, were republican rather than monarchical in character. We should now consider some of the major forms of composite polities that existed in late medieval and early modern Europe (figure 3.2).

---

[29] Collins 1995, xxx, 246–47.

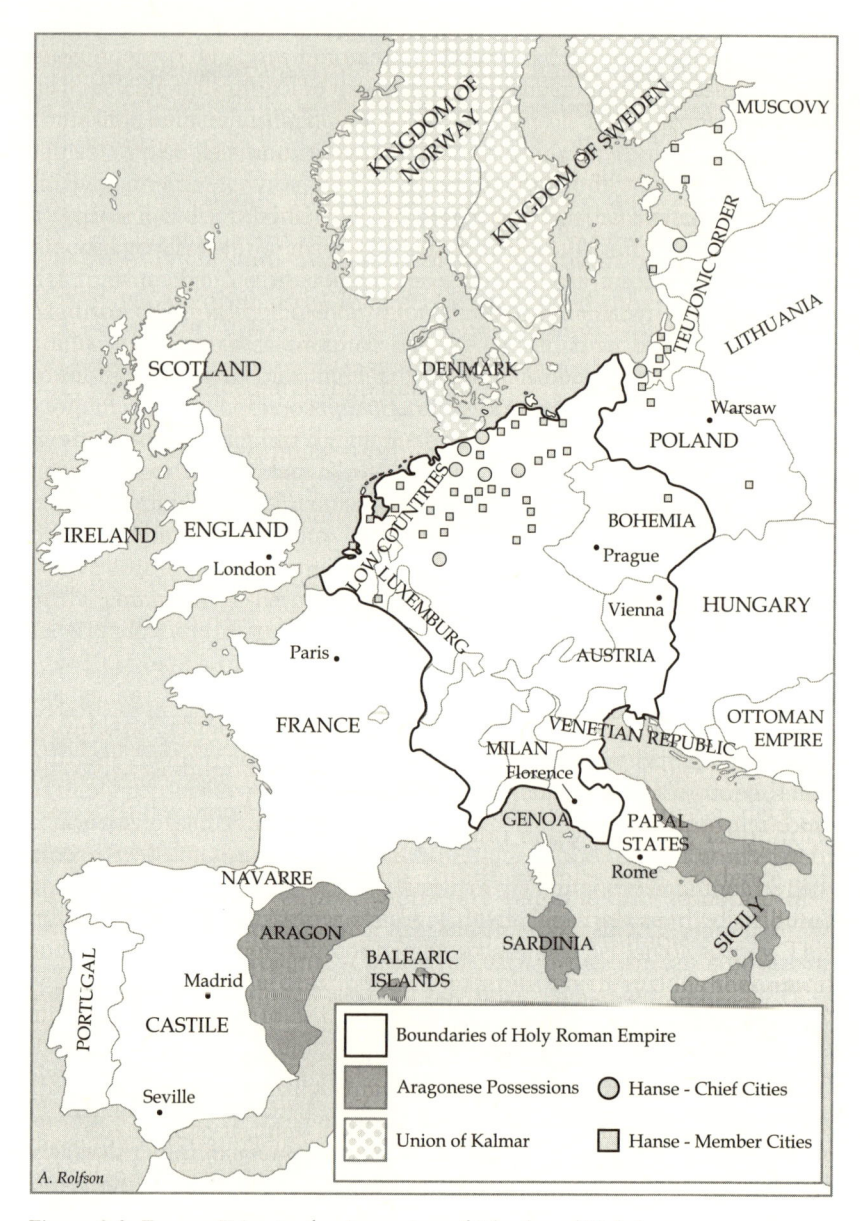

Figure 3.2 Europe Prior to the Ascension of Charles of Habsburg

FEDERATIVE ALLIANCES

Spruyt identifies city-leagues, along with city-states and the sovereign-territorial state, as one of the three major competing forms of the state in medieval and early modern Europe. His analysis of city-leagues focuses on the case of the rise and decline of the Hansa, a trading federation of urban centers based along the Baltic and North Seas.[30] He argues that the case of the Hansa reflects a general pattern of city-league formation. When urban centers could not compete with other political actors on their own but failed to receive support from monarchs, they formed city-leagues. Because the cities and towns of the Hansa traded "high-volume" but "low added-value" goods, they lacked the resources available to Italian communes; because the German emperors refused to back them against rival nobles and princes, they had little choice but to pool their resources to defend themselves and their market position.[31]

The Hansa, in fact, became a major player in European politics. At its height, the league "could dictate terms of peace to foreign potentates."[32] In 1522 the Hansa, led by the city of Lübeck, intervened in the struggle between the Danish king, Christian II, and the Swedish regent, Gustava Vasa, and thus played a decisive role in establishing an independent Swedish dynastic state. In 1523 the Hansa's support for the Duke of Holstein drove "Christian II from Denmark itself."[33] After 1523, however, the Hansa declined precipitously as a political force in Europe. As I argue in greater detail below, the reasons for the Hansa's decline are more complicated than Spruyt's econocentric logic implies. Changes in the nature of warfare, for example, played a key role in undermining the Hansa's relative position vis-à-vis dynastic states.

City-leagues, moreover, represented only one of the many kinds of federative alliances that developed in medieval and early modern Europe. Such federations often involved a strong urban component, but also included rural regions and even, as in the case of the Swabian League (formed in 1385), small principalities, knights, and monasteries.[34] As Spruyt's analysis highlights, such federations generally originated in alliances: their members joined together to secure some combination of common military, political, and economic objectives that they could not achieve through their own recognizance. The very heterogeneity of the European landscape—the existence of multiple centers of power within

[30] Spruyt 1994.
[31] Spruyt 1994, 62–76, 109–29.
[32] Westergaard 1953, 92.
[33] Koenigsberger and Mosse 1968, 66.
[34] Baron 1939, 222–23; Downing 1989, 217.

the formal jurisdiction of titular rulers—made such alliances possible and led to their formation under a wide variety of circumstances.

The Swiss Confederacy, for example, formed in 1291 out of an alliance of Alpine provinces that sought to maintain their independence against their nominal Habsburg overlords.[35] Economic changes played an important role in its development. Increasing agricultural productivity and expanding trade contributed to the development of important urban centers in what would become the confederation. These factors also made the region attractive to dynastic rulers, thus setting in motion the conflicts that led to the formation of the confederation. For the first few centuries of its existence, the confederation sought privileges within the empire rather than outright separation from it. Many of its cities won imperial freedoms that placed them under the direct authority of the emperor.[36]

The Swiss Confederation operated as a largely autonomous, but highly decentralized, political agglomeration within the Holy Roman Empire. Its members often pursued their own foreign policies.[37] During the Reformation, Catholic cantons fought a preventative war against Geneva.[38] Its composite nature—as a decentralized and linguistically heterogeneous union of different cantons—persists in present-day Switzerland.[39] In the sixteenth century the Swiss viewed one another as "league or oath comrades" rather than members of anything like a common nation.[40] The military tactics its members developed—involving highly coordinated pike-wielding infantry organized into "squares"—proved so successful against heavy cavalry formations that Swiss companies became highly sought after as mercenary forces in European warfare. In 1476 and 1477 Swiss forces defeated Charles the Bold, Duke of Burgundy. The second engagement left Charles dead and fragmented his own dynastic agglomeration. In 1499 Swiss forces fought off the pro-Habsburg Swabian League in one of the many wars through which it maintained their independence.[41]

Although many federations originated in the Middle Ages, they experienced something of a resurgence in the face of dynastic consolidation in the early modern period. As we have seen, a number of federations took on many of the characteristics of decentralized composite states. Even the Swabian League operated, at least in some respects, as an independent international actor: it negotiated external alliances and common policies among its members. Yet such federations remained subject to "internal"

[35] Baker 1993, 21.
[36] Bonney 1991, 95.
[37] Weart 1994, 303.
[38] See chapter 5 in the present volume.
[39] Bonney 1991, 95.
[40] Head 1995, 27.
[41] Koenigsberger and Mosse 1968, 59.

political and military struggles of the kind normally associated with international politics. Many also were themselves subject to more or less effective superordinate political authorities, such as the Holy Roman Empire or, in the case of the commercial urban leagues of Castile, the Castilian monarchy.[42]

CITY-EMPIRES

Many cities and towns in medieval and early modern Europe enjoyed varying degrees of autonomy as politically differentiated clusters of authority. As econocentrists and bellocentrists note, the rise of urban centers stemmed from a conjunction of factors: the growth of trade, alliances between urban leaders and princes, and a military-technical environment in which urban centers could support or purchase some degree of military capability. In some instances urban centers seized sufficient autonomy to act as states in their own right. They negotiated alliances, conducted warfare, and conquered surrounding territory.[43]

Some of the best known city-states of the late medieval and early modern era include Venice, Florence, Genoa, and Lübeck. Some, such as Lübeck, belonged to urban federations. Others operated as essentially autonomous political organizations.[44] The term "city-states," however, obscures the character of most early modern city-based political communities. It implies that the great city-states of Italy, for example, operated as self-contained entities whose jurisdiction extended to their own walls. The ascendant city-states of late medieval and early modern Europe, however, might better be described as "city-empires": they, at a minimum, controlled a *contado* composed of adjacent rural regions. Relations between city and *contado* generally took the form of core-periphery domination, in which *contadi* retained their distinctive identities and institutions. Powerful Italian city-states ruled *contadi* that included formerly independent cities and towns. As H. G. Koenigsberger and George L. Mosse note, "The defeated cities were rarely willing subjects."[45]

Italian urban communities, therefore, should not be described as "self-sufficient islands basking in their ancient privileges, immunities, and autonomy" but as members of a "regional network of political relations." Through their contracts with superordinate centers, "Local communities,

---

[42] For a theoretical discussion of the relationship between federations and alliances that treats the former as examples of "hierarchical" and the latter as "anarchical" relationships, see Lake 1996 and 2001.

[43] Downing 1989, Spruyt 1994, Tilly 1992.

[44] Spruyt 1994.

[45] Koenigsberger and Mosse 1968, 58. In contrast, the German city-states—whether "free imperial cities" or the "territorial cities" that were formally subordinate to local princes—never included other cities in a *contado*.

including client groups, institutional actors, and sectoral elites, continued to implement critical political functions."[46] Successful Italian autonomous cities, moreover, established overseas empires—that of the Venetian Republic stretched across the Mediterranean, and its governors (*podestàs*) oversaw the administration of subject political communities both in Italy and abroad.[47]

International-relations scholars often fail to recognize the degree to which city-empires functioned as composite political communities. Realists tend to treat the Italian wars of the Renaissance as an example par excellence of the timelessness of their claims about the realpolitik behavior of unitary states. The urban *cores* of city-states did represent, in some respects, dense social networks overlapping with a strong sense of collective identity. Yet "a feeling of community was precisely what was lacking in the city republics. That is to say, it existed in the cities themselves, but in each as purely local, civic patriotism." Almost invariably "the city republics were and remained brittle, in constant danger of rebellion from their subject cities."[48] The factionalism that eroded the strength of city-republics in the early modern period provides a stark example of how local networks of patronage and allegiance could split apart their urban cores.[49]

We should recall that city-states were themselves frequently embedded in other formal and informal political networks and institutions. For example, in the German domains of the Holy Roman Empire struggles within city-states were dependent upon their interaction with "outside forces—other cities, neighboring princes, and imperial commissions."[50] In this respect we should understand city-empires as occupying a particular place in a continuum of urban power that varied across Europe, in which only a few of the powerful (chiefly Italian) cities achieved something like full political autonomy in their own right.[51]

Thus, those who point to Renaissance Italy as an example of a sovereign-state system rely on fairly selective evidence. During the fifteenth century the Italian League (1455–1494) had as its fundamental clause

---

[46] Kirshner 1995, S6–7. For the full argument, see Guarini 1995.

[47] Kiernan 1980, 63.

[48] Koenigsberger 1986, 33. After all, Machiavelli understood himself as a republican theorist, and his discussion of Italian politics is strongly tied to his emphasis upon civic patriotism.

[49] Spruyt 1994, 148. Spruyt uses this evidence to show that city-states "never made the complete transition to sovereign, territorial statehood," but we could tell a similar story about the Western European monarchies of this period. See subsequent chapters in the present volume for an elaboration of this point.

[50] Vann 1986, S17.

[51] See Blockmans and Tilly 1989 and Tilly 1992.

"'the defense of the states,' that is, the mutual commitment to support the respective internal regimes or at least not interfere with them."[52] But this recognition of something like sovereignty occurred precisely as Italy came under pressure from external powers, and it proved to be quite short-lived.

THE HOLY ROMAN EMPIRE

The Holy Roman Empire was the formal descendent of the Carolingian Empire. For our immediate purposes, the empire combined elements of federative and imperial organization; although highly decentralized when compared to typical dynastic agglomerations of the period, it was far from deceased by the early modern period. If anything, Charles of Habsburg's ascension created an opportunity for the reformation of the empire into a more effective political community. Thus, we should not conclude, as some scholars of state formation do, that the thirteenth century marked the effective "end of the empire."[53]

After 887 the Carolingian Empire was permanently divided into three separate entities: West Francia (France), Lorraine, and East Francia (Germany). In 911 the last Carolingian ruler of East Francia died. After a brief period the monarchy passed to a Saxon dynasty that lasted until 1024, and under Otto the Great (936–973) gained the imperial title and founded the Ottonian Dynasty. He made effective use of Germany's comparatively intact monarchical authority to establish "a hegemony over west Francia and Burgundy," reimpose "the tributary status of the Bohemians," conquer "all of Italy as far south as Rome" in addition to defeating the Magyars and garnering the imperial title.[54]

The Salian dynasty (1024–1125) succeeded the Ottonians. Both faced "the entrenched power of dukes, margraves, and counts who, like their counterparts to the west, had taken advantage of Carolingian decline to render their offices largely hereditary." Against this centrifugal pressure both dynasties relied upon their imperial-religious authority, which gave them the right to appoint (invest) bishops and abbots.[55] By extending the right of Church communities to make and enforce their own laws (the "ban"), giving generous grants of land and authority to the Church, and appointing loyal followers to Church offices, the emperor brought substantial holdings effectively into imperial administration. According to

---

[52] Fubini 1995, S187–88.
[53] Spruyt 1994, 55. For a more comprehensive treatment of the empire in the context of international-relations theory, see Sharma 2005, 127–216.
[54] Ertman 1997, 229.
[55] Ibid., 229–30.

Horst Furhmann, "In this way the foundations were laid for the princely rank enjoyed by later bishops and abbots."[56]

In 1075 the Investiture Conflict began. Its roots lay in both practical political and ideological developments. Imperial and secular influence in the papacy sparked attempts at reforming the institutions and doctrines of the Church, while the presence of Norman armies in southern Italy gave the papacy an alternative base of military support to that offered by the emperor.[57] These attempts climaxed with the Gregorian reforms, which, among other important doctrinal changes, such as the prohibition of clerical marriages, asserted the absolute authority of the papacy over spiritual matters. This struck at one of the key sources of legitimacy used by the emperor to maintain his authority. In addition, the emperors had found in the right of investiture a way to create a body of regional administrators loyal to their persons.

The emperor, therefore, refused to accept the legitimacy of the reforms. As the conflict intensified, Pope Gregory VII excommunicated Henry IV and "deposed" him by proclamation, and many princes and nobles seized the opportunity to weaken imperial authority by siding with the papacy.[58] The Investiture Conflict sparked fifty years of civil war and gravely weakened imperial authority.[59] Future bids for centralization would founder upon conflicts between emperor and pope, conflicts that became even more acute with renewed imperial interest in Italy.

The Hohenstaufens (1138–1254) succeeded the Salians. Their ambitious program of expansion eventually led to a "partial collapse" of imperial authority. The Golden Bull of 1356 codified electoral procedures in the empire, and these procedures persisted without fundamental alterations until 1806. From 1273 until the ascension of the second Habsburg emperor (Frederick III) in 1440, the princes of the empire limited imperial power by refusing to elect successive members of the same dynasty. In fact, Frederick III showed so little interest in governing the empire that his reign provoked a major reform movement in the second half of the fifteenth century. Frederick's son, Maximilian I (Charles of Habsburg's grandfather) encouraged the reform effort in his attempt to seek support for his foreign interests, particularly his conflict with the French Valois in Burgundy and Italy.[60]

---

[56] Fuhrmann 1986, 34. In contrast, the monarchy in west Francia lacked an exclusive control of investiture. Thus, banal lordship provided another source of fragmentation.

[57] In fact, one reason for Gregory's delay in moving against the emperor can be traced, in part, to difficulty he was having with the Normans. See Barraclough 1968, 80.

[58] Ibid., 81–90; Fuhrmann 1986, 52–54; Keen 1991, 76–80; Spruyt 1994, 49; Thomson 1998, 94–97; Tierney 1988, 53–57.

[59] Ertman 1997, 234.

[60] Wilson 1999, 17–20.

A number of factors—including the relative size of the empire; the differential timing of the impact of economic change (by the sixteenth century Germany was the wealthiest region of Europe); military-technical change; the lack of a continuous dynasty between the thirteenth and fifteenth centuries; and the persistence of partible inheritance—contributed to the decentralized nature of political authority in the empire.[61] Many actors, however, turned toward federative alliances to preserve their autonomy and influence. By the fifteenth century "self-help . . . became unusually important in the German constitution, one of whose distinctive features was the formation of numerous leagues between towns, knights, princes and other nobles."[62]

Those concerned about the consolidation of power in the hands of larger principalities, most notably the Swabian League, looked to the emperor and imperial authority as the most obvious counterbalance to the princes. At the same time, regional federative alliances within the empire further eroded public order, since small-scale disputes and rivalries often escalated to involve a number of allies. Such circumstances created an odd situation: *both* the emerging territorial princes and their opponents saw benefits from expanding the authority of central institutions. Doing so might simultaneously enhance the influence of the territorial princes—if they could capture the process—while increasing public order.[63] This is one reason why, in a world in which religious divisions had not shifted the political landscape of Germany, the fate of the empire might have been very different.

In the early sixteenth century the empire combined features of ideal-typical empires and federations. Relatively uniform shared rights and privileges among members of the same orders—electors, princes, imperial cities, and the like—coexisted with many forms of heterogeneous contracting between them and the empire. The various leagues and other "self-help" arrangements within Germany created additional variations in formal and informal relations. Corporate and individual actors, such as princes, magistrates, and the regional leagues, occupied various intermediary positions between the emperor and his subjects.

---

[61] Central European rulers did not adopt principles of primogeniture but continued to divide their territories between their heirs. For a discussion of the significance of this difference for politics in the empire, see Sharma 2005.

[62] Bonney 1991, 95. See also Elton 1964, 24–26; Holborn 1959, 30–31; and Wilson 1999, 19. I should note that the question here is not the decline of the nobility as a social class, but rather the orientation of their political power toward princes. It may be true that, for instance, princely debts involved the shifting of " 'sovereign' rights into the hands of the nobility," but this was power mediated by territorial princes rather than operating independently of them. Cf. Stalnaker 1979, 34.

[63] Holborn 1959, 30–46; Wilson 1999, 19.

82 • Chapter 3

Given the extremely decentralized nature of authority in the empire, intermediaries enjoyed a great deal of practical autonomy to pursue their own interests and goals, regardless of whether they were consistent with those of the emperor. Sometimes, as with the Swiss Confederation, Milan, and the Venetian Republic, local rulers and institutions enjoyed such significant autonomy that it makes little sense to even speak of the empire as a system of indirect rule. Still, we should not lose sight of the fact that, at least with respect to the German regions of the empire, we are not looking at an anarchical system, but an extremely weak or "low-capacity" imperial composite policy which, in certain times and places, took on anarchical properties. German political relations involved nested structures of hierarchy and anarchy. The empire may have been dysfunctional by the sixteenth century, but it was far from politically irrelevant.[64]

DYNASTIC AGGLOMERATIONS

All dynastic agglomerations were ruled by individuals who occupied titular positions based upon medieval ranks and who claimed those positions by virtue of kinship ties. Dynasts expanded the territories of their agglomerations either by attaching them to the family line or to the "crown" of a particular kingdom or principality. The scale of dynastic agglomerations and their degree of integration, as noted above, varied tremendously. Charles of Habsburg's territorially discontiguous domains lacked much in the way of a central governing apparatus. Early modern France, in contrast, was both territorially compact and comparatively integrated.[65]

Such variation, however, does not change the basic fact that polities such as "Valois and Bourbon France, Stuart Britain and the Spanish monarchy all formed 'composite states' linked by dynastic rather than by national, geographic, economic or ideological ties."[66] The Capetian, Valois, and Bourbon kings of France, for example, expanded their territories by agglomerating heterogeneous populations and territories. "During the later middle ages the French monarchy had expanded the geographical area under its control by annexing—by agreement, by inheritance, or by conquest—a series of outlying sovereign territories previously independent from the crown."[67] Similarly, the Crown of Aragon was itself composed of three segments with independent institutions: the kingdoms of Aragon and Valencia, and the Principality of Catalonia.[68] The English monarchs also controlled a composite state, forged through the conquest

---

[64] For a different view of the "anarchical" quality of the empire, see Owen 2005.
[65] If the Valois kings had won the Italian wars, however, they would have ruled over a territorially discontiguous dynastic empire.
[66] Parker 1998, 113.
[67] Oresko, Gibbs et al. 1997, 8.
[68] Elliott 1963b, 4.

of the formerly independent kingdoms of Wales and their claims to Ireland.[69] As Koenigsberger argues, they "clung tenaciously to the remnant of the old Angevin empire, Calais, and when Calais was finally lost to the French in 1558, they tried for the rest of the century to recapture it." The Scandinavian monarchies, Poland-Lithuania, and the Burgundian state reflected the composite and agglomerative nature of dynastic states. The kings of Hungary, for their part, "wore three crowns and ruled over an ethnically even more diverse area of Europe than the kings of Poland."[70]

When dynasts successfully enforced their claims, through either military or legal means, or when voluntary unions brought multiple territories into a single dynastic line, rulers inherited pre-existing contractual obligations and patterns of patronage. On the one hand, political actors generally expected these contractual obligations to be maintained or modified only with their consent. On the other hand, a change in ruler or dynastic line also created opportunities for them to attempt to modify contractual and patronage relationships to benefit themselves, their kin, or their social class. In general, such modifications could only come at the expense of other political actors and groups.[71]

Whether segments of dynastic agglomerations were incorporated via conquest, inheritance, or dynastic unions, dynastic rulers held them through distinctive contracts that either preexisted their incorporation or were negotiated as conditions for compliance with resource and military demands. Dynasts sometimes ruled indirectly through appointed governors and viceroys. Even when they did not, the fact that rulers were dependent upon cooperation from and enforcement by quasi-autonomous actors meant that rule was largely indirect. One of the fundamental features of early modern dynastic rule was that kings and princes lacked the ability to enforce their authority without the cooperation of some coalition of important local actors: "No government of the period could reach into all areas or command all subjects within their borders."[72] When powerful local actors felt the terms of their contracts, especially their particular privileges, were in jeopardy, they might actively rebel, either simply demanding a restoration of their privileges or uniting behind an alternative claimant to the throne. As Geoffrey Parker notes, the failure of dynasts "to observe the terms of incorporation almost always led—often very swiftly—to disaffection and even to revolt, led by a local elite."[73]

---

[69] For a comparison of center-periphery relations between, on the one hand, the English monarchy and the medieval Welsh kingdom of Gwynedd, and, on the other, the French monarchy and the Languedoc, see Given 1990.
[70] Koenigsberger 1987, 48.
[71] te Brake 1998.
[72] Parker 1998, 133.
[73] Ibid., 113.

It followed that, in dynastic polities, central authorities acted as brokers between competing regional and local clusters of power who administered "public" authority with respect to specific and frequently overlapping jurisdictions.[74] In England, for instance, central administrative control remained extremely limited until after 1688.[75] In France regional parlements exercised sometimes competing, sometimes distinctive, and sometimes parallel jurisdictional authority with both local magnates and royal officials.[76]

The Rise of the Dynastic-Imperial Pathway

One of the central arguments of the present study is that the dynastic-imperial pathway of state formation comprised a vital and ascendant trajectory of European political development in the early modern period. Dynastic agglomerations rose in importance at the expense of other composite polities, such as federative alliances and city-empires. Each of the major approaches to state formation and international change—ideationalist, econocentric, and bellocentric—supply reasons for this trend.

First, norms and practices associated with dynasticism itself help explain the rise of dynastic agglomerations. Second, economic changes enhanced the viability of dynastic empire building. Third, shifts in the nature of warfare undermined many of the rival claimants to power and autonomy in early modern Europe. Some scholars associate these trends with the consolidation of sovereign territoriality in late medieval and early modern Europe. But these sources of change did not select for sovereign-territorial modes of organization over dynastic-agglomerative ones. The structure and practices of dynastic agglomerations, moreover, differed in important ways from those associated with a modern sovereign-territorial state system.

DYNASTICISM

The vitality of nondynastic composite states in medieval and early modern Europe—city-states, urban and rural federations, and so forth—should not give us license to forget a basic and hugely consequential feature of Europe's political topography: the European landscape was divided into jurisdictional holdings that belonged, in theory if not in actual practice, to dynastic lines or aristocratic families. Most towns and cities, and feder-

---

[74] Kettering 1986b.

[75] Brewer 1990, Scott 2000.

[76] See, e.g., Collins 1995, 5–10; Knecht 1996a, 20, 230–33; and Major 1971. Royal legislation had to be ratified by each regional parlement to enter into effect. The autonomy of the regional parlements waxed and waned in the early modern period, but both the Paris and regional parlements became important players in the conflicts of the sixteenth and seventeenth centuries, most notably the Wars of Religion and the *Fronde*.

ations of all kinds, resided in territories that owed some form of obedience to a dynastic overlord. Thus, no matter how much de facto independence a federative alliance or particular town enjoyed, it was likely to be at least nominally part of a territory or territories over which titular authority could be claimed or transferred according to dynastic practices.

In the fifteenth century, for example, the Habsburgs nominally ruled many of the Swiss cantons; those that acquired imperial liberties owed allegiance to the emperor, which created a problem for them when the empire elected Habsburg dynasts as kings of the Romans. Similarly, many of the towns of the Hansa were located in a variety of German principalities, as well as in non-German kingdoms, duchies, and counties. In the German Empire the highest authority was, arguably, the Imperial Constitution, but the emperor would always be a dynast in his own right. If a communal polity, such as many of the Italian "city-states," achieved a status that rendered dynastic claims largely irrelevant, it still operated amongst duchies and kingdoms that were directly implicated in dynastic claims and counterclaims.

The political topography of Europe thus positioned dynasts and dynastic lines, almost invariably, as brokers in the relations between members of federative alliances and city-empires. Although such conditions did not make the triumph of dynastic states inevitable, it did provide dynastic-empire builders with social and political resources unavailable to competing state-like organizations.

Dynastic marriages and the likelihood that, over time, dynastic families would face succession crises also facilitated the dynastic-imperial pathway of state formation. As Vivek Sharma argues, once Western Europeans adopted principles of primogeniture the number of dynastic lines in Europe decreased and the scope of dynastic agglomerations grew. In 1300 Europe contained thirteen major dynasties; by 1500 that number dropped to eight.[77] Dynastic practices themselves favored dynastic empire building and the formation of dynastic agglomerations.

The logic of dynastic accumulation extended even to the city-empires of the Italian peninsula. By 1494 every major power center in Italy, with the exception of the Venetian Republic, was implicated in dynastic-empire building.

> It is important to stress . . . that rather than attaching "petty states" to "new monarchies," "Renaissance diplomacy" attached Italian dynasties to foreign dynasties. On the eve of the French invasion of 1494, there were five major power complexes of European importance in the peninsula: the Kingdom of Naples, Medicean Florence, the Papal States, the Duchy of Milan, and the Venetian Republic. The family of

[77] Sharma 2005, 92–93.

86 • Chapter 3

the Aragonese Alfonso ruled as kings in Naples. Florentine republicanism had broken its back on family faction, the avoidance of which was guaranteed by the triumph of a single family, the Medici, who were princes in all but name. The Pope, Alexander IV, schemed to ensure the continuation of Borgia power in the Romagna: hence the campaigns of his son, Cesare. The Sforza had succeeded the Visconti in Milan and had extinguished the Ambrosian Republic to do so. . . . In the interstices of this power network, we find microcosmic empires, often identified with the dominion of a family. . . . This was the world on which the Valois invasion fell.[78]

ECONOMIC CHANGE

Econocentrists, as we have seen, argue that various changes in the European economy and forms of production drove many crucial institutional developments in medieval Europe. Increasing trade, monetarization, and other factors promoted the rise of urban clusters of capital and rendered cities and towns important players in power-political competition. Princes and monarchs, particularly in Western Europe, enhanced their position by playing towns off against land-holding nobles. They chartered towns and granted them exemptions, thus undermining the position of the local nobility. The revenues they collected from the towns allowed them to expand their military capabilities; such revenues also were an important source of patronage by which princes and monarchs could render their aristocratic inferiors dependent upon them.[79] As Norbert Elias notes, monetarization also broke, however slowly, the cycle of rise and decline characteristic of early medieval kingdoms and principalities. Rulers could now substitute monetary payments for extensive grants of land as a reward for military and political service.[80]

The early modern "price revolution"—the inflation that began to take hold in sixteenth-century Europe—generally favored entrepreneurial merchants and the higher nobility. The latter not only benefited from the increasing price of agricultural goods, but could also derive income from patronage and military activity. Ironically, their comparative fortune made them more dependent on the crown, not only with respect to patronage but also because monarchical brokerage became, at least in some regions, essential to the ability of large landowners to raise rents and squeeze profits from the peasantry.[81] Some theorists argue

[78] Mackenney 1993, 222–23.
[79] Spruyt 1994, 86–105.
[80] Elias 1994, 355–421.
[81] The possible citations here are too numerous to list. For overviews, see Koenigsberger and Mosse 1968, 22–46; and Wallace 2004, 119–23.

that, in the context of these economic changes, more modern forms of state administration proved better at providing and securing the kinds of property rights necessary for capitalist economies.[82] Economic changes thus concentrated power in the hands of magnates, monarchs, cities, and federative alliances. They produced composite states even though they did not decisively select for dynastic agglomerations over alternative composite polities.

MILITARY CHANGE

Bellocentric theorists of state formation often focus on the political ramifications of the so-called military-technical revolution. Historians dispute both the timing and existence of the military revolution, but sometime between the late fifteenth and seventeenth centuries new techniques and technologies of warfare influenced the nature of military conflict. The introduction of pike squares, pioneered by the Swiss Confederation and used decisively against Charles the Bold, undermined the effectiveness of modes of warfare based upon charging heavy cavalry into enemy lines. When combined with advances in personal firearms, which could penetrate the sophisticated armor of late medieval men-at-arms, organized pikemen rendered the last remnants of the old "feudal hosts" obsolete—at least in the Western European context.[83] At the same time, more effective artillery easily destroyed old stone castles, and led to the development of more advanced—and much more expensive—fortification techniques. The coordinative action required by pike formations, especially when combined with firearms, made the training of ordinary infantry more complicated and time-consuming.

Thus, during the sixteenth and seventeenth centuries the frequency and expense of warfare in Europe escalated. As the offensive firepower of armies increased, military commanders adopted techniques of siege warfare that added to the already great expense of the new armies by increasing the importance of logistical support and supply.[84] Although "individual states faced the consequences of these changes at different points in time," all eventually came under pressure to expand and reform their administrative infrastructure, borrow money, increase their resource base, or seek subsidies from wealthier states.[85] As Koenigsberger argues,

---

[82] North 1990, North and Thomas 1973.

[83] As Robert I. Frost notes, "While cavalry may well have been all but useless in the siege warfare which played a central role in the Eighty Years War between Spain and the Dutch rebels, it remained central to operations in eastern Europe throughout the period." See Frost 2000, 311.

[84] See Bean 1973, Downing 1992, Eltis 1995, Ertman 1997, Glete 2002, Hintze 1975, Howard 1976, Parker 1976 and 1988, Roberts 1967, and Tilly 1975 and 1992.

[85] Braddick 2000, 61.

The traditional armies of feudal knights and retainers had proved themselves unable to stand up to new, highly trained professional infantry which the Swiss had pioneered and which the Spaniards perfected. The old feudal castles crumbled before the fire power of the new siege artillery; and in the raising and deploying of these new weapons, kings had an enormous advantage over even their most powerful vassals.[86]

Yet once cities and towns adapted by employing new styles of fortification, siege warfare, as previously noted, necessarily became an expensive and time-consuming proposition.[87] Thus, while military-technical change facilitated the rise of dynastic power, it did not open an easy doorway to sovereign-territorial state building.

Configurational Effects

Taken together, these factors—dynastic practices, economic change, and alterations in the nature of warfare—undermined without necessarily destroying many competing logics of political organization, such as federative alliances and city-empires.[88] Urban centers of power and lesser nobles, in particular, came under severe pressure from dynasts and dynastic states. Yet these factors did not conjoin to set Europe on an inevitable pathway toward a sovereign-territorial state system. They favored, at least in their proximate effects, dynastic-agglomerative state formation without tilting the balance towards sovereign-territorial state building.

THE LOSERS

Processes of change in late medieval and early modern Europe undermined a variety of alternative forms of composite polities. We have already seen how processes of dynastic competition transformed most of the Italian city-empires into microdynastic empires. By the end of the sixteenth century most of the formerly independent city-states of Italy—with the exception of Venice—had been or were soon to be incorporated into local dynastic states, and Italian polities were bit players in the great dynastic struggle

---

[86] Koenigsberger 1987, 42. Nevertheless, nonstate actors with access to sufficient resources were able to mobilize military power despite its increasing costs. During the French Wars of Religion, for example, the major armies of all sides—led and raised largely by princes and other great lords—made use of the new techniques to slaughter one another. See Eltis 1995, 18, 44.

[87] See, e.g., Wood 1996, 32.

[88] Sharma argues that the social institution of "dynasticism," rather than "Darwinian selection" through economic and military competition, explains the contours of early modern state formation. But such analysis neglects the degree to which economic and military competition, under changing conditions, made possible the expansion of dynastic power at the expense of rival actors and forms of political organization. See Sharma 2005.

between the Habsburgs and first the Valois and then the Bourbons.[89] In 1509 the French decisively defeated the Venetian army at Agnadello and put an end to Venice's great-power status within continental Europe.[90] The Swiss Confederation survived largely because its mountainous terrain made it difficult to attack. Geography also played perhaps a crucial role in the emergence and survival of the Dutch Republic.[91] Watery terrain allowed for the construction of effective fortifications, and the rebels could always open a region's dikes to flood besieging armies.[92] As we shall see in subsequent chapters, the rebellion nevertheless almost failed.

The Hanseatic League also faced growing problems. The rising influence of dynastic states created difficult challenges for the league; some historians question whether the Hansa should be thought of as a coherent federation by the early part of the fifteenth century. The defeat of the Teutonic Order—whose alliance with the Hansa helped provide security for its members—by Poland-Lithuania seriously eroded the autonomy of many Hansa towns.[93] Although the Hansa scored, as we have seen, impressive military victories in the early part of the sixteenth century, long-term economic changes eroded the common interests holding the league together.

The rise of maritime and commercial activity in the Low Countries created major problems for the Hansa.[94] Shifts in economic production and the rise of credit-based financing, in particular, limited the Hansa's ability to extract concessions by denying towns access to its markets and merchant fleets. In the early sixteenth century Netherlandish towns financed the construction of their own merchant ships rather than continuing to pay the Hansa to transport their goods. As towns defected from their concessions with the league, its market leverage quickly declined.[95] Since the Hansa lacked land forces comparable to those held by princes and since its members resided within the jurisdiction of other political authorities, it could not rely on coercive capacity to maintain its position over the long term. Spruyt points out that many of the league towns sim-

---

[89] Koenigsberger and Mosse 1968, 59–64. For the example of Turin, see Symcox 1997. See, generally, Elliott 2000.

[90] Koenigsberger and Mosse 1968, 65. Venice's commercial power soon recovered, only to be eclipsed in the eighteenth century by the Dutch and the English.

[91] Israel 1995, Parker 1972.

[92] Parker 1972, 16–17. In 1574 the Revolt was saved from imminent military defeat at Leiden by heavy rainfall, which, given that the rebels had opened the dikes, flooded the countryside and forced the Spanish to retreat. As Israel notes, "So weakened were the defenders that scarcely anyone in the town could stand." Israel 1995, 181. See also Geyl 1958, 137–38.

[93] Malowist 1966, 25.

[94] Bonney 1991, 439; Mackenney 1993, 88; Winter 1948, 285–86.

[95] Winter 1948, 285–86.

ply defected from it and reaffirmed their position within the kingdoms and principalities in which they resided.[96]

Another important factor in its decline, however, stemmed from the naval dimension of military-technical change. As a federation centered upon maritime trade, the Hansa's great strength lay in its merchant fleet. But developments in warfare rendered merchant vessels less and less useful as fighting ships. As Robert I. Frost argues, "The construction of ever-larger warships designed to carry a growing number of heavy guns shifted the balance decisively. The new warships were unsuitable for use as merchantmen, and Hanseatic merchants, who had largely protected themselves in the past, could not afford the vast expense of maintaining dedicated warships on a large scale."[97] After its intervention in Denmark during the early sixteenth century, the Hansa never achieved another major victory.[98]

By the end of the sixteenth century, writes J. P. Morgan, the "independence and direct political power of towns declined everywhere in Europe, except in the United Provinces and Switzerland."[99] Urban centers continued to be important sources of power in early modern Europe, but they saw a steep decline in their capacity to act as autonomous forces in interstate politics. Indeed, as we shall see, religious conflicts played a not insignificant—if secondary—role in this process. Towns and cities, nevertheless, remained barriers to the consolidation of nation-state styles of governance and thus one factor in the persistence of dynastic-agglomerative, rather than sovereign-territorial, state formation.

THE WINNERS: DYNASTIC AGGLOMERATIONS RATHER
THAN SOVEREIGN-TERRITORIAL STATES

Economic and military changes in the early modern period generally gave an advantage to polities with significant territories, populations, and access to capital sufficient to finance more expensive forms of warfare. But the "economies of scale" in early modern Europe belonged, as we have seen, to relatively large dynastic agglomerations. Dynastic composite states could also provide property rights, security, and access to commercial markets; this should be particularly clear if we consider that almost all of the putatively sovereign-territorial states of the period were composite dynastic states.

What about increasing bureaucratic and administrative governance? Growth in administrative technology—spurred by the expansion of liter-

[96] Spruyt 1994, 165–70.
[97] Frost 2000, 6.
[98] Bonney 1991, 439; Koenigsberger and Mosse 1968, 66–67.
[99] Cooper 1971, 15.

acy, the rise of trade and long-distance travel, advancements in communication, and the adoption of new techniques of record keeping—provided a counterbalance against the centrifugal pressures that had undermined central control over heterogeneous territories and populations in the early medieval period. In other words, it facilitated the administration of composite entities.[100]

One exception can be found in Germany, where the *relative* weakness of imperial institutions, the Turkish threat, and, as we shall see, the spread of the Reformation, enabled princes to consolidate their authority. Yet at least two factors caution against reading too much into the aspirations of German princes. First, in the sixteenth century, towns and local actors were significant obstacles to the development of territorial princedoms in the empire, particularly in northwestern Germany.[101] Second, it was not clear until after the Thirty Years' War whether the emperor or the princes would emerge triumphant. As Walter Hubatsch argues,

> the full development of the sovereign territorial state . . . did not come about until the imperial dignity had been reduced to a mere adornment and the Habsburgs had turned aside to pursue the interests of their dynasty. Charles V . . . was still perfectly able to assert his own will in the Schmalkaldic War: it may have caused a considerable stir for princes of the Empire to be taken prisoner and sentenced to death, but at this time it was still completely within the realms of the possible, even though it was never repeated.[102]

To make matters even more complicated, economic change in Poland actually increased the power of the nobility, particularly at the expense of the monarchy. As Thomas Ertman argues, the comparatively late arrival of sustained warfare in the Western European model helps account for Poland's trajectory.[103] But Poland itself was also a dynastic agglomeration, and, as a result of the 1385 ascension of Jagiello, the Grand Duke of Lithuania, an extremely large one. Once it became an elective monarchy, foreign dynasts such as Henry of Anjou (1572)—later, Henry III of France—and Sigismund Vasa (1587) of Sweden won election to its throne. The nobility elected Vasa, for example, to gain Swedish support for Poland-Lithuania's wars with Muscovy, and hence to avoid having to pay the cost for military campaigns.[104] The resulting Swedish claim to the Pol-

---

[100] Lynch 1991, 99–100.
[101] Schilling 1983, 445.
[102] Hubatsch 1971, 198.
[103] Ertman 1997.
[104] Koenigsberger and Mosse 1968, 222–23.

ish crown led to "a half-century of futile and destructive wars between Sweden and Poland."[105]

Few of the forces at work in late medieval and early modern European state formation favored the emergence of sovereign-territorial states. The great monarchies of Europe were composite, dynastic states with only some elements of sovereign territoriality; there was little reason to believe those elements would become the central features of their political systems. Rulers continued to look to magnates and nobles for the provision of (at least some of their) military forces, and a variety of local actors operated as military and political intermediaries within dynastic conglomerations.[106] In France, for example, many local royal officials were clients of the nobility, and "they were expected to exhibit higher loyalty to their patrons than to their kings."[107] Because of the agglomerative nature of even the "new monarchies" of Western Europe and the central importance of "transnational" dynasticism, "ordinary political subjects . . . acted in the context of overlapping, intersecting, and changing political spaces defined by the often competitive claimants to sovereign authority over them."[108] According to Mark Greengrass, in

> the sixteenth and seventeenth centuries, sovereignty was still the exercise of authority within different domains (seigneurial, ecclesiastical, juridical, etc.). These domains were often not delineated with great precision and, if they were, their limits often did not coincide with one another. Sovereignty was still alienated to princes in the form of specific grants of a feudal nature, such as the appanage to a prince.[109]

In the empire, shifting struggles between emperor, prince, Church, and urban centers left a fluid political landscape. Nondynastic composite polities found themselves on the defensive. The dominant political relations in dynastic agglomeration were more imperial than sovereign and territorial.

International Relations in an Era of Dynastic Composite States

International-relations scholars need to be particularly careful about how they assess arguments about the origins and development of the sovereign-territorial state system in late medieval and early modern

---

[105] Ibid., 220.
[106] Cohn 1971, 29; Koenigsberger 1971a, 7–8.
[107] Major 1971, 52–54.
[108] te Brake 1998, 14.
[109] Greengrass 1991, 3.

Europe. Many aspects of sovereignty did develop in these periods. The sixteenth century witnessed, for example, the culmination of some very important developments in theories of sovereign authority. Throughout the early modern period, European rulers claimed sovereign authority while theorists elaborated the nature of sovereign power.[110] But a major thrust of international-relations scholarship on political change involves not the emergence of aspects of sovereignty, per se, but the search for the origins of the kind of international system idealized in international-relations theory: one composed of sovereign nation-states pursuing their interests in a generally anarchical environment. In the last chapter I argued that such a system should be conceptualized, at least in part, as a relational structure composed of (relatively) categorically homogeneous and densely tied social sites operating in (relatively) categorically heterogeneous and sparsely tied environments.

Early modern Europe did not approximate such a system. Even though we can find elements of sovereign territoriality within it, we should not make the logical leap of assuming that such elements produced an international system that conformed with our ideal-typifications of international politics. The logic of international politics generated by an order dominated by dynastic agglomerations departed from realist conceptions of world politics in a number of important and highly consequential ways.[111]

First, "reason of dynasty" rather than modern conceptions of state interests drove international-political competition. As Garrett Mattingly remarks in his discussion of the Valois-Habsburg struggle for Italy, "The sixteenth-century struggle for power had a dynastic, not a national orientation. . . . Whether such conquests would be worth to [a prince's] people the blood and treasure they would cost was an irrelevant, absurd question. Nobody expected that they would.[112] Even when dynasts pursued policies designed to promote commercial or economic advantage, they did so with the aim of securing revenue for their own ambitions. The Valois kings of France proved willing to throw wealth and manpower down the drain to make good their dynastic claims in Italy, but "the alternative of pushing towards a Rhine frontier, in the pursuance of a supposedly 'French national interest,' was not even considered; for in the climate of sixteenth-century opinion it would have been very difficult to justify."[113]

---

[110] See, e.g., Armitage 1998b, Bodin 1992, Mackenney 1993, Muldoon 1999.
[111] For similar arguments, see Nexon 2006; Sharma 2005; and Teschke 1998, 2002, and 2003.
[112] Mattingly 1988, 140.
[113] Koenigsberger and Mosse 1968, 217. See also Knecht 1996c, 32–33. During the Valois-Habsburg conflicts that marked the first half of the sixteenth century, the driving force was contested dynastic claims in Italy, not the balance of power. See Garrisson 1991,

Marriage and inheritance played, unsurprisingly, a central role in interdynastic alliance formation and negotiations between dynasts and lesser lords.[114] European politics, in consequence, involved a patchwork of hereditary claims to kingdoms, counties, and principalities. Prudent dynasts recognized the dangers that might follow from making marriage alliances a central component of peacemaking and coalition building, but dynastic norms and practices made such marriages an frequent component of many political negotiations. For example, "In 1550 secretary Paget, negotiating for the return of Boulogne to the French, was questioned on a French marriage for Edward VI [Henry VIII's short-lived son]. An Italian merchant, working for England, told him a treaty with France without a marriage alliance was 'but a drye peace.' "[115] Marriage alliances served other important interests: they preserved the future aspirations of dynastic lines even as they made specific concessions in a particular treaty.

For lords, marriages with one another or with dynasts provided important conduits for familial influence and patronage. Such practices created both dangers and opportunities for dynasts because "dynastic rights were considered to be perpetual and inalienable." As Richard Bonney argues, "Valois claims to Naples and Milan and Habsburg claims to Burgundy were difficult, if not impossible, to negotiate away in a peace treaty."[116] Long after the English had been routed at the end of the Hundred Years War, Elizabeth I's royal title referred to her as the King of France.[117]

Early modern European politics also lacked a fundamental feature of contemporary politics: nationalism. The tight connection between nation and the state represented by the ideal of "national self-determination" simply did not exist in dynastic agglomerations. Individuals usually considered their affiliations to "Normandy or Provence, Aragon or Castile, Bavaria or Saxony," let alone their immediate personal loyalties, rather than those of "Frenchman, Spaniard, or even German."[118] Local identities remained far more important than the still inchoate notions of *patria*, or

---

137; and Knecht 1996b, 62. Even though the decisive stages of the conflict frequently involved northern France and the Low Countries, the primary objective of the fighting remained Italy. See Knecht 1996a, 45.

[114] As it did in the patron-client networks, both dynastic and nondynastic, that formed the sinews of politics in polities such as France. See Kettering 1986a.

[115] Russell 1986, 85–86.

[116] Bonney 1991, 79.

[117] Koenigsberger and Mosse 1968, 216.

[118] Koenigsberger and Mosse 1968, 213. Koenigsberger and Mosse argue that peasant "xenophobia" is a better model for ethnic identity in the sixteenth century than modern nationalist discourse. These "rhetorics of foreignness" played a key role in many of the revolts of the early-modern period.

nation.[119] Subjects often preferred rule by their own ethnic group, but proved willing to tolerate foreign dynasts. Subjects favored such arrangements largely because they believed that an indigenous ruler would better protect the customary practices of their political community, would be less likely to dispense patronage to outsiders, or would be less inclined to seek to expropriate revenue for interests with no connection to their own immediate concerns.[120]

Dynasts might, often through propaganda, argue that their dynastic interests and the interests of their holdings were synonymous. Sometimes they succeeded, but there was nothing obvious about the harmony of dynastic ambitions and the interests of a kingdom or principality.[121] As J. H. Shennan remarks, "We should beware of misinterpreting aspects of the consolidation of princely authority in the late fifteenth and early sixteenth centuries as evidence of proto-national sentiment."[122] A dynast's desire to prosecute his or her claims, however, often found support among the nobility—even among those who harbored their own dynastic ambitions—since warfare provided ample opportunity for their enrichment and advancement.[123]

Dynastic norms and practices, therefore, drove European political struggles. As Richard Mackenney explains,

> For those who governed, the interests of the family were all important. The word "dynasty," which denotes a succession of rulers of the same family, could in itself mean "sovereignty" or "power." Indeed, the survival or extinction of the dynasty was the difference between peace and war, and the accidents of inheritance shaped the power blocs of Europe as a whole.[124]

Dynastic ties and claims provided the critical context for late medieval and early modern articulations of "sovereignty." They shaped most political struggles in early modern Europe; at the same time, notions of territorial control remained, at best, embryonic.[125]

---

[119] Mackenney 1993, 59.

[120] Hale 1985, 43.

[121] For an illuminating study of the use of and rhetoric of Valois propaganda during the League of Cambrai, in which France fought in an Italian alliance against the Venetian Republic, see Sherman 1977.

[122] Shennan 1974, 40. See also Cooper 1971, 2–4.

[123] Koenigsberger and Mosse 1968, 218. Hale argues that the period from the sixteenth to the seventeenth century saw a significant decline in aristocratic participation in warfare. These arguments are not incompatible, as this was a process that unfolded during the major changes in the state that took place during the period this work considers. See Hale 1985.

[124] Mackenney 1993, 219.

[125] For a cultural analysis of territorial power and its changing nature from the fifteenth to the seventeenth century, see Mukerji 1997.

Second, the heterogeneous nature of dynastic agglomerations and the logic of dynastic practices ensured that international politics contained what we would now call a significant "transnational" component. Scholars of international relations are accustomed to thinking of states as the fundamental units of international politics. It should not be surprising, therefore, that we view rulers of states largely as individuals who decide and implement state policies. Some approaches to international politics, particularly in the game-theoretic tradition, treat leaders as independent actors, with an interest in holding onto power and, possibly, of achieving financial gain. In early modern Europe, however, dynastic rulers and even dynastic lines operated as units in their own right.[126]

Consider the complicated career of Ludovico Gonzaga. Gonzaga, the brother of the Duke of Mantua and Monferrato, was sent to France either, depending on the account, to facilitate his naturalization and, hence, his inheritance of his grandmother's holdings, or so that the Gonzagas, who had allied with the Habsburgs, could hedge their dynastic bets. In 1565 he married Henrietta of Kleve, who was not only a co-heiress to the cadet branch of the House of Kleve (in the Holy Roman Empire) but also to the duchies of Nevers and Rethel in France. Through the marriage Ludovico also obtained Bois-Belle-en-Berry and the principality of Arches, which were both "sovereign territories" in France. Thus, Ludovico was a *prince étrange* through his brother, a sovereign prince in his own right, and a French *grand*, as well as an individual with dynastic ties to "a complex network of German princely families. As duc de Nevers and Rethel," he "owed allegiance to . . . the king of France, yet was not juridically a subject of the French king."[127]

Gonzaga's career not only demonstates how dynastic lines functioned as actors in their own right, but also how the European political landscape remained crisscrossed by real or potential claims of dynastic authority to a variety of kingdoms, principalities, and other political units. As Mark Greengrass notes, international "treaties and aristocratic declarations of loyalty to a sovereign lord continued to contain expressions of political relationships in terms of personal oaths of allegiance."[128] We have already seen that, even as their significance declined relative to the preceding centuries, federative alliances and individual towns operated as international actors. Magnates, displaced dynasts, and a variety of other individuals also participated in the shifting power-political formations of early modern Europe. Dynasts routinely conspired with malcontents—whether nobles or urban oligarchs—in one another's territories. Local actors seeking

---

[126] Sharma 2005, Teschke 2002 and 2003.
[127] Parrot 1997, 154–57.
[128] Greengrass 1991, 3.

to extend or conserve their rights and privileges negotiated with foreign dynasts, who themselves often exploited these relationships to further their own claims.[129]

The papacy, for its part, continued to function both as a quasi-dynastic state in Italy and as a transnational actor. There is little doubt that, by the fourteenth century, Western European monarchs had gotten the upper hand over the Church: papal authority, and its ability to derive revenues by taxing the Church, became dependent upon royal authority. Yet networks of papal authority still played an important role in the Western European monarchies, as long as the papacy's activities did not interfere with royal power.[130] These trends accelerated in the latter part of the fourteenth century, as sovereigns "exploit[ed] the pope's need for allies" against both secular opponents in Italy and rival seats of power within the Church. In particular, the papacy accepted a number of concordats that, while ceding important powers to kings and princes, at least maintained the pretense that the concessions were based upon contracts rather than outright annexations of papal authority.[131]

THE IMPACT OF THE REFORMATIONS

The European political order of the sixteenth and seventeenth centuries clearly fails to reflect the principles and practices associated with a sovereign-territorial state system. In consequence, we cannot sustain a number of arguments about the timing and development of the modern state system. The dynastic-imperial pathway and the composite quality of early modern European political communities also raise doubts about any approach to international change that takes the *transition* between "medieval heteronomy" and the modern state as its fundamental puzzle, insofar as doing so misses the significance of early modern political relations as objects of analysis in their own right.

In this light, we can identify a few ways in which the Reformations contributed to the development of the modern state system. First, the division of Latin Europe into different confessional camps limited the future possibilities for dynastic-empire building. It became progressively more difficult for dynasts to conclude marriage alliances in which one partner was Catholic and the other Protestant.[132] Second, the Reformations accelerated the development of conceptual innovations related to

---

[129] Subsequent chapters in the present volume contain many examples of these dynamics.
[130] Thomson 1998, 175–76.
[131] Barraclough 1968, 187–88.
[132] Flemming 1973; Kann 1973, 388–89.

sovereignty and the sovereign-territorial state system, such as doctrines of "necessity" and "reason of state," as well as theories of sovereignty itself.[133] Third, religious differentiation created conditions of possibility for the development of nationalism and the nation-state. Dynamics associated with so-called confessionalization, in which religious beliefs hardened into distinctive identities and those identities became tied to territorially demarcated churches, helped push European political relations in the direction of our models of sovereign-territorial states.[134] I deal with these indirect effects in chapter 8.

But the Reformations produced a number of more direct changes to the European political landscape, such as the failure of the Habsburg bid for hegemony, the associated independence of the United Provinces, and other developments that limited, for the time being, the territorial expansion of intra-European dynastic empires.[135] Indeed, the most immediate impact of Reformations was the defeat of the Habsburg dynasty as the dominant force in Europe. This is a far from insignificant consequence, as it suggests that transnational religious networks helped determine the future configuration of power relations in early modern Europe.

The next chapter provides a theoretical account of some of the key mechanisms and processes through which the Reformations shaped European political developments. These mechanisms and processes were tied to the structural dynamics of dynastic agglomerations and composite states. My exploration of European state formation through the beginning of the early modern period, therefore, not only helps us to assess debates about the origins of sovereignty, but provides the necessary infrastructure for understanding why the Reformations led to a crisis, if not an unambiguous turning point, in European state formation.

[133] Armitage 2004, 102–3.
[134] See Bendix 1978, 267–68; Elliott 1992, 59; Gorski 1993, 1999, and 2000; Marx 2005; and Schilling 1992.
[135] Tilly 1992, 167.

CHAPTER 4

Religious Contention and the Dynamics of Composite States

IN THIS CHAPTER I theorize the impact of the Reformations on European state formation through a relational-institutionalist lens. Composite states combined indirect rule with heterogeneous contracting; in dynastic agglomerations, rulers occupied titular positions that linked together their different domains based on explicit and implicit contractual obligations between rulers and subjects. Contractual obligations differed not only across these domains, but between different groups and classes within them. Some contracts provided for comparatively direct rule but, in general, dynasts controlled their holdings through a variety of local intermediaries. Such characteristics of early modern states suggest an ideal-typical account of their relational structures that shares important characteristics with what network theorists call "star-shaped" or "spoked" networks.[1] The network-structure of ideal-typical early modern European states accounts for their routine patterns of collective mobilization, resistance, and rule.

- Such structures create barriers against cross-regional and cross-class resistance to central authority: they produce institutionalized patterns of *divide-and-rule* that tend to limit the capacity of local actors to overcome the capabilities of central authorities. These same features also produce strong *cross pressures* on rulers stemming from the different interests and identities of their territories.
- Indirect rule limits *governance costs* for rulers; it also, however, leads to inefficiencies and principal-agent problems. Local intermediaries—such as viceroys, governors, magnates, and urban oligarchs—often already have, or develop, their own interests and ambitions. Not only might they disregard the policies and goals of their rulers, but they sometimes seek to expand their own autonomy or even, whether de facto or de jure, secede from central control.
- Rulers more effectively extract resources and negotiate with their subjects if they find ways to legitimate their rule across diverse audiences: that is, if they engage in what social scientists call *multivocal*

[1] Montgomery 2005, 169–70; Padgett and Ansell 1993, 1278.

or *polyvalent* signaling. Failure to do so, however, worsens cross-pressures and generally narrows the scope of mutual accommodation for rulers and ruled.

These conditions facilitated the rise of religious heterodoxy that we now call the Reformations. The structure of composite states in general, and dynastic agglomerations in particular, also accounts for *why* the Reformations led to a crisis in early modern state formation. The emergence of cross-region and cross-polity networks centered around religious beliefs and identities undermined the various ways that rulers managed their heterogeneous domains. Once disputes over theology and ritual entered into ongoing struggles over central and local control, rulers found it more difficult to legitimate their authority across different political coalitions. As Richard MacKenney argues, "The obstacles to sovereign national entities, universalism and localism, took new forms and indeed acquired new vigor—and in their novelty became more recognizably modern as political forces precisely because of the expanding importance of religion as an ideological and social force."[2]

I begin by elaborating the ideal-typical form of dynastic agglomerations in terms of their network properties. I next discuss how these properties produce routine dynamics of resistance and rule, drawing not simply upon evidence from early modern Europe but from a broad range of imperial composite polities. The next section discusses patterns of resistance and rule in early modern Europe; I demonstrate that these patterns represent specific manifestations of the broader structural logic of imperial composite states. In the final section, I discuss how the introduction of religious contention in early modern European states, depending upon the specific vectors and ideas of religious movements, triggered conditions that increased the threat posed by resistance in early modern Europe.

The Ideal-Typical Structure of Dynastic Agglomerations

We find a great deal of organizational variation among dynastic agglomerations, not to mention among different forms of composite states. The structure of royal authority in Castile differed from that in Aragon, Catalonia, and Valencia. The organization of representation and rule, for example, in the Tudor monarchy, Imperial Germany, and the Netherlands was, as we have seen, far from identical. We can, nevertheless, construct an ideal-typical description of "composite polities" that covers the variety of dynastic agglomerations found in early modern Europe. Doing so pro-

---

[2] Mackenney 1993, 81.

vides a ceteris paribus account of their dynamics of resistance and rule; we should expect, furthermore, that the degree to which, and in what ways, a particular early modern state departs from our ideal type should have implications for specific historical processes and outcomes.[3]

A relational-institutionalist approach to ideal typification focuses on the network structure of political authority. Early modern composite states often combined indirect rule with heterogeneous contracting. In this respect they involved elements that look more like ideal-typical empires than ideal-typical nation-states.[4] Like empires, they had a core-periphery structure in which peripheries are differentiated—or segmented—from one another: the "most striking aspect of such a structure is not the hub and spoke, but the *absence of a rim* . . . of political and economic relations between and among the peripheral units or between and among them and non-imperial polities [original emphasis]."[5] Actual composite states, like real-world empires, vary in the degree of connectivity between constituent political communities. Such variation, of course, shapes patterns of resistance and rule, but the institutional structure of composite polities usually produces intrasegment ties that are denser than cross-segment connections.

We should begin by specifying four kinds of social sites: central authorities, local intermediaries, substitutable elites, and ordinary people.[6]

- *Central authorities*. Any actor, or collection of actors, that sits at the highest level of central administration, such as an emperor, monarch, sovereign prince, or oligarchs ruling a city with a *contado*. Central authorities may or may not be embedded within a specific segment, which would then constitute a "core" or imperial "metropole." For our purposes, cores are simply privileged segments.
- *Local Intermediaries*. Governors, viceroys, regional magnates, or any group of administrators who directly govern a segment or subsegment of a composite state. Local intermediaries may hail from the territory they govern, from a core segment, or be recruited from elsewhere (A_1-D_1 in figure 4.1).
- *Substitutable Elites*. Any group whose members could become local intermediaries without disrupting the underlying political organization of a constituent segment of a composite state. These actors in early modern Europe often, but not always, included great magnates and other members of the aristocracy (A_2-D_2 in figure 4.1).

[3] On ideal-typical methodology, see Mommsen 1989, 125–26; Ringer 1997, 5–6, 17, 23, 110–116; and Weber 1949 and 1978.
[4] Tilly 1997a, 3.
[5] Motyl 2001, 16–20.
[6] Borrowed and adapted from te Brake 1998.

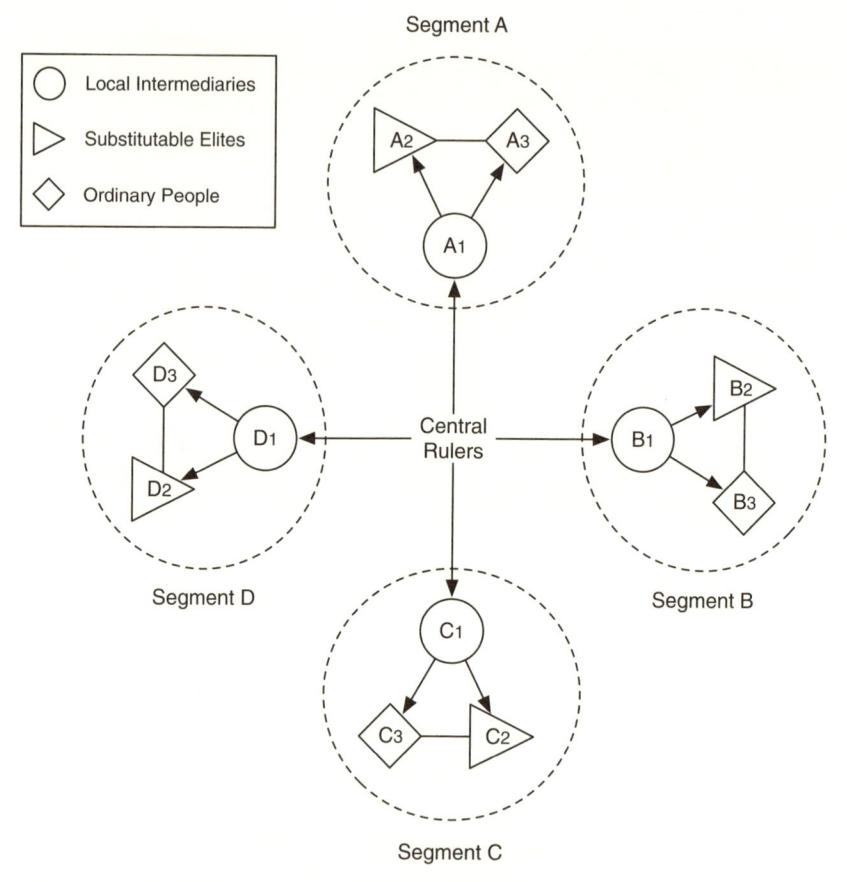

Figure 4.1 Ideal-Typical Structure of Imperial Composite States

- *Ordinary People.* Those local actors who, if they assumed control of a segment, would, by definition, overthrow the old order. In early modern Europe, the most common sites of this type were composed of burghers organized politically into towns or communes, or of peasants (A_3-D_3 in figure 4.1).

Actual processes of resistance and rule in composite states involve many more constellations of actors, such as different factions of substitutable elites and ordinary people. We need not, however, increase the number of political sites—either by paying attention to within-group cleavages or by adding other clusters of political actors—in order to understand the basic dynamics of dynastic agglomerations.

Figure 4.1 captures the ideal-typical network structure of an early modern composite state with four constituent segments. Central authorities, usually dynasts and their advisors, exercised authority over local intermediaries who, in turn, administered substitutable elites and ordinary people. Networks of authority, therefore, ran from central authorities *through* local intermediaries to various local actors.

As noted above, the combination of heterogeneous contracting and indirect rule produces a structure similar to a "star-shaped" or "spoke" network. This network represents *only routine authority relations*. Central authorities may, for example, bypass local intermediaries and negotiate directly with local actors. Other kinds of ties may also exist in the overall network (for example, economic, social, and kinship), but we will consider those as they become relevant to specified dynamics of resistance and rule. This ideal-typical representation, furthermore, ignores the fractal qualities of early modern composite states: the fact that these relations reproduced themselves, in various ways, as we move from the overall composite state to the level of towns and rural localities. Such complications also need not concern us for the present; they represent the kind of variation in the actual structure of particular polities analyzed over the next few chapters. At our current stage of abstraction, we should focus on two important "levels" of the ideal-typical network structure represented in Figure 4.1: its aggregate structure and its within-segment structure (for example, central authorities A_1, A_2, and A_3).

Aggregate Structure

If we look at figure 4.1 at the aggregate level, we can see that central authorities are directly connected to A_1-D_1 and indirectly connected to A_2-D_2 and A_3-D_3. In contrast, no actors within a constituent segment are directly connected—in terms of authority relations—to any actors in a different segment. For example, A_3 is not connected to B_3, C_3, and D_3; B_1 is connected to B_2 and B_3, but not to A_1-A_3, C_1-C_3, and D_1-D_3. Thus, ties *between* segments are comparatively weak and sparse, while ties *within* segments are comparatively strong and dense. This aggregate structure gives rise to a number of significant, though interdependent, network characteristics.

CENTRALITY AND BROKERAGE

Both in terms of the hierarchy of authority within dynastic agglomerations, and in terms of patterns of ties, central authorities occupy a central position with respect to the overall network. In some respects this is just another way of saying that dynastic agglomerations have a kind of core-periphery structure, but it has important implications.

In network analysis centrality is often a proxy for power and influence. The underlying mechanism involves informational asymmetries: actors with more connections have more information about the preferences and orientations of others than those with fewer connections.[7] In dynastic agglomerations central authorities occupy a *brokerage* position between local intermediaries and aggregate segments: they negotiate relations between different segments.[8] This political position gives central authorities an advantage in terms of power and influence vis-à-vis actors in the rest of the network. The fact that these networks involve authoritative relations of super- and subordination only reinforces those other structural sources of asymmetric power.

PERIPHERAL SEGMENTATION AND COLLECTIVE MOBILIZATION

Figure 4.1 does not adequately capture one important consequence of heterogeneous contracting: the ties that run from central authorities through each of their local intermediaries (A_1-A_4) to local actors (A_2-A_4 and B_2-B_4) in each segment all represent a different combination of rights, rules, and obligations. The identity inhering in the relationship between central authorities and each segment is different, as is the categorical identity associated with each segment. This tends to prevent a concordance of interests between segments.

Moreover, the organization of dynastic agglomerations involves structural holes between segments: that is, comparatively sparse and weak intersegmental ties.[9] Constituent regions were relatively disconnected from one another, at least with respect to authoritative or institutional ties. These structural holes work against cross-periphery coordination and collective mobilization.[10] Since actors in each segment tend to be isolated from one another, segments will trend toward greater institutional, attitudinal, and normative differentiation over time.

Within-Segment Structure

If we look at the local structure of relations we see a rather different picture. In the relationship between central authorities and any given segment, local intermediaries display a higher degree of network centrality.

---

[7] Freeman 1977, 35–36; Lange 2003, 375; Nye 2002, 94.

[8] On brokerage as a property of network location, see Burt 1992 and Gould and Fernandez 1989, 91.

[9] On the concept of "structural holes," see Burt 1992. See also Granovetter 1973 and 1983 and Lange 2003.

[10] Lange 2003, 374.

B_1, for example, is directly connected to central authorities and to Segment B's local actors (B_2 and B_3). C_1 is directly connected to central authorities and to Segment C's local actors. Thus, local intermediaries occupy the key brokerage position in the relationship between central authorities and their domains. In terms of local relationships, they are *more powerful* than central authorities although that power will, in important respects, be undermined by their comparative lack of authority vis-à-vis central authorities.[11]

The comparatively dense nature of ties also facilitates within-segment collective mobilization. Simply put, it is easier for actors in one segment to resist dynastic authority than it is for them to coordinate or collaborate with actors in another segment. As I argue below, however, this was often more true of ordinary people (A_3-D_3) than of substitutable elites (A_2-D_2), particularly when those elites were aristocrats. Kinship ties and political relations between nobles often crossed segments, making it easier for them to coordinate their activities than it was, for instance, for peasants or even townsfolk.

Aggregate Structural Tendencies: Divide-and-Rule

The persistence of differentiated local institutions create limitations on central control. When central authorities implement centralizing policies, they frequently confront entrenched local interests. Both substitutable elites and ordinary people often see little to gain—and much to lose—from conceding their political autonomy. They, in fact, often view their autonomy as part of the fundamental bargain between rulers and subjects; attempts by central authorities to transfer power away from local institutions, therefore, not infrequently triggers crises of legitimacy. But the structure of imperial composite states confers important advantages to central authorities. It favors and facilitates processes of across-segment divide-and-rule.

Many realists stress the centrality of the balance-of-power mechanism in world politics: actors seek to form, they argue, countervailing coalitions against rising powers. Divide-and-rule processes, in contrast, work to prevent the formation of countervailing coalitions by exploiting divisions among potential challengers. The logic here is straightforward: as the number of actors resisting control increases, and as they increasingly pool their resources through coordination and collaboration, the ability of dominant actors to maintain their position diminishes. Divide-and-

---

[11] In terms of network analysis, see Stevenson and Greenberg 2000, 656.

rule, therefore, is a means of *maintaining hierarchy*, while the balance of power works to maintain anarchical relations.[12]

Why does the combination of indirect rule and heterogeneous contracting create structural proclivities for divide-and-rule? First, heterogeneous contracting makes bargains between central authorities and many of their subordinate segments distinctive. Disputes over rights and responsibilities in one segment thus often remain localized. Second, the existence of structural holes between segments creates "firewalls" against the spread of resistance: the absence of cross-cutting ties and sources of collective identification across peripheries makes it difficult for actors in multiple peripheries to collectively mobilize against dynastic rule (see figure 4.2). When rebels or usurpers manage to seize control of the organs of government in a particular locality, moreover, they do not automatically gain access to governmental networks in other segments of the composite polity. In sum, resistance to central control is less likely to spread and rebels are less likely to coordinate or collaborate than they would be in the context of uniform contracts or cross-cutting ties. Central authorities, in principle, can bring overwhelming force—by drawing on resources from elsewhere in the composite state—against an isolated rebellion or uncoordinated uprising.[13]

Many uprisings and rebellions in late medieval and early modern Europe fit this pattern. In the *gabelle* revolt of 1542, for example, the people of France's Atlantic marshes rose up against changes in the administration of the salt tax, which imposed additional fiscal burdens and revoked what they understood as their traditional privileges. As R. J. Knecht argues, "The feudal levy was mobilized, but the rebels, knowing that the king was engaged on several fronts at once, stepped up their agitation." Francis I relented, "for he was still engaged in a foreign war" and "he would have been unwise to create bitterness in parts of France so vulnerable to English intervention."[14] In 1548 Francis's heir, Henry II, imposed changes in the salt tax again, prompting another rebellion. The local governor could not suppress the uprising on his own, so he requested aid from a nearby governor. The rebels defeated this force and expanded their attacks on tax collectors. Henry's agents responded with overwhelming force and they savagely suppressed the rebellion.[15]

---

[12] Similarly, divide-and-conquer strategies aim to *establish hierarchy* by disrupting the balance-of-power mechanism. Divide-and-conquer strategies follow broadly similar logics to those found in divide-and-rule, but take place in the absence of pre-established domination. See Baumgartner, Buckley et al. 1975 and Hui 2004.

[13] For discussions in the context of imperial rule, see Cohen 2004, Luttwak 1976, Pollis 1973, and Rosen 2003.

[14] Knecht 1996c, 179.

[15] Ibid., 209–10; Zagorin 1982a, 284.

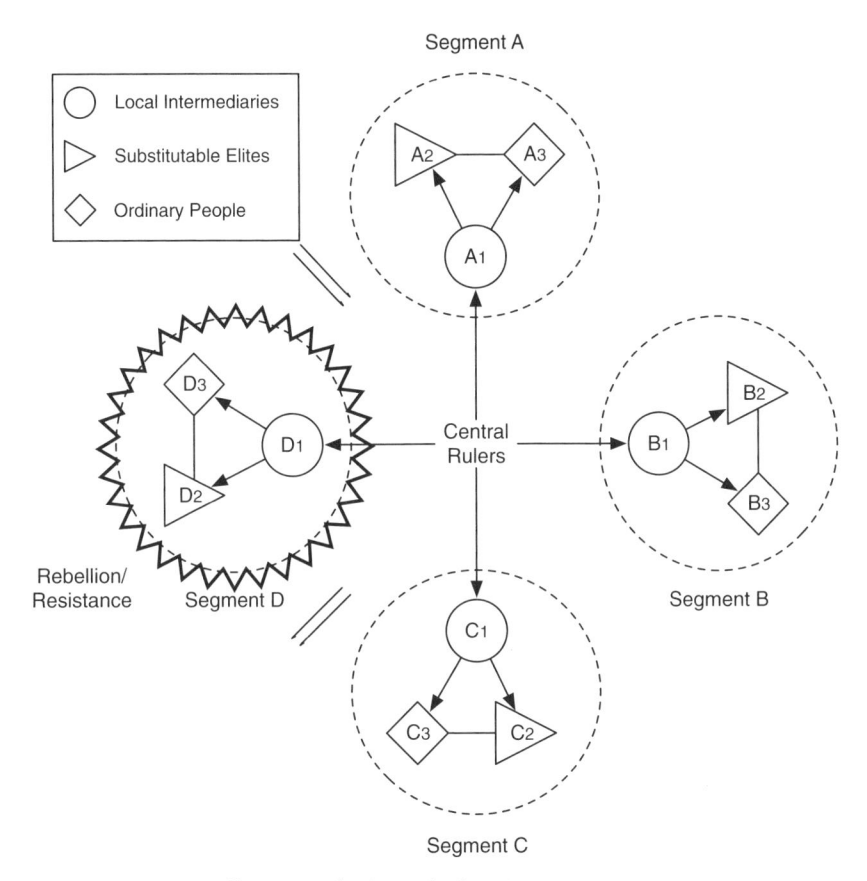

Figure 4.2 "Firewalls" Limit the Spread of Resistance

In 1632 the Crown extended the *gabelle* yet again, prompting another revolt (the "Nu-pieds" uprising) that found support among aristocratic elements. Perez Zagorin describes the uprising as a "provincial" revolt—it appealed to "Norman patriotism, imploring both noble and peasant to act in the name of provincial liberty." Royal troops again suppressed the localized rebellion over a specific contractual relationship between center and periphery.[16] During the *Comuneros* revolt (1520–1522), directed at Charles's policies and fiscal demands in Castile, regional differences precluded the spread of resistance to Andalusia. At roughly the same time, Valencia experienced the revolt of the *Germanías* (1519–1522), but the two groups of rebels made no attempt to coordinate or collaborate

[16] Zagorin 1982a, 8–12.

against their sovereign. Both saw their concerns as local and, regardless, lacked any social ties to facilitate collaboration. Forces loyal to Charles in each domain separately defeated the uprisings.[17]

FACTORS THAT UNDERMINE DIVIDE-AND-RULE

What kinds of developments undermine divide-and-rule in star-shaped political networks? The first involve increasing peripheral connectivity. Greater collective identification between actors in disparate segments and increasing network density between segments expand the opportunities and potential motives for collective resistance to central control.[18] The second involve exogenous and endogenous triggers for simultaneous resistance, such as particular policies adopted by central authorities or exogenous shocks that lead to independent, but simultaneous, uprisings in multiple peripheries.

Decreasing peripheral segmentation. Leaders of star-shaped political systems often, either deliberately or inadvertently, encourage connections between peripheries. For example, stable rule often facilitates the growth of interperiphery trade, which brings with it increasing ties between actors in segments of composite polities.[19] Imperial composite states often wind up diffusing aspects of imperial culture; the Romans and various Chinese dynasties created large zones of cultural commonality and interaction within their domains.[20] The Japanese engaged in varying degrees of "assimilative practices" within their empire, and often aimed (with mixed success) to build emotional ties between colonial subjects and the symbols of the Japanese Empire.[21] Such developments correlate with the diminished salience of across-segment divide-and-rule. Alexander J. Motyl notes that "because Britain's American colonies had developed extensive economic and political linkages long before 1776, they could mount organized opposition to His Majesty's imposition of various taxes and successfully rebel."[22]

We can find a variety of examples of this process at work in late medieval and early modern Europe. The formation of the Hanseatic League stemmed from increasing economic activity that tied together a variety of towns subject to different composite polities. In fact, the Hansa's emer-

[17] Nexon 2006, 269. For a more detailed discussion, see chapter 5 in the present volume.
[18] Nye 2002, 91–94.
[19] The political success of the Roman Empire, for example, facilitated high levels of economic interdependence and functional differentiation within its territories. See Ward-Perkins 2005, 87–104.
[20] Howe 2002, 41–43; Pagden 2001, 24–30.
[21] Peattie 1984, 189.
[22] Motyl 1999, 137; and 2001.

gence as an autonomous political actor can be treated as a partial secession from, for example, the German Empire.[23] The Burgundian dukes' attempts at state building in the Low Countries imposed a variety of superordinate institutions that linked together nobles, towns, and regions in the Netherlands. These patterns of interconnection facilitated cross-segment collective action in at least two generalized uprisings—in 1477 and, for a time, during the Dutch Revolt.[24]

Thus, processes that often enhance the loyalty of substitutable elites and ordinary people to composite polities—through acculturation and the benefits derived from greater economic exchange—also create conditions of possibility for expanded collective resistance against central control. Interperiphery "transnational" movements may spread through such cultural and economic connections; alternatively, their vanguards may generate increasing connections between peripheries. If such development create common categorical identities among actors in different peripheries, they may undermine the institutional basis of divide-and-rule in star-shaped political systems. Figure 4.3 illustrates how connections between local actors (D_2—A_2, D_3—A_2, D_2—A_3, D_3—A_3) might overcome the firewalls between segments and lead to more generalized resistance or rebellion.

The spread of reformation and counterreformation movements often produced precisely this effect: it linked actors in different regions and provided them with common orientations toward the policies of the center. Indeed, reformation movements enhanced not only intersegmental connectivity but crossed the boundaries of composite states. During the French Wars of Religion, for example, Calvinists in Geneva supplied arms to Huguenot forces. They also negotiated on their behalf for fiscal and military assistance from third parties.[25]

I explore this process more below and in subsequent chapters, but for the present we should recognize that common confessional identities were not always sufficient to overcome intraregional differences. In the Pilgrimage of Grace, Catholics from different regions of Britain marched on Henry VIII and nearly brought him to terms. A variety of factors doomed the movement, such as its leadership's loss of nerve when it came to chal-

---

[23] Spruyt 1994, 123–28.

[24] Israel 1995, 21–25. Kiser and Linton (2002, 900) test aspects of this hypothesis in early modern France and find negative evidence: during periods of time when the Estates General met, they report, rebellions against fiscal demands were half as likely. They argue that "this finding suggests that the Estates General worked not as a collective action mechanism facilitating revolt, but as a forum for negotiation and information exchange that provided a less costly alternative to revolt." This finding, though, is orthogonal to the claim made here: that growing connectivity undermines the modular quality of resistance associated with composite states.

[25] Elliott 2000, 74–75. See also Kingdon 1967; and Koenigsberger 1971b, 224–52.

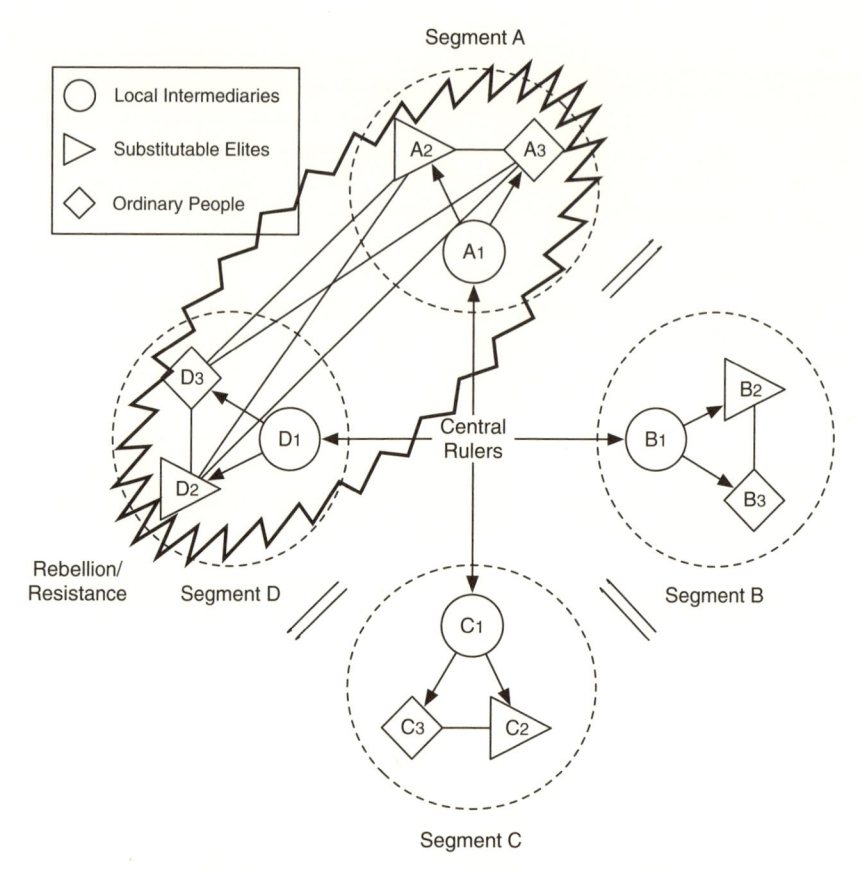

Figure 4.3 Trans-Segment Ties Lead to Coordinated Resistance

lenging their monarch and their naïve faith in his promised concessions, but it also floundered upon regional differences stemming from the composite nature of the Tudor dynastic polity.[26]

Such patterns need not involve dense ties between actors. The existence of common religious categorical identities across imperial composite polities has often proved a sufficient basis for simultaneous resistance. The British were very aware of this potential problem; they often shaped their policies toward the Ottoman Empire with an eye to how those policies would be received by their Muslim subjects. The Ottomans themselves attempted, unsuccessfully, to encourage a jihad against the British in Egypt.[27]

[26] Zagorin 1982a, 19–31.
[27] Karsh and Karsh 1999, 96, 117, 180.

Triggers of simultaneous resistance. A variety of exogenous and relatively autonomous developments may undermine divide-and-rule in composite polities. Any shock—such as widespread famine, economic downturns, or the strains imposed by warfare—that provokes unrest in multiple segments might lead to cross-segment resistance to imperial composite rule. Similarly, ideological forces and social movements can create simultaneous resistance to imperial rule in multiple segments even if they do not create cross-cutting ties or common identities. A good example of this kind of process is the role of the rise of nationalism in the unraveling of the European colonial empires. The diffusion of ideas of national self-determination to local elites and subjects led to multiple movements against colonial rule in the imperial territories of Britain, France, and the Netherlands. The rise of nationalist movements in so many different peripheries certainly undermined the ability of the European colonial empires to maintain control over their extensive territories.[28]

Central authorities may also promulgate policies that lead to resistance in multiple segments at the same time. A confluence of attempts to extract more resources from different segments may trigger simultaneous rebellions. Central authorities may attempt to impose uniform bargains across a number of segments, thereby triggering simultaneous—but often uncoordinated—uprisings. In such instances they do away with the divide-and-rule advantages of heterogeneous bargaining.

These sorts of situations (figure 4.4) are not, all things being equal, as dangerous for composite polities as coordinated cross-segment uprisings. But they still undermine the ability of central authorities to mobilize effective countervailing force. Moreover, such processes may produce patterns of modular devolution: simultaneous, but localized, resistance detaches one or more segments that afterward retain their rough territorial, and sometimes institutional, contours. We can observe this pattern not only in the collapse of many European colonial empires but also, as Mark Beissinger demonstrates, in the fall of the Soviet composite polity.[29]

Aggregate Structural Tendencies: Cross-Pressures

The same structural features that facilitate divide-and-rule strategies also expand the vulnerability of central authorities to cross-pressures: that is, the existence of simultaneous and contradictory (or potentially contradictory) demands on actors occupying a brokerage position in a network of relations.[30] Recall that the combination of heterogeneous contracting and

---

[28] Brunt 1965, Philpott 2001.
[29] Beissinger 2002.
[30] Arguments involving "cross-pressures" are common in studies of the influence of multiple identities and overlapping social relations on individual behavior, political preference,

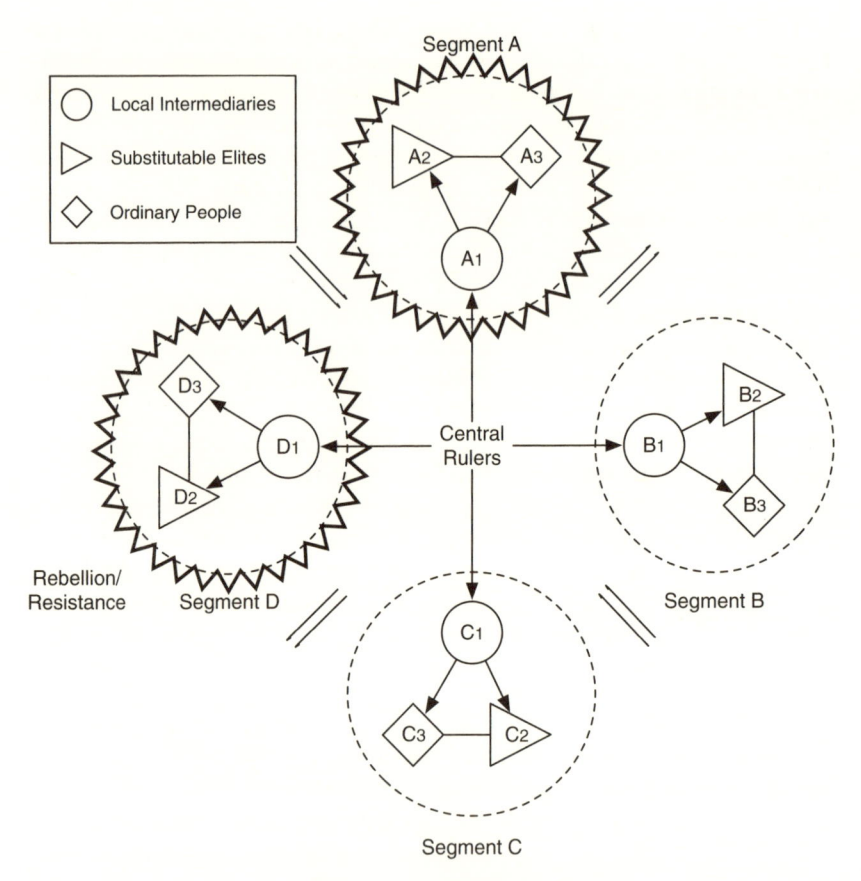

Figure 4.4 Uncoordinated Resistance in Multiple Segments

peripheral segmentation reinforces, and sometimes creates, distinctive identities and interests. Thus, central authorities navigate between different "pushes and pulls" as actors in peripheries attempt to shape central policies in favorable ways.[31] When central authorities, for example, seek to expropriate revenue and manpower to fight conflicts in the interest of specific peripheries they may face stiff resistance from segments that have no stake in those conflicts.

---

and compliance with social norms. See, for example, Brittain 1963, Covington 1988, and Seshia 1998.

[31] Padgett and Ansell (1993, 279) associate cross-pressures with network density; that is, they argue that individuals in dense networks may be subjected to too many "simultaneous and contradictory" demands to effectively mobilize. The key issue here, however, is that central authorities become the focal point for heterogeneous demands.

The structural potential for cross-pressures stems from a number of factors. First, it increases with the number of segments. Each new segment creates an additional contractual tie between central rulers and subjects that the latter expect the former to uphold. It also brings with it sets of local interests—economic, ideological, and security—and concordant demands upon the time and resources of central authorities. Second, the potential for cross-pressures increases with the relative heterogeneity of constituent political communities. The more differentiated the contractual relations, local identities, and local interests of segments within a composite polity, the more likely it is the central authorities will be pushed and pulled in conflicting directions by their subjects.

My claim that star-shaped networks give rise to cross-pressures on central authorities refines a key argument associated with hegemonic-stability and power-transition theory. In both theories strategic overextension represents a crucial mechanism of hegemonic decline. As they attempt to conserve or expand their preferred order, hegemonic powers take on an increasing number of commitments; they often find themselves pulled into peripheral conflicts of increasingly marginal strategic importance. Hegemonic powers, in consequence, tend to deplete their resources and long-term capacity to maintain their preponderant position in international politics.[32] Strategic overextension, however, often stems from an inability to manage cross-pressures. The risk of strategic overextension increases, ceteris paribus, with the number and heterogeneity of the ties between central authorities—whether a hegemon, a dynast, or imperial rulers—and subordinated political communities.

The British, for instance, experienced the dangers associated with cross-pressures in the eighteenth century when they adopted policies designed to aid the East India Company. As H. V. Bowen notes, "Parliamentary action had been designed to enable the hard-pressed East India Company to dispose of its large accumulated stocks of tea in London, but in the ports of Boston, New York, and Philadelphia the measure was interpreted as a calculated attempt to force cheap but highly taxed tea onto colonial consumers." Propaganda directed against the East India Company generated a widespread perception that "powerful Eastern influences emanating from one periphery of Britain's overseas empire were thus seen to have weakened the imperial core and it appeared that, in turn, they were now being brought to bear upon another periphery."[33]

Although heterogeneous contracting tends to isolate each bargain in composite states, the British example demonstrates how poorly managed cross-pressures can effectively link different peripheral bargains. When a

---

[32] See chapter 2 in the present volume.
[33] Bowen 2002, 292–95.

core engages in strategies associated with "credible commitments" toward one periphery, it may convince actors in other peripheries that their interests are being "sold out."[34] This most likely occurs under conditions of mounting cross-pressures, since actors in a given periphery already tend to be concerned—as they were in British North America—about a core's favoritism toward another periphery.

Central authorities may attempt to limit the impact of cross-pressures through the judicious use of side payments or other incentives to actors within different segments. The problem with this approach is that it often accumulates obligations while draining resources. Every time core authorities renegotiate a core-periphery bargain on terms favorable to the periphery, they reduce their access to revenue and resources. Such strategies may also, over time, worsen relations between central authorities and particular segments. Actors in a periphery may come to believe they are getting a comparatively poor deal with respect to other segments of the empire. Central authorities can also ignore demands coming from the periphery and bank on their ability to localize and suppress resistance, but doing so also increases the risks of resistance in an ever expanding number of segments.

Central authorities may minimize cross-pressures through legitimation strategies that are *multivocal* or *polyvalent*: that is, they signal different identities and values to different audiences. Heterogeneous audiences, in consequence, attribute shared (but inconsistent or incompatible) identities and values to imperial authorities. Because agents more willingly accommodate, sacrifice for, and support those they see as members of an ingroup, mutivocal legitimation strategies expand the "win set" of imperial authorities in dealing with different peripheries and make resistance to their demands less likely.[35]

This is one of the crucial insights in John F. Padgett and Christopher F. Ansell's seminal treatment of network structures and multivocal signaling. Cosimo de' Medici occupied a central location in the segmented network structure of elite interaction in Florence. The Medici family spanned the structural holes in Florentine elite interaction. Cosimo was able to exploit his resulting informational and resource advantages by engaging in "robust action"—that is, "multivocal action leads to Rorschach blot identities, with all actors constructing their own distinctive attribution of the identity of ego." Multivocal signaling usually works best when the

---

[34] Rector (2004) suggests that such linkages are unlikely. On credible commitments and conflict, see Fearon 1998, Powell 2006.

[35] On how collective identification impacts the willingness of actors to settle for less favorable resource distribution, see Mercer 1995 and Tajfel 1978

two audiences either cannot or do not communicate with one another. If they do compare notes, they may demand clarification from the signaler.[36]

Multivocal signaling enables central authorities to engage in divide-and-rule tactics without permanently alienating other political sites and thus eroding the continued viability of such strategies. To the "extent that local social relations and the demands of standardizing authorities contradict each other, polyvalent [or multivocal] performance becomes a valuable means of mediating between them" since actions can be "coded differently within the audiences."[37] Multivocal signaling, therefore, can allow central rulers to derive the divide-and-rule benefits of star-shaped political systems while avoiding the costs stemming from endemic cross pressures.

In subsequent chapters we will find many instances of the failure of multivocal signaling contributing to crises in European rule. The spread of reformation, in particular, made it difficult for dynasts to engage in polyvalent signaling across religiously differentiated audiences. Claims about the "true" religious orientations or policies of dynastic rulers became part of the repertoire of actors seeking to mobilize resistance against their rulers.

Even in the absence of religious polarization, dynasts sometimes had difficulty convincing their heterogeneous subjects that they shared common interests. Dynastic rulers could usually do so by signaling their willingness to uphold the customary rights of their subjects in different holdings. Dynasts, however, confronted difficulties if they appeared to their subjects as "foreign" rulers. Charles's status as a Flemish ruler and his reluctance to comply with certain identity-oriented demands of his Castilian subjects, such as marrying an Iberian princess, formed part of the backdrop of the *Comuneros* revolt. Philip II, in contrast, appeared to

---

[36] Padgett and Ansell 1993, 1263.

[37] Tilly 2002, 153–54. For a similar argument about the use of multivocal signaling to hold together disparate interest groups in American politics, see Hacker and Pierson 2005. Many pundits and observers of contemporary politics note the rise of "dog-whistle politics," in which politicians and political parties send favorable signals to particular—and usually more extreme—audiences that will be coded differently, if at all, by moderates. See Safire 2005. Another example comes from the 2000 U.S. presidential campaign. George W. Bush ran as a "compassionate conservative." The term was carefully designed to signal different identities and values to different audiences. To conservative Christians, one of the most important special interests within the Republican party, "compassionate" and "conservative" are redundant: to be a "compassionate conservative" is to be a hard-right conservative. To moderates and swing voters, however, the addition of "compassionate" presented Bush as a softer, less hard-line conservative: that is, the exact opposite of what the slogan signaled to hard-right conservatives. See Lemann 2003. In each of these cases, actors deploy polyvalent signaling to reconcile the demands of heterogeneous—and structurally disconnected—audiences.

many Netherlanders as a "Spanish" ruler; his opponents in the Low Countries successfully framed his policies as attempts to impose "Spanish" rule at the expense of their customary rights. In such cases, identity and material interests, which international-relations theorists sometimes treat as discrete phenomena, become intertwined in processes of resistance and rule.

Local Structure: Intermediary Autonomy

Indirect rule minimizes governance costs for central authorities.[38] Tilly argues that empire "has proven to be a recurrent, flexible form of large-scale rule for two closely related reasons: because it holds together disparate smaller-scale units without requiring much centrally-controlled internal transformation, and because it pumps resources to rulers without costly monitoring and repression."[39] As long as intermediaries are left to tailor rule making and enforcement to local conditions, central authorities can avoid the various costs that come with direct entanglement in peripheral governance.

The imposition of direct rule turns central authorities into intimate participants in local factional and political struggles, thereby eroding their ability to function, in pretense if not in fact, as "impartial" brokers in such conflicts. When intermediaries assume the costs of participating in local factional politics central authorities are able to maintain some degree of plausible deniability. If intermediaries make and enforce unpopular or politically disruptive policies—even when those policies are approved by central authorities—central authorities can triangulate between intermediaries and their subjects.

Niccòlo Machiavelli describes a rather extreme version of this kind of triangulation strategy. After conquering the Romagna, Cesare Borge put Remiro d'Orco in charge of restructuring the province and bringing order to it. But, since "he knew the harsh measures of the past had given rise to some enmity towards him," the duke decided to make clear that d'Orco, not he, was responsible. Thus, "one morning, in the town square of Cesena," Cesare Borge "had Remiro d'Orco's corpse laid out in two pieces, with a chopping board and a bloody knife beside it.[40]

The Habsburgs routinely tied unpopular policies to their viceroys and governors. Koenigsberger remarks of Philip II's decision to dismiss his chief intermediary in the Netherlands, Antoine Perrenot de Granvelle, that

---

[38] Cooley 2005; Lake 2001; Lal 2004, 34.
[39] Tilly 2003, 4.
[40] Machiavelli 1994, 24–25.

Philip's action in this case was very much part of a pattern of political behaviour which he followed consistently whenever one of his ministers, viceroys or governors ran up against local opposition that seemed for the moment insuperable. So it was with Margaret of Parma and, later, with her son, Alexander Farnese, with the marquis of Mondéjar in Andalucia, with Antonio Pérez and with the Duke of Alba himself. Machiavelli had recommended making a show of sacrificing unpopular ministers. In fact it was difficult to avoid doing this where an early modern ruler had to rely on the co-operation of a local elite. The almost universal contemporary lament of the fickleness of princes has much justification, for such fickleness was built into the system of early modern government. Granvelle had faithfully carried out Philip's policy in the Netherlands. In the process he had become unacceptable to a large section of the local elite.[41]

There are two main downsides to indirect rule. First, the more indirect central administration, the more room there is for licit and illicit diversion of resources into the hands of intermediaries. Indirect rule also decreases the efficiency of response to central directives; as in all principal-agent relations, the less central authorities monitor and enforce compliance with policies, the more latitude they create for subversion of those policies.[42]

Second, because intermediaries occupy a position of relative centrality with respect to central authorities and a given segment, they may gain asymmetric leverage over the relations between central authorities and imperial subjects. Their position enables them to build or develop their own patronage networks and sources of loyalty within a particular segment. If they use the resulting power and influence to pursue their own interests in power and wealth, they may not merely subvert particular policies but decide to break away from central control. Such cases were endemic during periods of the Roman Empire; indeed, military leaders, governors, and local rulers did not only set themselves up as, in effect, autonomous local rulers, but often sought to claim the imperial title for themselves.[43]

More limited variants on this theme occurred persistently in late medieval and early modern Europe. For much of the Dutch Revolt, William the Silent sought to enhance his own political position at the expense of Habsburg authority. Magnates and noble families in early modern France jockeyed not only for relative position, but to maintain and expand their control over regions of the country throughout the fifteenth and sixteenth

---

[41] Koenigsberger 1986, 117. For Granvelle's fate as an example of legitimating strategies that insulated the ruler from blame for his own decisions, see Bercé 1987, 28–29.

[42] Pratt and Zeckhauser 1991; Tilly 2003, 4.

[43] Isaac 1992, Ostrogorski 1969.

centuries. These conflicts took on renewed virulence when they became embedded in religious conflicts. The religious war in Germany involved, in many respects, limited *patrimonial secessions* by princes seeking to wrest greater autonomy from the Habsburg kings of the Romans.[44]

Indirect rule and intermediary autonomy thus create important tradeoffs. They lower governance costs and give central authorities plausible deniability for unpopular policies—and hence the ability to triangulate between local actors and local intermediaries. On the other hand, they lead to constant principal-agent problems, produce inefficiencies in resource-extraction, and diminish the likelihood that central directives will be enacted in segments. Local intermediaries may even seek to enhance their power at the expense of central authorities. Central rulers in star-shaped political systems often must balance the tradeoffs from expanding or limiting the autonomy of local intermediaries; the choices they make shape the relevant salience of these various processes, as they did for European dynastic rulers.

Local Structure: Within-Segment Divide-and-Rule

The ideal-typical structure of composite states not only institutionalizes across-segment divide-and-rule but also leads to a variety of patterns of within-segment divide-and-rule. Control over individual segments depends, in no small part, on avoiding the formation of extensive coalitions *within peripheries* that oppose central revenue, resource, and political demands. The different strategies central authorities pursue in this respect have direct implications for the tradeoffs created by intermediary autonomy; they also shape pathways of structural transformation within composite states.

In keeping with our simplified model of composite political systems, within-segment divide-and-rule involves four classes of actors: central authorities, local intermediaries, substitutable elites, and ordinary people. All things being equal, the fewer the number of significant sites (actors and groups of actors) that resist central control at any given time, the easier it is for central authorities to maintain control over a segment. If we recall figures 4.3 and 4.4, a coalition of D_2—D_3, for instance, is more dangerous than an uprising confined to either D_2 or D_3. Similarly, a patrimonial secession, involving D_1 and some combination of D_2 and D_3, will

---

[44] On patrimonial secessions, see Eisenstadt 1963, 29. The archetypal case of such patrimonial secessions is, perhaps, Muhammad Ali Pasha's uprising against the Ottoman Empire. Appointed governor of Egypt in 1805, he immediately consolidated his personal power by massacring the extant Mamluk elite. From there he set about to substitute his own empire for that of the Ottomans. Only foreign intervention prevented his dismemberment of much of the Ottoman Empire. See Karsh and Karsh 1999, 27–41.

often be more dangerous than an ordinary rebellion, since local intermediaries control at least some of the institutions of local governance—including, often, the ability to raise and field a military force.

Within-segment divide-and-rule takes a number of different forms. In *binding strategies*, composite states develop a class of local actors—often substitutable elites who themselves may act as intermediaries—whose status, material position, or ideological orientations tie them closely to central authorities. The aim is to create relatively strong and dense ties with some subset of significant local actors. These actors, whether they serve as local intermediaries or as adjutants to imperial rule, are thus (central authorities hope) removed as a potential site of resistance.[45] After the *Comuneros* revolt, Charles adopted a binding strategy toward the Castilian elite; in doing so, he thrust most fiscal burdens onto other sectors of the Castilian economy, with disastrous long-term results.[46]

In *pivoting strategies*, central authorities maintain the ability to triangulate between different local factions, and even their own intermediaries. This prevents imperial rule from itself becoming dependent on the goodwill of a single local group. The Jurchen used a pivoting strategy to prevent the emergence of a threat to their rule from the Mongolian steppe. This worked well until the Jurchen's miscalculations facilitated the rise of Chinggis Khan.[47] The British, for their part, made extensive use of such within-segment divide-and-rule strategies.[48] The Capetians, according to Spruyt, played burghers against nobles as it built the medieval French monarchy.[49]

Because of the absence of institutional firewalls generated by a rimless hub-and-spoke structure, within-segment divide-and-rule is inherently more difficult than across-segment divide-and-rule. Thus within-segment divide-and-rule depends upon exploiting categorical differences: class, status, identity, religion, ethnicity, and so forth.[50] Binding strategies, therefore, will often be easier to implement than pivoting strategies: it is less difficult to rely on a particular group to enforce imperial commands than to repeatedly shift commitments between categorically distinctive groups without, in turn, undermining the credibility of imperial bargains. Thus, te Brake argues that whether princes threw their lot in with the aristocracy or with ordinary people explains important divergences in pathways of early modern state formation.[51]

[45] For examples from historical empires, see Allsen 1987 and Barrett 1995.
[46] See chapters 5 and 6 in the present volume.
[47] Barfield 1989, 177–84.
[48] Pollis 1973.
[49] Spruyt 1994, 77–108.
[50] Baumgartner, Buckley et al. 1975, 422.
[51] te Brake (1998) focuses on issues of absolutism, constitutionalism, and other aspects of state formation outside of the purview of this work.

On the other hand, by turning one class of local actors into, in effect, local intermediaries, binding can increase their bargaining power vis-à-vis central authorities. It can reciprocally enhance the dependency of central authorities upon substitutable elites.[52] Central authorities, in consequence, lose some of the flexibility and autonomy associated with pivoting strategies. In general, this tends to increase aggregate-level cross-pressures, since central authorities cannot respond to the claims of one class of local elites by credibly threatening to switch their support to another set of local actors. Binding strategies, if they involve acculturation into a cross-polity or metropolitan culture, may also contribute to the creation of cross-periphery ties at the elite level. Finally, although binding strategies tend to produce a loyal subgroup of subjects, they also risk creating a class of permanently disenchanted local have-nots.

Rulers of composite polities often combine aspects of these strategies: they attempt to make elites and non-elites socially, politically, and culturally tied to the center while manipulating fault lines between local populations. Although this represents an extremely effective means of maintaining control over a segment, it can be very difficult to implement because of the tradeoffs discussed above.

Overextension in Composite Polities

In my discussion of cross-pressures I already noted the connection between the structural tendencies of star-shaped political systems and overcommitment. Cross-pressures, and how central authorities manage them, shape the likelihood that a composite polity will suffer from strategic overextension. Paul MacDonald makes a similar point in the context of empires: imperial overextension, he notes, is often "more the result of pressures in the periphery that lead to unintended, unanticipated political developments that generate reactions that pull great powers more deeply into the politics of other polities."[53] For example, this was one of the dilemmas the British faced throughout the eighteenth century vis-à-vis the North American colonies: the interests of their colonists pulled them into struggles on the North American continent that, from a strategic perspective, were genuinely peripheral. When the British government demanded, after the Seven Years' War, that their colonists pay part of the costs of these struggles, they set in motion events leading to the American Revolution.[54]

---

[52] When binding strategies target ordinary people, they often transform them into substitutable elites by virtue of elevating them within the socio-political structure of a segment.

[53] MacDonald 2004, 9.

[54] Lenman 2001.

Cross-pressures provide one mechanism for overextension in composite polities. At a more general level, overextension, rather than simply resulting from "foreign policy" dynamics, often stems from the failures of central authorities to manage their diverse segments. The Spanish Habsburgs' wars with England—which scholars often cite as a key factor in Spanish overextension—were a byproduct of a peripheral uprising in the Netherlands. Both Philip II and Philip III hoped that, by either conquering England or forcing it to capitulate to Spanish hegemonic control, they could cut off England's strategic support for the Dutch.[55] However peripheral entanglements, failures of local management, and external warfare combine, all are often present in the process of overextension and decline. Thus, predominant international-relations accounts of overextension are often incomplete rather than incorrect; a relational-institutionalist account allows us to focus on how external pressures interact with the endogenous dynamics of various forms of political organization in processes of international-political expansion and decline.

Patterns of Resistance and Rule in Early Modern Europe

Many of the effects the Reformation had on European state formation, as I have argued, were not due to any of its putatively sui generis qualities. The spread of religious heterodoxy in early modern Europe reconfigured processes of resistance and rule, but did so in ways consistent with pre-existing patterns of collective mobilization. The structural dynamics of ideal-typical composite states provide insights into these patterns: what kinds of resistance, in general, triggered different levels of threat to the power and authority of early modern rulers.

The basic parameters of continuity and change in early modern Europe, as we saw in chapter 3, stemmed from three factors: dynastic practices, economic change, and shifts in the conduct of warfare. Dynastic polities competed with one another to add new political units into their domains, but followed a model in which significant local autonomy and pre-existing institutional arrangements of agglomerated political communities remained, at least in part, in place. The fifteenth, sixteenth, and seventeenth centuries were also marked by almost constant warfare: Europe experienced only very short periods of time in which two or more major powers were not engaged in military conflict.[56] Even though economic and military changes altered the balance of power in favor of those capable

---

[55] See chapters 5 and 6 in the present volume. For general discussions, see Allsen 1991 and Kamen 2003.

[56] Koenigsberger 1971a, 6.

of mobilizing substantial resources for warfare—particularly kings and sovereign princes—the high costs of military conflict forced rulers to make increasing fiscal demands on their subjects.

Military competition was not the only source of fiscal pressures in early modern polities. Economic changes in the fifteenth and sixteenth centuries produced a great deal of social dislocation. Price inflation and the rise of entrepreneurial capitalism undermined older relationships between class and wealth, bringing "new men" into the ranks of the wealthy. In the process, personal bonds became more fluid, and also more dependent upon the actual exchange of resources and goods. Patronage networks grew in importance: "Instead of standing at the apex of a feudal pyramid, kings now came to stand at the apex of a pyramid of a complex patronage system; or, to use a more appropriate metaphor, at the center of a nationwide network of patron-client relations. The greater a king's resources, the more easily he could bind his subjects to his service."[57]

We see here something of a paradox. As I have argued, rule through intermediaries and the maintenance of local institutions carries with it important advantages in terms of the political costs of control. Conversely, it places constraints upon what rulers can and cannot do. In early modern Europe, rulers ignored local contracts at their peril; failure to balance the demands of local actors risked provoking costly rebellions.[58] At the same time, the pressures of warfare, combined with the importance of patronage for the maintenance of early modern European rulers' authority, created strong incentives to renegotiate, override, or otherwise disrupt local exemptions, institutions, and factions when they interfered with fiscal extraction. Almost invariably, these pressures led to conflicts between local interests and rulers, with rulers attempting to expand their ability to extract resources at the expense of local rights, factions, and institutions.

What kinds of patterns, then, do we find in resistance and rule in early modern Europe? Consider three uprisings in the Netherlands between 1477 and 1540. After Charles the Bold's death in January of 1477, almost all of the provinces and towns of the Low Countries rose against his daughter, Mary of Burgundy; they sought to reverse many of Charles's centralizing reforms. His policies, Jonathan Israel argues, had been "straightforward: to expand his army, conquer more territory, advance administrative centralization, and raise more taxation. His methods were heavy-handed and unpopular."[59] Ghent took the leading role in the rebellion; the French Valois seized the opportunity to weaken their rebellious

[57] Ibid.
[58] te Brake 1998, 14–15.
[59] Israel 1995, 27.

cadet branch and invaded Burgundian territory. Faced with a widespread revolt, and lacking her own military resources, Mary capitulated and granted the "*Grand Privèlege* . . . a charter that gave the States General of the Burgundian Netherlands" extensive rights and privileges, including an effective veto over taxation and military policy. Holland and Zeeland, however, sought to balance Flemish and Brabantine influence by seeking their own contractual grant of greater autonomy—which they received that same year.[60]

The year 1487 witnessed a widespread rebellion in Flanders against Mary's husband, Maximilian of Habsburg. Ghent and Bruges emerged as the central axis of the uprising, but remained divided by their own rivalry with one another. Ghent invited the French to send a garrison to the city. In response, Maximilan's father, the emperor Frederick II, sent German troops to intervene against the rebels. Many Netherlanders were outraged by Frederick's actions; the rebellion spread to Brabant and Holland. But, unlike in 1477, regional and particularistic interests precluded effective cross-segment mobilization. By 1492 the Habsburgs defeated most of the rebels: only Gelderland established its autonomy from Habsburg control.[61] In 1539–1540 Ghent again rose up against Charles of Habsburg's fiscal and political demands, but no one rallied to its aid; Charles defeated the city and humiliated its officials.[62]

The uprising of 1477 combined four of the features typical of resistance dangerous to the authority of dynastic rulers:

1. The existence of a common front between substitutable elites and ordinary people;
2. A coordinated uprising in many segments of a dynastic agglomeration;
3. Intervention by another dynastic ruler—the French Valois who, in this instance, advanced territorial claims to the Burgundian patrimony.[63]
4. Subjects who viewed their dynastic rulers as engaging in ongoing violations of their contractual rights.

Between 1487 and 1492 some of these features were present, but Maximilian's efforts to reverse the concessions of 1477 won support from the great magnates while regional differences proved a greater barrier to rebellion than they had a decade before. Ghent's uprising of 1539–1540

---

[60] Ibid., 28.
[61] Ibid., 29–30.
[62] Blockmans 2002, 151–52, 164–65; Bonney 1991, 413.
[63] The Valois maintained, among other things, that because Philip lacked a male heir, any territory he held by virtue of an appanage grant now reverted to the French crown. Bonney 1991, 82.

was, in many ways, more typical of early modern resistance: a single locality rose against its ruler, but almost no one saw anything to be gained by supporting it. Mary of Hungary, Charles's regent, stressed the basic point that Ghent, and Ghent alone, refused to pay for "the reasonable cause of the defense of the Netherlands." In doing so "Mary and her council were able to keep the city isolated . . . very much in contrast to the 1480s."[64] Indeed, as te Brake writes, "The fact is that the political bargains by which dynastic princes typically constructed their composite states created local privileges that distinguished one piece of the composite from another."[65] In consequence, only very specific conditions were likely to overcome inter- and intrasegment rivalries and produce a truly dangerous uprising against dynastic rule. We should consider each of these four conditions in turn.

Substitutable Elites and Ordinary People

Numerous historians note the importance of linkages between aristocratic elements and ordinary people in early modern European rebellions.[66] As J. H. Elliott notes, "A revolt stood some chance of success only if it could count on the active participation of at least a section of the traditional ruling class, and on the neutrality, if not the goodwill, of the greater part of the political nation."[67] Further, Zagorin remarks that "the substantial participation and leadership of elites was nearly always necessary to make an early modern revolution really dangerous to the ruling powers."[68]

Ordinary people lacked the resources and military capacity to mount sustained challenge to dynastic authority on their own. They could have a profound influence on European politics, they could resist administrative centralization, and they could, particularly when operating in the context of pre-existing vertical networks (towns, guilds, and the like), mount serious challenges to dynastic authority. In the end, though, they tended to lose, and lose badly. As we shall see in chapter 5, the German Peasants' Movement of 1526, despite achieving significant geographical scope and loose coordination as a result of its religious component, was crushed by the Swabian League; the decision by Castilian magnates to turn against the *Comuneros* doomed that uprising. The growing expense of warfare and the comparative advantage held by dynastic rulers in access to re-

---

[64] Koenigsberger 1994b, 147.
[65] te Brake 1998, 28.
[66] Forster and Greene 1970; Francois 1974, 22; te Brake 1998.
[67] Elliott 1970, 112.
[68] Zagorin 1982a, 24.

sources and manpower, on the other hand, undermined the ability of aristocrats to mount successful rebellions in the absence of links to other members of the "political nation" and ordinary people.

The participation of substitutable elites also influenced the likelihood of cross-segment collaboration. In many composite states, such as Valois France and the Tudor monarchy, aristocratic intermarriage—as well as participation in common political and court rituals—embedded nobles within cross-segment networks of the kind that might be mobilized against central authorities. Urban leaders forged connections through participation in centralizing institutions—such as estates—and through networks of economic exchange. The fact that members of these groups also acted as local intermediaries gave them access to military capabilities, not to mention revenue collection and other "state" functions. But this was not the case across many of the segments of more heterogeneous and disconnected composite states; aristocrats and urban leaders in Castile, for example, were structurally isolated from their counterparts in the Netherlands, Naples, and other Habsburg domains.

Cross-Regional Collaboration

Cross-segment and cross-regional collaboration made resistance to dynastic authority extremely serious. The different contractual arrangements between rulers and constitutive regions tended to localize rebellions, in that subjects who feared for their privileges in one segment, region, or position had difficulty linking their specific complaints to potential sources of opposition in other segments. For this reason, the structure of dynastic agglomerations facilitated divide-and-rule efforts across constitutive political communities, which accounts, in part, for the failure or Ghent's rebellion in 1540.

As we should expect, given the structural dynamics of composite polities, simultaneous but uncoordinated rebellions might also prove a serious threat to dynastic rule. There could, moreover, be tensions between the potential for cross-segment rebellion and the establishment of linkages between ordinary people and elites. Of the Catalan revolt, Koenigsberger remarks that the normal disdain aristocrats felt for popular movements could be overcome if "the leading groups could make use of a strong regional tradition and a deeply felt local patriotism which gave their alliance with a popular movement a great air of respectability."[69] Of course, such a movement was unlikely to form linkages with sites of resistance in other segments without some strong additional basis for rebellion.

[69] Koenigsberger 1986, 164. See chapters 7 and 8 in the present volume.

For example, overreaching attempts by dynastic rulers to expand central authority over resource-extraction might be sufficient to anger enough disparate groups to accomplish cross-segment collaboration even in the face of disparate local identities. This was the case in the Netherlands in 1477, but less so in 1487–1492. The French *Fronde* united a wide variety of actors from different regions against the expansion of central authority at the expense of local rights and privileges.

Foreign Assistance

French intervention in 1477 contributed to the success of the uprising against Mary of Burgundy, while half-hearted support in 1487–1492 helped doom the one against her husband, Maximilian. The expense of warfare and the asymmetric capabilities of dynastic rulers meant that, as in some of the above examples, foreign assistance often made the difference between successful and unsuccessful resistance. The messy and often overlapping character of authority in early modern Europe facilitated external assistance for rebellions, as did the nature of dynastic competition. But it also meant that, "by choosing to oppose the claims of putative sovereigns . . . Europeans were often deliberately reinforcing the claims of constitutionally alternative or competitive rulers who were willing, at least temporarily, to legitimate their political actions."[70] The importance of foreign assistance—in some form—to successful resistance tended to mitigate against the deployment of republican scripts; these scripts alienated potential dynastic supporters of an uprising.

Legitimating Frameworks

We cannot, however, view the previous three factors in isolation from the justifications and assertion of identity that variously accompanied, motivated, and justified resistance against dynastic authority. The grounds upon which movements of political resistance justified their actions shaped, and was shaped by, the potential coalitions against the consolidation and expansion of dynastic authority. At the same time, rhetoric deployed by dynasts shaped and was shaped by the potential coalitions they could build to expand their authority. Roughly three scripts predominanted in instances of resistance before the spread of the sixteenth-century Reformations: first, violations of customary rights; second, alternative dynastic claims; and third, republican principles. These different justifications often appeared in a variety of configurations.

[70] te Brake 1998, 15.

CUSTOMARY RIGHTS

Many historians have remarked upon the tendency of resistance movements toward conservativism in late medieval and early modern Europe. Such movements almost always couched their justifications for resistance in terms of defending traditional prerogatives and correcting deviations from prior, and presumably better, practices. Although often represented as primordial, such rights and privileges were not infrequently of relatively recent origin. Sometimes political movements invented them during the claims making and counterclaims making of bargaining between rulers and subjects.[71] Regardless, since the consolidation of dynastic authority invariably involved the abrogation or renegotiation of customary rights, it is not at all surprising that their defense provided a common rallying cry for rebels and resistors. In 1477, 1487–1492, and 1539–1540 Netherlandish rebels justified their resistance to dynastic rulers in terms of customary rights. Indeed, nearly every rebellion in early modern Europe involved claims and counterclaims about the traditional privileges of various localities and social groups.

DYNASTIC CLAIMS

Marriages between dynastic lines and nobles meant there were often no shortage of individuals with secondary or tertiary claims to a dynastic holding. In turn, high rates of infant mortality, other forms of premature death, and infertility meant that succession crises were an inevitable and relatively common occurrence in medieval and early modern Europe. The importance of personal relationships and patronage in the smooth functioning of monarchies and principalities also meant trouble—in the form of factional jockeying and conflict—if a young child or incompetent individual succeeded to power. The bloody baronial conflicts in England during the fourteenth century provide a stark example of the dangers for political stability inherent in personal and dynastic rule. The Tudor dynasty that eventually emerged to control England during the fifteenth century was, in fact, of extremely dubious legitimacy—which provides one explanation for Henry VIII's desperation to find a wife who might produce a healthy male heir.

---

[71] Whig historical writings were a later and extremely developed manifestation of this tradition of finding the "ancient" constitutional order violated by expanding dynastic authority. The more scholarly discussions of customary rights took on a specific importance in late medieval and early modern Europe as a counterbalance to the appropriation of Roman legal traditions by princes seeking to establish their "sovereign" powers. One of the significant aspects of Jean Bodin's influential formulation of sovereignty is that he moved beyond *simply* borrowing from Roman legal traditions and grounded his analysis in surveys of customary law in Europe.

Such situations highlight the importance of dynastic status as a basis for the legitimation of resistance to a particular dynast. An individual who had such status, even if he was the member of a cadet branch of a dynastic line or the illegitimate offspring of a dynast, had a much better chance of brokering political coalitions than other individuals. They were part of a "national" and "transnational" network of prestige. In consequence, they could exploit vertical clientele networks for military and resource mobilization. Their participation in political movements also conferred legitimacy on the support foreign powers might give to resistance movements. It is not surprising that foreign princes preferred to deal with those who belonged to the same status groups. In an era of dynastic states, dynasticism could easily emerge as a double-edged sword for rulers seeking to consolidate and expand their authority.

REPUBLICAN PRINCIPLES

Republican ideas often came into play in justifications centered around customary rights, and sometimes even when opposition involved alternative dynastic claimants or someone of dynastic stature. The more thoroughly republican rationales for resistance generally involved some of the most radical justifications for resistance and rebellion, although they could be thought of as "conservative" when they involved attempts to restore the lost status of, for instance, Italian communes. Nevertheless, in polities with a long tradition of hereditary rule, such as the kingdoms of Western and Northern Europe and the lay principalities of the empire, republican justifications had what we would now recognize as a revolutionary character.

LEGITIMATION MATTERS

The particular configuration of these scripts often shaped—and was shaped by—what kinds of coalitions formed against dynastic authority. Which customary rights came into play, for example, impacted the possibility for alliances between substitutable elites and ordinary people. One reason the nature of heterogeneous contracting in early modern dynastic agglomerations worked against such alliances stemmed from the zero-sum character of local privileges. There was almost no way, in practice, to simultaneously expand the rights and privileges of dynasts, substitutable elites, and ordinary people. Dynastic rulers could, therefore, offer selective incentives to one group of local actors at the expense of the other.[72] If ordinary people or substitutable elites sought to create a common front they, in turn, needed to find legitimation frameworks that appealed to

[72] te Brake 1998.

both groups *against* dynastic authority. Republican frameworks generally foreclosed this possibility, because, when invoked by ordinary people, they tended to alienate aristocratic elites.

In contrast, claims about customary rights and questions of dynastic legitimacy often conjoined in those uprisings that seriously threatened dynastic authority. The Catalans invited Louis XIII to become their monarch on the grounds that Philip IV had failed to respect the traditional rights and privileges of Catalonia. This was only after some actors floated the alternative of declaring Catalonia a republic; although the right to transfer sovereignty to a different dynast found support in ideas drawn from republican theory, straightforward republicanism proved too revolutionary for the more prudent members of the rebellion. Similarly, the participation of the house of Orange in the Dutch Revolt conferred an important element of legitimacy to those foreign powers with an interest in assisting the rebellion—an element that might very well have been lacking if the revolt had come to rest exclusively on republican principles. Indeed, the Dutch joined the Swiss as an inspiration for rebels and insurrectionists, even if both polities were hardly models of democratic governance.[73]

THE IMPACT OF THE REFORMATIONS

The presence of heterodox religious movements increased the chances that an uprising would combine each of the various factors that would make it of greater concern to central authorities. Under the right conditions, it made alliances between substitutable elites and ordinary people more likely; created cross-segment networks that facilitated collective mobilization against dynastic rulers; enhanced the chances of foreign support (usually by co-confessionals); and attached powerful legitimating frameworks to ongoing struggles over customary rights and local privileges. At the same time, religious disputes undermined the ability of dynastic rulers to project polyvalent identities to rival factions. Religious aspirations combined with religious repression to provide motivations for resistance and rebellion. Religious conflicts led to new rounds of military mobilization, which put additional fiscal pressure on constitutive segments of dynastic agglomerations and increased their populations' grievances against central authorities. The Reformations, in short, exacerbated all of the problems inherent in dynastic states.

[73] Ibid., 172.

The Reformations and Polyvalent Legitimation

As the Reformations spread and matured, the divisions between Protestants and Catholics intensified to the point where actors from both camps lacked an easy way to reconcile their theological differences. Moreover, the emergence of new Protestant movements, including Anabaptism, Calvinism, and Zwinglism, created new, intense religious cleavages. In other words, where the Reformation spread, it introduced new, and increasingly polarized, categorical identities. These circumstances undermined the ability of dynasts to project polyvalent identities—both across segments and within segments bifurcated by religious differences.

ACROSS SEGMENTS

Dynasts whose composite states contained segments that remained heavily Catholic and segments with a significant Protestant presence confronted a particularly acute dilemma. For a dynast to countenance Protestant activity meant undermining his or her legitimacy with Catholic segments, and vice-versa. The Habsburgs found themselves particularly hard hit, which should not be surprising since the Spanish Habsburgs ruled the most disconnected holdings of any European dynastic line. Moreover, authority in the Holy Roman Empire was both conceptually and practically—through ecclesiastic holdings—tied to Catholicism. But these effects also undermined—sometimes temporarily, sometimes for much longer—dynastic rulers' positions across their holdings in Britain, France, and Poland, to name only a few polities.

As composite states increasingly came to identify with Catholicism or particular Protestant sects, the ability of rulers to agglomerate polities grew correspondingly limited. Subjects often preferred that their rulers share their own confessional identities. For a variety of reasons, German princes had an easier time adopting new religious identities than rulers who held large composite states, although, as we shall see, even in small polities religious differences between rulers and subjects could undermine central authority.

WITHIN SEGMENTS

Religious differences also undermined polyvalent signaling to different audiences within a segment. We might think of religious difference as *extruding* a new coalition of actors from three sites (local rulers, substitutable elites, and local actors) in the minimal-actor model of imperial rule. In fact, it proved very difficult to engage in multivocal action across these two coalitions. During the Dutch Revolt, figures such as William the Silent ultimately failed in their attempts to hold Catholics and Protestants together against the Spanish. Rulers lost a great deal of their capacity to broker disputes and, in consequence, saw a diminishment in their ability both to prevent local revolts and to maintain shifting divide-and-rule strategies.[74]

Processes of religious differentiation also had important effects on the relationship between rulers, territory, and subjects. The particular form of Christianity embraced by a ruler, and what variations of Christianity a ruler tolerated, gave subjects of all stripes new and direct interest in the nature of their government. Religious distinctions between political communities also produced a new, highly charged source of societal differentiation that was increasingly coterminous with territorial authority. If rulers found it more difficult to engage in multivocal action across newly formed religious cleavages, they also found a powerful new weapon to bind their subjects to the state. These processes, often worked out through military struggles and religious repression, played an important role in the legitimation of, for example, the newly independent Swedish state.[75]

Cross-Segment Networks

The injection of religious differences into early modern European social and political relations created networks of co-confessionalists that transcended local and social cleavages. The result was the creation of movements involving both common identities and cross-cutting ties, both of which brought together social groups that, in the early modern context, often shared few concerns and interests. These networks undermined the divide-and-rule advantages of composite states, even in situations when important actors lacked strong religious convictions. As Koenigsberger notes of the wars of religion in Western Europe, "Religious belief alone, no matter whether it was held with fanatic conviction or for political expediency, could bring together the divergent interests of nobles, burghers, and peasants over areas as wide as the whole of France."[76]

If Lutheranism produced such ties—once a number of German princes threw in their lot with it—its effects paled in comparison to those of Calvinism. Particularly as repression of heterodox ideas intensified in France and the Low Countries, Calvinists formed networks that a number of historians have compared to revolutionary cells.[77] In France, Calvinists deliberately targeted powerful lords—and frequently their wives—thus

---

[74] Wallace 2004, 118.
[75] Ringmar 1996.
[76] Koenigsberger 1971a, 227–28. See also Francois 1974, 31–32.
[77] Koenigsberger 1955; Rublack 2005, 121.

ensuring that a single conversion would bring an entire clientele network with it.[78] In the second half of the sixteenth century, Calvinism's opponents saw the movement as a great international conspiracy. They found their own recourse in the Jesuits and the ultra-Catholic parties.[79]

We should not, however, lose sight of the fact that religious networks played upon, followed, and congealed with pre-existing tensions in early modern polities. Many French nobles, a majority of whom adopted Calvinist doctrine, sought to regain and extend privileges lost to the monarchy. At the same time, religious differences split along factional lines within the ranks of the great nobles, resulting in a combustible mix between court politics and religion. In the Netherlands, religious uprisings and repressions played out against the backdrop of regional cleavages, urban factional politics, and resentment of the Habsburgs' resource demands. In the empire, Lutheranism provided both pretext and motivation for princes to secure their current autonomy in the face of Charles V's political power. The Valois aided them with financial and military support; indeed, the Valois' rivalry with the Habsburgs inclined them not only to form alliances with heretics but with the infidel Ottomans.

Foreign Assistance

The addition of religious differences "into the mix" of dynastic politics, as I already argued, undermined traditional divide-and-rule strategies and produced rebellions that could not easily be localized and, in the process, crushed. It also tended to "internationalize" conflicts. The French Wars of Religion brought Habsburg intervention to support the ultra-Catholics, and led to Huguenot intervention in the Low Countries to support their Calvinist co-confessionalists. In the first half of the seventeenth century, the often confusing relationship between religion and politics produced what many historians refer to as a European-wide "civil war."

Yet religious cleavages could also open up new avenues for divide-and-rule strategies. Charles V skillfully exploited divisions in the empire to crush his enemies in the Schmalkaldic War. Yet religious division soon reappeared, convincing an exhausted and depressed Charles to abdicate his many titles.[80] Whatever contingent effects they had, the nationalization and transnationalization of religiously inspired rebellions shifted the rules of the game of dynastic control.

[78] Knecht 1989, 14–15; Koenigsberger 1971a, 224–52.
[79] Dunn 1970, 9.
[80] Mackenney 1993, 274–81.

Feedback Effects

The effects of religious conflict were not isolated from ongoing proclivities in early modern European political structures. Religious conflict did not engulf all of Europe. For example, with a few exceptions, such as a Muslim revolt, the Habsburgs' Iberian domains remained relatively impervious to religious conflict. But conflicts produced by religious strife forced rulers to place increasing resource burdens on those localities and segments where they maintained effective authority.

Doing so exacerbated the fiscal crises endemic to all early modern composite states, because the increasing expense of warfare far outpaced the extractive or economic capacities of early modern European states. A lack of finances, for example, proved a constant problem for the French state as it struggled with religious parties. Indeed, religious collective mobilization made it possible for some towns and cities to grind down opposing forces in protracted sieges, both because of advantages in their morale and because access to resources enabled them to construct new-style defensive works.[81] As James Wood notes of France,

> Not all towns, of course, could have mounted such a defense [as La Rochelle], which depended not just on works and weapons, but also on the fanatical discipline of a ruthless religious minority faced with possible extermination. But the lesson surely must have been that in the presence of a suitably motivating ideology, a relatively small number of urban defenders could fight an entire royal army on equal terms and even in defeat, as the bitter siege of Sancerre . . . showed, inflict terrible damage on it.[82]

For the Habsburgs, generally at war not only with heretics and other dynasts, but also with the Turks, religious conflict led to imperial overexpansion and the failure of their bid for long-term dynastic hegemony. These resource strains generally meant that those polities that already contained stronger national-state elements, or those that could adopt them, ultimately became better equipped to compete in an altering European landscape.

Conclusions

The Reformations led to a crisis in European state formation because of the ways it intersected with ongoing processes of rule and resistance.

---

[81] Compare the English New Model Army during the English Civil War, which owed its formidable capabilities to religious enthusiasm. See Gentile 1994.

[82] Wood 1996, 274.

It undermined traditional practices of divide-and-rule, increased crosspressures upon central authorities, diminished the capacity for polyvalent legitimation, and otherwise made serious resistance to central control more likely. It activated certain dispositional tendencies in the formal structure of composite states that track with empirical patterns of resistance and rule in early modern Europe. Over the next few chapters, we will see how these complex processes and interactions unfolded in historical time: how the decisions of actors, accidents of chance, and other contingencies intersected with more general structural processes to produce a crisis in early modern European politics that, in the end, diminished the salience of the dynastic-agglomerative pathway of European state formation.

CHAPTER 5

The Rise and Decline of Charles of Habsburg

CHARLES OF HABSBURG ruled a dynastic agglomeration of unprecedented scale and heterogeneity (figure 5.1). At its height it included Castile and its New World territories, Aragon-Catalonia, Sicily and Naples, the Netherlands, Franche-Compté, and significant holdings in Central Europe. Charles's election (in 1519) as King of the Romans and his subsequent coronation as emperor made him the titular head of the Holy Roman Empire. Yet Charles's dynastic agglomeration failed to outlive his reign. He met military and political defeat in Germany at the hands of a Protestant alliance; he divided his titles and territories between his brother, Ferdinand I, and his son, Philip II of Castile.

Extant international-relations theories supply a number of explanations for this outcome. Hegemonic-order theory suggests the intersection of processes of strategic overextension with challenges by anti-Habsburg "revisionists" such as France, the Ottoman Empire, and Protestant German princes. Balance-of-power realism focuses our attention on the threat posed to these, and other, actors by Habsburg power. James Tracy argues that for Charles, "The fundamental problem was that post-Roman Europe had never seen a dynasty whose territories bestrode the continent from the Low Countries to Sicily and from Spain to Transylvania—not to mention Spain's overseas possessions."[1] Constructivist theories might point in the direction of the impact of the Reformation. In such accounts, insurmountable religious conflicts in Germany first undermined and then collapsed Charles's dynastic ambitions. We might also focus on specific choices and bargains. Victoria Tin-Bor Hui, for example, argues that Charles's reliance on external loans and fiscal expedients played a decisive role in Habsburg overextension.[2]

None of these factors, however, operated in isolation from the others. Charles's demands for revenue to finance wars against the French Valois, Ottoman Turks, and heretical German princes strained his relations with his subjects. Francis I and Henry II exploited the pressures created by religious reformation in Germany to weaken Charles's international position. International-relations theorists often seek to reduce political out-

[1] Tracy 1999, 143.
[2] Hui 2004 and 2005.

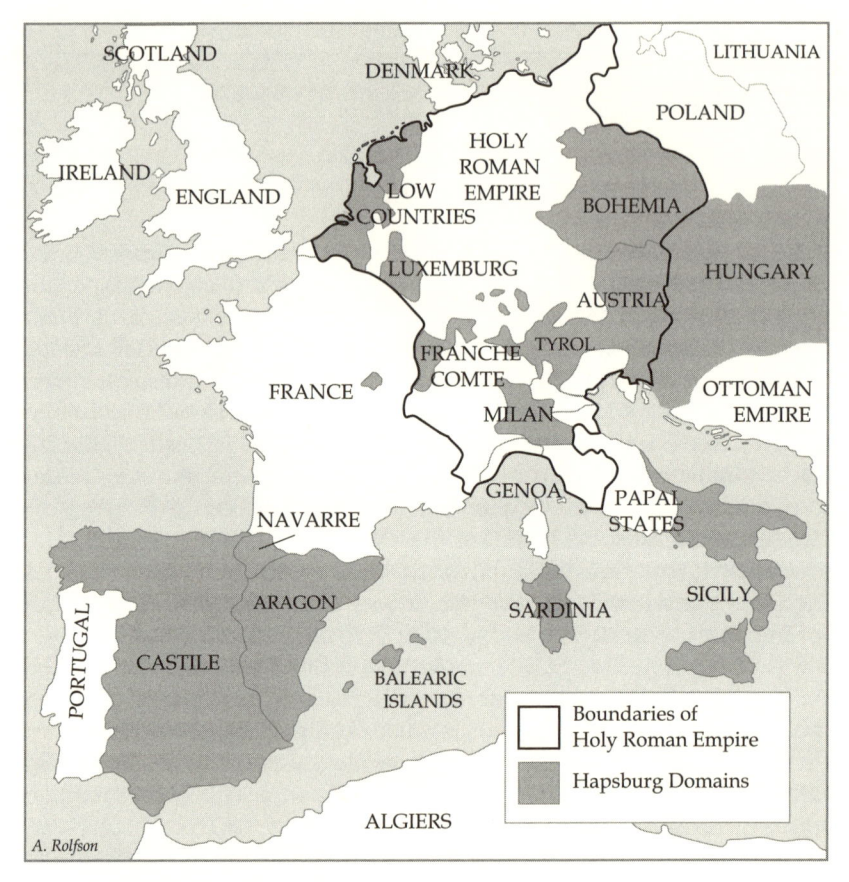

Figure 5.1 The Domains of Charles V

comes to single classes of causes, whether the balance-of-power mechanism, processes of hegemonic overextension, or the force of ideas. As I have argued in previous chapters, we should avoid this blind alley if we want to understand the collapse of Charles V's imperial ambitions. As Wim Blockmans reminds us, "The Ottoman expansion, American silver, Reformation, and military technology, each in its own way, threw the strategic plans of Charles's reign into total confusion."[3]

Rather than choose among these forces, we should focus on how they *interacted* with the underlying logics of early modern European composite states. This chapter does so by focusing on dynamics of resistance and rule in Iberia—particularly the 1520–1521 *Comuneros* revolt—and in

[3] Blockmans 2002, 45.

Germany from the advent of the Reformations until the 1555 Peace of Augsburg. Recall the major processes and mechanisms that I outlined in the previous chapter: cross-pressures and multivocal signaling, the trade-offs associated with different degrees of intermediary autonomy, and the collective-action dynamics resulting from variations in across-segment and within-segment network density. Charles of Habsburg faced, from the very early years of his reign, tremendous cross-pressures generated by the scale and heterogeneity of his domain and, in consequence, he probably could not have avoided some degree of strategic overextension.[4] In the absence of major resistance, however, Charles might well have adequately navigated these cross pressures.

Charles's failure to engage in persuasive multivocal signaling toward his Castilian subjects—in the context of revenue demands—triggered a major uprising against his policies and even, for some, the nature of his authority in Castile. It failed for reasons that should by now be familiar, such as the ways in which the structure of the composite state interfered with cross-segment and within-segment collaboration among sites of extant or potential resistance against dynastic rulers. Charles offered targeted concessions to Castilian notables, who subsequently moved with full force to suppress the uprising. These concessions ultimately formed the basis of a within-segment binding strategy focused on the nobility at the expense of other social groups.

These choices, in conjunction other actions Charles took to signal his commitment to Castilian interests, implicated the long-term development of the Habsburg monarchy. They placed a disproportionate extractive burden on the most vibrant elements of the Castilian economy, which ultimately contributed to Habsburg resource overextension. They gave the Habsburg monarchy an increasingly "Castilian" flavor, which undermined across-segment multivocal signaling in Germany and the Netherlands.

The German Reformations, in contrast to the *Comuneros* movement, created vectors for cross-regional collective mobilization while simultaneously reducing Charles's ability to engage in polyvalent legitimation strategies. The evidence I present in this chapter, however, demonstrates the limitations of a purely "ideationalist" account of Charles's ultimate defeat in Germany. Charles often prioritized other strategic interests over a religious resolution in Germany; cross-pressures prevented him from taking decisive action at many stages of the struggle. Moreover, composite-state barriers to joint-action across social and geographic divisions fre-

---

[4] The cost of early modern warfare, combined with the structural limitations of state extraction in the period, meant that any major conflict would likely overextend the resources of dynastic rulers. See Parker 1998.

quently resurfaced to undermine resistance against Charles. Charles's victory in the first Schmalkaldic War derived from his skillful manipulation of these barriers, as well as his framing of the conflict as "political" rather than "religious." His inability to consolidate his victory, and his eventual defeat at the hands of his Protestant subjects, stemmed from the degree of religious polarization within the empire, Charles's own commitment to restoring Catholic unity, and how these factors intersected with balance-of-power dynamics.

RULE AND REBELLION IN IBERIA

On 14 March 1516, at a ceremony in Brussels, Charles's advisors proclaimed him and his mother, Juana, co-rulers of Castile. Ferdinand's decision to declare Charles his successor stood on dubious legal ground. Juana, not Charles, was next in the line to the throne, but she suffered from bouts of mental illness. After Isabella's death, Castile passed through a series of regency governments controlled by Cardinal Cisneros and Ferdinand of Aragon. Ferdinand, as regent, probably lacked the authority to promote his grandson over his daughter. At least one prominent historian, Joseph Pérez, describes Charles's assumption of de facto rule over Castile as a coup d'état.[5] Few politically astute Castilians believed that Juana would be able to assume rule. Many, however, worried—with good cause—about the implications of a Habsburg ruler for both their personal positions and for Castile's interests. Charles's ascension threatened to shift patronage away from Castilian notables toward his own, foreign advisors. They also knew that Charles might treat Castile as little more than a source of resources for Habsburg dynastic ambitions in Italy, France, and Germany.[6]

Charles confronted the basic problem identified by Machiavelli: how to effectively legitimate control over a newly acquired territory. The heterogeneity of Charles's domains, combined with his rapid succession to them, placed especially difficult burdens on his capacity to engage in multivocal signaling. Between 1516 and 1520, Charles failed miserably at this task. Many of the towns and cities of Castile rose against his demands in what would come to be known as the *Comuneros* revolt. The uprising highlights a number of other dynamics typical of resistance and rule in early modern states—most notably how the structural tendencies of com-

---

[5] Pérez 1970, 83–85. See also Blockmans 2002, 18. In 1518, Charles arranged for Juana's almost total isolation. See Haliczer 1981, 155–56.
[6] Lynch 1991, 48-50.

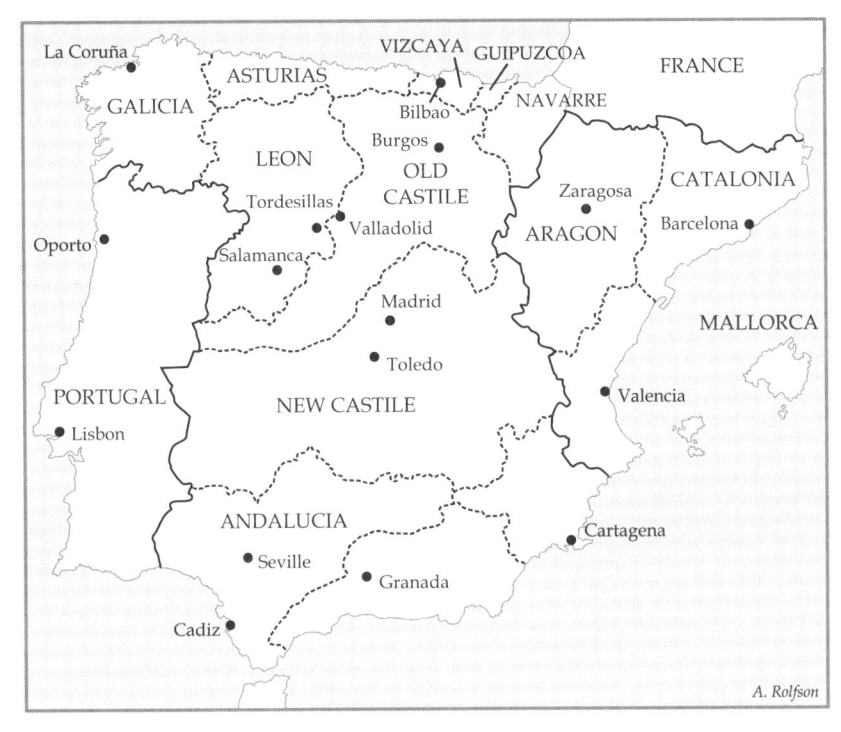

Figure 5.2 Iberia at the Time of Charles V

posite states often frustrated attempts by subjects to build cross-class and cross-regional collective resistance of the kind necessary to emerge victorious over central authorities.

Charles remained in the Netherlands for a year after assuming the title of King of Castile. On 18 September 1517 he arrived off the coast of Asturias on the first leg of his tour of his Iberian possessions. According to John Lynch, the "local inhabitants fled to the hills armed with staves and knives and only returned when their scouts reported the arrival not of an enemy but of their king."[7] From October 1517 to May 1520, Charles's court toured the country. Charles dispensed patronage, in the form of important positions, to his "Fleming" (as they were known in Castile) advisors and their relatives. His court threw ostentatious celebrations in the tradition, alien to Castile, of Burgundian court culture. These actions reinforced Castilian concerns that Charles was, first and foremost, a foreigner appropriating the throne of Castile for his, and his cronies',

[7] Ibid., 49.

own ends.⁸ Charles's behavior struck a growing reformist coalition as "the end process of forty years of royal misrule."⁹

By the summer of 1520 Charles's signals to elites and ordinary people in Castile established him firmly as a "foreign" dynast. His failure to project a polyvalent identity across his domains reduced his ability to gain concessions from his Castilian subjects. This was a very serious problem insofar as Charles faced considerable financial pressures. The voyage to Iberia itself cost a great deal of money. The expense of maintaining his court alone exceeded his ordinary revenues from Castile. In February 1518 Charles summoned a meeting of the *cortes*—legislative bodies roughly equivalent to France's Estates-General— at Valladolid. There he sought a *servicio*—a grant of extraordinary revenues to cover his expenses.

The meeting began poorly; members of the *cortes* discovered that Jean de Sauvage, a Walloon in Charles's entourage, would preside over the assembly. Delegates from the towns delivered speeches protesting the policies of the king, and particularly "the presence of foreigners in their deliberations." Representatives in the *cortes* requested, among other things, that Charles learn Castilian, that he exclude all foreigners from Castilian offices, and that he retain Ferdinand in the kingdom. They voted, despite their reservations, to grant Charles an unconditional subsidy of six hundred thousand ducats.[10]

Having secured the *servicio*, Charles proceeded to Aragon and an even less favorable reception. The Aragonese challenged Charles over appointments of foreigners and the status of his mother. Charles managed, after some difficulty, to negotiate an additional *servicio* of two hundred thousand ducats. Charles met with less trouble in Catalonia, where he secured both recognition as its ruler and a small extraordinary subsidy. Before he could continue on to Valencia, however, Charles received news of the death of his grandfather, the emperor Maximilian. This meant a new election for the position of King of the Romans. Despite being head of the Habsburg dynasty, Charles could not treat his election as a foregone conclusion. A successful candidacy required, among other things, significant largesse. Charles returned to Castile, the wealthiest of his Iberian domains, and sent his tutor, Adrian of Utrecht, to meet with the *cortes* of Valencia. This presented something of a double insult to Valencia, since Charles sent a foreign agent in his place; his strained relations with Valencian notables complicated resolution of the rebellion of the *Germanías* of Valencia.[11]

[8] Elliott 1963b, 153; Esteban 2001, 80–81; McElwee 1936, 28–29.
[9] Haliczer 1981, 138–39. See also Elliott 1963a, 144–45; Lynch 1991, 51; Pérez 1970, 121, and 1989, 23–24.
[10] Lynch 1991, 51.
[11] Esteban 2001, 17; McElwee 1936, 31–35.

In June 1519 Charles secured election as King of the Romans. Historians disagree about whether Francis I, Charles's principal opponent and the Valois King of France, ever posed a serious challenge to Charles's election. Although Charles was a native francophone who had "never set foot in the German Empire," as a Habsburg, he could make a more credible claim than Francis to represent German interests. His propagandists repeatedly drove this point home during the campaign. Regardless of whether Francis I enjoyed any real chance of becoming King of the Romans, his candidacy allowed German princes to extract major financial and political concessions from Charles. Charles's agents spent great sums of money on bribes; Charles guaranteed continued princely autonomy and promised never to transform the imperial title into a hereditary position. Charles financed his campaign through loans from the banker Jacob Fugger, which saddled him with significant debts. Charles also needed cash to pay for his trip to Germany and for the costs of his coronation ceremonies. To meet his needs, Charles turned to the Castilian *cortes* for a second *servicio*.[12]

In October 1519 Charles outraged popular opinion in Castile by reforming the process of ordinary revenue collection. Instead of relying on local officials to collect taxes (the *encabezamiento*), he decided to let individuals bid for the right to do so. Charles thus violated his promise to the *cortes* at Valladoid that he would retain the *encabezamiento*.[13] Charles's new tax policy proved too much for the city of Toledo, which soon declared its opposition to a second *servicio*. Toledo also raised objections to Charles's adoption of a new title for official documents: "Don Carlos, rey de Romanos, semper augusto, electo emperador, y doña Juana, su madre, y el mismo don Carlos, por la gracia de Dios reyes de Castilla, etc."[14] Toledo insisted that the only titles appropriate for Charles in Castile were the traditional ones of the kings of Castile; although symbolic, the change in titles—which placed his imperial titles before his Castilian ones—convinced many that Charles had every intention of subordinating Castilian interests to those of dynasty and empire. Charles's election as

---

[12] Blockmans 2002, 50–51; Garrisson 1991, 140–41; Wilson 1999, 22–23. The principal question is whether the electors ever took Francis's candidacy seriously, or whether they used it as an excuse to wring concessions and money from Charles. For the latter viewpoint, see Knecht 1996a, 106–7. Garrison (1991, 140), in contrast, argues that some electors were simply willing "their vote to the highest bidder" and that the election was in doubt until "the last moment." The fact that the pro-Habsburg Swabian League defeated supporters of Francis I also proved decisive.

[13] Haliczer 1981, 158; Lovett 1986, 30; Pérez 1970, 142–43.

[14] Quoted in Pérez 1970, 144 ("Don Carlos [Charles], King of the Romans, *semper Augustus* [part of the formal title of the King of the Romans: "always exalted" or "eternal Augustus"], elected Emperor, and Dona Juana [Joanna], his mother, and that same Don Carlos, by the grace of God, King of Castile, etc.)"

King of the Romans brought to a head concerns about the shape of Charles's rule. Many other local actors raised similar objections, but Toledo's demands went further: the communes ought to have a greater share in the operations of government, particularly during periods of royal absence from the country.[15]

Each step that Charles took further undermined his ability to signal common interests and identities with his Castilian subjects. His decision to break his promise concerning the *encabezamiento* violated, in the eyes of many of his subjects, his contractual obligations as their dynastic ruler. The sum total of his actions since his arrival in Iberia simultaneously diminished his legitimacy and threatened local privileges. The towns, who took the lead against Charles's policies, were particularly jealous of their prerogatives.[16]

Thus, officials in Salamanca authorized a group of Augustinians, Dominicans, and Franciscans to develop a platform of opposition to Charles's policies. Just as Toledo's demands went further than those of many representatives at Valladolid, Salamanca's added concerns relating to the royal succession. Charles should not leave Castile until he was married and the succession assured. Failing that, Charles should return his brother Ferdinand to Castile to guarantee an orderly succession if anything should happen to Charles. In sum, the *cortes* should not consent to the *servicio*; the resources of Castile should be employed only for the defense of Castile; and, if Charles would not assent to these demands, "the comunidad of Castile would be able to take matters into its own hands in order to protect the kingdom's resources from exploitation."[17]

Charles confronted a rapidly deteriorating position when the *cortes* finally met at Santiago. There his representatives attempted to broker an alliance between moderates and officials on the Crown's payroll. Even though neither Toledo nor Salamanca participated in the deliberations, the remaining representatives refused to vote in favor of the *servicio* until the Crown moved to resolve their grievances. In response, the Crown relocated the meeting to the more remote city of La Coruña. Through bribery, threats, and the pledge that Charles would not appoint a foreigner to act as regent in his absence, Charles's representatives managed to put together a narrow plurality in favor of the *servicio*.[18]

The proceedings at La Coruña provide us with an example of a failed attempt by Charles's agents to legitimate his multiple interests and identities to his Castilian subjects. Prior to the vote at La Coruña, Mota (the

---

[15] Lynch 1991, 52–53; Pérez 1970, 173–74.
[16] Haliczer 1981, 66–113.
[17] Ibid., 158–59. See also Pérez 1970, 149–51, and 1989, 26.
[18] Lynch 1991, 53–54; McElwee 1936, 36.

Bishop of Badajoz and one of Charles's Castilian supporters) put forth a conceptualization of Charles's relationship to Castile—and Castile's relationship to his empire—that the Crown hoped might convince the *cortes* to approve the *servicio*. According to Mota, Castile should rejoice that its king was the emperor, the most important office in the world. It was clear that God had willed that Charles become emperor.[19] Divine providence had placed Charles in this position for one purpose—to save Christendom from the Turkish menace: "En nuestros días emprender la empresa contra los infieles enemigos de nuestra santa fe católica."[20] It was up to the *cortes* whether, and under what conditions, Charles could pursue his divinely appointed task: "Su Majestad parte de España con amor de sus vasallos y ellos quedan en gracia dél, porque sola España es aquella que puede impedir o adelantar la ventura de Su Majestad."[21]

Mota sought to persuade a hostile group of Castilians that they shared the same fundamental interests as their ruler: that there was no contradiction between his imperial dignity and his identity as king of Castile. Mota argued that Charles was no different than his Iberian predecessors: he was simply taking up those titles that were his by right. If Castile supported Charles—by granting him the *servicio*—it would take its place as appointed by God: as part of the struggle to preserve Catholicism and Christendom.[22] Mota's speech failed to sway his audience.[23] Even taken at his word, Mota's vision still subordinated Castile to Charles's larger interests. Charles, for his part, consistently signaled that he had no intention of living up to Castilian expectations concerning the proper role of its rulers. Few Castilians saw Charles as "one of their own," and, in consequence, lacked the inclination to make sacrifices for his dynastic ambitions. After the *Comuneros* revolt, when Charles took clear steps to signal his commitment to Castile and to his office, his subjects embraced, in fact, a very similar ideology of empire to that proposed by Mota. Even then, his Castilian subjects would not allow Charles to use his imperial title on Castilian soil.[24]

The Crown's blatant manipulation of the *cortes* at La Coruña precipitated the revolution of the *Comuneros*. In April of 1520 Charles's oppo-

---

[19] Pérez 1970, 156. See also Pérez 1989.

[20] Quoted in Pérez 1970, 156 ("Today embarking on a venture against the infidel enemies of our holy Catholic faith.").

[21] Quoted in Pérez 1970, 157 ("His Majesty takes leave of Spain with love of his vassals and they will always be in his grace, because only Spain can hinder or advance his happiness.").

[22] Pérez 1970, 156.

[23] Otto von Habsburg's contention that Mota's "eloquence worked wonders" is patent nonsense. See Habsburg 1967, 77.

[24] Pagden 1995, 40.

nents seized control of Toledo. Charles departed for Germany on 20 May 1520, leaving Adrian of Utrecht as regent—in violation of his promise to the *cortes* not to appoint a foreigner to that position. On 20 May 1520 a mob in Segovia seized one of their representatives who had voted for the *servicio* and hanged him. The mob soon purged the Crown's representatives. By 30 May 1520 Charles faced a serious rebellion in Castile.[25]

The Revolt of the Comuneros

The uprising of the *Comuneros* of Castile (1520–1521) and the near-simultaneous revolt of the *Germanías* of Valencia (1519–1522) were the first major rebellions Charles faced (uprisings in Palermo in 1516 and 1517 proved only minor annoyances). The *Germanías* initially directed their ire against the aristocracy, but, fueled by leaders who cast their struggle in religious terms, they soon turned against the Muslim population, engaging in murder, forced baptism, and the destruction of property. Royal troops put down the rebellion. The *Comuneros* rebellion, for its part, followed the general patterns of an urban provincial revolt: a movement centered in cities seeking greater autonomy from the encroaching authority of both their dynastic ruler and the rural nobility.[26]

The success of the *Comuneros* movement depended, as did nearly every other early modern rebellion, upon its ability to forge cross-cutting coalitions. The *Comuneros* never developed the kind of cross-segment collaboration that provided an important advantage for early modern uprisings. The composite structure of Charles's Iberian holdings ensured wide regional divergences in institutional structures, identities, and interests. Valencia was, of course, a separate kingdom within the composite state of Aragon. Thus, the *Comuneros* and *Germanías* fought against different regimes and for different political concerns. They lacked any cross-cutting networks or identities that might have formed the basis for a collaborative effort.[27]

Although technically part of Castile, the cities of Andalusia—the recently conquered Kingdom of Granada—not only spurned the *Comuneros* but even formed a league against them. A number of factors contributed to the failure of the *Comuneros* to broker an alliance with key actors in Andalusia. Some elements of the population expressed sympathies with the *Comuneros*, but they lacked the strength to seize power in

[25] Haliczer 1981, 3. See also Habsburg 1967, 90–91; and te Brake 1998, 26.
[26] Elliott 1963b, 156; Lynch 1991, 60–61. On the *Comunidades* as an urban movement, see Maravall 1983.
[27] Bonney 1991, 414; Haliczer 1981, 216n17; Koenigsberger 1986, 136; Lynch 1991, 60.

an Andalusia dominated by the aristocracy. Many Andalusians, moreover, viewed the Morisco population as their greatest threat. They worried that joining the *Comuneros* revolt would imperil the gains of the Christian Reconquest. But as Stephen Haliczer notes, "The fundamental reason for Granada's hostility to the Comunero Revolution was that it came from Castile. . . . In the minds of the Castilian city councilors and in the minds of many Andalusians, Castile and Andalusia were different nations."[28] The *Comuneros* lacked an ideological focus capable of spanning regions and classes; in consequence, it remained confined to a single segment of Charles's empire. In the end, the Castilian aristocracy used their private armies to crush the rebellion.

At the beginning of the rebellion both Toledo and Segovia established revolutionary juntas. Adrian's regime vacillated over how to proceed. Adrian decided to proceed swiftly against the uprising rather than to pursue a conciliatory policy toward it, but he lacked sufficient troops to take Segovia.[29] The "bulk of Castilian revenues was earmarked for repayment of foreign loans, and many Castilian cities did not transmit the funds they collected to the royal treasury." Without Castilian revenue to service Charles's debts, Adrian could not even obtain additional loans.[30]

Adrian therefore decided that taking control of the stores of royal artillery in Medina del Campo presented the best opportunity to gain an advantage over the rebels. Medina's city council, however, refused to hand over the artillery. Royal forces subsequently attacked Medina. The town's forces repulsed the royal army, but not before the battle devastated its key commercial districts. These events prompted a wave of popular outrage against the regency government. Many cities moved into open support of Toledo and Segovia. In August *Comunero* forces seized Tordesillas. Thirteen cities now belonged to the Holy Junta. At Tordesillas, representatives of the Junta met with Queen Juana. Juana's response was cautious—she voiced support for the Junta but declined to sign any documents to that effect. Nevertheless, the Junta took her verbal support as a grant of legitimacy for their assumption of rule in Castile during Charles's absence.[31]

The city juntas debated whether to declare Charles's rule illegitimate and back Juana as the sole rightful sovereign of Castile. Juana's mental instability, however, recommended against doing so.[32] The *Comuneros* instead opted for a formula in which the *cortes* represented the public

[28] Haliczer 1981, 183–84.
[29] Ibid., 163; Pérez 1989, 34–35.
[30] Haliczer 1981, 164.
[31] Esteban 2001, 83; Haliczer 1981, 5, 167; Pérez 1970, 181–83, and 1989.
[32] Pérez 1970, 197–200.

interest of the commonwealth. Besides calling for more effective representation—such as regular meetings of the *cortes*—and reforms designed to make government more efficient and less corrupt, the *Comuneros* demanded:

> that the government should be thoroughly nationalized. Charles should dismiss his foreign advisors; when he returned to Castile, he should "Castilianize" his household by following the formulas and court ceremonies as they had been in Isabella's time and by finding Castilian knights and gentlemen to serve in his court. In order to give his reign a thoroughly Iberian flavor, he should marry the Portuguese princess, since this would avoid the dangers that followed when a "foreigner" (Charles) sat on the Castilian throne. Not only was the Princess Isabel of Portugal an "excellent person" and "very beautiful," but "she is a firm friend of our nation and of all Castilians and she speaks Castilian as we do."[33]

During September 1520 the regency government occupied a precarious position. Many royal soldiers defected to the Junta, which, unlike the regency government, could afford to pay its troops on a regular basis. The Junta increasingly assumed responsibility for daily governance in Castile. Castile's magnates, unhappy with Charles's pattern of appointments and Adrian's status as regent, remained officially neutral—a stance that benefited the *Comuneros* more than the regency government. If the magnates moved into direct opposition, Charles would face the worst-case intrasegment scenario for a dynastic ruler: a full-scale revolt involving both significant sectors of the urban population and the nobility. In October the regency government began to regroup, but the success or failure of the rebellion depended on whether the Junta could, first, form an alliance with significant Castilian magnates and, second, maintain support among other moderate factions. Its failure at both tasks sealed its fate.[34]

As the movement grew in power, it also showed signs of radicalizing. Its democratic tendencies alienated a growing number of urban moderates, as did its heavy-handed revenue expropriation and military policies. When the Junta suspended the Council of Castile, Burgos defected to the royalist camp. Indeed, the Junta advocated an ambitious reform program designed to shift power to the cities, which meant, in practice, diminished influence for the aristocracy. As with other composite states, the structure of rights and privileges in Castile—in which greater autonomy for one group tended to lead to diminished prerogatives for others—created strong pressures for the emergence of such a conflict of interest between

---

[33] Haliczer 1981, 178.
[34] Ibid., 168–76; Lovett 1986, 32.

potential sites of resistance to dynastic authority. The Junta's difficulty in garnering support from the aristocracy, in turn, encouraged its radical elements to stoke antiseigniorial passions. In the face of mounting antiseigniorial violence, an increasing number of nobles reconciled with the regency government.[35]

Charles and his advisors exploited this growing rift by making selective concessions designed to appease the nobility and moderates. He appointed both the admiral and constable of Castile to the regency government. He agreed to suspend the *servicio*, to appoint no more foreigners to offices in Castile, and to re-establish the *encabezamiento* system. That left, in the main, only the towns' more radical grievances outstanding. Rival nobles, for their part, set aside their differences in order to confront their common foe.[36] On 1 November the admiral of Castile described the realm as divided between two parties: one of the communes, the other of the grandees and nobles.[37] Charles's bid to divide and rule Castile—facilitated by the underlying structure of the Castilian composite state—isolated the more radical elements of the movement from the rest of the country. In response, the Junta at Valladolid now cast the conflict as one against both the king and the grandees. Additional troops from the magnates' private armies joined the Crown's forces. Over subsequent months, combined royal and aristocratic forces reversed the gains made by the Junta. At Villalar on 24 April 1521 the *Comuneros* suffered a decisive defeat, although Toledo held out until October 1521.[38]

Consequences

Resistance and rebellion against Charles's demands in Iberia reflected the general dynamics of composite states and dynastic rule in early modern Europe. The political signals sent by Charles and his agents—both in terms of their rhetoric and their concrete policies—led his subjects to see him as an outsider who sought to subordinate their own interests to "foreign" dynastic ambitions. He violated, in their eyes, the underlying contracts that governed relations between rulers and ruled. He met not only increasing resistance to his demands but, in Castile, an outright rebellion against them. Charles emerged chastened but victorious, because the structural effects of composite states created strong pressures against generalized cross-segment and intrasegment resistance. The rebels in Castile

---

[35] Bonney 1991, 415; Haliczer 1981, 185–87; Lovett 1986, 32–33; Ortíz 1971, 51; te Brake 1998, 28.
[36] Elliott 1963b, 153; Haliczer 1981, 190; Pérez 1989, 43.
[37] Pérez 1970, 46.
[38] Haliczer 1981, 187–97; Lynch 1991, 58; Pérez 1970, 473–76; te Brake 1988, 27–28.

and Valencia lacked cross-cutting ties of the type that might have led them to coordinate their uprisings. Highly institutionalized practices of rule in Castile, for their part, undermined efforts by the *Comuneros* to reach out to the aristocracy. Charles and his advisors exploited these categorical tensions by offering concessions that appealed to magnates and urban moderates. By gaining their support, he successfully divided and ruled Castile.

The defeat of the *Comuneros* averted an immediate threat to Charles's authority, but it nevertheless also left the future of his position in Castile uncertain. The nobility delivered victory to Charles; he remained at the mercy of their goodwill. Charles, therefore, returned to Castile and set about implementing many of the moderate reforms demanded by the *Comuneros*. Charles bought off urban magistrates and bound them to royal service through largesse. This coalition, between local rulers and the Crown, would make it possible for Charles and his successors to, more often than not, effectively extract subsidies from the *cortes*.[39] Over the next decade Charles's compromises with the nobility left them largely exempt from taxation. Their financial support became limited to *juros*—bonds sold at high interest rates. The nobility became strong supporters of Charles's military activities: they gained both military honors and profited from the Crown's need to finance warfare.[40] As Koenigsberger writes, "Their early hostility to Charles soon changed to enthusiastic support" for Charles's "crusading and imperial ideals."[41]

Charles set about learning Castilian; he married Isabella of Portugal, the sister of Portugal's king, in 1526. Charles only opted for the marriage after his negotiations with Henry VIII for Mary Tudor's hand came to naught, but it both secured him a dowry to finance his Italian campaigns and enhanced his legitimacy with the *cortes*, who had long advocated the marriage. They, in turn, proved more ready to provide him with financial assistance. Charles also appointed an increasing number of Spaniards and Castilians, not just to posts in Iberia but to ones throughout his empire. Despite his later prolonged absences from Castile, Charles left his son, Phillip, to be educated as a Castilian and learn the arts of rulership there.[42]

Charles's actions signaled his commitment to play the part of a Castilian king. As I noted earlier, they help legitimize a conception of his empire—and Castile's role within it—quite similar to the one Mota proclaimed before the *cortes* at La Coruña. Castile and the rest of Spain, as a practical matter, continued to take second place to Charles's imperial

[39] te Brake 1998, 29.
[40] Lynch 1991, 66.
[41] Koenigsberger 1971b, 25.
[42] Blockmans 2002, 58, 118; Elliott 1963a, 208–9; Lynch 1991, 67.

interests. His commitments elsewhere remained distinctly "foreign" to Castile. "His feud with the King of France, his war against the Protestant princes of Germany," to name just two of Charles's strategic preoccupations, failed to resonate with Castilians. Even his pursuit of hegemony in Italy reflected more of an Aragonese than a Castilian temperament.[43]

Charles, as J. H. Elliott remarks, nevertheless "succeeded in making many Castilians identify themselves and their country with his crusade" against the Ottoman Empire. Castilian intellectuals wove an account of the relationship between Castile and empire that saw "Spain, as the new focal point of the empire and the God-appointed scourge of Islam"; Spain was not only Rome's heir, but its subjects' devotion to Christian and Catholic mission elevated it beyond even Rome's glory.[44] This image may have remained far from the minds of the average Castilian, but we can see evidence of the emergence of a new identity—centered around Castilian "hegemony" and the defense of Christendom. These rationalizations of Castile's position, under kings who also ruled many other kingdoms, gained increasing credibility with Philip II's ascension to the throne.[45] In short, Charles's reaction to the *Comuneros* rebellion set his empire on a course toward Castilianization. While his actions sent signals and built coalitions that cemented his control over Castile, they would have costs for his rule over Germany. In particular, they made it highly unlikely that Philip would ever succeed his father as King of the Romans.

The German Reformation and the Collapse of the Unified Habsburg Monarchy

The Iberian rebellions were only the start of Charles's difficulties in holding together his domains. After the collapse of the *Comuneros* revolt, Charles returned to Castile; he left Germany just as the process of reformation accelerated. A confrontation with the French Valois also loomed; Charles proved lucky that Francis failed to act with sufficient alacrity to take advantage of the *Comuneros* rebellion. Meanwhile, the Ottoman Turks threatened Charles's territories and interests in both Eastern Europe and the Mediterranean. Charles "believed that his supreme mission as Holy Roman Emperor was first to establish peace within Christendom, and then to wage war against its major enemy, the Ottoman Empire."[46] From 1517 to 1520, Europe buzzed with discussion of a Crusade against

---

[43] Elliott 1963a, 168.
[44] Pagden 1995, 41.
[45] Elliott 1963a, 162–63.
[46] Fischer-Galati 1954, 47.

the Turks. A peace arrangement with France gave Charles and his Burgundian court the breathing room they needed to secure the Castilian and Aragonese thrones. It also opened up the possibility—or so some believed—of a united front against Islam.[47] Charles's election as emperor, however, doomed hopes—however unrealistic—for a lasting European peace. In March 1521 Francis backed Henry d'Albert's attempt to recapture Spanish Navarre and Robert de La Mack's invasion of Luxembourg. Within a year the Valois-Habsburg rivalry returned to its traditional epicenter: direct confrontation in Italy. This was the first of five open wars between Charles and the Valois kings of France.[48]

The Reformation presented a multifold challenge to Charles's ambitions (figure 5.3). As we saw in chapter 3, some of the emperor's power derived from his special status within the Catholic faith, as well as from his particular relationship to ecclesiastical territories. Scholars who focus on the role of the Reformations in shattering this status, however, run into a basic problem of timing: these aspects of imperial authority, as Spruyt argues, had already lost much of their significance by the fifteenth century.[49] The impact of the Reformations on Charles's hegemonic aspirations, rather, stemmed from the way that new religious identities and ties intersected with the institutional dynamics of dynastic composite states. Charles's commitment to a religiously unified empire, and the way that commitment factored into the legitimating narratives of his reign, made it difficult for him to speak across confessional divides—that is, to sustain polyvalent signaling. The process by which the Reformations spread through Germany, combined with aspects of its various doctrines, created opportunities for princes to expand their territorial authority at the expense of imperial state building. It facilitated, in other words, limited patrimonial secessions by intermediaries. In order for Charles to effectively combat heresy in Germany, in turn, he needed to enforce and acquire prerogatives that threatened the autonomy of Protestant and Catholic princes alike.

Religious disputes in Germany intersected with conflicts over local and central authority. The same kinds of imperial reforms, in fact, that Maximilian's subjects viewed favorably eventually lost much of their appeal when Charles became King of the Romans. Charles controlled a greatly expanded and far wealthier dynastic base than that of his grandfather. He, unlike Maximilian, could harness improvements in imperial governance to weaken the authority and independence of the German princes

---

[47] For discussions, see Koenigsberger 1971b, 6–7; and McElwee 1936, 18–21.
[48] Elton 1964, 79; Garrisson 1991, 142–44.
[49] Spruyt 1994, 51–54.

Figure 5.3 The German Empire at the Election of Charles V

and cities. Religious reformation raised the stakes for all in terms of who would gain, and who would lose, from expanded imperial authority.

Cross-pressures generated by the scope and heterogeneity of Charles's dynastic empire also influenced the fate of the German Reformations. Ottoman incursions in Hungary and Central Europe, for their part, increased the urgency of imperial reform—indeed, the Habsburgs eventually proved willing to make concessions to the Protestants in order to meet the Turkish threat, and less willing to do so when the threat receded. Political rivalry with the Valois and the papacy also contributed to Charles's inability to consolidate his position—and his eventual defeat at the hands of Protestant princes. Both, at various times, took steps that undermined religious unity in Germany: the Valois by actively supporting German Protestants, the papacy by refusing to compromise with the reformers and even by placing balance-of-power considerations over a Habsburg—and, in consequence, a Catholic—victory in Germany.

Reformation and Empire, 1520–1525

In the early days of Charles's reign, the movement for reformation appeared to most observers—Charles included—as a minor irritant to Habsburg power. Luther himself celebrated Charles's ascension as an opportunity for German spiritual renewal. One can find, already, however, signs of an impending crisis. Strong antipapal sentiment among the German princes led Charles to pledge, as a condition of his election, to impose limits on the use of the imperial ban. Even those German princes who did not embrace religious reformation wanted to limit papal jurisdiction in Germany.[50]

Charles believed that the Church needed reform; he hoped for a smooth reconciliation between the papacy and its critics. Yet he also showed little sympathy for heretics in his other domains, such as the Netherlands. In Germany, however, he lacked the institutional prerogatives to effectively suppress heresy. German princes and towns, as local intermediaries, enjoyed far more legal and practical autonomy than magnates and urban centers in most of Charles's other domains. In retrospect, Charles should have recognized his comparative weakness in dealing with religious dissent in Germany from the very start of his reign. Luther's patron, Elector Frederick the Wise of Saxony, came quite close to winning the imperial election before he decided to withdraw from the contest. Charles needed Frederick's continued support in his quest to consolidate his new authority in the empire.

Thus, soon after his election, Charles acceded to Frederick's wishes and invited Luther to present his views at the Diet of Worms. He granted him a guarantee of safe conduct, despite the fact that Luther had already been excommunicated. The meeting proved a fiasco. Luther refused to back down from his heretical positions. Members of the imperial Diet sought to condemn papal influence in Germany. Some even called for the elimination of all ties between the papacy and the empire. Antipapal feeling, however, did not incline most of the members of the Diet to support Luther. On 19 April 1521 the Diet condemned Luther; within a month Charles published the Edict of Worms, which banned Luther's writings and ordered his existing works burned.[51]

---

[50] Holborn 1959, 147; Shoenberger 1977, 66.
[51] Blockmans 2002, 80–83; Bonney 1991, 15–16; Grimm 1965, 139–41; McElwee 1936, 60–64.

Charles sought to resolve a number of issues at Worms that, from his perspective, took priority over the question of what to do with Luther. He needed to make preparations to return to Castile—to deal with the aftermath of the *Comuneros* rebellion—and wanted aid in prosecuting his growing conflict with Francis I. He gained only very limited assistance from the Diet, but fared rather better in his attempt to reform imperial institutions. At his urging, the Diet established the *Reichregiment*, a regency council that, ironically, shared much in common with the one forced upon Maximilian by his German subjects.[52] Charles appointed Ferdinand as his deputy, and prepared to depart, first for the Netherlands and then for Spain; it would be nearly a decade before Charles returned to Germany (in 1530). In the intervening years reformation further spread throughout Germany and won converts among many German princes.[53]

COMPOSITE-STATE DYNAMICS AND RELIGIOUS MOVEMENTS
IN THE EARLY GERMAN REFORMATIONS

The political implications of religious differentiation in early modern Europe stemmed from institutional dynamics of composite states. The Reformations produced trans-segment, transregional, and even transnational connections between a variety of local actors, local intermediaries, and central authorities. These ties proved particularly dangerous to central authorities when they also crossed class and social divisions. Analysis of the effects of the German Reformation on the empire, therefore, requires some exploration of the Reformations not only as religious phenomena but also as *collections of social and political movements*. Differences in the vectors by which reformation spread—and the movements it created—had political consequences for Germany.

Charles, in fact, profoundly underestimated the problems posed by religious heresy in Germany. Luther's works and ideas spread widely prior to Worms; no imperial edict was likely to suppress them. Luther may have been the most visible figure of reformation, but others also pressed for major changes in doctrine and ritual. While elites debated the finer points of the Lord's Supper, justification by faith, and other complex theological issues, most of those pressuring for reform "in the trenches" focused on less intellectual concerns. The growing challenge to Church doctrine created a general atmosphere favoring many kinds of dissent. As the spirit

---

[52] The *Comuneros* revolt was not simply an impetus for Charles to return to Castile. It also made Charles acutely aware of the danger of rebellion in his absence in any of his realms. Thus, he pushed reforms at Worms that were aimed to avert another rebellion of the type he had already faced in Iberia.

[53] Blockmans 2002, 83; McElwee 1936, 65–66.

154 • Chapter 5

of religious renewal spread through Germany, it sparked grass-roots activism for religious-political reform.[54]

Wayne te Brake argues that the process of urban reformation in the period roughly from 1520 to1540 was dominated by pressure "from below" upon civic officials to appoint reformist preachers, resist attempts by higher authorities to discipline evangelicals, or otherwise to abet religious reformation. Sometimes it was radically successful, sometimes it was defeated, but more often popular pressure for religious reform led to religious-political bargains that produced incremental reforms. Only a few urban officials led reformation themselves.[55] Such processes predominated in Upper (Southern) Germany, but, taking a variety of forms, also operated in Lower (Northern) Germany. Although the specifics varied, desire for religious reformation often came together with pressure for communal rule.[56]

The aspirations of many social groups, as Philpott argues, certainly displayed an elective affinity with Protestant ideas.[57] But the comparative advantage of reformers in building and exploiting networks of popular mobilization proved crucial to the spread of reformation. In many areas of Germany a kind of "vanguard," however unorganized, of dissidents soon emerged. Artisans, merchants, former soldiers, converts, and defrocked clerics fanned across Germany preaching various versions of reform, contrasting clerical abuses to the scriptural "word of God."[58] Until the forces of counterreformation finally organized, the Catholic Church lacked not only a set of coherent and vital anti-Protestant ideas, but also any means of forming comparable networks. With a few exceptions, the Church depended either upon more-or-less locally organized—and sometimes spontaneous—antiheretical mobilization or the coercive power of rulers to counter Protestant agitation.[59] Coercion often succeeded at con-

---

[54] te Brake 1998, 48–49.

[55] Ibid., 35–49. See also Moeller 1982, 61–69. "Bottom-up" activity, as te Brake notes, did not end in 1540 but continued as a force in the process of religious reform in the empire. The heuristic distinction between "bottom-up" and "top-down" phases of the Reformations captures important differences in the character of early modern religious change. But we should not overplay this distinction: such processes of reform often coexisted in time and, less frequently, even in specific places. Even in the seventeenth century, the process of reformation escaped the exclusive control of princes and urban leaders. See Schilling 1992 and Wolfart 2002.

[56] Schilling 1992, 190–92.

[57] Philpott 2000 and 2001.

[58] Bercé 1987, 17; Ozment 1975, 123–25.

[59] On the 1536 British Pilgrimage of Grace, which provides a partial exception to this rule, see Zagorin 1982a, 19–31. On the more successful—at least in the short-term—Catholic popular mobilization in Scandinavia, see te Brake 1998, 54–55. Both examples involved attempts by sovereigns to impose versions of Protestantism in the absence of substantial

taining reform movements, but as long as the Church depended upon "state" power, Catholic orthodoxy remained vulnerable to the shifting religious allegiances of rulers, whether magnates, urban councils, lay and ecclesiastical princes, or sovereigns.[60] Indeed, these disadvantages explain why Habsburg inaction in the face of religious heresy during the 1520s proved crucial to the success of the German Reformations.

FAILED UPRISINGS: THE IMPERIAL KNIGHTS
AND THE GERMAN PEASANTS' MOVEMENT

Soon after its inception, therefore, reformation led to the formation of transregional networks through which religious ideas, passions, and aspirations flowed. Such connections created a basis for significant political mobilization. Political and military conflict followed. During 1522–1523 a group of Imperial Knights rose against ecclesiastical authority, but failed to gain support from either princes or towns. Traditional cleavages associated with composite polities doomed their efforts: the Swabian League suppressed the uprising—and destroyed the Imperial Knights as important political players in German politics.[61] The brief conflict frightened moderates and conservatives, who already worried that reformation would bring with it political instability. The German Peasants' War seemed, for a time, to confirm those fears.[62] It also provides a particularly good example of how religion could produce cross-segment mobilization, but how that mobilization faltered if it could not draw in significant elite support.

In his discussion of the "Revolution of 1525," te Brake points out that the war was really a combination of barely coordinated uprisings against local rulers. It demonstrated, nevertheless, the tremendous potential for collective mobilization around the banner of religion: "In all, hundreds of thousands of ordinary people served at one time or another in the 'peasant' armies; as many as 130,000 may have died in the fighting or the subsequent repression; virtually all areas of Central and Southern Germany, with the notable exception of Bavaria, were touched by the conflicts."[63] As Thomas F. Sea notes, "The extent of the major rebellion that

---

popular support. The Pilgrimage of Grace, in particular, demonstrates the limitations of depending upon such forms of countermobilization: one of the reasons the Pilgrimage failed was that it lacked any basis by which it could overcome regional division within England and Wales. Henry VIII divided and conquered Catholic opposition.

[60] For examples, see Brodek 1971, 398–99.
[61] On the Swabian League, see chapter 3.
[62] Grimm 1965, 200–201; Holborn 1959, 169–70. For an extended discussion of the origins of the revolt, see Hitchcock 1958.
[63] te Brake 1998, 32–33. See also Sessions 1972, 26–27.

developed in early 1525 took everyone by surprise. No one was prepared to respond, either militarily or through more peaceful means."[64]

Religious identities and social ties, created by the process of popular reformation, account for the scale and simultaneity of the uprisings. Evangelical networks circulated grievances, along with scriptural justifications for action, among geographically dispersed groups. The disconnect between biblical ideals of equality and the radical inequality inexperienced by ordinary people provided a solid ideological basis for the movement. Scriptural ideals and images of justice resonated with pre-existing grievances but, at the same time, transformed them into something more radical. Because participants in the movement could point toward a scriptural basis for their demands for social justice, they gained an enormous sense of legitimacy and urgency. Common religious orientations, however inchoate, joined together individuals from different walks of life; they brought into the movement experienced soldiers who could direct its campaigns.[65]

Much of this, of course, was not unique to the Reformations era. The Hussite movement produced a crisis in the empire precisely because it had some of these features. In that case, however, linkages between ordinary people and elites succeeded once the movement became associated with the regional aspirations of Bohemia, which meant, in turn, that it could not become a basis for building solidarity between disparate regions—at least until the growth of the more general Reformations in the first quarter of the sixteenth century.[66]

The "social gospel," in fact, had long been a feature of peasant rebellions; when members of the German Peasants' movement asked "When Adam delved and Eva span / Who was then a gentleman?" they were repeating lines from a popular song also sung during the Wat Tyler rebellion in 1381.[67] As te Brake argues, "In this sense, the scenario of 1524–1525 was well rehearsed; the claims, the claims makers, and the basic forms of claim making must at least have been familiar to those involved." The 1520s, however, witnessed a widespread cross-communication and cross-fertilization of the social gospel; Luther's challenge to the Church appeared to many, including Luther, to presage the great conflict between Christ and Antichrist envisioned in the Book of Revelation.[68]

The German Peasants' War demonstrates how "once Luther's preaching had challenged the religious and social teachings of the old Church,

[64] Sea 2007, 219.
[65] Blickle 1984, 8; Grimm 1965, 168–74; Mommsen 1984, x.
[66] On this comparison, see Graus 1976.
[67] McNeil 1966, 19. "Span" is an archaic past participle of "spin," not a reference to sexual activity.
[68] te Brake 1998, 32–33. See also Sessions 1972, 26–27.

and had in addition made the secular power and property of the Church suspect, much larger masses could stand up against social and political abuses or even demand the realization of the 'divine' or, as it was called now, 'evangelical law.' "[69] The grievances of the peasants' movement held little appeal to elites in Germany, however. Its ideological content precluded it from forming vertical networks between elites and ordinary people. Some of the "armies" disintegrated of their own accord—as we should expect from a high-category—low-network group—while others were quashed once the Swabian League belatedly mobilized against them.[70]

Throughout the development of the Reformations, in fact, reform movements that embraced the social gospel and more radical doctrines of equality generally ran up against the interests of those whose support made the difference between victory and suppression. They might gain many converts, but they could not usually overcome the coercive power of the nobility, princes, and urban oligarchs. In the imperial cities, "The connection of demands for Reformation with desires for social and economic reform more likely retarded than accelerated the victory of the Reformation."[71] The Anabaptist movement, for example, which formed a tighter theological grouping and put forth a more radical program of social change than most early Reformations sects, saw its future as a political movement collapse after the takeover, siege, and capitulation of the city of Münster during 1534–1535.[72]

In fact, the German Peasants' War significantly influenced the political fate of the Reformations, particularly in Upper Germany.[73] Its social radicalism inspired Luther, along with many of the more conservative reformers, to expand upon those elements of his theology that attracted both dynastic rulers and urban magistrates. In the period following the war, a rash of princes entered the Protestant camp. James D. Tracy contends that

---

[69] Holborn 1959, 62.

[70] Sea 2007, 239–40; te Brake 1998, 32–33.

[71] Moeller 1982, 57.

[72] During 1534–1535 radical Anabaptists seized control of the city of Münster and set about establishing a rather bizarre "New Jerusalem" organized along pseudo-biblical lines. Anabaptists rejected infant baptism as, they argued, infants could not choose to embrace Christ, and instead advocatated adult baptism. See Bonney 1991, 25–26; and, more generally, Stayer 1991.

[73] The identification of 1525 as a key turning point is prevalent in Marxist interpretations of the Reformations. See Blickle 1985. For problems with the argument, see, for example, Kittelson 1986, S128; Schilling 1992, 191–201; and Scribner 1994. Blickle's argument treats the Upper German Reformation as distinctively "communal." The category of "communalism," however, remains hotly contested. Many German towns did not seek self-government as part of Reformation; as Scribner (1994, 206) notes, "Exactly what 'communal' meant was a political matter. . . . It was certainly not a universal whose meaning was fixed or invariable."

the German Peasants' War convinced even Catholic princes that "religious order imposed by heretical governments was better than the chaos that seemed to loom on the horizon."[74]

Reformation and Empire, 1525–1555: Religious Polarization, Imperial Management, and Civil War

In a recent international-relations treatment of processes leading to Charles's defeat at the hands of German Protestants, John Owen argues that the rise of Protestantism triggered a security dilemma and "ideological" spiral that ultimately polarized Germany between Protestants and Catholics and led to open warfare.

> Spreading transnational ideologies set up conditions under which alliances formed along ideological lines. Governments that adhered to one ideology were threatened by a rival transnational ideology, and opposed that ideology, entering domestic-security agreements. Those agreements in turn raised fears among governments of the opposing ideology, which responded by increasing cooperation as well. The first set of governments reacted by increasing their own cooperation; the second reacted in kind; and these interactions eventually produced alliances that correlated to ideology.[75]

Owen's account captures key dynamics in the onset of religious warfare in Germany. Only a few princes overtly backed religious reformation during the first half of the 1520s. As Heinz Schilling notes, the "princes were less susceptible than the municipal oligarchs to pressure from below to give evangelical preachers a pulpit." Frederick of Saxony, Luther's first protector, supported—albeit carefully—reformation relatively early. Philip of Hesse abandoned Rome in 1524. In 1525 Albrecht von Hohenzollern embraced Luther's teachings, dissolved the Teutonic Order, and became the first Duke of Prussia.[76] The unfolding of the German Peasants' War helped convince a number of Catholic rulers—including Ferdinand and the dukes of Bavaria—to agree to suppress religious heresy in their domains. Internal disputes, particularly between the Habsburgs and the Bavarians, stymied any real cooperation. In 1526 John of Saxony and Philip of Hesse formed the Gotha-Torgau (League of Torgau) alliance to protect themselves against aggression. But not much came of this alliance either, in part because Protestant cities feared its political implications:

---

[74] Tracy 1999, 73. See also Sea 2007, 220, 235–40.
[75] Owen 2005, 93
[76] Schilling 1992, 196–97. On the politics of Albrecht von Hohenzollern's conversion, see Hubatsch 1971.

they worried that opposing their ruler would ultimately undermine their position in the Imperial Estates.[77]

The limited success of the League of Torgau highlights how processes of religious polarization in Germany should be contextualized within the broader dynamics of resistance and rule in early modern composite states. Although they enjoyed significant political and military autonomy, even the princes and Imperial Cities of the empire were not "sovereign" actors in an international environment.[78] They were local intermediaries, although quite autonomous ones, in a composite state. In consequence, the various attempts of co-religionists to form alliances ran up against the routine ways in which composite-state structures worked against cross-class and cross-regional collective mobilization. In this sense, the fact that religious identities and ties ultimately overcame these divisions proves crucially important to the arguments of the present study. Religious polarization shaped the ability of actors, most notably Charles and Ferdinand, to broker political compromises—even those that involved nonreligious issues.

At the same time, the Habsburgs faced both opportunities and dilemmas that stemmed directly from their positions within a system of composite states. Charles's authority as King of the Romans mattered a great deal for dynamics of bargaining and negotiation in the German Reformations. His role as the leader of a broader dynastic agglomeration accounts for the cross-pressures that shaped his policies in Germany: those emanating from the *Comuneros* rebellion, the Valois-Habsburg rivalry in Italy, Ottoman expansion in Hungary and Central Europe, and conflicts in the Netherlands.

FROM 1525 TO THE SECOND DIET OF SPEYER IN 1529

While German rulers cobbled together ineffectual religious alliances, Charles pursued war in Italy. In 1526 Charles achieved a spectacular victory at Pavia. His forces destroyed Francis's Italian army and captured the French king himself. Charles's ally, Henry VIII, argued that "not an hour is to be lost": the two should dismember the French monarchy in accordance with their alliance's objectives.[79] Charles, however, decided— in part due to fiscal and military constraints—not to push his advantage. He believed, rather naïvely, that he could negotiate a binding agreement with his captive. Charles therefore rejected Henry's pleas; he concluded a treaty in which Francis agreed, however conditionally, to restore

---

[77] Blickle 1984, 18; Bonney 1991, 31–32; Elton 1964, 62–64; Müller 1977, 126; Owen 2005, 88; Tracy 1999, 74–75.
[78] Owen 2005, 85–86.
[79] Quoted in Bonney 1991, 103.

Burgundy to Habsburg control and to eschew his claims to Milan and Naples. Charles released Francis, taking Francis's two sons as hostages in his place.

Francis, however, promptly renounced the treaty; since he accepted it under duress, he argued, he need not abide by it. By 1526 Charles faced a new alliance between Francis, Pope Clement VII, Florence, Venice, and Milan (League of Cognac).[80] Charles's brother, Ferdinand, needed support against the Turks in Hungary. These strategic pressures precluded direct conflict with the newly Protestant princes in Germany, whose support for Ferdinand "was conditional on a tacit acceptance of their faith and the secularization of church lands in their principalities."[81] Thus, a brief window available to Charles in 1525 to turn his attention toward the spread of the Reformations in Germany closed.

France's League of Cognac, however, proved a failure. In 1527 Habsburg forces compelled Pope Clement VII to accept a separate peace, and not long after that the infamous sack of Rome by unpaid Habsburg troops left the papacy firmly under Charles's control. The pattern of previous French campaigns in Italy resurfaced: initial French gains gave way to defeats. In the Peace of Cambrai (1529), Francis formally abandoned all of his claims in Italy. From then until 1536, the struggle with France returned to the character of a "cold war," allowing Charles to return to the empire.[82]

Charles, despite these eventual victories, still lacked both the military and political resources to combat the spread of reformation in Germany. Both committed Catholics and supporters of Luther, for their part, wanted to resolve growing religious dissension in the empire through a general Church council that, they hoped, would produce a reform-oriented compromise. Charles opposed this proposal as late as 1524, but by 1526 the Ottoman threat convinced him to reverse course. Ferdinand desperately needed assistance from the Imperial Estates to support his wife's brother, Louis II of Hungary, against an Ottoman offensive.[83] In 1526 the Recess of Speyer effectively rescinded the Edict of Worms "by accepting that, in anticipation of a council, 'in religious matters every section of the Empire could behave in a way that it hoped and believed could be justified before God and His Imperial Majesty.'"[84] Speyer created three years of breathing room for advocates of reformation to consolidate and expand their position.[85]

[80] Knecht 1996c, 35–38; McElwee 1936, 65–85.
[81] Bonney 1991, 115. See also Fischer-Galati 1954; and Grimm 1965, 197–202.
[82] Bonney 1991, 105–7.
[83] Fischer-Galati 1954, 56–59.
[84] Blockmans 2002, 84.
[85] Bonney 1991, 32.

Between 1525 and 1529 the reformers made impressive gains in Germany, winning converts among princes and dominating imperial cities. Charles still failed to appreciate the nature of the religious problem. In 1526 he wrote to his brother Ferdinand:

> With regard to the report you inform me of, that certain cities and towns of our Empire, fearing to be included in the punishment of Luther's excesses, are practising upon such Princes and persons as they know to be unfavorable to our interests, in order to move and attract them towards themselves, and thus to join in common cause against us, I could wish, that you had, at the same time, pointed out to me some speedy remedy.[86]

Even in 1529 Charles still believed that the majority of Protestants pursued purely political objectives.[87] He was wrong. The vast majority of city-dwellers who adopted Protestant beliefs and rituals did so out of religious conviction. Princes, for their part, derived important benefits from abandoning the Catholic Church, such as the ability to appropriate and sell ecclesiastical property. But most were quite sincere in their beliefs.[88] Tracy points out that despite the political benefits ultimately associated with conversion to Protestantism, "We should be wary of imputing overly calculating motives to princes and their councilors. They too were caught up in a spirit of enthusiasm for the great enterprise of making a more godly world."[89] Princes who adopted Protestant confessions during the 1520s and early 1530s risked a great deal: to do so brought with it possible conflict with the emperor and the many princes who remained committed to some form of Catholicism. Finally, if religious orientation was merely an expediency for political ends, we would be hard pressed to explain why the dukes of Bavaria (dynastic rivals of the Habsburgs, who sometimes allied with Protestants against Charles) remained staunch Catholics.[90]

If we reduce the high politics of the Reformations to instrumental concerns, then we simply cannot make sense of the political conflicts and negotiations that dominated the period between 1529 and 1555. Princes and cities alike sought to balance their theological convictions with their sense of political necessity. Protestant princes, of course, allied with Catholic France and Bavaria against Charles. Yet their concerns about French persecution of Protestants often shaped German Protestant relations with

---

[86] Quoted in Bradford 1971 [1850], 259.
[87] Blockmans 2002, 86.
[88] Fischer-Galati 1954, 54.
[89] Tracy 1999, 28.
[90] Bonney 1991, 31.

France. Some Protestant princes, in fact, eventually fought on the side of the Habsburgs. But here they weighed religious considerations against other strategic and normative interests. Carl C. Christensen's assessment of John of Saxony's diplomacy might be applied to many, but not all, of the important players in Germany: they adopted policies of realpolitik in the service of religious—and, we might add, dynastic—interests.[91]

Only days after the end of the Recess of Speyer, Louis II fell in battle against the Turks. Ferdinand laid claim to Hungary through his marriage to Louis' sister. A majority of Hungarian nobles rejected Ferdinand's claim and elected John Zápolyai as their king, but a minority, meeting separately, opted for Ferdinand.[92] The Ottomans exploited the divisions in Hungary for their own benefit. Charles, however, focused his attention on Italy and the Valois. Ferdinand sought aid from a group of German princes, but they refused to provide it in the absence of a general Diet. Negotiations at the Diet of Regensberg (1527–1528) came to little. As Stephen A. Fischer-Galati argues, the "Catholics, and the majority of the Lutherans, refused to help out Ferdinand because they thought he was asking for money to fill the Habsburg coffers for Charles's western affairs or for possible diversion into Italy."[93]

Philip of Hesse and John of Saxony, on the other hand, feared that if Ferdinand's position in Hungary improved—particularly if he defeated Zápolyai—he might "be in a position to retract some of the concessions made at Speyer."[94] The failure of Regensberg presaged greater setbacks in Hungary. By the end of 1528 Ferdinand determined to try yet again, and arranged for another Imperial Diet to meet at Speyer in 1529. There he met continued resistance. Advocates of reformation made their support conditional on religious concessions; Catholics "alarmed by the progress of the Lutherans, desired to obtain a religious settlement which would check their opponents" and would only "take up the question of substantial aid to Ferdinand" if he met their demands. Unable to move either side, Ferdinand threw his support behind the Catholics.[95]

The 1529 Diet of Speyer, in consequence, effectively reaffirmed the Edict of Worms.[96] Reformers responded that the Diet could not exercise

---

[91] Christensen 1984, 430. See also Bonney 1991, 27–28; Hendrix 1994; and Holborn 1959, 215–16. On the relationship between French persecution and alliance politics, see Baumgartner 1988, 125–26; and Knecht 1996c, 393–407.

[92] Bonney 1991, 242–43; Fischer-Galati 1954, 58.

[93] Fischer-Galati 1954, 60–61.

[94] Ibid., 61.

[95] Ibid., 62–63. One reason for the growing Catholic-Protestant split was Philip of Hesse's abortive invasion of the Catholic Mainz and Würzburg, an invasion resulting from Philip's mistaken belief that the Catholic parties were preparing a war against reformed princes and cities. See Owen 2005, 89.

[96] Blockmans 2002, 84.

authority over spiritual matters, protesting that "in matters touching God's honor and our eternal life and salvation, everyone has to stand before God and give account for himself, so that here none can excuse himself with the decisions of others, whether a minority or a majority."[97] Their formal legal protest against Speyer earned them the appellation "Protestants."

The spread of Protestantism clearly frightened Catholic parties; thus, their pressure on Ferdinand to rescind the 1526 Recess of Speyer in exchange for aid against the Ottomans. The processes that led to the outcome of 1529 Diet of Speyer, however, reveal more than an ideological spiral of threat between Protestants and Catholics. Habsburg inaction during the 1520s resulted from Charles and Ferdinand's inability to effectively navigate the cross-pressures imposed by their dynastic interests and the heterogeneity of the Habsburg domains. In 1527–1528, Ferdinand failed to convince Catholic parties that their aid would not be used to forward Habsburg dynastic ambitions elsewhere. The increasingly strained relations between Catholics and Protestants made it difficult for Ferdinand, at the 1529 Diet of Speyer, to negotiate a solution to his fiscal and military needs without abandoning one of the two sides. Although the 1526 Recess did the most to demobilize alliances among co-religionists, variations in regional interests and between those of princes and towns remained persistent problems for both sides.

INTRA-REFORMATION DISPUTES AND THE EARLY FAILURE
OF AN ANTI-HABSBURG ALLIANCE

Events at the 1529 Diet of Speyer convinced many Protestants of the necessity for a military alliance. Divergent interests between various princes, as well as between princes and cities, continued to bedevil their efforts. Disagreements over religious issues magnified these rifts. While the Diet was still in progress, Philip of Hesse took the lead in negotiating a defensive league, to include himself, John of Saxony, and the cities of Nuremburg, Strasbourg, and Ulm. A number of factors made John of Saxony reluctant to conclude the alliance. It was of questionable utility for Saxony, which was far from any of the other potential members but bordered directly on Habsburg lands. Moreover, the alliance risked jeopardizing the ability of Saxony to collect on significant debts owed by the Habsburgs, and, more importantly, John's presumed future investment as an imperial elector.[98]

---

[97] Quoted in and translated by Schulze 1986, S50. Speyer convinced many Protestant theologians to adopt theories of resistance that denied the spiritual authority of the emperor. See Shoenberger 1977 and 1979.

[98] Christensen 1984.

Ideological and theological differences proved particularly intractable. The South German cities had strong "republican tendencies" that "grated on the monarchical sensibilities of a conservative prince like John of Saxony and involved a degree of citizen participation which seemed to raise the spectre of instability and popular excess." It was, furthermore, "unprecedented for a North German prince to enter into a religio-political alliance with South German cities."[99] The debate between Lutherans and Zwinglians over the Lord's Supper also created problems for alliance negotiations. Both rejected the Catholic denial of the lay chalice, and both refused to accept that the Eucharist literally became the body of the sacrificed Christ. But they differed on the nature of Holy Communion. Luther held that the body and blood of Christ "coexisted with the bread and wine after it had been consecrated." Zwingli, in contrast, maintained "that 'is' in Christ's words ['this is my body . . . this is my blood'] really meant 'signifies' " and that Holy Communion was a commemorative ceremony of thanksgiving for Christ's sacrifice. Luther responded that "is" meant "is" and that one could not deny the plain meaning of the Bible. These differences produced much ill-will between reformers.[100]

Thus, widespread suspicions about Zwinglian leanings among the South German cities made John of Saxony reluctant to join with them in an alliance. The Lutheran theologian Philip Melanchthon left the 1529 Diet of Speyer convinced that "a more clear-cut rejection of Zwinglianism by the Saxons would have won greater concessions from the imperial government. He wrote frantic letters to friends . . . containing phrases such as 'I would rather die than see our cause polluted by a union with the Zwinglians.' "[101] His reading of Speyer was not without merit: the Diet called merely for a halt to Lutheran expansion and freedom of Catholic worship, but demanded complete suppression of Zwinglianism.[102] Luther himself sent instructions to John that he should not participate in an alliance. Luther argued that it would lead to military conflict, force Lutherans to defend doctrinal errors, and contradicted biblical condemnation of human alliances. Subsequently, John wrote instructions to his representative at the intra-Protestant negotiations forbidding him "to enter into an alliance with those who accept Zwinglian views of the sacrament."[103]

[99] Ibid., 420-21.
[100] Bonney 1991, 27-28. See also Christensen 1984; Grimm 1965, 194-97; Hendrix 1994; Müller 1977; Tracy 1999, 60-62; and Wallace 2004, 114. Despite superficial similarities, it would be unfair to label Zwingli's argument "Clintonian."
[101] Christensen 1984, 422.
[102] Ibid., 420.
[103] Ibid., 422-23. Luther's pacifist leanings factored into his reluctance to sanction a Protestant military alliance. His attitudes seem, however, to have changed as Protestants grew more convinced of the impossibility of coming to terms with the emperor. See Shoenberger 1977 and 1979.

In 1530 Pope Clement VII crowned Charles V Holy Roman Emperor. As G. R. Elton remarks, "If the emperor seemed to stand on a pinnacle of power, the Protestants were markedly ill-prepared to face him." All efforts to build an anti-Habsburg coalition "broke down over the theological differences" between Protestants "on the one hand, and on the other over the conservative reluctance of Saxony and Nuremberg to contemplate political action against the Emperor."[104] Philip of Hesse could not broker an alliance in the face of these theological and ideological differences; religious issues proved as much a problem for intra-Protestant solidarity as for cross-confessional negotiations. News that Charles would hold a Diet in Augsburg, and that there he intended to resolve the question of religion through compromise, brought the progress of alliance negotiations to a standstill.

THE FORMATION OF THE LEAGUE OF SCHMALKALD

The 1530 Diet of Augsburg, in fact, helped the Protestant camp overcome its differences and form a military alliance. Catholic German princes, meanwhile, exploited divisions within the empire to enhance their autonomy and strategic position vis-à-vis the Habsburgs. They often proved unwilling to lend significant aid against Protestantism if doing so would enhance Charles's power and authority at their own expense.[105]

The 1530 Diet of Augsburg did not meet with the sole purpose of resolving religious disputes. Charles and Ferdinand placed many items on the Diet's agenda. Not long after the end of the 1529 Diet of Speyer, Ottoman forces laid siege to Vienna. Despite the unfavorable outcome at Speyer, Protestant princes rallied to the Habsburgs' aid and helped repel the invasion. At Augsburg the Habsburgs resumed their pressure for permanent assistance against the Ottomans. They viewed the Ottoman threat as their most important concern. Charles also wanted to secure the election of Ferdinand as King of the Romans, an unprecedented move that appeared to be the first step in transforming the emperorship into an hereditary Habsburg title. He saw the other two items on the agenda—resolving religious differences and imperial reform—as means to these ends. Charles, despite his apparent position of strength, still lacked the political and fiscal resources to resolve the breach in Latin Christendom through force of arms. Religious issues, nevertheless, dominated the proceedings at Augsburg.[106]

---

[104] Elton 1964, 141–42. On Philip of Hesse's attempts to justify resistance in the face of Nuremberg's conservative interpretation of imperial authority, see Shoenberger 1977, 69.

[105] Elton 1964, 142–49. The Bavarians, in particular, put their dynastic rivalry with the Habsburgs ahead of their religious convictions.

[106] Elton 1964, 142–43; Fischer-Galati 1954, 63–64; Krodel 1982; Müller 1977, 134.

The summons for the 1530 Diet of Augsburg included conciliatory language; the Protestant participants believed that Charles was genuinely interested in an open discussion of theological disputes.[107] Once the diet began on 20 June, Catholic representatives presented a document that exhaustively listed the "errors" of Lutherans, Anabaptists, and Zwinglians. The Saxons presented the emperor with the Confession of Augsburg. Originally intended only to enumerate the Saxon position, the Confession had, by the time of the Diet, mutated into a collective statement of Lutheran doctrine, signed by a number of Protestant princes and two imperial cities. In response, the Catholic representatives produced the *Confutatio*, a refutation of the Confession. The fact that the *Confutatio* was written at Charles's request damaged his position as a broker between the two sides; his explicit rejection of the Confession also undermined his ability to negotiate with the Protestants.[108]

Nevertheless, the next few months of the Diet were given over to negotiations between representatives of both sides. Melanchthon, the chief spokesman for the Lutherans, proved eager to compromise. His readiness to negotiate, however, strengthened the intransigence of the papacy, which became "less inclined to make concessions, and particularly less amenable to the emperor's entreaties for the convocation of a Christian council."[109] The Diet of Augsburg ended badly for the cause of peaceful reunification. It confirmed the Edict of Worms; Charles called on the Protestants to return to the fold within six months or face prosecution as violators of the national peace and, in consequence, potentially face military action. Ferdinand became King of the Romans, which seemed to many to consolidate the Habsburg position in Germany.[110]

The outcome at Augsburg produced important changes in the calculations of Protestant princes and cities: intra-Protestant disputes suddenly seemed less important than the threat of imperial intervention on behalf of Catholicism.[111] As far as many Protestants were concerned, it was now clear that they needed to form a military alliance to defend their faith.

---

[107] Blockmans 2002, 86; Christensen 1984, 426.

[108] Blockmans 2002, 86–87; Christensen 1984, 427; Holborn 1959, 212–13; Owen 2005, 90–91; Spitz 1980, 3.

[109] Holborn 1959, 213.

[110] Blockmans 2002, 87–88; Bonney 1991, 33; Holborn 1959, 13.

[111] Owen 2005, 90. Stephen Walt argues that actors do not counterbalance power, but rather balance against threat. In his recent extension of his argument, he contends that revolutionary regimes almost always constitute a threat to existing powers. See Walt 1985, 1987, and 1997. Although we need to be sensitive to the degree that the category of "threat" may produce a tautological theory, it seems clear that after 1530 the threat posed by Catholic and imperial forces to the survival of Protestantism appeared greater than the "threat"—if we can call it that—that siding with sacramentarians posed to the spiritual purity of Lutherans.

On 27 February 1531 six princes and ten cities formed the League of Schmalkald, which quickly began to grow in membership.[112] As Abe J. Dueck argues, "It was in direct response to this recess [of Augsburg 1530] that the Protestants finally were able to overcome their earlier difficulties and organize the Schmalkaldic League, which, although it was solely defensive in character, did not exempt resistance to the emperor as earlier defensive alliances had."[113]

The formation of the League accelerated Charles's efforts to end religious divisions in Germany. He had little other choice; although the Catholic estates were perfectly happy to condemn heresy and insist that Charles suppress it, they showed no interest in aiding their emperor in that task. Moreover, Ferdinand's election as King of the Romans split the Catholic camp.

> The elevation of Ferdinand to this rank, however, seemed to establish the Habsburgs on a hereditary throne. If the Catholic princes had been so brave in urging Charles to fight the Protestants, but so chary in offering active support, it had been for fear that their political liberties, their so-called Libertät, would be placed in jeopardy by the subjugation of their Protestant confreres. How could the Catholic princes hope to maintain their relative independence against a victorious monarch?[114]

Once again, Charles turned his hopes toward a general council. In the meantime, he agreed to let the Electors Albrecht of Mainz and Louis of the Palatine treat with the Protestant camp. Negotiations began at Schweinfurt on 1 April 1531–at roughly the same time as Charles convened the 1531 Diet of Regensberg. Albrecht and Louis presented the Protestants with a statement of terms: those who had submitted to the Augsburg Confession must not introduce further ecclesiastical innovations or allow anyone to advocate such innovations; they were to eschew alliances with Zwinglians and Anabaptists; they must not harbor religious refugees from elsewhere in Germany; and must agree to support a general council, aid the emperor against the Turks, and to recognize Ferdinand's election.[115]

In October 1531 the position of Zwinglianism changed dramatically. Zwingli's propaganda against the Catholic cantons of the Swiss Confederation and his repeated calls for a militarily expansionist policy by the Protestant cantons led the "Five States" (an alliance of Catholic cantons) to launch an attack against Zwingli at Zurich. Zwingli died in battle, and

---

[112] Holborn 1959, 216.
[113] Dueck 1982, 55.
[114] Holborn 1959, 215.
[115] Blockmans 2002, 88–89; Dueck 1982, 57–58.

Zwinglian influence—and that of the Swiss Reformation in general—in Southern Germany quickly deteriorated. Zurich could no longer provide military support to Protestant Southern German cities.[116]

Philip of Hesse, for his part, managed to negotiate an alliance with the Catholic Bavarian dukes against Habsburg interests.[117] The status of the Augsburg Confession, however, still divided the Protestant camp during negotiations with Catholics in 1532. Philip of Hesse argued for the right of Lutherans to form alliances with Zwinglians. John of Saxony again opposed their inclusion in an alliance. Zwinglian-leaning cities finessed the issue by accepting the Augsburg Confession while also affirming their adherence to their separate confession, the Tetrapolitana. Alliance negotiations with England, for their part, broke down over Electoral Saxony's insistence that the English must first accept the Augsburg Confession.[118]

Philip and John of Saxony also stood at odds over whether the League should agree, as the imperial negotiators demanded, not to support the spread of Protestantism. John was willing to accept the proposal; Philip was not. Philip almost certainly recognized that these terms would significantly undermine the Protestant position over time, but "whatever Philip's real motive was, he knew that his attempt to keep open the possibility for further expansion was more likely to succeed if he was able to formulate convincing theological counterarguments to those of the Wittenberg theologians [Luther and his cohorts]."[119]

But such disagreements surfaced again during bargaining at Schweinfurt. Philip claimed that failing to support future converts amounted to a sin against God. A number of Protestant theologians soon entered the fray. Philip and John exchanged letters debating the theological implications of the peace terms, but such exchanges only widened the rift within the Protestant camp. Highly technical disagreements over the form of a proposed general council to resolve religious divisions also divided Protestants and Catholics, as well as the Protestants themselves.[120]

After the failure of the Schweinfurt negotiations, the parties reconvened in Nuremburg, where they again made little progress. John of Saxony opted to make a separate peace with Charles. Before word of his decision could reach the conference, however, Charles unexpectedly agreed to accept a temporal rather than religious peace—meaning that religious disputes were now off the table. He pledged all of the estates to peace, which, in essence, ensured that the spread of Lutheranism would not be opposed

---

[116] Bonney 1991, 28–29; Elton 1964, 73–74; McElwee 1936, 120; Rublack 2005, 79.
[117] Müller 1977, 136; Owen 2005, 90.
[118] Dueck 1982, 60–61; Müller 1977, 135.
[119] Dueck 1982, 62.
[120] Ibid., 64–70.

by military force. Most of the issues debated at Schweinfurt and Nuremberg remained effectively unresolved. By this point, Charles's central concern was again the Ottoman threat. Neither he, nor his representatives, could broker an agreement between Protestants and Catholics, but he could attempt to table the issue while he (and Ferdinand) focused on their dynastic interests. The Nuremburg agreement required the Protestants to commit themselves to the defense of the empire against the Ottomans; for the time being—at least until a general council could be convened—Charles was willing to provide de facto recognition of Protestantism within Germany in exchange for strategic support.[121]

THE SCHMALAKDIC LEAGUE EXPANDS

After Nuremburg a growing number of princes and towns entered the Schmalkaldic League. In 1534 the League attacked the Habsburgs themselves. It intervened in the Duchy of Württemberg, which the Habsburgs had controlled since 1520–following the disgrace and military defeat of its ruler, Duke Ulrich.[122] A thoroughly unpleasant character, Ulrich attracted Philip of Hesse's attention for two reasons: first, he was a Lutheran, and second, restoring him to his strategically important Southern German duchy would be a direct blow to the position and prestige of the Habsburg dynasty. Financed by Francis I, Philip's army captured Württemberg while the Swabian League, paralyzed by internal religious divisions, stood on the sidelines. They were joined in their inaction by the dukes of Bavaria, who preferred a Protestant victory over continued Habsburg control of Württemberg.[123]

The crisis dealt a final blow to the existence of the Swabian League. Its collapse left the Habsburgs bereft of one of its major pillars of power in Southern Germany. Neither the loss of Württemberg nor the collapse of the Swabian League prompted Ferdinand to action; he remained "preoccupied with his dynastic interests in Hungary . . . and he was fearful of the prospect of French intervention in Imperial affairs."[124] Charles, for his part, was distracted by other commitments: his attack on Tunis in 1534 and, later, the resumption of conflict with France.[125]

Charles's inability to balance cross-pressures emanating from other segments of his empire, combined with the tendency of intermediaries to

---

[121] Blockmans 2002, 89; Dueck 1982, 71–74; Holborn 1959, 217–219.

[122] Ulrich murdered a knight whose wife he desired. The Swabian League forced him into exile and turned over the administration of the Duchy to the Habsburgs.

[123] Bonney 1991, 96, 117; Elton 1964, 154–55. Elton notes that the Bavarians would have preferred that Ulrich's Catholic son succeed him, which would have satisfied both their religious and anti-Habsburg interests.

[124] Bonney 1991, 117.

[125] Blockmans 2002, 90; McElwee 1936, 131–32.

pursue their own interests (for example, Ferdinand's prioritization of his own dynastic position in Hungary over control of Württemberg), ensured Philip of Hesse's victory. Religious concerns, however, motivated the Schmalkaldic League's show of strength. The Swabian League's collapse in the face of Philip's aggression stemmed from its own religious divisions. Bavaria may have put dynastic rivalries before religious convictions, but confessional polarization accounts for the reconfiguration of Germany's political landscape in ways that directly eroded Habsburg authority.[126]

Philip's success in 1534 emboldened the Schmalkaldic League; it soon acted as "a visible unit negotiating with Henry VIII of England and playing its part in the politics of Scandinavia."[127] Confessional ties and identities yoked together a new international actor in the form of a Protestant alliance. The Schmalkaldic League's expansion, in turn, prompted the formation of a Catholic counteralliance—including a number of important dukes, such as those of Bavaria, and archbishops—in 1538.[128]

STRATEGIC OVERREACH

In 1535 Francesco Sforza, the Duke of Milan and a Habsburg puppet, died without a male heir. The Valois-Habsburg rivalry immediately reignited. By May 1536 the two dynasties were once again engaged in open conflict. Charles's invasion of France floundered on his lack of adequate finances. Mutual bankruptcy led to a truce in January 1538. The truce produced four years of peace, but Charles lacked the resources for renewed conflict in Germany. He therefore accelerated his calls for a general council and allowed the arrangement negotiated at Nuremberg to continue.[129]

The strategic problems associated with a far-flung, heterogeneous dynastic empire continued to dog Charles. In 1539–1540, during a period of peace between Charles and Francis I, the Flemish city of Ghent, dominated by its guilds, rebelled against Charles's revenue demands and administrative policies. Ghent declared that Charles was no longer its sovereign. Class and regional antagonisms, however, prevented Ghent from finding allies among the other cities of Flanders and foreign powers. France not only failed to intervene on Ghent's behalf, as it had done during Maximilian's reign, but Francis, in a gesture of goodwill, granted Charles the right of passage through French territory on his way to crush the rebellion. Having done so, Charles revoked Ghent's privileges and

---

[126] Owen 2005.
[127] Elton 1964, 156.
[128] Blockmans 2002, 91.
[129] Ibid., 91; Bonney 1991, 106–7.

exemptions. Additionally, in 1541 Charles led a second expedition to Tunis. This time he was defeated, not by the forces of Islam, but by a seasonal storm.[130]

During this period Charles took an especially conciliatory line toward the German Protestants. At the 1540 Diet of Hagenau, Charles agreed to treat the Augsburg Confession as the starting point for future religious negotiations. At the 1540–1541 Diet of Worms, negotiations continued. From April to July of 1541, six moderate theologians from both sides met at Regensburg to work out a compromise. Among them was Cardinal Gasparo Contarini, a moderate Catholic who believed that the Lutheran rejection of Catholicism was based mainly upon misunderstandings of the true doctrines of the Church. The negotiations went well on a range of issues, and a solution appeared to be in sight, but the theologians could not come to an agreement on papal authority and the continuing hobgoblin of the Lord's Supper (although they did reach agreement on justification by faith, opting for a compromise). Even if the negotiators had succeeded, it seems unlikely that either Luther or Pope Paul III would have accepted any agreement. Once again, doctrinal disputes precluded compromise.[131]

In 1542 the Schmalkaldic League attacked the duchy of Brunswick-Wolfenbüttel and forcibly brought it into the Protestant camp.[132] By 1545 "all of northeastern and northwestern Germany had become Protestant, as well as large parts of southern Germany."[133] While the League made war on Brunswick-Wolfenbüttel, Charles soundly defeated Duke William V of Jülich-Cleves. William was in the process of consolidating a Protestant and anti-Habsburg dynastic agglomeration in northwest Germany. Charles's victory in 1543 finally ended the chronic threat to his Burgundian patrimonies emanating from Gelders—which Charles added to his dynastic holdings—and restored William's territories to official Catholicism.[134]

The war against William was linked to renewed war with France. Francis's attempt to exploit Charles's weakened position resulted in stalemate. Charles and Henry VIII both invaded France, but their forces failed to score a decisive victory. Indeed, Charles did not really aim for a joint conquest of France, but instead wanted Francis's support for his "long-

---

[130] Blockmans 2002, 151–52; Bonney 1991, 413.
[131] Bonney 1991, 58–59; Holborn 1959, 226; Tracy 1999, 89.
[132] Bonney 1991, 118.
[133] Holborn 1959, 221.
[134] The Schmalkaldic League did nothing to protect William. After Philip of Hesse committed the crime of bigamy, he received imperial clemency from Charles in return for not concluding foreign alliances and excluding Duke William from the League. See Grimm 1965, 218–20; and Holborn 1959, 223.

contemplated and much-delayed punitive expedition against German Protestants."[135] His finances once again stretched to their limit and his invasion out of steam, Charles signed a separate peace with Francis at Crépy-en-Laonnais on 29 August 1545.[136]

The terms of Crépy reflected these shifts in Charles's priorities since his early wars with France. Charles renounced all territorial gains since 1538 (the Treaty of Nice). Francis's heir, Charles, Duke of Orléans, would marry either Charles V's daughter Mary or Ferdinand's daughter Anne. If the Duke of Orléans married Mary, he would receive Franche-Compté and the Netherlands as dowry. If he married Anne, he would receive Milan. Charles was, in essence, agreeing to surrender—from a position of relative strength—one of the two dynastic inheritances that had defined the Valois-Habsburg rivalry for the length of his reign.[137]

In return Charles received Francis's pledge to aid him against the Turks. Francis also agreed to renounce his claims to Savoy and Piedmont, as well as alienate a number of duchies to his son, the Duke of Orléans. These were the public articles of the treaty. According to secret provisions, Francis would assist Charles in his goal of reforming the Church through a general council. If these strategies failed to end religious divisions in Germany, and Charles resorted to military means to bring religious unity to Germany, then Francis would come to aid.[138] For Charles, the fate of the empire and its heretics now took precedence over all other considerations.

After some delay Charles decided that the Duke of Orléans would marry his niece, Anne. The decision came too late: Francis's son died on 9 September 1545, leaving Henry II as heir to the French throne. Francis remarked that in losing his son Christendom had lost "he by whom Christianity might have remained in perpetual repose and quietude; he would have nourished peace and tranquility among the princes."[139] In fact, Henry II's attitude toward the Habsburgs was far more belligerent than that of his elder brother; some speculate that the former took his youthful captivity in Spain far harder than the latter.[140]

THE SCHMALKALDIC WAR

Additional events conspired to force a resolution to the religious question in Germany, including a truce with the Ottoman Empire in October 1545 and the opening of the long-awaited general Church council at Trent in December of the same year. The Council of Trent did not go as Charles

---

[135] Blockmans 2002, 154.
[136] Knecht 1982, 370.
[137] Tracy 1999, 140.
[138] Grimm 1965, 222; Knecht 1982, 370–71.
[139] Quoted in Knecht 1982, 371.
[140] See Baumgartner 1988.

hoped. The Church proved intransigent, and in January 1547, the Council condemned the positions and theology of the reform camp. The German Protestants responded by abandoning the Council when it relocated outside of Germany in March 1547. The Council of Trent, which continued (in multiple session) until 1563, solidified the division between Protestants and Catholics and inaugurated the so-called Counter-Reformation.[141]

The failure of Trent, already evident in 1546, convinced Charles that he would have to achieve religious unity in the empire through force. Specifically, he must attack the Schmalkaldic League. Charles wrote to his sister Mary, his representative in the Netherlands, that "we have no other recourse than to resist these apostates strenuously and to use all means to force them to some sort of acceptable conditions. . . . If we do not take a strong line the risk to the faith is enormous. The consequences could be so harmful that there could be no turning back, namely the estrangement of the rest of Germany from our holy faith."[142]

Charles, by this time, had few obvious allies among the German princes and towns. Many now belonged to the Protestant camp (figure 5.4). Even the staunchly Catholic Bavarians saw little advantage in aiding an expansion of Habsburg power in Germany; they were willing only to provide what Wim Blockmans calls "passive support" for Charles in exchange for a marriage between Duke Albrecht and Ferdinand's daughter, Anne.[143]

Charles confronted a dilemma: he sought to suppress heresy but he required the support of Protestant princes. His solution was twofold. First, he (mis)represented his goals as merely political: the suppression of disobedience to imperial authority. As he wrote to his son, the future Philip II, "As you know, the restoration of the faith is our aim and intention, but it seemed useful to make known right from the beginning that our concern is to punish those who disobey, especially the margrave, the Duke of Saxony [John Frederick, who succeeded his father, John, in 1532] and all those like them."[144]

Enframing the conflict as "merely" political facilitated Charles's attempts to divide and conquer his opponents: it provided cover for alliance negotiations with Protestant princes, many of whom subordinated confessional allegiances to their financial and dynastic interests. The existence of Protestant allies, including the main recruiters for the imperial army, also signaled the apparently "political" nature of his activities. To his sister Mary, in the same letter quoted earlier, Charles wrote that "I decided to embark on war against Hesse and Saxony as transgressors of the peace

---

[141] Bonney 1991, 56–76; Elton 1964, 176–209; McElwee 1936, 177.
[142] Quoted in Blockmans 2002, 118.
[143] Ibid., 94.
[144] Quoted in ibid., 94.

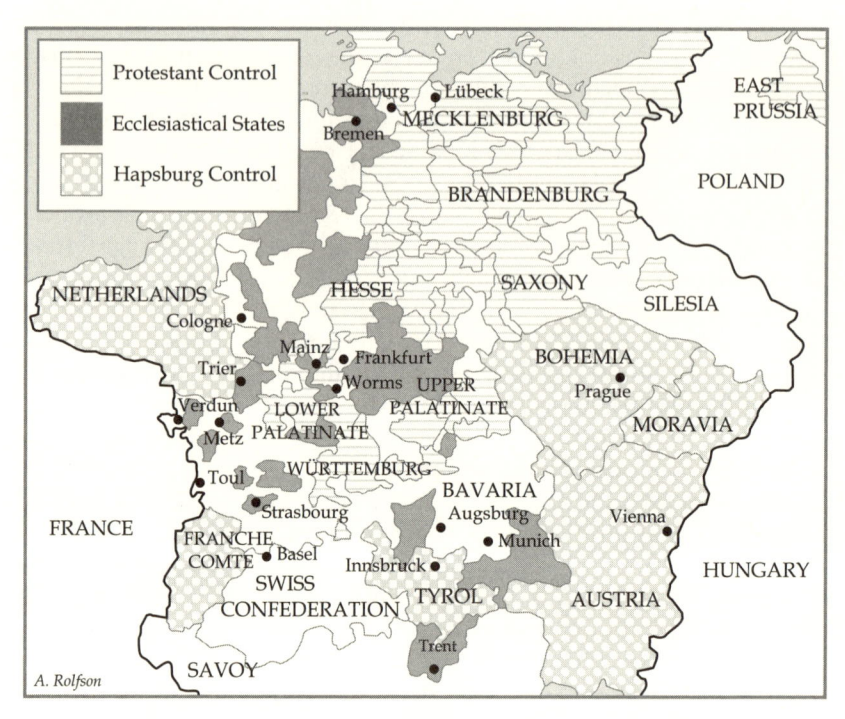

Figure 5.4 The German Empire on the Eve of the War of Schmalkald

against the Duke of Brunswick and his territory. And although this pretext will not long disguise the fact that this is a matter of religion, yet it serves for the present to divide the renegades."[145] In fact, the League mobilized their forces pre-emptively; on 20 July 1545, Charles declared war on Elector John Frederick of Saxony and Philip of Hesse on the grounds that they and the Schmalkaldic League were violators of the imperial peace.[146]

Many Protestant princes and towns remained, at this point, on the sidelines. The League, moreover, suffered from a lack of effective leadership and consensus over its strategic objectives. Ever since the northern princes of the League invaded the Catholic duchy of Brunswick-Wolfenbüttel, major differences emerged between the northern Princes and the southern Protestant cities. The princes saw reformation as depending upon "a fusion of restored gospel with princes' liberty," while the cities understood the threat contained in this formula to their own autonomy.[147]

---

[145] Quoted in Bonney 1991, 118. See also McElwee 1936, 182–84.
[146] Bonney 1991, 118; McElwee 1936, 182–84.
[147] Brady 1994, 51.

Despite the impact of religious ties, composite-state dynamics still worked against collaboration.

The longer the war dragged on, the more time it allowed for Charles's Netherlandish and Spanish forces to reinforce his German troops (as well as those supplied to him by the papacy). The French court, for its part, suffered from factional divisions, while its ongoing persecution of French Protestants undermined its negotiations with the German princes. It failed, in consequence, to move decisively against Charles.[148]

In October 1545 Maurice of Saxony, a Protestant prince, broke his neutrality and invaded Electoral Saxony.[149] The temptation presented by Electoral Saxony—combined with the growing risk that Ferdinand might seize it first—led Maurice to take military action against the League. He justified his decision to his people on the grounds that "the attack on their fellow Lutheran was . . . the only way to preserve their own religion and the best means of checking the designs of the Catholic Ferdinand." Charles, in turn, offered John Frederick of Saxony's electorship to Maurice.[150]

Ferdinand and Maurice's invasion of Electoral Saxony forced John Frederick to abandon his allies in Upper Germany. It did not take long for Philip's army, demoralized by lack of pay, to disintegrate. The remaining southern German Schmalkaldic towns, as well as Frederick, Elector Palatine, and Ulrich of Württemberg, surrendered to Charles. The emperor publicly humiliated both princes and forced them to pay reparations for their aggression, but allowed them to retain their lands and titles. Similarly, those towns that capitulated paid heavy taxes, but, with the exception of Augsburg, Charles did nothing to proscribe Protestant worship within their territories.[151]

In Saxony, however, Maurice and Ferdinand ran into difficulties. Popular outrage at Maurice's actions allowed John Frederick to easily retake his own lands—and to conquer Maurice's, as well. The presence of Spanish Catholic soldiers in Bohemia frightened the Bohemian Ultraquists into joining with the League against Ferdinand,[152] and the "Hansa cities at last bestirred themselves. . . . Charles faced a solid union of North Germany

---

[148] On the failure of the French monarchy to support the German Protestants, see Potter 1977.

[149] Absent the practice of primogeniture, the Saxon lands were subdivided many times amongst many heirs; the electorship itself, however, could only be inherited by a single person.

[150] Blockmans 2002, 95; Elton 1964, 249; McElwee 1936, 188–89.

[151] Elton 1964, 249; Holborn 1959, 228–29; McElwee 1936, 185–88.

[152] The Ultraquists, moderate Hussite reformers, were supporters of the lay chalice. For a discussion of the history and pathways of Ultraquism and Hussitism, see Lambert 1977, 283–360.

emerging against him."¹⁵³ Increasingly strained relations with Pope Paul III also created problems for Charles. The Council of Trent's decision to reject justification by faith (on 13 January 1547) angered Charles and his representatives, who recognized that the direction of the Council made compromise on religious questions impossible. On 22 January 1547 Pope Paul III ordered his troops to abandon the imperial forces and return to Italy, most likely out of balance-of-power considerations raised by Charles's position in Upper Germany. The papacy also began to see renewed potential for an anti-Habsburg coalition with France; Francis's declining health raised the prospect of the imminent succession of his son, Henry, to the French monarchy.¹⁵⁴

The lack of coordination among Protestant forces balanced out these difficulties. Once Charles mobilized his forces to move on Saxony, the end came quickly. On 24 April 1547 Charles and the Duke of Alba, at the head of a Spanish Army, routed John Frederick's forces at Mühlberg. Charles arranged for a court to sentence John Frederick, now in custody, to death on 10 May 1547. John Frederick refused, even in the face of execution, to renounce his faith. On 19 May 1547 the two sides reached an agreement. John Frederick transferred those territories to Maurice that invested the latter with the Electorship. In exchange, Charles commuted John's death sentence. In June Hesse's surrender all but ended the war.¹⁵⁵

THE ROAD TO RUIN

Charles could not convert his military success into a political victory. He alienated his allies by denying them what they saw as their fair share of the spoils. Charles allowed John Frederick's heirs to retain some of their territory in Saxony in order to prevent Maurice from accumulating too much power. His treatment of the Elector Palatine precluded the transfer of his territory to Bavaria, thus frustrating the long-standing aspiration of the co-dukes of Bavaria for an electorship and what they believed to be their just territorial compensation for their support of their Habsburg rivals.¹⁵⁶

At the 1547–1548 Diet of Augsburg, Charles was stronger than he had ever been in Germany, yet his scheme to create a standing imperial army collapsed under fierce opposition from the princes. Charles finally took religious matters into his own hands, announcing an "Interim" religious settlement worked out by a commission of his own choosing. The Augsburg Interim conceded to the Protestants the lay chalice, clerical marriage,

[153] McElwee 1936, 190.
[154] Blockmans 2002, 95.
[155] Bonney 1991, 119; Esteban 2001, 117–18; Holborn 1959, 230; Tracy 1999, 140.
[156] Holborn 1959, 230

and other matters of doctrine but took no position on the key issue of justification by faith. At the same time it put in motion procedures for reform of the Catholic Church in the empire and mandated that Protestant towns and territories allow the conduct of Catholic worship.[157]

Elton characterizes the Interim as "little more than an assertion of Catholic orthodoxy with a few insignificant concessions to the Reformation";[158] an overwhelming majority of Protestants found its terms unacceptable. Throughout Germany local rulers obstructed implementation of the Interim. As Wim P. Blockmans notes, "Protestant pamphlets decried the Interim as a diabolical trick and popery in disguise."[159] As long as Charles had kept religious questions off the table, he had been capable of building cross-religious coalitions. Once the Interim became public, however, that coalition began to unravel.[160]

Charles made matters worse by his decision to press for Philip to succeed Ferdinand as King of the Romans, instead of Ferdinand's son Maximilian. Maximilian would, under this arrangement, only become King of the Romans once Philip was emperor. This arrangement effectively transformed the position of King of the Romans into an hereditary office. It thus violated the pledge Charles had made to the electors as a condition of his own election. It also played into German fears of foreign domination. Charles, after all, had won the Schmalkaldic War with troops from the Netherlands and Spain, and Germans already chafed at their presence on German soil. Charles's new position also, naturally, angered his brother and nephew.[161]

In 1550 a small number of Protestant German princes formed a new defensive league and made overtures to the new King of France, Henry II. Duke Maurice meanwhile secretly schemed against Charles. With Charles's position eroding and a new Protestant League forming, Maurice had every reason to believe he would become a prime target of his co-confessionalists' ire. Maurice sought to improve his relations both with the Protestant camp and with Ferdinand himself, while at the same time pretending his continued loyalty to the emperor. Thus, when Maurice was put in command of the imperial army sent to besiege Magdeburg—which alone had refused to submit after the Schmalkaldic War—Maurice dragged out the siege, draining imperial coffers while preserving his own access to military power. In November 1551 Maurice lifted the siege but did not disband his army. "Charles shut his ears to the urgent warnings

---

[157] Blockmans 2002, 97; Bonney 1991, 119; Holborn 1959, 231–32.
[158] Elton 1964, 254. See also Wallace 2004, 115–16.
[159] Blockmans 2002, 97; Holborn 1959, 235.
[160] Ibid.
[161] Blockmans 2002, 98; Bonney 1991, 120; Holborn 1959, 236–37; Lynch 1991, 28.

he received from Ferdinand and from his regent in the Netherlands" about Maurice's likely intentions. Meanwhile, Ferdinand was once again at war with the Ottoman Turks.[162]

In January 1552 the allied Protestant princes signed an agreement with Henry II. Henry agreed to support the Protestants against Charles in exchange for control over imperial territory—specifically, Metz, Toul, and Verdun. In March Henry attacked Lorraine. In April Maurice's forces marched against Charles at Innsbruck. Charles barely escaped capture. Maurice, however, made further overtures toward Ferdinand—and thus continued to exploit the divisions between the King of the Romans and the Holy Roman Emperor. In July 1552 Ferdinand and Maurice negotiated the Treaty of Passau. Although Charles had authorized Ferdinand's negotiations, he would not accept Passau's provisions for religious toleration.[163]

Charles, exhausted and ill, had failed to resolve religious schism. The French held their gains in the empire. Through his push for Philip's succession, Charles strained his relations with Ferdinand. The Imperial Diet next met at Augsburg in February of 1555. Charles, not wanting to involve himself in any agreement that granted permanent toleration for German Protestantism, left the negotiations to Ferdinand. The Religious Peace of Augsburg recognized the Protestant Confession of Augsburg and ratified existing seizures of Church lands by Protestants, but also held that any future clerical converts to Protestantism would have to transfer their benefices to a Catholic cleric. The agreement amounted to what te Brake refers to as a "thoroughly authoritarian settlement" to the question of religion. Henceforth, each autonomous town's, region's, or princedom's religion would be determined by its representative in the Estates. This was the principle *cuius regio eius religio*: rulers would decide the religions of their subjects.[164]

---

[162] Elton 1964, 263. As A. W. Lovett (1986, 54) remarks, "The renegade prince played a highly dangerous game. He continued to lead the imperial army in Germany while conducting a treasonable correspondence with his former co-religionists, the Lutherans, and with the French king. He knew that the imperial army, of which he was the field commander, acted as a guarantor of Charles's shaky pre-eminence; therefore, he must set about undermining its efficiency. To do this, Maurice continued to campaign against isolated Lutheran cities which had refused to surrender after the collapse of the Schmalkaldic League, since this would drain the emperor's resources. The siege of Magdeburg, undertaken from 1550 to 1551, was intended not to reduce the town but to dissipate the imperial war chest; and this is exactly what it did." Historians have offered the betrayal of his father by Maurice as one explanation for Philip's heavy-handed attitude toward local elites in many of his domains, most notably the Netherlands.

[163] Elton 1964, 263–64.

[164] te Brake 1998, 48. See also Blockmans 2002, 99; and Wallace 2004, 116.

Between 1555 and 1556 Charles abdicated his titles, granting the emperorship to the "Austrian" branch of the family and reserving his Italian, Burgundian, and Spanish inheritances for his son, Philip II. The move stunned his contemporaries. His abdication speech in the Low Countries brought his audience to tears.[165] Although Philip would not become King of the Romans, Charles contented himself with a marriage alliance (July 1554) between Philip and Mary Tudor. This held out the possibility of a successful Catholic restoration in England, and, if Philip and Mary produced an heir, a consolidated Habsburg agglomeration including England and the Burgundian inheritances, as well as a possible regency government in England headed by Philip himself.[166]

Consequences

Historians and social scientists have long debated the impact of the Religious Peace of Augsburg and Charles's abdication on the future of the European state system. Did Augsburg mark the start of a fully sovereign state system in Europe? When Charles abdicated, did he put an end to one of the last remnants of the medieval order? Did the sixty-odd years between Augsburg and Westphalia constitute a unique phase in the transformation of the European state system or simply a period of Spanish Habsburg hegemony? These issues have been partially addressed in chapter 3: Augsburg and abdication were important moments, at the very least for the constellation of European politics. Their immediate significance for something like the origins of the modern state system are less clear. Charles's abdication did not put an end to the viability of the dynastic-imperial pathway of European state formation, but rather split the Habsburg domains into two dynastic-imperial composites.

Augsburg represented an outcome to religious conflict in the empire that favored territorialization under princes to alternative forms of political organization. The confessional alliances between Protestant princes and towns put the former in a position of relative power. Once Lutheran and Catholic princes alike joined together to preserve the imperial peace, it was their erstwhile allies among the towns and localities who found themselves isolated.

Nevertheless, the change in the relative balance of political forces within the empire only became clear over the long haul. James Kittelson sums up the differences between the German political order in 1500 and 1600 by pointing out that, on the surface, little changed as a result of reformation and Augsburg: "The Empire still did not function like a true

---

[165] Koenigsberger 1971b, 59.
[166] Bonney 1991, 122–23.

state, and it still had difficulty keeping the peace among competing cities, principalities, bishoprics, and the like, nor could it decisively defend its borders against the Turk."[167]

THE DIVISION OF THE HABSBURG LANDS

Charles's abdication split the Habsburg domains into two parts (and possibly three, if Philip II and Mary produced an heir and proceeded with Charles's strategy). Both Philip II and Ferdinand now controlled dynastic agglomerations with less manpower and wealth than that of Charles V. Yet, in important respects, the division provided advantages to both "Austrian" and "Spanish" Habsburg rulers. Ferdinand and his heirs no longer directly contended with the Valois-Habsburg rivalry. Philip could focus upon building the power and influence of his Spanish monarchy. By ending religious conflict in the empire, if only on a temporary basis, the Peace of Augsburg facilitated these aims.[168]

Philip inherited a more manageable empire, one in which Castile became the unequivocal metropole. In truth, this process had already begun after the *Comuneros* revolt, as Charles leaned more and more upon Castilian wealth and manpower to service his dynastic ambitions. But as long as Charles ruled, the Habsburg domains remained polycentric; after his abdication,

> Castile became, and was to remain, the centre of an empire which was now indisputably Spanish. As a consequence of this new alignment the overseas possessions became, even more so than they had under Charles, the focal point of the monarchy, while those areas, most crucially the Netherlands, Milan, and Naples, which had been central to the older imperial structure, now found themselves on the periphery.[169]

Even though Philip would not possess the title "Emperor," Castile was still "the only viable candidate for a true universal empire" in Europe, a fact recognized by the rest of Latin Christendom and acknowledged by Charles's heirs in their court culture and political style.[170] In this respect the significance for the empire of the first forty years of the Reformations

---

[167] Kittelson 1986, S136.

[168] Nevertheless, we should not decide that Ferdinand's conclusion of the Peace of Augsburg showed an indifference to religion in the face of political calculations. As Paula Fichtner (1980, 27) remarks, "He certainly did not regard the Augsburg settlement as permanent. But his support of the reform position within the church, with its attendant conviction that the Protestant heresy was the result largely of moral weaknesses within the Catholic hierarchy, was so consistent that to see it merely as a reflection of Realpolitik or the result of bad judgment is to trivialize its function in his thinking."

[169] Pagden 1995, 44.

[170] Ibid., 43.

was not the ending of "universal empire," but the concrete fragmentation of the particular dynastic agglomeration cobbled together under Charles V, as well as the turn of the Austrian branch toward dynastic consolidation in its patrimonial domains.[171] Both of these developments were of enormous import for the future of state and system formation in early modern Europe.

THE RELIGIOUS PEACE OF AUGSBURG

The Peace of Augsburg succeeded in bringing nearly seventy years of stability to the empire. The principal of *cuius regio eius religio* established a connection between rule, territory, and religion and served to shift the balance of forces in the empire further toward territorial (and princely) authority. The right of religious dissenters to emigrate from territories that did not practice their faiths further expanded the territorially exclusive nature of rule and religion.[172] Yet the Peace's provisions failed to resolve disagreements over who exactly was a territorial ruler, and thus who had the right to implement religious practices. This led to a number of "peculiar local solutions" that often undermined the religious status quo Augsburg was supposed to maintain. In general, the progress of the Reformations did not slow or stop with Augsburg.[173]

The manner in which religious conflicts unfolded under Charles's reign strengthened princely power at the expense of cities and towns. Princes emerged as the key political and military actors in the various leagues and alliances that took shape during confessional conflict. At the same time, the push for "national" churches among Protestant princes and the concurrent spread of state-sponsored Catholic orthodoxy in Catholic lands further crystallized the relationship between state, territory, and religion discussed above.

> Even in northern and northwestern Germany the system of imperial peace and territorialization was maintained, supported by a solidarity among the territorial rulers that crossed confessional lines. It was the individual princes who felt the full impact of the "new commotion" present within the Hanseatic cities when the they attempted to integrate the local, home-grown Protestant city churches into their territorial

---

[171] See Evans 1979; Ingrao 2000; and Kann 1974.

[172] John Gerard Ruggie (1993) is among those social scientists who emphasize this connection as crucial to the development of sovereign territoriality. We should keep in mind, however, that the original principle was "*Ubi unus dominus, ibi una suit religio* ["Where there is one lord, there should be one religion"]. . . . [T]he territorial was not directly expressed but only hinted at in the Peace of Augsburg, in which *religio* did not originally mean religious confession but the public practice of religion." See Tüchle 1971, 155.

[173] Tüchle 1971, 160–61.

churches according to the principle of *cuius regio eius religio*. The religious confrontation was especially fierce during the confessional age, and the princes used it to break the medieval freedom and autonomy enjoyed by cities and to replace it with the unified authority and sovereignty of the early modern state.[174]

These same factors also hardened theological and ritual differences between religious confessions—again, often along territorial lines. Princely co-optation of Lutheran and Catholic impulses, now under the rubric of Augsburg, worked—although only gradually and not without reversals—as a vector of political influence over rival pockets of power.[175] Such processes of "confessionalization" are sometimes given more weight than they deserve in explaining sixteenth- and seventeenth-century state formation, but to the extent that Augsburg ratified and forwarded them, the Peace reinforced trends toward sovereign territoriality.[176]

Finally, Augsburg only recognized the validity of Catholicism and the Augsburg Confession; it provided no toleration for Calvinism, which was rapidly emerging as the most vibrant and influential movement of the Reformations. This, in addition to the ambiguities it contained with respect to control over local Churches, undermined the Peace and finally led to its collapse in the events that precipitated the Thirty Years' War.

Conclusions

A confluence of dynamics shaped the fate of Charles's dynastic ambitions. Economic changes and military-technical developments greatly impacted Charles's fortunes. Fiscal strains, inflation, and the difficulty of mounting long-term offensive operations in the face of advancements in defensive warfare contributed to Habsburg overextension. So did a host of individual deaths, recoveries, and mistakes in diplomacy and on the battlefield. The personalities of many individuals, not least of all Charles, played their part as well. In the fabric of historical events, it is often impossible to isolate and remove individual threads and still maintain the overall pattern.

In this chapter we have seen how foolish it would be to dismiss the politics of identity as a causal factor in Charles's ability to manage his empire. In Castile, Charles's actions confirmed the rhetoric against him: that he intended to turn Castile into a playground for his Flemish "favorites" and bleed its resources in far-off military campaigns. The

---

[174] Schilling 1992, 36.
[175] te Brake 1998, 48.
[176] Gorski 1999 and 2003, Schilling 1992.

resulting uprising failed because of the inability of the *Comuneros* and the nobility to bridge their differences. Charles and his advisors exploited their rift by offering selective incentives and concessions that won the aristocracy over to the royal cause. The importance of Castile to Charles's dynastic interests led him to make a series of commitments that laid the groundwork for the Castilianization of his empire. These commitments, ironically, made credible the very arguments for Castilian support—the defense of Catholicism and the glory of Castile—that Mota had found fruitless before the *cortes*.

Perhaps even more striking was the role of religious polarization in the ultimate division of the Habsburg domains and the end of the largest composite political community Europe had yet seen.[177] Disputes over doctrine broke alliances and paved the way to civil war in the empire. Yet however historically specific the doctrines and personalities of Reformation Germany, the dynamics they triggered fit the more general pattern found in low-capacity empires. Religious polarization destroyed the old tools of Habsburg authority—such as the Swabian League. At the same time it allowed Protestant Princes to concentrate practical power into their own hands and to forge alliances with towns and other princes—those whom the emperor would normally seek to play off against them. The process of "territorialization" that the Reformations accelerated was, in many ways, an example of the broader dynamic of patrimonial secession.

Some social scientists, particularly in the field of international relations, dismiss the importance of religious beliefs to political outcomes, arguing that they mask underlying material interests or power-political calculations. There is an irony here, in at least two respects. In the first decade of his reign Charles's greatest mistake in understanding the implications of the Reformations was to see them in precisely those terms: as nothing more than "political" maneuvers by malcontents against their emperor. As a result, he consistently underestimated the damage anti-Protestant policies would do to his position in Germany. Once Charles finally understood the challenge, and had the opportunity to move against it, Charles masked his religious goals behind political rhetoric. His victory gave way to defeat because, in part, Charles pushed forward a religious settlement that alienated Protestant allies.

But just as religious interests could trump power-political ones, so, too, could power-political interests overcome religious scruples. We have seen

---

[177] Rome at its greatest extent may have controlled more contiguous territory, but we should not forget that Charles ruled over the Castilian New World empire. If we count the Mongol Empire as a "European" composite political community—because of its territory west of the Urals—then Charles' empire was merely the second largest.

in this chapter, as we will see in subsequent chapters, that the interplay between various identities and interests can elicit different behaviors, even from the same individuals. In Germany, at least, the Peace of Augsburg represented a genuine desire for peace among many on both sides; that desire helped keep the peace until it was finally undone by a series of disputes involving religion and authority.

Charles's abdication did not end the quest to secure and maintain Habsburg hegemony; the dominant political force in Europe now became a Spanish empire headed by Charles's son, Philip II. Like father like son: many factors contributed to the strategic overreach of Philip's empire, but questions of religion and identity helped spark rebellions that would prove his undoing. The most important of these was the Dutch Revolt, an uprising whose seriousness was made possible by the spread of international Calvinism and perceptions of Philip's Castilian identity.

What of Charles's reign as a whole? Blockmans's judgment seems apt: "Charles would have wanted peace among all Christians and the defense of the Catholic Church as the themes of his reign; because of the policies he followed, however, his reign ended in more warfare, higher taxation, decreasing prosperity and growing repression."[178]

---

[178] Blockmans 2002, 166.

CHAPTER 6

The Dynamics of Spanish Hegemony in the Sixteenth and Early Seventeenth Centuries

NEITHER THE PEACE OF AUGSBURG nor Charles's abdication brought an end to military conflict in Western Europe. Charles's son, Philip II, prosecuted the Habsburg-Valois rivalry with renewed vigor. Free of German entanglements, Philip routed the French in Italy and in northern France. But the costs of chronic warfare once again outstripped the capacities of early modern rulers to extract revenue and resources from their domains. In 1557 Philip's government entered into bankruptcy; Henry II's court soon followed suit.

Other factors also inclined both monarchs toward peace. Henry II, whose manipulation of Protestant grievances against Charles had proven so successful in advancing French interests, became increasingly concerned about the growth of a new, more militant heresy among his own people. According to Frederic J. Baumgartner, "It is difficult to escape the conclusion that Henry wanted most of all to turn his attention to the religious problems in France." Both Philip II and Henry recognized the threat Protestantism posed to domestic stability in their respective monarchies.[1]

Fiscal collapse and religious dissent brought the two parties to the table, but another pressing event precluded an immediate peace. On 17 November 1558 Mary Tudor, Queen of England and Philip's wife, died. Elizabeth, her sister, succeeded her. Mary's death had far-reaching implications. Philip was no longer king of England; his loss of influence had ramifications for the religious and military balance in Western Europe. Observers, moreover, remained unsure about what policies Elizabeth would adopt concerning both foreign affairs and religious doctrine.[2] Both the Castilian and French courts jockeyed for influence. Since Mary Stuart, Henry II's daughter-in-law, stood as next in line to the throne, Philip

---

[1] Baumgartner 1988, 231. See also Elliott 2000, 4–5; Kamen 1997, 66–71; and Koenigsberger 1994a, 176. I should note a parallel here with the notion of "omnibalancing": that leaders in weak states balance not simply against external but also against internal threats. In these terms, Henry II changed his alliance policies because of the pressing nature of internal challenges to his regime. See David 1991a and 1991b.

[2] Elliott 2000, 4.

found himself taking steps to protect a Protestant-leaning regime against a Catholic power.[3]

The Treaty of Cateau-Cambrésis, signed by Castile and France in 1559, represented the new realities faced by Habsburg and Valois. It, in some respects, inaugurated an era of dynastic peace, during which time Western European politics became dominated by confessional conflicts. If Henry had lived longer, Cateau-Cambrésis might have proven as empty a peace as the previous half-century of Habsburg-Valois agreements. But Henry II's death, the result of an injury from a jousting accident at the ceremonies celebrating Cateau-Cambrésis, helped guarantee that France would descend into religious warfare (see chapter 7).[4]

International-relations scholars often treat the history of Spain from the ascension of Philip II until the Treaty of the Pyrenees (1659) as a near-paradigmatic case of hegemonic overextension (figure 6.1). Paul Kennedy calls it "one of the greatest examples of imperial overstretch in history."[5] The Spanish Habsburgs did, indeed, find themselves fighting too many wars on too many fronts. At one point or another they engaged in some combination of campaigns against the Turks, French, Danes, Swedes, and the English (among others). They fought in Italy, in Germany, in the Low Countries, in France, and in the Atlantic. Consistent with expectations of hegemonic-cycle and power-transition theorists, the Habsburgs sustained these multifront engagements by depleting their resources and ruining the economy of Castile.[6] The key blow to Spain's hegemonic aspirations, however, came from rebellion at home. The Count-Duke Olivares's attempt to spread the burdens of warfare across the Spanish Habsburg's

---

[3] Kamen 1997, 72. These sorts of behaviors give credence to realist interpretations about the relative influence of religious identities and power-political concerns. But, as I argued in previous chapters, we lose analytic purchase on such dynamics if we reduce them to a test between "logics of appropriateness" and "logics of consequences." Philip, in this case, rationalized conflicting dynastic and religious interests in one particular way at one specific moment.

[4] Baumgartner 1988, 260–61.

[5] Kennedy 1987, 112. See also Kupchan 1996, 35. Kennedy stresses the interplay of religion and great-power cycles, but realists often downplay or ignore this conjunction.

[6] There is significant historical debate over whether Castile's economy--and the Spanish Empire more broadly--was "in decline" during the latter part of the sixteenth century. Elliott (1989, 239) argues that the final collapse of Spain was simply "the logical dénouement of the economic crisis which destroyed the foundations of Castile's power, and of the psychological crisis which impelled it into its final bid for world supremacy." Consistent with power-transition expectations, Castille's domestic economy appears to have stagnated under the twin pressures of foreign warfare and economic mismanagement. See Flynn 1982. At the same time, the fate of Spanish military power does not correlate well with economic stagnation, which suggests we should be cautious about mapping long-term expectations derived from theories of hegemonic decline with actual political events in the sixteenth and seventeenth centuries. See Stradling 1994, 8–9.

Figure 6.1 The Domains of Philip II

non-Castilian subjects led to a series of rebellions that rapidly tilted the strategic balance against the empire (see chapter 8).

In the previous chapter, I focused upon the counterfactual problem posed by the existence of multiple mechanisms that each worked to undermine Charles's dynastic ambitions and the dynastic imperial trajectory of state formation. We face a similar problem when considering the reigns of Philip II, Philip III, and Philip IV. Many processes—nascent balance-of-power politics, financial strains, contingencies of weather and military encounters, religious conflicts—came together in particular historical configurations to bring about outcomes that shaped the future of European states and political relations.

However we weigh these factors, the failure of Spain's bid for hegemony cannot simply be written off, contra realist analysis, to the balance-of-power mechanism. Steven Walt is only partially correct when he argues that the "overwhelming tendency for states to balance . . . defeated the hegemonic aspirations of Philip II."[7] Spanish power and the fears it invoked in other polities did not, by themselves, lead to overstretch. Nor did the purported inefficiency of Spanish resource-extraction and fiscal policy.[8] The Dutch Revolt played a major role in Spanish decline; we cannot understand it, in turn, without reference to the interplay of religious contention and imperial structures.

> For eighty years (1568–1648) the revolt drained tax revenue from Castile and its American empire and weakened the fragile links connecting the Habsburg possessions in Europe. The revolt also disrupted Castile's lucrative wool trade with Flanders, a trade that had been synonymous with Castilian prosperity since long before the discovery of the New World.[9]

According to Geoffrey Parker, although the French destroyed the Spanish Empire, the Dutch Revolt amounted to "a weakening hold which, long applied, debilitates a wrestler so that he will more easily submit under a more deadly attack from a different quarter."[10] Protracted conflict in the Netherlands and the eventual loss of the northern provinces proved an enormous blow to Spanish Habsburg power. It drew the Spanish monarchy into conflicts with England; it transformed the great territorial arc encircling France into a strategic liability.[11] A stable Netherlands, as Jonathan Israel notes, "was, from many points of view, the ideal strategic base for Habsburg power in Europe," one that gave the Spanish Habsburgs the ability "to penetrate into France almost at will, while the French could effect little against the Netherlands."[12]

This chapter continues my analysis of Habsburg overextension in terms of the dynamics of resistance and rule in early modern composite states. I focus on the Netherlands from Philip II's ascension until the conclusion of the Twelve Years' Truce of 1609. The Dutch Revolt deserves special attention not only because of its significance for Spanish Habsburg overextension, but also because it provides further evidence for how the spread of heterodox religious movements triggered critical mechanisms and processes associated with the relational structure of dynastic agglomerations. I also survey other cases of resistance against Habsburg rule, however. Many of these cases highlight some of the different configura-

---

[7] Walt 1985, 15. For Walt's "balance-of-threat" argument, see Walt 1987.
[8] G. Parker 1998, 112–13.
[9] Phillips and Phillips 1977, 312–13.
[10] G. Parker 1972, 267.
[11] See Allen 2000, and G. Parker 1972, 1977, and 1998.
[12] Israel 1995, 131–32.

tions of rule and resistance that predominated in the absence of polarized religious contention, or that developed amidst different religious distinctions—such as that between Catholics and Muslims.

I begin with a discussion of the Spanish monarchy at the start of Philip II's reign. The steps toward "Castilianization" taken under Charles V reached fruition under Philip, not only because the loss of the eastern Habsburg domains left Castile the clear epicenter of its "Spanish" successor, but also because of the decisions taken by Charles to consolidate his position in Castile after the *Comuneros* revolt. Catholicism and Castile conjoined under Philip in ways that limited his ability to engage in multivocal signaling with respect to other domains.

Philip also faced a major challenge from the Ottoman Empire. Philip prioritized his Mediterranean interests, in part because of the threat posed by linkages between external Islamic rivals and the Moorish population in Castile. This decision, generated by the inevitable cross-pressures associated with the heterogeneous character of the Spanish monarchy, entailed a relative neglect of developments in the Netherlands. Had Philip decided to bring overwhelming force to bear against the rebellion early on, it would almost certainly have failed.[13]

The next section, which comprises the bulk of this chapter, carefully traces processes of resistance, rule, brokerage, and signaling in the Netherlands. The Dutch Revolt provides crucial evidence for my theoretical claims. If alternative, sparer theories make sense of the revolt, then we have little need to resort to the claims I make about understanding the impact of the Reformations on early modern European politics. But, of course, I reject alternative accounts that focus simply on ideational or material causes.

Thereafter I explore additional developments during the reigns of Philip II and Philip III. I focus on Philip II's acquisition of Portugal and instability in Catalonia and Aragon. I then consider all of these developments in light of the geopolitics of the Spanish Empire. The final section takes our story into the seventeenth century and sets the stage for my discussion of the Thirty Years' War in chapter 8.

PHILIP II TAKES CONTROL

Philip embraced, at first, many aspects of Charles's strategy of imperial management. Philip spent time in the Low Countries in order to prosecute the war against the Valois and to arrange for the peace established by Treaty of Cateau-Cambrésis. He appointed Margaret of Parma, an

[13] Darby 2001a, 5; León and Parker 2001.

190 • Chapter 6

illegitimate daughter of Charles, to serve as viceroy in the Burgundian inheritance. She was assisted by a Council of State that included, among others: William of Orange (Count of Nassau, also appointed stadholder, or steward, of Holland, Zeeland, and Utrecht); Lamorall (Count of Egmond, also appointed stadholder of Flanders and Artois); and two members of the royal bureaucracy—Vigilius van Aytta and Cardinal Antoine Perrenot de Granvelle.[14]

Margaret's appointment continued Charles's practice of ruling the Low Countries through a deputy of the Habsburg—and thus, dynastic—bloodline. Doing so signaled a commitment to the importance of the Netherlands in the monarchy. Furthermore, Orange's presence in the Council of State affirmed that Philip would consult with local notables over important matters of policy and administration, while Granvelle was known for his loyalty both to the Habsburgs and the Catholic cause.[15]

Such a mix made a great deal of sense. Habsburg rule faced serious ongoing challenges in the Low Countries. Locals resented the presence of Spanish troops. The spread of religious nonconformity, combined with Habsburg policies to suppress heresy, supplied an ongoing source of tensions. Many debts remained from the recent Habsburg-Valois conflict. The provinces added under Charles V remained unstable. But problems elsewhere required Philip's attention.[16]

Philip returned to Castile in September 1559. In a marked departure from the roving court of his father, he would never again leave Iberia. At home he confronted a number of pressing concerns: the apparent discovery of Protestant cells in Seville and Valladolid, food shortages, and a deteriorating war with the Ottoman Turks. To make matters worse, the crown's fiscal situation proved desperate. The gravity of the crisis in Castile soon became apparent: "I have to admit," he wrote, "that I never thought that while I was in the Netherlands that things could be so bad here."[17]

Castile and Catholicism

Philip's reign witnessed the Castilianization of the empire he inherited from his father. The seeds of this process began under Charles. In order to solidify his position in Castile, Charles promised to respect Castile's traditional privileges and to give Castile a place of priority among his

[14] Israel 1995, 139.
[15] Ibid., 138–39; Kamen 1997, 75; Ortíz 1971, 70–71.
[16] Israel 1995, 137; Kamen 1997, 75; G. Parker 1977, 42–43.
[17] Quoted in G. Parker 1977, 43–45. See also Elliott 1970, 212–24; Kamen 1997, 79–89; and Lovett 1986, 124–25.

domains. Charles required Castilian wealth and military capabilities for his imperial ambitions. By the end of Charles's reign, Castile and Castilians enjoyed a place of increasing predominance in the Habsburg Empire.

Over the next few decades, most observers came to recognize this reality. The very fact that Philip had been born and raised in Castile risked marking him as a Spanish ruler; as Koenigsberger writes, the "overwhelming impression which Philip gave to his contemporaries was that he was a Spanish king, ruling a Spanish empire in the interests of Spaniards."[18] Indeed, Philip's return to Castile meant that "events were seen and judged from Spain, in a Spanish ambience, by Spanish personnel, and in Spanish interests."[19] Philip's identity, his removal to Castile, and the changes in the Habsburg domains brought about by their division shifted the Netherlands to a peripheral position in the empire.[20] By the early 1590s few could harbor "any doubt as to the nature of Philip II's monarchy" as a "Spanish empire."[21]

Philip was a devout Catholic, but he also proved willing to make alliances with Protestant states. He even utilized Protestant troops in Flanders. Henry Kamen points to evidence that Philip considered permitting religious toleration in England in the event of a Spanish victory against Elizabeth.[22] Nevertheless, Philip refused to tolerate heresy in his own dominions. Parker notes that he "felt he possessed a direct mandate to uphold the Catholic faith at almost all times and in almost all places."[23] Although Philip saw himself as the ruler of many different, equally important polities, he also believed that he could override the customary rights and privileges of his holdings if required to do so by the imperative of preserving the Catholic faith. Neither strict claims about the primacy of power politics nor religious concerns explain Philip's decisions.[24]

Philip's unwillingness to countenance Protestantism involved other, more complicated rationales. First, Philip, along with many of his contemporaries, believed that policies of toleration led to sedition and rebellion. The outbreak of civil war in France only reinforced this view. Philip became "convinced that any concessions to the nobles would lead to a rapid collapse into the situation France was currently facing."[25] Second, in 1567, at a crucial moment in the evolution of the Dutch Revolt, Philip received news of a failed plot to overthrow his authority in Mexico. This

---

[18] Koenigsberger 1986, 115.
[19] Lynch 1991, 253.
[20] Koenigsberger 1986, 83. See also Elliott 1963a, 211; and Pagden 1995.
[21] Koenigsberger 1986, 85.
[22] Kamen 1997, 230, 233.
[23] G. Parker 1998, 93.
[24] Koenigsberger 1986, 112–13.
[25] Kamen 1997, 230, 233.

reinforced the view of Philip and his advisors that if his authority was undermined in *any* of his dominions, sedition would soon spread.[26] Third, Philip also needed a strong policy against heresy to reassure the papacy, whose support Philip required for his wider geostrategic interests.[27] Finally, the clear failure of Charles's cosmopolitanism left Hispano-Catholic imperialism as the main ideological alternative for the rump Habsburg domains. Philip's reign marked his empire as one part Spanish, one part Catholic.[28]

Conflict with Islam

In 1560 a Spanish-Italian campaign to capture Tripoli ended in disaster, making an already bad situation in the Mediterranean worse. Islamic corsairs stepped up their raids along the coast of already-unstable Granada. Agents of the Crown encroached on the economic activities and property of the Moriscos while conducting an on-again, off-again campaign of religious persecution. The combination of intermediary autonomy, local grievances against royal power, and religion created problems for imperial rule. The Ottomans hoped to rally the Morisco population against Philip. They made ample use of Morisco spies throughout Philip's Mediterranean possessions, and one of their agents revealed, under torture, the existence of a plot by the Turks to seize the coast of Granada.[29]

In 1565 Turkish forces laid siege to Malta. In the ensuing atmosphere of crisis, the local authorities in Granada decided to forcibly assimilate the Moriscos. Morisco officials responded by opening negotiations with Philip and his administrators, but Philip, unlike his father, refused to accept their protestations of loyalty. His position triggered a significant Morisco rebellion, concentrated in the rural hinterland of Granada, that lasted from 1568 to 1570. At its peak, the insurgency involved roughly thirty thousand combatants. Once the uprising was over, Philip approved a series of mass deportations designed to weaken Morisco cohesion and bring about assimilation by dispersing the Morisco population throughout Castile. This policy, however, only widened the geographic scope of the Morisco "problem."[30]

The Turks took advantage of the insurgency to improve their strategic position in the eastern Mediterranean; they attacked Venetian-controlled Cyprus. The Venetians and Spanish put aside their usual rivalry and

---

[26] Ibid. For a general discussion of this "domino" theory, see G. Parker 1998, 89.
[27] Kamen 1997, 116.
[28] Pagden 1995.
[29] Elliott 1963a, 239; Kamen 1997, 129; Lynch 1991, 312–13.
[30] Elliott 1963a, 240, and 2000, 123–25; Kamen 1997, 129–31; Lynch 1991, 313–18.

formed, with the pope's blessing, a "Holy Alliance" against the Turks. Meanwhile, the temporary success of stadholder Duke of Alva in the Netherlands (about whom see below) freed additional resources to support offensive operations in the Mediterranean. On 7 October 1571 the combined Italian and Spanish forces defeated the Turkish fleet at Lepanto. Soon afterwards the Venetians broke ranks and began negotiating with the Turks. Nevertheless, Philip's decision to make the Mediterranean a strategic priority turned back the Ottoman tide. Although defense of the Mediterranean continued to consume money and resources into 1572, the Turks no longer posed an imminent threat to Italy and Iberia, even less so as the Ottomans shifted their attention to their border with Persia.[31]

Whatever victory Philip could claim, these troubles stemmed in no small part from failures of imperial management in the context of religious contention and local grievances. Despite forcible conversion, the Moriscos' distinctive identity and a continued sense of Islamic religious orientation among some of their ranks—reinforced through persecution—provided important linkages to external powers. These linkages facilitated the uprising and distracted Philip from developments in Northern Europe tied to the spread of religious heterodoxy, particularly the rising force of Calvinism. Thus, it was only after Lepanto that Philip was able to turn the resources of his empire toward the deteriorating situation in the Netherlands.

REBELLION IN THE NETHERLANDS

Historians have long disagreed about the causes of the Dutch Revolt. Some have seen it as a struggle for national independence. Others stress economic interests, such as resistance to fiscal demands or new social relations brought about by economic change. Some even portray the revolt as an early revolution of the bourgeoisie. Still others argue that the defense of local privileges against the growing centralization and absolutism of Philip's reign provided the key motivation of the rebels. Another venerable tradition paints it as primarily a religious conflict, either one between Protestants and Catholics or one on behalf of religious liberty. Yet another set of scholars locate the underlying causes of the revolt in the incompatible interests of the northern and southern Low Countries—differences dating back to the formation of the Burgundian state. Another debate cuts across all these traditions: whether or not to characterize the rebellion as "revolutionary."[32]

---

[31] Chudoba 1969, 86–93; Elliott 2000, 125–31; Lovett 1986, 67–78.
[32] For an excellent summary, see Nierop 2001b, 30–32. See also Griffiths 1960, 454; and Rowen 1990, 570.

We should not treat the Dutch Revolt as a single episode. Contention in the Netherlands during Philip's reign involved a series of linked conflicts and a number of different phases of resistance. At various times, different actors, coalitions, and interests took the leading role. At one point or another, magnates, lesser nobles, Calvinists, and townsfolk—or coalitions of these groups—played key roles in contestation and resistance.[33] No matter how we choose to view it, however, the causes of the uprising stemmed from a conjunction of two dynamics: first, grievances relating to processes of centralization; and, second, the political effects of religious divisions.

Indeed, the questions of heresy and centralization intertwined such that central authorities and local actors—whether intermediaries, elites, or ordinary people—faced enormous barriers to concluding peaceful settlements of their disputes. Although Philip's policies produced alliances against him that crossed religious divisions, cleavages between Protestant extremists and Catholic moderates ultimately destroyed the possibility of a Netherlands-wide rebellion. By 1590, when the States General declared the existence of a "sovereign republic," the northern provinces and Calvinist forces dominated the revolt. Indeed, the revolt evolved into a conflict between two polities: the Dutch Republic and the Spanish Monarchy. Even after Philip III succeeded his father as king and economic and strategic interests perpetuated the conflict, religion remained one of the crucial obstacles to some form of reconciliation, let alone peace. The Twelve Years' Truce of 1609 represented the de facto recognition by the Habsburgs of the Dutch Republic's independence, but only in 1648 did Spain finally officially recognize its sovereignty.

Background

I have already discussed some of the political history of the Netherlands, particularly the rebellion following Charles the Bold's death in 1477 and the uprising in Ghent in 1540, in previous chapters. Still, some additional background is in order. First, Habsburg policies of administrative centralization had, since Maximilian's reign, eroded civic autonomy and the relative position of the guilds in the Netherlands. These changes also effectively expanded the power of the Estates as regional governing bodies. Second, upon assuming the throne, Charles stepped up military pressure on those northwest provinces that remained independent. Third, the spread of the Reformations to the Netherlands led to a variety of shifts in the region's political dynamics (figure 6.2).

[33] Darby 2001b, 16–25.

Figure 6.2 The Netherlands Prior to the Dutch Revolt

Such centralizing policies alienated many nobles and produced tensions with local elites. During his reign, Charles placed stadholders (intermediary governors) throughout most of the provinces of the Low Countries. Only Brabant and Mechelen escaped, largely because of their proximity to the capital in Brussels. Furthermore, Charles strove to increase the efficiency of his administration: he both reduced the number of administrative officials and staffed his administration largely with university-trained jurists. The nobility found themselves gradually sidelined from many of the organs of state. Charles sought to maintain their support by compensating them with pensions and land, as well transforming them into counts and dukes. Church patronage provided for their younger sons.[34]

Almost immediately upon assuming the throne, Charles began his campaign to unify the Netherlands with a major incursion into Friesland and Groningen. After some initial successes, the operation lost momentum.[35] With neither the time nor the resources to mount a prolonged campaign, Charles allowed Holland to take over the effort of subjugating the remaining independent states. Holland eventually succeeded in defeating the anti-Habsburg forces in most of the northwest, and with Charles's victory over the Schmalkaldic League in Germany, the "Burgundian 'circle' " was finally established in 1548.[36]

Despite Holland's importance in this struggle, Charles prevented it from reaping much in the way of territorial benefits. He annexed those provinces conquered between 1516 and 1548 as part of the Netherlands. This created significant grievances in Holland.[37] The conflict also had at least one important side effect: the States of Holland gained experience, expertise, and infrastructure for managing credit and loans.[38]

During the same period, reformation penetrated the Low Countries. For economic, social, and cultural reasons, the Netherlands proved amiable territory for reformation.[39] But reformation in the Low Countries, at least before the 1550s, lacked much in the way of coherence. Martin Luther's writings influenced many there, but organized Lutheranism faltered. Charles's quick organization of an effective repressive apparatus stifled Lutheran activities; however, the powerful humanist strain in the intellectual life of the Low Countries also worked against formal Lutheranism. Repression ultimately forced "the country's intellectual élites to draw a veil of concealment over their religious beliefs, discussions, and

---

[34] Israel 1995, 34–39; Nierop 2001b, 49–50; Rosenfeld 1971, 257–64.
[35] Israel 1995, 34.
[36] Bonney 1991, 113; Tracy 1990, 64–89.
[37] Israel 1995, 56–70.
[38] Darby 2001b, 15; Tracy 1990, 115–46, and 1999, 135. Charles financed his wars, in general, through means that devolved fiscal responsibility to the States.
[39] For greater elaboration, see Bonney 1991, 9–13; and Israel 1995, 43–54.

reading." Thus, while German Protestantism split between often antagonist confessional camps, reformation in the Low Countries operated mostly through crypto-Protestantism by the 1520s.[40]

Anabaptism emerged as the first major organized reformation movement the Netherlands. Anabaptism made significant inroads, involving ordinary people and nobles alike. Some noble families actively sought to shield Anabaptists from persecution, in a pattern Gary Waite argues presaged the formation of strong coalitions between the gentry and Calvinists in the period of the Dutch Revolt.[41] The radicalism associated with Anabaptism—reinforced by the takeover of Münster—combined with Charles's outwardly successful antiheresy campaign, worked to limit the spread of Anabaptism. The result: "In general, the broad response of the Netherlands élites was to strive for one or another theological *via media*, enabling them to reject the old Church inwardly, and partake of new theologies, while, at the same time, outwardly conforming to Catholicism." The tradition of humanism, widespread crypto-Protestantism, and the sorry state of the Church in the Netherlands meant that a large proportion of the population of the Netherlands resented Charles's suppression of heresy.[42]

Despite these tensions, Charles had many reasons for optimism when he turned over the throne to Philip. Of the Netherlands, Charles commented, "There were no people in the world, who, governed mildly (*paternellement*), were more docile to the wishes of their prince than those of the Low Countries."[43] If Philip could maintain their sense of independence, their customs, and the status of the magnates, then all would be well.

The Struggle for Control of Governance (1559–1565)

The first phase of political contestation in the Netherlands involved a classic struggle between local elites and centrally appointed intermediaries. For more than fifty years processes of centralization undermined the authority and autonomy of local actors and institutions, including the magnates—yet Charles's stature and a general harmony of interests between him and his Netherlandish subjects limited serious resistance to the city of Ghent.[44] Since Philip lacked Charles's unique relationship with the Netherlands, he faced more resistance in continuing, let alone accelerat-

[40] Israel 1995, 83.
[41] Waite 1992, 485.
[42] Israel 1995, 94.
[43] Quoted in Bonney 1991, 146.
[44] Rowen 1988, 5.

ing, administrative centralization. The perception that he put Spanish interests before those of his other holdings reduced the willingness of his subjects to implement policies they found burdensome and, often, distasteful.[45] Broader shifts in the nature of governance also spelled trouble: by 1550, as I have noted, civil servants, rather than the nobility, dominated day-to-day royal administration in the Netherlands. Thus, substitutable elites had little to gain from centralizing reforms.[46]

When Philip departed the Netherlands in 1559, he left behind a garrison of Spanish troops to guard against the possibility of renewed French aggression. This rather sensible decision stoked fears that Philip intended to diminish local autonomy and violate the "customary rights" of the Low Countries. Cardinal Granvelle wrote that "people here universally display discontent with any and all Spaniards in these provinces. It would seem that this derives from the suspicion that *one might wish to subject them to Spain and reduce them to the same state as the Italian provinces under the Spanish crown*" [my emphasis].[47] The states responded with fiscal pressure. They not only refused to pay for the garrison, but also blocked the release of the Nine Years' Aid Philip needed to set his treasury in order. Philip conceded to their demands, and the garrison force departed in 1561.[48]

A majority of the Netherlander magnates chafed at the concentration of power in the hands of Granvelle. Granvelle's personality and his aggressive use of patronage on behalf of his family and friends during Charles's reign had already made him many enemies at court. These traits exacerbated the inevitable rivalries created by his privileged position in the administration of the Low Countries. Granvelle's control of patronage, however, assured him support in the judiciary and some corners of the Church; he developed a coalition with a few of the magnates, including the Duke of Aerschot. His political relations with the rest of the magnates, particularly Orange and Egmond, soon frayed.[49]

William, dubbed "the Silent" by Granvelle for his carefully chosen language—he frequently hid his true beliefs—was a proud and skilled political operative. As Prince of Orange, an Imperial fief in southern France, he had a unique status among his fellow magnates: he was a dynastic head of state in his own right, enjoying "juridical equality with the king of Spain himself" despite the actual insignificance of his dynastic holding.[50] Orange and his allies most likely aimed at monopolizing control over the

---

[45] Israel 1995, 139; G. Parker 1977, 45; Rowen 1988, 5–6.
[46] Waite 1992, 459.
[47] Parker 1998, 117.
[48] Ibid.
[49] Elliott 2000, 83–84; Israel 1995, 138–39.
[50] Rowen 1988, 11. See also Israel 1995, 139; and Koenigsberger 1986, 102.

daily functioning of the Low Countries and the access to patronage that went with that control. They saw themselves as the proper group to act as the king's intermediaries and expected a degree of autonomy comparable to that which regional lords enjoyed throughout Europe at the start of the sixteenth century.

They also disliked the ongoing persecution of heretics; although Granvelle himself believed in religious moderation, he represented the policies of the Habsburgs. Granvelle presented both an obstacle to Orange and his allies and, as a civil servant by background, an affront to their sense of status and prestige. Orange was a "constitutional conservative, accepting the established traditions in the Low Countries, where for centuries the dukes and counts had governed with the participation of States assemblies in conformity with hallowed practices and with respect for the power and wealth of the towns."[51]

Nevertheless, Orange's friendship with Granvelle and their tacit agreement to divide patronage between themselves helped ameliorate these tensions. That friendship ended by the summer of 1651, and the relationship between the two men turned venomous. The split occurred for a number of reasons, including Orange's failed attempt to secure the governorship of Franche-Compté for himself over a Granvelle protégé and Orange's decision to marry Anna of Saxony, niece of the Lutheran Elector of Saxony and daughter of Charles's betrayer, Maurice of Saxony. The match made financial and political sense for Orange, but it infuriated Granvelle and Philip: "The regent, the king and Granvelle did all they could to dissuade Orange and to sabotage his marriage plans; they even had the matter discussed by the Council of State. Orange was humiliated, but he persevered." In August of 1561 Orange married Anna.[52]

Orange and Egmond's rivalry with Granvelle harbored particularly dangerous possibilities for the existing order. The aristocracy of the Netherlands comprised a fairly cohesive group tied together through "intermarriage, government service, and patronage."[53] They also "had close ties with the nobility of the Empire," a factor that would prove important later on.[54] Therefore, if matters came to a head, Orange and Egmond had behind them a powerful, cross-regional coalition.[55] The crisis came when Philip decided to implement an ecclesiastical-reorganization scheme developed during Charles's reign.

[51] Rowen 1988, 10–11. See also Koenigsberger 1986, 102–3.
[52] G. Parker 1977, 51. See also Elliott 2000, 84–85; Israel 1995, 140; and Koenigsberger 1986, 98.
[53] G. Parker 1977, 49.
[54] Elliott 2000, 83; Nierop 1999, 84–85.
[55] On the importance of the magnates in the Netherlands, see Israel 1995, 139.

ECCLESIASTICAL REORGANIZATION AND THE ANTI-GRANVELLE CAMPAIGN

Reforming the ecclesiastical structure of the Netherlands made sense at a number of levels, as it had remained virtually unchanged since the Merovingian era. There were only four dioceses for the entire region, and the two that covered the bulk of the Low Countries, Rheims and Cologne, sat in German territory not subject to Habsburg authority. In 1559 the papacy agreed to create fourteen new bishoprics, with boundaries based upon linguistic groupings rather than the existing political divisions in the Netherlands. The financial structure of the Church in the Low Countries was also outmoded and inefficient, and so a new scheme was developed to draw revenues from existing abbeys. The plan aimed to increase the effectiveness of antiheresy measures. Hence, it expanded the number of inquisitors, and provided a means for putting in place "efficient, reliable churchmen, selected by virtue of education, and zeal, rather than aristocratic connections."[56]

We have already seen that much of the political impact of the Reformations derived from their intersection with conflicts between localism and centralization. While many of these connections involved contingent synergies, the suppression of heresy in the Netherlands depended upon political centralization. Its opponents stressed this relationship in their propaganda: they argued that the plan violated the privileges of the Netherlands and the contract between Philip, as sovereign prince, and his subjects.[57]

The plan itself could not have been better designed to trigger widespread resistance. From its development in relative secrecy, to Granvelle's appointment as the new archbishop of Mechelen to oversee its implementation, to its many provisions that threatened to erode local privileges and deny patronage to the nobility, to the threat it posed to religious dissent at a time of growing Protestant sympathies among the population, it threatened nearly everyone yet benefited very few. It provides a stark example, then, of the way central authorities might trigger cross-regional and cross-group resistance through poorly chosen policies. Opposition from all sides soon stymied attempts to implement the plan. The general backlash it engendered emboldened the anti-Granvelle faction to finally make their move.[58]

The plan united the Orange and Egmond faction with a large segment of the greater and lesser nobility, as well as ordinary townspeople and urban leaders. It brought together religious dissenters and nondissenters. The Habsburgs' intensifying antiheresy campaign further inflamed opin-

---

[56] Ibid., 143. See also Lovett 1986, 148; and G. Parker 1977, 47.
[57] Gelderen 1992, 110–15.
[58] Darby 2001b, 16; Duke 1999, 117; Geyl 1958, 74; Israel 1995, 143–44; G. Parker 1977, 48; Rowen 1988, 6–7.

ion. Granvelle and Philip alienated nearly every potential base of support within the Netherlands. The plan, in other words, sparked a complete failure of the divide-and-rule policies heads of dynastic agglomerations pursued to make their authority effective. Egmond and Orange, already operating as local intermediaries within the organs of state, emerged as crucial brokers between these disparate groups, while Granvelle lacked any significant local actors to which he could turn for support. As Parker dryly notes, "This was a remarkable achievement," given the traditional tensions between the nobility and the towns."[59]

The magnates, joined by the lesser nobility and led by Orange and Egmond, began a campaign to remove Granvelle from office. Montigny, one of the great nobles, left for Castile in 1562 to request Granvelle's withdrawal. When he failed, Orange, Egmond, and Hornes (another magnate in the Council of State) sent an ultimatum to Philip: unless Granvelle went, they would stop participating in the Council of State. Philip stood firm, and all three made good on their threat in July of 1563. Brabant opted to apply fiscal pressure: it withheld tax revenue from the king. Margaret soon decided to abandon Granvelle and, in August 1563, instructed her private secretary to convince Philip to dismiss him. Philip capitulated, and Granvelle left the Low Countries in March 1564. The possibility of continuing troubles in the Netherlands presented a major problem for Philip, as it undermined his plans to intervene in France against Huguenot forces (see chapter 7) and to prosecute the conflict in the Mediterranean.[60]

Philip faced a classic problem in composite-state management. His policies engendered resistance serious enough to produce strategic overextension. He could, therefore, pursue some combination of tactics. First, he could exploit the advantages provided by intermediary autonomy to insulate himself against blame for unpopular policies. Second, he could co-opt some group of powerful local actors and hope to use them to restore smooth governance in the Netherlands. Third, he could reverse some significant components of the unpopular policies and thereby restore local support. Philip's strategy emphasized the first two courses of action: he scapegoated Granvelle and empowered Orange and his supporters. "Granvelle," notes Koengisberger, had "faithfully carried out Philip's policy in the Netherlands. In the process he had become unacceptable to a large section of the local elite."[61]

Orange and his allies seemed on the verge of achieving their political goals. Working side by side with Margaret in the Council of State, they

---

[59] G. Parker 1977, 48.
[60] G. Parker 1977, 53–55, and 1998, 118–19. See also Elliott 2000, 86; and Geyl 1958, 75.
[61] Koenigsberger 1986, 117. See also Bercé 1987, 28–29.

now assumed chief responsibility for governing the Netherlands. They hoped to relax the antiheresy laws; if they succeeded, they would establish themselves as crucial brokers between not only the various factions in the Netherlands, but also between them and their sovereign.[62]

The Beggars, Iconoclasm, and Polarization (1565–1566)

Granvelle's departure failed to restore smooth relations between the Council of State and both the towns and regional states. Orange and his allies could not easily secure their cooperation in the face of traditional class-based and regional tensions, particularly given continued popular anger at antiheresy measures. At the same time, Habsburg-Tudor tensions led to a temporary suspension of English wool and cloth exports to Flanders; a war in the Baltic closed off trade and much-needed grain imports; and a bad winter in 1564–1565 further depressed the economy. The poor economic and political conditions facilitated the spread of heresy; Calvinists expanded their activity in the Low Countries, spurred on by the instability in France and the successes of Calvinist cells there.[63]

Starting in 1564, Calvinist preachers began to flout the antiheresy laws. The Council of State faced a delicate situation. Any attempt to enforce the antiheresy legislation would alienate the people. On the other hand, if it relaxed the antiheresy laws, it would arouse the anger of the king.[64] Orange's faction sought to convince Philip to change his mind. They continued to decry the aggressive suppression of Protestantism. The Council of State, with Margaret's support, dispatched Egmond to persuade Philip of the wisdom of moderation. In 1565 Egmond met with the king and his ministers, and deceived himself into believing he was making significant progress. Philip tried to engage in multivocal signaling: he opted for "an ambiguous reply" that he hoped would "maintain the integrity of his principles without stirring up more trouble."[65]

Upon his return to the Netherlands, Egmond claimed that the king was ready to accept a compromise. Local officials reacted by further relaxing enforcement of the antiheresy laws, which only facilitated the spread of religious heterodoxy in the Netherlands. Thus it came as a great shock when Margaret received instructions, drafted on 13 May 1565, to execute six Anabaptists rather than grant them clemency. Orange, Egmond, and their associates believed that Philip had played them for fools. The enor-

---

[62] Elliott 2000, 86; Israel 1995, 144.
[63] G. Parker 1977, 56–57. See also Elliott 2000, 86–87; and Pettegree 2001, 71–72.
[64] Elliott 2000, 87.
[65] G. Parker 1998, 119. See also Elliott 2000, 87; and Kamen 1997, 99.

mous backlash against the news, in fact, prompted the Council of State to recommend toleration. It even declined to execute the Anabaptists.[66]

The magnates and Margaret tried to square the circle created by Philip's intransigence, but their influence and prestige suffered badly from their miscalculation. They lost credibility as brokers between the king and his subjects. A small group of lesser nobles, made up mostly of Calvinists and Protestant sympathizers, met secretly in November 1565 to draft a petition known as the "Compromise" protesting the antiheresy laws and setting up a "League of Compromise" to achieve its implementation. Its leaders made skillful use of their patron-client and family networks to build support. About four hundred nobles—very few of them magnates—signed on. In April 1566 two hundred lesser nobles forced their way into Margaret's presence and delivered the document to her. Critics dubbed them "the Beggars," a name that they appropriated. Margaret agreed to order the magistrates to exercise greater leniency pending another delegation to the king.[67]

The triumphant Beggars made their way from town to town, holding public ceremonies at which many nobles signed onto their program. The number of eventual signatories to the Compromise may have reached two thousand. The success of the Beggars demonstrated a breakdown in the authority of the regency, while Margaret's renewed attempt at moderation satisfied neither the expanding and increasingly emboldened Calvinists, nor Orange, Egmond, and their allies. The latter declared their intentions to leave for Germany; Margaret would have to either take steps to increase their power and prestige or risk losing their assistance in coping with the rapidly deteriorating political situation.[68]

The Calvinists took full advantage of Margaret's suspension of the antiheresy laws. Calvinist preachers streamed into the Netherlands and held large, open-air meetings. They established numerous Reformed Churches and Calvinist cells. Alarmed by the rapid course of events, the Council of State decided in July of 1566 that their best hope was an alliance with the Beggars. Orange and Egmond met a delegation of the Beggars, where "they were shown a 'second Request' . . . which demanded full toleration for non-Catholics and a firm promise that the States-General would be summoned immediately." Egmond and Orange presented the demands to an outraged Margaret. The three sides agreed to wait for the king's deci-

[66] Kamen 1997, 100.
[67] Bonney 1991, 148–49; Darby 2001b, 17; Duke 1999, 120–21; Elliott 2000, 120; Gelderen 1992, 38; Israel 1995, 145–46; Ortíz 1971, 71; G. Parker 1977, 70. On the composition of the Beggars and the wide range of allegiances--Catholic, Erasmian, Calvinist, Lutheran, and so forth--represented in their ranks, see Wyntjes 1981.
[68] G. Parker 1977, 71–72; Zagorin 1982a, 92–94.

sion; in the meantime, the Beggars would "keep the peace, to do nothing further to achieve their ends, and to aid the local authorities to suspend" Calvinist "hedge-preaching," as the open-air meetings were called, "for twenty-four days."[69]

But the Beggars lacked any practical control over the activities of reformation supporters. Calvinist hedge-preaching intensified. Many preachers openly called for the smashing of images and the desecration of Catholic altars. Starting on 10 August 1566, with an attack on a convent in Flanders, both spontaneous and organized violence spread through much of the Low Countries. By the end of August every church in Antwerp had been attacked. Soon, nobles and prominent citizens began to direct the attacks. The number of governmental officials and subjects who refused to obey the regency government demonstrated its weakness and isolation.[70]

On 31 July Philip issued a letter indicating limited agreement to a more moderate course; by the time the letter reached Margaret it was hopelessly outdated. On 23 August she agreed to an "Accord" that allowed limited freedom for Protestant worship in exchange for an end to iconoclasm. The Beggars and the moderate magnates received responsibility for enforcing toleration. The Accord failed, however, to halt a growing breakdown in governance. The Calvinists rejected any limitations on their activities. The most militant—and openly Protestant—ranks of the Beggars, led by Hendrik Brederode, denounced the terms of the agreement.[71] The Accord also alienated some leading magnates, such as Aerschot, Aremberg, and Meges, who remained loyal to Philip and his policies.[72]

The bargain, therefore, failed to resolve the deteriorating situation. Orange, Egmond, and Horne all negotiated agreements to allow full rights for Calvinists and Lutherans. These agreements went well beyond Margaret's compromise. Nevertheless, their crackdown on the iconoclasm alienated many of the very Calvinists they sought to protect. Indeed, the Calvinists sought not only freedom of worship, but the *suppression* of Catholicism and Lutheranism alike. Growing polarization eliminated the middle ground. The moderates could not credibly broker between the various sides. Of Orange, Egmond, and the other moderates, Parker writes that "theirs was a middle-of-the-road position, and it was rapidly becoming untenable—and they knew it."[73]

[69] G. Parker 1977, 74.
[70] Elliott 2000, 88; Israel 1995, 147–52; G. Parker 1977, 71–72.
[71] Brederode had orchestrated the League of Compromise in the first place.
[72] Elliott 2000, 90; Israel 1995, 152; G. Parker 1977, 81.
[73] G. Parker 1977, 82. See also Duke 1999, 129; Elliott 2000, 92; Israel 1995, 152; Nierop 1999, 94; and Woltjer 1999, 189–90.

The First Revolt (1566-1567)

The outbreak of the 1566–1567 revolt confounds both materialist and ideationalist accounts. On the one hand, economic interests and realpolitik considerations obviously played an important role in the deteriorating situation in the Netherlands, but we cannot make sense of both triggers of resistance and patterns of collective mobilization without reference to religious identities and concerns.[74] On the other hand, a focus on how actors followed "logics of appropriateness" dictated by religious beliefs provides very little explanatory leverage over the shifting policies, bargains, and coalitional dynamics that culminated in the First Revolt. Instead, as we have already seen, religious identities and networks altered the conditions of possibility for resistance, brokerage, and rule. These processes, in turn, influenced the salience of religious identities and the structure of political ties.

By 1565–1566 the Netherlands saw a particular concatenation of these dynamics. First, many actors in the Low Countries perceived Philip as a "Spanish" ruler who, at best, cared little for their specific interests and, at worst, might try to impose unfavorable contractual terms on the region. This state of affairs undermined the legitimacy of Philip's policies toward the Netherlands and made local actors less willing to make fiscal and political concessions to him and his agents. Second, mechanisms associated with indirect rule, such as principal-agent problems, contributed to factional struggles that undermined Habsburg policies and repeatedly threatened dangerous coalitions between specific intermediaries and other social sites. Third, religious polarization exacerbated these dynamics by, among other processes, restricting the room for brokerage and compromise by local intermediaries. Fourth, the spread of religious networks facilitated specific forms of cross-regional and cross-class collective mobilization against central authorities.

But the events leading to the outbreak of the First Revolt also raise some interesting questions about the relative importance of different dynamics associated with rule and resistance in composite states. In particular, might Philip have avoided the outbreak of militarized hostilities through actions that, first, demonstrated a stronger commitment to his identity as ruler of the Netherlands and, second, reduced the endemic principal-agent problems that undermined governmental authority?

In April 1565 Philip and his advisors started seriously to contemplate military intervention in the Netherlands. From October 1565 onward, the major debate in Madrid over policy toward the Netherlands concerned whether Philip should travel to the Netherlands to personally resolve the

---

[74] See also G. Parker 2004, 40.

problems there. Many significant figures in both Madrid and the Netherlands argued that doing so would resolve the developing crisis through the mechanisms discussed above: his personal presence would dispel Philip's image as a solely "Spanish" king and resolve ongoing uncertainty about governmental policy.[75] No less an authority than Geoffrey Parker believes that Philip could have prevented the Dutch Revolt, without giving much ground in religious issues, if he had traveled to the Low Countries: his presence, among other things, would have made it impossible for Orange to protest his loyalty to Habsburg authority while working against Philip's policies.[76] In any event, the First Revolt overtook such plans and, for a variety of reasons, Philip never made good on his future determinations to depart Spain.

Once Margaret's delegation arrived in Castile, Philip met with his counselors and made two decisions: to go to the Netherlands in person in the spring and to reject the demands of the moderates. When news of the explosion of hedge-preaching reached Madrid, Philip wavered—sending the 31 July letter agreeing to a limited relaxation of the antiheresy campaign. "No sooner had the letters gone than Philip regretted even his few concessions. In a small legal ceremony . . . he retracted the offer of a pardon, on the grounds that he had issued it under duress. Shortly after, he instructed Margaret to raise troops in Germany."[77] Thus, Philip still opposed compromise when news of the iconoclastic riots and increasing Calvinist militancy reached him. He decided to send the Duke of Alva at the head of an armed force.[78]

Back in the Netherlands, the Calvinists and remaining Beggars marshaled their forces and sought aid from German Protestants and the French Huguenots. Margaret responded by banning Calvinist worship and preparing for armed confrontation. Only two options remained: armed revolt or submission. The Calvinists and their allies opted for armed revolt. They did so with some justifiable optimism. Common religious affiliations only partially account for their transnational reach and quick mobilization for revolt: the church infrastructure developed during 1564–1566 allowed the Calvinists and radical Beggars to raise money and organize resistance. They created a central treasury, based in Antwerp, and ordered local churches and cells to levy troops.[79]

The iconoclastic riots, however, alienated most Catholics in the Netherlands. The Calvinist rebels would have faced significant difficulties, re-

---

[75] Kamen 1997, 111–14.
[76] G. Parker 2004.
[77] Kamen 1997, 114–15; G. Parker 1977, 84–90.
[78] Bonney 1991, 151; Kamen 1997, 116–17; G. Parker 1998, 121.
[79] G. Parker 1977, 92–94; Zagorin 1982a, 96.

gardless, in expanding their base of support. The Beggars had capitalized not on any widespread affinity for Protestantism, let alone militant Calvinism, but from a general distaste for the repression of religious pluralism and concern for the Netherlands' "customary rights." Calvinist intolerance shocked and appalled many of the same people who had supported the Beggars. It angered the Lutherans, most of whom remained neutral or actively joined to suppress the revolt. Although many of the important regional, class, and religious factions worried about maintaining their customary rights, they remained unwilling to cross into open rebellion. The coalitional dynamics of the First Revolt thus favored the regency government.[80]

The rebels hoped for widespread noble support for their cause, but this support never materialized. Only a few of the magnates, among them Louis of Nassau, came to their aid; others, such as Orange and Egmond, vacillated before openly siding with the government. News that Philip was preparing for military intervention further eroded support for the rebellion. In December 1566 and January 1567 the rebels suffered setbacks. Significant foreign support never materialized, and the defection of moderate magnates made the position of the rebels even more precarious. The revolt collapsed by May 1657.[81]

The fighting itself, together with the collapse of the rebellion, prompted an exodus of Protestants out of the Netherlands; many fled to Protestant areas in Germany. The exodus intensified after the arrival of Alva and the king's army. Despite having sided with the government, Orange fled in April. So did Brederode, leader of the Beggars and the most important noble leader of the rebellion.[82]

Alva's Regime between the Two Revolts (1567–1572)

Philip's court engaged in considerable debate over whether or not to send a military expedition to the Netherlands. On a number of occasions, Madrid came close to aborting the plan in favor of, for example, sending a replacement for Granvelle in preparation for Philip's eventual arrival. In the end Margaret's letters convinced Philip that the situation called for nothing less than a significant military commitment. Alva should go to assert royal power, and afterwards Philip would come to sort things out in person. By the time an emissary, dispatched by Margaret, arrived at Court on 27 April 1567 to explain that the revolt was virtually over and that no Spanish forces were needed, Alva had already departed.[83]

---

[80] Marnef 1999, 60; Nierop 2001a, 61; Zagorin 1982a, 95–96.
[81] Bonney 1991, 150; Kamen 1997, 117; G. Parker 1977, 94–99.
[82] Israel 1995, 153–58; Nierop 2001b, 61–62; G. Parker 1977, 99; Wallace 2004, 141.
[83] Kamen 1997, 113–17; G. Parker 1977, 99–102.

From the outset, Philip envisioned a temporary presence for Alva and his forces. Alva carried with him few concrete instructions about how to proceed after his arrival. But a number of factors precluded Philip's departure for the Low Countries. For one, the Morisco uprising and the campaign in the Mediterranean kept him in Iberia from 1567 until 1572. For another, Philip could no longer ignore the mental instability of his son and only heir, Don Carlos. Don Carlos, whose deformities, sadism, and erratic behavior alarmed those around him, had suffered a serious accident in 1561. Afterwards, his mental condition further declined. Philip could not leave Don Carlos alone in Castile. Don Carlos certainly could not, as originally planned, be installed as governor in the Netherlands. Once Don Carlos realized his likely fate—to die a powerless bachelor—he plotted to escape from Madrid. In January 1568 Philip had him arrested. Once confined, Don Carlos's behavior became self-destructive. In 24 July 1568 he died—probably from a combination of self-inflicted tortures, but some contemporaries speculated that his death was a bit too convenient and suspected foul play. Don Carlos's death left Philip without an heir for another decade. Given Philip's own poor health, he could not, he reasoned, risk a trip to the Netherlands.[84]

No one, of course, anticipated Philip's permanent absence from the Netherlands when Alva arrived there in August 1567. Alva's relations with Margaret quickly soured. She never desired his presence; Alva, for his part, insisted that his ten thousand Spanish and Italian troops be billeted in Brussels and a number of nearby cities. Only if they were close at hand, he argued, could they ensure Philip's safety when Philip arrived in the Low Countries. Margaret objected that Alva's plan placed the burden of quartering the troops upon those towns that had supported the government during the revolt. In doing so, it risked alienating those who remained loyal to the government. Alva "firmly and rather gracelessly" overruled her complaints. Margaret's predictions quickly proved accurate: "The troops were unruly and insolent, regarding the Netherlanders as heretics and traitors to a man." Alva, moreover, forced Margaret to disband her own forces, partly on the grounds that many were German Lutherans. Both moves humiliated Margaret.[85]

Only five days after he arrived, Alva implemented the strategy developed in Castile to establish a "Council of Troubles" for the purpose of rooting out and punishing heretics and rebels. He initially kept the existence of the council a secret; Alva aimed to lure those magnates who had fled in the wake of the First Revolt back to the Low Countries.

---

[84] Kamen 1997, 119–22; Lovett 1986, 119–22; Lynch 1991, 262–67; G. Parker 1977, 112–13.
[85] G. Parker 1977, 104–6.

Among them, Hornes, Egmond, and the former burgomaster of Antwerp, Antoon van Stralen, returned; Alva quickly had them arrested for trial. Margaret, unaware of Alva's plans, had personally invited Van Stalen to Brussels. She also objected to the treatment of Hornes and Egmond—both pious Catholics and men whom, as far as she was concerned, had proved their loyalty during her regency. Margaret resigned in protest, swore in Alva as her replacement, and left the Netherlands for good on 30 December 1567.[86]

Over the course of Alva's governance, the council investigated something on the order of ten thousand people, of whom it executed more than a thousand. Horne and Egmond numbered among those condemned to death; they were beheaded before an "appalled crowd" in the Grand-Place of Brussels ten months after their arrest. The council seized books and pamphlets in 1569.[87] The reign of terror proved so complete that one official, as Parker notes, attempted to commit suicide "for fear that he would be blamed for not stopping the disorders of 1566 single-handed."[88]

INITIAL SUCCESS . . .

In 1568–1569 Alva's style of rule appeared to be working. Many of the nobles implicated in the revolt escaped, but the Council of Troubles managed to capture a surprising number of conspirators. Entire cells of Calvinists fled the Netherlands. Between the first mass exoduses after the failure of the revolt and this second wave, approximately sixty thousand people left the Low Countries. Either by driving out religious dissenters and their supporters, or by catching and prosecuting them, the council made substantial progress against heresy. Alva implemented the decrees of the Council of Trent and resumed the aborted ecclesiastical reorganization plan. More importantly, his oppressive policies stifled internal opposition.[89]

Alva's strategy, however, created a number of serious—if not yet obvious—problems. First, by sentencing and convicting the exiled nobles in absentia, Alva ensured that the "sole way for the exiles to recover their inheritances was to regain control of the Brussels government. This, of course, could only be done by an armed invasion which would overthrow the military basis of Alva's power."[90] Second, Alva's repression—and particularly the execution of Hornes and Egmond—produced widespread international outrage against the Spanish monarchy. It did enormous

---

[86] Israel 1995, 156; G. Parker 1977, 106.
[87] Israel 1995, 156–57.
[88] G. Parker 1977, 108.
[89] Ibid., 159–61.
[90] Ibid., 108.

210 • Chapter 6

damage to Philip's relations with the Austrian Habsburgs. Maximilian, who had strong Protestant sympathies, was particularly upset by the actions of the council.[91] Third, the mass exodus consolidated Calvinism's place as *the* religion of opposition, both because of its superior organizational infrastructure and the large number of Calvinists among the exile communities.[92]

The greatest success for Alva came in 1568, when he crushed an invasion orchestrated by Orange. After his sentencing, Orange lost any hope of a peaceful return to status, power, and wealth in the Netherlands. With Brederode dead, Orange became the public face of the struggle against Alva's governorship. His movement challenged, he argued, *not* the right of Philip to rule the Netherlands but the actions of a dangerous and corrupt intermediary. Orange's propagandists focused on Alva's "tyranny," while minimizing the importance of religious issues. They took pains not to portray their movement as a Calvinist one.[93]

William's status as a dynast helped him immeasurably in rounding up international support: "He negotiated with other German princes, and European rulers, as one sovereign to another, as a German (Protestant) prince himself and sovereign of Orange, in southern France." The international outrage at Alva's policies greatly aided Orange's efforts.[94] Once they amassed financial and military support—their armies included French Huguenots and German and English Protestants—the exiles decided to launch an invasion. One after another, the forces went down to defeat; the support they expected from within the Netherlands largely failed to materialize. William's foreign supporters repudiated him, and the armed struggle transformed into one of low-level harassment against Habsburg interests.[95]

... TURNS TO FAILURE

The propaganda of the exile opposition met with little overt response in the Netherlands during 1568–1569. Despite discontent with Alva's regime, few in the Low Countries were prepared to join a new uprising. Alva, for his part, faced a basic difficulty: his policies sought to prepare the Netherlands for Philip's arrival, but Philip never arrived. Alva was left to administer the Netherlands on his own.

Alva's mission soon expanded beyond stabilizing the Low Countries. He had to ensure that they would not be vulnerable to another invasion

[91] Kamen 1997, 123–26.
[92] Pettegree 2001, 77–78.
[93] Duke 1999, 129–30; Israel 1995, 162; Pettegree 2001, 78.
[94] Israel 1995, 161–62.
[95] Ibid., 162–65; G. Parker 1977, 108–11.

attempt. With the continuing religious struggles in France, the Netherlands resumed their place as an important staging ground for Spanish operations in northwestern Europe. Already in 1569 Alva and his troops had intervened in the French Wars of Religion on behalf of French Catholics. But all this cost the monarchy dearly; Philip's treasury, already stretched by conflict in the Mediterranean, lacked the resources to support Alva's forces. Philip wanted Alva to make the Netherlands self-financing, a point reiterated in a letter from his chief minister to Alva in 1569: "The amount of money which the Castilian Exchequer has had to provide the Netherlands does not cease to cause us grave concern. And, indeed, if you do not arrange things so that the outlay stops, I am concerned that it will be impossible to go on any longer."[96]

Alva therefore convened the States and requested three new taxes. The States agreed to a one-time capital tax but refused to assent to the other two: a five-percent tax on land sales (the "Twentieth Penny") and a ten-percent sales tax (the "Tenth Penny"). Alva's plan to administer the taxes through a staff independent of the States proved particularly contentious. The States, under pressure, voted a one-time extraordinary subsidy, but they refused to give up their control over taxation. After two years of unsuccessful efforts to bring the States to heel, Alva, in July 1571, made the fateful decision to impose the taxes on his own authority. Adding insult to injury, Alva set about collecting the tax by threatening to fine civic officials who did not immediately comply with his demands.[97]

The imposition of the tax contributed to the worsening economic situation in the Netherlands. The Netherlands and England were, at this point, in the midst of a trade war sparked by Queen Elizabeth's refusal to release five ships carrying money to Alva from Southampton and Plymouth, where they had sought refuge from Huguenot pirates. The halt in trade; a bad winter in 1571–1572; the breakdown of shipping commerce caused by the pirate activities of the Sea Beggars (about whom see below); an outbreak of plague; and the hardship caused by the new taxes together created a serious economic crisis in the Low Countries. Hunger, unemployment, and poverty ran rampant.[98]

All of these factors wrecked Alva's legitimacy. His blatant disregard for the customary rights of the States in pushing through a deeply unpopular tax, one that exacerbated the poor economic conditions in the Netherlands, produced a serious political backlash. Alva had, over time, alienated a major proportion of the political actors in the Low Countries. The

---

[96] Quoted in G. Parker 1977, 114. See also Israel 1995, 166.
[97] G. Parker 1998, 124. See also Darby 2001b, 18; and Israel 1995, 167.
[98] G. Parker 1977, 123–29. See also Kamen 1997, 133.

Tenth Penny also undermined his own magistrates, as they found themselves tasked with implementing the unpopular tax.[99]

Such developments increased the chances of significant resistance in the Netherlands. Deteriorating relations between England and the Spanish Monarchy, moreover, ensured another vector of support for Netherlandish rebels—as well as anti-Habsburg Huguenots in France. The trade debacle with England was only the start of the problem. In September 1568 Spanish forces destroyed a fleet of English ships involved in illegal trade in Mexico. Factions in Madrid began scheming to overthrow Elizabeth. Philip initially refused to support such plans, including one involving an attempted rebellion in the north of England in 1569. Despite English piracy against Spanish ships, Philip still sought to maintain his ties with England so as to ensure its neutrality. But he eventually succumbed to temptation and backed a plot, involving the Duke of Norfolk, to arrest Elizabeth. In 1571 Philip ordered Alva to prepare for an invasion of England in the event of Elizabeth's capture. The discovery of the plot destroyed Philip's relations with Elizabeth. England would now pursue an anti-Spanish—and pro-Protestant—policy on the Continent.[100]

By 1571–1572, therefore, we find almost all of the conditions for serious resistance within a composite-state segment: Alva's policies prompted cross-class and cross-regional hostility, the conjunction of religious and geo-strategic pressures enhanced the prospects for external support of resistance, and signaling failures undermined collective identification between Philip and his Netherlandish subjects. Religious contention triggered, either indirectly or directly, many of these developments. Orange and his allies, meanwhile, exploited these developments and rebuilt support for a major invasion of the Netherlands. But Orange's plans were quickly overtaken by a strange turn of fate.[101]

The Second Revolt (1572–1576)

The Sea Beggars, a group of privateers with a strong Calvinist contingent, emerged as an important force during the First Revolt. Prior to 1572 they operated out of English ports, but on 1 March 1572 Elizabeth expelled them because of complaints from the Hanseatic League. They settled on Brill, a town in South Holland, as a new base of operations. The town was, for the moment, without its normal garrison of Habsburg troops. The Sea Beggars took Brill on 1 April 1572. Heavy winds prevented a

[99] G. Parker 1977, 130–31. See also Bonney 1991, 151–53.
[100] Kamen 1997, 133–34; G. Parker 1977, 124–25, and 1998, 124.
[101] G. Parker 1977, 125–26.

counterattack by a hastily assembled, but otherwise adequate, Spanish force and gave the Sea Beggars time to reinforce their position.[102]

The capture of Brill produced a collapse in Habsburg authority. Alva and his officials, as I noted earlier, lacked cooperative ties with almost every major social site in the Netherlands. Town magistrates, charged with collecting the hated Tenth Penny, lacked the legitimacy they needed to mobilize support against invasion. All of this created enormous opportunities for those seeking to yoke together a coalition against Habsburg policies based on appeals to common interests and identity. Orange, for his part, exhorted his fellow Netherlanders to rise up in order to "attain the freedom of His word and your conscience and your fatherland, your bodies, wives, children, and the preservation of your privileges, rights, and goods, all in the true service of the King."[103] Common religious ties between organized resistance movements and Calvinist cells within the Netherlands, moreover, facilitated collective mobilization against the regency government.

The rebellion quickly spread. The Sea Beggars moved into the northwest Netherlands; town after town capitulated. The Sea Beggars skillfully exploited opposition to the Tenth Penny. Indeed, in some towns the Calvinist minority threw open the gates. In order to undermine Catholic opposition to their campaign, the Sea Beggars promulgated an edict issued in the name of Orange—and, for that matter, in Philip's name, since Orange still claimed to be a rightful stadholder, and thus an agent of the king—promising to respect Catholic worship. The Sea Beggars soon held most of northern Holland. Despite their pledge to respect other confessions, they almost immediately began to suppress Catholic activity; they also handed over religious and educational jurisdiction to agents of the Reformed Church.[104]

Alva still might have repulsed the Sea Beggars, but a small invasion from France—led by Louis of Nassau—forced him to focus his attention on protecting Brussels. Orange, in turn, invaded Brabant in August; he quickly took control of a number of towns. Other towns rose up on their own. Alva now faced open revolt in much of the Low Countries, yet he could not move decisively against the spreading rebellion for fear it would leave the Netherlands vulnerable to a full-fledged French intervention.[105]

The St. Bartholomew's Day Massacre of 23–24 August 1572, however, ended the immediate threat of a major French invasion (see chapter 7). Alva annihilated Orange's forces. But he lacked sufficient resources to

---

[102] G. Parker 1977, 126, 131–33, and 1998, 125.
[103] Quoted in Rowen 1972, 42.
[104] Israel 1995, 172–74; Koenigsberger 1971a, 234–39.
[105] G. Parker 1977, 136–38, and 1998, 125–26.

recapture every rebellious town. Alva, therefore, "chose a strategy of selective brutality" to bring the rebellious towns to heel.[106] The campaign ended the revolt outside of Holland and Zeeland, but the rebels remained firmly ensconced in the northern provinces. Their religious policies, moreover, precluded surrender. They understood full well their likely fate if, having suppressed Catholicism, they capitulated to Alva. One of Alva's subordinates, in fact, rejected overtures from a delegation from Haarlem. The resulting seven-month siege destroyed Alva's hope that he could quickly bring the rebellion to an end.[107]

A number of factors made a Spanish military victory unlikely: inadequate manpower, the difficult terrain of the north, and the fact that many of the towns enjoyed advanced fortifications. The Spanish inadvertently stiffened the resolve of the rebellious towns when, violating a promise to spare Haarlem if it surrendered, their victorious forces launched bloody reprisals against its citizens. No northern town would again surrender to Spanish forces.[108]

The sack of Haarlem also undermined already waning support for Alva in Madrid. Philip and his advisors recognized that the human and financial costs of the conflict placed Spanish power in jeopardy. On 30 January 1573 Philip ordered Luis de Requeséns to replace Alva. Still, the Spanish could not defeat the insurrection; the rebels held on in a few remaining strongholds. Philip and his court sought to end the impasse, but even the suspension of the Tenth Penny in 1573 failed to alter popular opinion in the Netherlands. The financial position of the army worsened. In late 1574, after a desperate defense of Leiden by the rebels saved the revolt, Requeséns decided to open negotiations.[109]

The issue of religious toleration, however, prevented a negotiated settlement. As Israel argues:

> Here then, fully evident in 1575, as it had been in 1565, was the stumbling-block precluding a negotiated solution to the Dutch Revolt. If Orange had been a less skillful, and tenacious, leader, the Revolt might well have been overwhelmed militarily. But the ideological framework prevailing in the Holland and Zeeland towns, from the very outset, in 1572, based on rejection of Catholicism and insistence on Protestant worship—with Catholic support too weak to mount any real challenge—meant that no negotiated settlement, even if Orange had been more pliant, was possible.[110]

[106] G. Parker 1998, 127.
[107] Gelderen 1992, 43–44; G. Parker 1998, 126–32.
[108] G. Parker 1977, 156–60.
[109] Darby 2001b, 19; Israel 1995, 179–81; Kamen 1997, 153–55; G. Parker 1998, 136–38.
[110] Israel 1995, 183–84.

As Requeséns himself wrote, "If we were talking about a peace that could be settled by transferring four towns or four kingdoms," success might be possible, "but it all depends on religion, which has caused this war. . . . I have no hope whatever for a settlement [since] . . . we cannot meet any of the [rebels'] demands on the religious question."[111] Historians dispute whether or not the parties could have struck a deal on some of the issues at stake, but religious compromise proved impossible.[112]

The Third Revolt (1576–1581)

In September 1575 Spain's finances collapsed. Philip was bankrupt, his credit ruined. Requeséns had a difficult time financing his military campaign; his death in 1576 exacerbated Habsburg fiscal troubles in the Netherlands. On 2 July 1576 Spanish troops staged their first mutiny; frustrated with their lack of pay, they turned on the local population. A panicked Council of State authorized the States of Brabant to raise their own troops to stop the pillaging. The States of Brabant then, on its own recognizance, summoned the States General of the Netherlands to find some way to end the broader conflict. On 30 October its negotiators signed an armistice with the States of Holland and Zeeland, the aim of which was to "drive the mutinous Spanish contingents out of the country and confer on the subject of religion."[113]

In November the mutineers attacked Antwerp in what came to be known as the "Spanish Fury." For two days the city was subjected to "slaughter, pillage, and rape." Orange and his propagandists grossly exaggerated the death and destruction wrought by the Spanish troops—which was, in truth, considerable, but hardly the some eighteen thousand murdered that they claimed. The sack led directly to the "Pacification of Ghent" (1576), in which the States agreed to drive out the troops and set up their own provisional government. They also agreed on a temporary compromise on the religious question, one roughly following the parameters of the Augsburg settlement of 1555. Only two provinces, and part of another, rejected the agreement and continued to support Madrid.

The mutiny of the Spanish troops provided, with suitable framing by opponents of the government, the kind of trigger for collective action associated with high-category/low-network relational contexts. The Pacification of Ghent effectively placed all of the Netherlands in revolt against Philip's authority. But, as we should expect with such pathways of collective mobilization, internal differences involving a complex interplay between class resentments and religious divisions soon fractured the rebel-

---
[111] Quoted in G. Parker 1998, 142.
[112] Gelderen 1992, 44–45.
[113] Israel 1995, 185.

lion. Starting in 1577 and accelerating in 1578, a coalition of Calvinists and burghers mounted coups d'état in many moderate and loyalist towns. Waves of iconoclasm and, frequently, the suppression of Catholic worship, followed their takeovers. Although these coups d'état provided impetus to the revolt by moving important cities, such as Ghent and Antwerp, into the hard-line faction, they also alienated staunch Catholics and moderates, splitting the ranks of the rebellion.

Orange tried to broker between the various factions in an attempt to maintain a unified revolt, but his efforts failed. Spanish victories under Alexander Farnese, Prince of Parma, encouraged defections from the rebellion, particularly among the southern nobility. Meanwhile, the frontlines of the rebellion slid into chaos. France and England jockeyed for influence in the Netherlands, and external events—English aid, the failure of the Spanish Armada, and the Spanish intervention in France against Henry of Navarre—saved the revolt from total disaster. The Third Revolt ultimately divided the Netherlands between the northern provinces, who declared themselves an independent state, and the south (figure 6.3).

THE NETHERLANDS PRECARIOUSLY UNITED (1576–1578)

From the very start of the Third Revolt, the States of Brabant and the other newly rebellious actors saw their actions as temporary expedients. They recognized the new governor, Don Juan of Austria, on the condition that he dispatch the mutineers and affirm the new order. They therefore agreed to so-called Eternal Edict of February 1577. Orange responded by siding with the burghers in the south against the "firmly Catholic" nobles and urban elites. Don Juan's attempt to reassert royal authority through an alliance with the nobles and patricians who controlled the States General broke down when his negotiations with Orange failed. Again, the religious disposition of Holland and Zeeland emerged as the key obstacle: both refused to come to terms, since the Edict "provided no guarantees for the Reformed Church and would have stripped . . . [them] of all control over the military." In any event, neither Orange nor his allies in the north trusted the Spanish.[114]

Don Juan, unable to forge a compromise, fled to Namur—one of the remaining loyal provinces—and recalled the Spanish troops. He thus violated the Edict and brought himself into direct confrontation with the States General. Orange triumphantly returned to Brussels in September 1577. Tensions among the rebels intensified, particularly between Orange and a faction of staunchly Catholic nobles—all of whom distrusted and resented Orange. Orange outmaneuvered one of his chief foes, Aerschot,

---

[114] Ibid., 186–87; G. Parker 1977, 179–84.

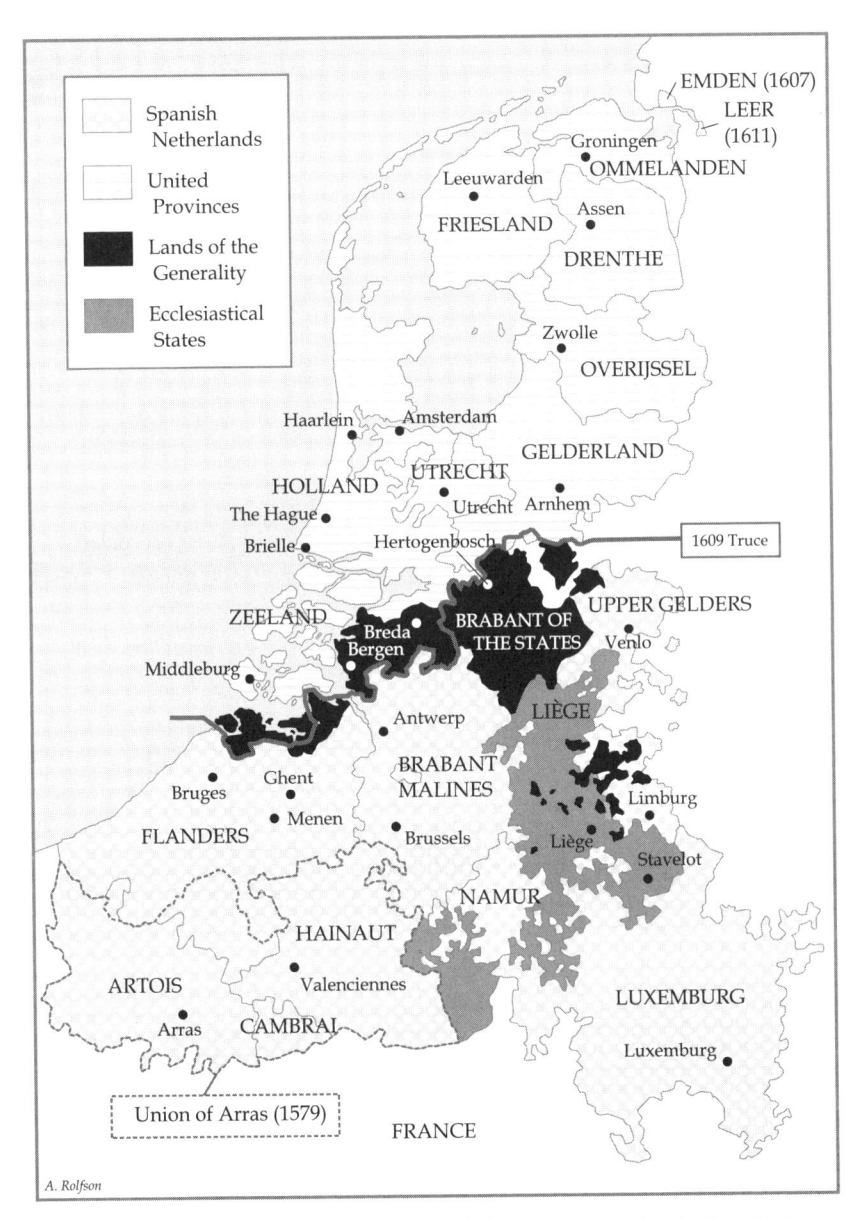

Figure 6.3 Disposition of the Provinces of the Low Countries during the Later Phases of the Dutch Revolt

stadholder of Flanders, by having the States Generals reinstate Ghent's privileges (see chapter 5) on 22 October 1577, whereupon two Calvinist magistrates arrested Aerschot. Ghent, one of the three most important cities in Brabant, proceeded to place its weight behind the cause of continued rebellion.[115]

Into this political climate walked Archduke Mathias, a young son of the late Emperor Maximilian II. Loyalist and moderate magnates championed Mathias as a successor to Don Juan, but Orange outmaneuvered them by arranging for the States to place severe restrictions upon Mathias's authority. These factional struggles had little immediate impact, however, as two developments created favorable conditions for Don Juan to seize the initiative. First, Philip negotiated a peace treaty with the Ottoman Empire, thus averting renewed distractions in the Mediterranean. Second, a particularly rich treasure fleet arrived in 18 August 1577. Its bounties allowed Philip to re-establish his line credit.[116]

With fresh financing, Don Juan mounted a military offensive. A Spanish military victory at Gembloux, close to Brussels, forced the representatives of the States General to evacuate in January 1578.[117] The revolt strained under growing factional struggles. During 1577–1578 Groningen and Friesland split between pro- and anti-Orange rebels. Mathias appointed a conservative Catholic magnate as stadholder of the two provinces. The new stadholder failed, however, to prevent a coalition of local nobles and townsfolk from conducting purges against royalist officials and asserting Calvinist authority. In Gelderland, the struggle between Catholics and Calvinists led to a compromise: Orange's brother, Count Johann von Nassau, was appointed stadholder. Nassau, however, had recently switched religious affiliations from Lutheranism to Calvinism; he "refused to swear allegiance" to Philip II and "took every opportunity to promote the cause of the Reformed [that is, Calvinism] in Gelderland." The urban elites—compromised by their earlier cooperation with Alva—could not stem the tide of the small, but organized, Calvinist militants; the militants sacked Catholic churches and suppressed Catholic worship.[118]

During 1578 Orange's supporters increased their pressure on the Catholic holdouts in Holland and Zealand, including the towns of Haarlem and Amsterdam. On 16 February 1578 militant Calvinists from Ghent seized control of the town of Oudenaarde. In that same month Don Juan's forces made advances in the south. Intensifying tensions between Catho-

---

[115] Israel 1995, 187; G. Parker 1977, 183–86.
[116] Darby 2001b, 20; Kamen 1997, 160–61; G. Parker 1977, 186–88. On the "General Settlement" in particular, see Lovett 1982 and 1986, 128.
[117] G. Parker 1977, 186.
[118] Israel 1995, 191–92.

lics and Calvinists led to coups d'état in a number of towns located within Brabant. Militants took control over Arras, the capital of Artois. Over two days, 26–27 May 1578, Calvinists seized control of Amsterdam and then Haarlem. On 10 June 1578 Utrecht, despite having agreed to Orange's call for religious toleration, fell to Calvinist plotters and their allies. Nearly everywhere that Calvinist-burgher coalitions took control, they followed the same pattern: iconoclasm and the suppression of Catholicism.[119] Despite his best efforts, Orange could not persuade the Calvinists to relent; militant Calvinists and Catholics alike ridiculed his pleas for moderation.[120] These developments left both Catholic moderates and militant Calvinists even less inclined to compromise with one another. Of the regional States and towns not under Calvinist control, only Antwerp agreed to tolerate open Calvinist worship. Still others firmly rejected the possibility of toleration within their jurisdictions.

The States General sought help from France and invited Francis, Duke of Anjou and the younger brother of the king of France, to bring military aid in exchange for a position of leadership. Queen Elizabeth, fearful of French influence in the Low Countries, agreed to finance an army under John Casmir, the administrator of the Rhine Palatinate. Such offers of support did nothing to improve matters—French intervention served the interests of the Catholics, German and English intervention that of the Calvinists.[121] On 15 October the States of Hainaut proposed an alliance against Brabant and Flanders, and six days later Catholic parties mounted their own coup d'état in Arras. On 29 September Don Juan, terminally ill with typhus, appointed his secretary, Alexander Farnese, prince of Parma and son of Margaret, the new stadholder of the Netherlands.[122]

The States General was already running out of money, and could not support its troops—which now numbered more than fifty thousand. Regiments in the south mutinied, and "within a month they were joined by their Walloon commanders who, horrified by the excesses of the Calvinists in Ghent and by Orange's domination of the States-General," captured the town of Menen, thirty miles away from Ghent. They opened negotiations with the "Walloon estates meeting at Arras to discuss a Catholic Union," as well as with the Anjou. The frightened leadership in Ghent invited John Casimir, elector of Palatine, and his German troops to their defense, and by October his forces were clashing with the Walloon troops.[123]

[119] Ibid., 192–94; Koenigsberger and Mosse 1968, 262; G. Parker 1977, 189–90.
[120] Elliott 2000, 177; Gelderen 1992, 50–51.
[121] G. Parker 1977, 191–92.
[122] Israel 1995, 194–95; G. Parker 1977, 193.
[123] Elliott 2000, 192; G. Parker 1977, 192–93.

THE UNION OF UTRECHT AND THE COLLAPSE
OF THE UNITED REVOLT (1579–1585)

On 23 January 1579, Gelderland, Holland, Zeeland, Friesland, Utrecht, and Ommerlanden formed the "Union of Utrecht." The union marked a formal alliance between those provinces and towns dominated by Calvinists or other extremist elements. Modeled after the Swiss Confederation, the union maintained the autonomy of each province but pledged them to act as a single entity with respect to military and foreign affairs.[124] While Article XII of the Treaty enjoined every province—except Holland and Zeeland, which were exempted from the Religious Peace—to maintain individual freedom of religion, it also went on at length about the rights of each province to introduce "such regulations as they consider proper for the peace and welfare of the provinces."[125] As Parker notes, "It made virtually no mention of the king's authority or the maintenance of the Catholic faith, and it did not envisage reconciliation with Spain. . . . Henceforth, they [the signatories] were committed to fight for total victory."[126]

The formation of the Union created a new crisis for the revolt. Anjou returned, for the moment, to France, John Casimir to the Palatine, and on 6 January—stirred in part by news of the negotiations for the Union—Hainaut, Artois, and Walloon Flanders formed the Union of Arras as a Catholic counterweight. Political opposition in Gelderland and Friesland blocked their ascension to the Union of Utrecht until March and August 1579, respectively.[127]

Orange was reluctant to swing his support behind the Union. He, as well as many of his supporters, worried that the religious implications of the Union would splinter Brabant and Flanders while driving the Walloon provinces, "already teetering on the edge, into the arms of Spain."[128] Orange, along with the States of Brabant, began work on an alternative Union centered around the States General and confirming toleration of Catholic worship. Orange, however, could not broker an agreement. Holland and Zeeland opposed Orange's proposal, and the Union of Arras opted to enter into negotiations with Parma. The mutinous Walloon troops joined the royal army on 6 April, and on 17 May, the Treaty of Arras brought the Walloon provinces back into the Spanish fold.[129]

---

[124] Darby 2001b, 20–21; Israel 1995, 199–200; G. Parker 1977, 149.
[125] From the text of the Treaty in Kossman and Mellink 1974, 169.
[126] G. Parker 1977, 194.
[127] Israel 1995, 201–2; G. Parker 1977, 194–95.
[128] Israel 1995, 202.
[129] Ibid. See also Elliott 2000, 202; Lovett 1986, 167; and G. Parker 1977, 194–95.

The rebellion had irrevocably splintered, but a majority of the Netherlands still battled against the forces of their sovereign. The States General accepted a proposal by the Austrian Habsburgs to mediate their dispute with Philip; negotiations began at Cologne in May 1579. Spanish forces continued to make military gains, capturing the city of Maastricht in June. The negotiations floundered over religion: the Spanish negotiators would settle for nothing less than exclusive Catholic worship in every province except Holland and Zeeland.[130]

Indeed, Madrid, now under Granvelle's helm, had already decided to opt for a divide-and-conquer strategy. They aimed to strip away Catholic rebels with offers of amnesty and financial inducements. Some supporters, no longer able to countenance Calvinist intolerance, abandoned the rebellion of their own accord. The Union of Utrecht decided to take matters into its own hands; its members pushed through additional policies virtually guaranteed to alienate Netherlandish moderates. The Union, in its most provocative act, decided to actively support rebellious towns in non-Union provinces: it provided both financial and armed assistance to Calvinist minorities against Catholic magistrates. In December 1579 the Union invaded north Brabant to secure Hertogenbosh for their Calvinist supporters; the Catholic majority of Brabant entered, in response, into an alliance with the Spanish. Groningen, under the direction of the count of Rennenberg, who was also stadholder of four other provinces, followed suit in March 1580. The defections in turn sparked a massive anti-Catholic backlash, not only in those provinces under Rennenberg's governorship, but also elsewhere in the Union and parts of Brabant. Militants, in a pattern that should by now be familiar, sacked churches and banned Catholic services.[131]

All things considered, 1580 was a bleak year for the rebellion. Yet Spain could not yet capitalize on the Treaty of Arras. The Treaty required that all foreign troops be withdrawn from the Netherlands. This left Parma with a small and ineffective army. Only in 1582, after being softened by Parma's diplomacy and persuaded of the impossibility of victory without the return of Spanish troops, did the magnates agree to allow Spanish troops to return.[132]

Parma's position remained precarious, but Orange desperately struggled to prevent further defections from the revolt. Orange remained convinced that "the only way to prevent total defeat was to regain the support of those moderates alienated by Calvinist radicalism and—by making the northern provinces more accommodating to Catholicism (and Lutheran-

---

[130] Israel 1995, 205; G. Parker 1977, 195.
[131] Israel 1995, 205–6; G. Parker 1977, 195–96.
[132] Elliott 2000, 193–94; G. Parker 1977, 208–9.

ism)—reassure Catholics in the south, as well as gain the confidence of the king of France and Lutheran princes in Germany."[133] Orange settled on a radical strategy: to offer the sovereignty of the Netherlands to Anjou. As both a moderate Catholic and the brother of the king of France, Anjou offered hope to secure these objectives simultaneously. The States of Brabant and Flanders acquiesced, and Anjou, after much negotiating, became "prince and lord of the Netherlands" on 23 January 1581.[134]

This was a radical strategy, in no small part because it required the States General to make a final break with Philip II. Orange might not have gone so far but for the fact that in 1580 Philip declared him an outlaw and offered a reward for his assassination. William "the Silent" no longer had anything to lose by formally breaking with his sovereign. On 26 July 1581 the States General issued a placard, the "Act of Abjuration," divesting Philip of his sovereignty over the Netherlands. The act drove a number of officials to quit the rebellion.[135] On the other hand, many of the rebel provinces, including Holland and Zeeland, refused to recognize Anjou's sovereignty. Indeed, the Act of Abjuration and the ascension of Anjou merely deepened the divisions in the revolt, as did the vitriolic propaganda now exchanged by all sides. Anjou's troops proved ineffective, and Parma's advances continued.[136]

Anjou, for his part, chafed under the restrictions placed on his sovereignty; the treatment of Catholics in many of the provinces appalled him. Indeed, one of his advisors related that "I cannot describe the anger and discontent that seized His Highness over [the] barbarous humiliation" that Anjou suffered upon learning of widespread repression of Catholicism.[137] In January 1583 Anjou attempted to mount a coup d'état in Flanders and Brabant. In June, Anjou threw in the towel and left for France.[138]

Even before Anjou fled, the tide had begun to turn against the revolt. Now Parma could do more than bribe his opponents—he could conquer them. By August of 1582 he had sixty-thousand men at his command, many of whom were disciplined veterans. From 1582 to 1585 Parma systematically rolled back the rebellion. Catholic distaste for Calvinist magistrates led many towns to surrender without a fight. Holland was fast be-

---

[133] Israel 1995, 208–9.

[134] G. Parker 1977, 197.

[135] Recall my discussion of legitimating frameworks in chapter 4. Many subjects might take up arms on behalf of their customary rights—and, by extension, the very sovereign whose forces they fought—but it was another thing altogether to depose a rightful ruler.

[136] Israel 1995, 212–13.

[137] Quoted in Holt 1986, 170.

[138] Holt 1986, 166–84; Israel 1995, 212–13.

coming the last center of revolt; there, a radical Catholic assassinated Orange on 10 July 1584.[139]

AND YET IT LIVES . . .

With Parma on the verge of total victory, the survival of the rebellion depended upon a new source of foreign assistance. Queen Elizabeth and her councilors decided to present the rebels with an offer of military aid: the English would enter the conflict through an attack on the Spanish West Indies and an expeditionary force sent to the Netherlands. The States General declined the offer. They once again sought aid from France. Indeed, they offered sovereignty to Henry III in exchange for his intervention in the conflict. On 9 March 1585 Henry declined. On 12 May 1585, with Antwerp besieged, the States General made their own offer to Elizabeth: sovereignty over the Netherlands, or, failing that, military cooperation. On 20 August 1585 the two parties signed the Treaty of Nonsuch—the first treaty of the United Provinces as a sovereign state—and Elizabeth agreed to dispatch troops and subsidize the war. The Earl of Leicester would lead the war effort in the United Provinces. He arrived in December of 1585. In February of 1586 a newly created Council of State declared him governor of the Netherlands.[140]

The Treaty of Nonsuch was concluded too late to save Antwerp from Parma, but it gave the beleaguered rebels a new lease on life; they even

---

[139] G. Parker 1977, 216–18. See also Darby 2001b, 22; Israel 1995, 212–16; Rowen 1988, 29–30.

[140] Israel 1995, 219–20; G. Parker 1977, 217–18. Zeeland objected to the deal, since it offered two ports in Zeeland—as well as Brill—as collateral for the subsidies. Why did Elizabeth decide to enter the fray? Even after Spain and England resolved their trade war in 1574, their relations had continued to worsen. Philip knew well of Elizabeth's support for anti-Spanish privateering operations; Elizabeth and her council worried about the strategic implications of Philip's addition of Portugal to his domains (see below). But Elizabeth endeavored to avoid open war with the Spanish monarchy. Three factors worked to change her mind. First, continuing Spanish complicity in plots against her doubtless poisoned relations. Her propagandists cited these plots as part of the effort to justify her move against Spain. Second, the complete failure of the Dutch Revolt would place Elizabeth in a difficult strategic position. She well remembered the plan in 1571–1572 for a Spanish invasion of England. Third, mounting anger at Spain, fear of Spanish-Catholic plots, and Orange's propaganda efforts inflamed Protestant sensibilities in England. Elizabeth faced strong political pressures to support Protestant co-confessionals against the "oppressive, bloodthirsty, and Papist" Spaniards. But Elizabeth also feared a complete victory by either the Habsburgs or the rebellious provinces. The best outcome, as far as she was concerned, was for a protracted struggle that kept Philip occupied, poorer, and unable to use the Low Countries as a base of operations against the Tudor monarchy. Nevertheless, with the imminent collapse of the revolt, Elizabeth and her advisors chose to intervene directly. See Elliott 2000, 204–5; Kamen 1997, 255–56; Ortíz 1971, 78; and G. Parker 1977, 218, and 1998, 172.

managed to make a limited counterattack. Philip's advisors, in the Netherlands and in Madrid, came to the conclusion that if they wanted to destroy the revolt once and for all they would need to knock England out of the conflict. Leicester's presence, however, exacerbated underlying tensions between Holland and the many in the United Provinces who resented its dominance. Leicester's limited skills proved inadequate to both the political and military challenges faced by the rebels. Parma's advance continued into 1587. That same year, Leicester left the Netherlands. But the growing impact of English harassment on Spanish naval interests increased the attractiveness of a knockout blow; Madrid dispatched the famous Spanish Armada in 1588 to depose Elizabeth and, if all went well, establish Philip's daughter, Isabella, as Queen of England.[141]

With better planning, more effective implementation, and less unfavorable weather conditions the Armada might very well have succeeded. If Habsburg forces had landed on English soil, they faced good odds of seizing London and, at the very least, forcing Elizabeth to accept peace on Spanish terms. Nevertheless, the invasion failed—and at tremendous expense to the Spanish treasury and available military manpower; the failure also shifted the psychological balance against the Spaniards.[142]

On 22 September 1588 the Venetian Ambassador reported from Madrid: "His Majesty outwardly displays a fixed resolve to try his fortune once again next year; though it is quite possible that he may have a different design in his head, perhaps because he recognizes the actual impossibility of carrying out the enterprise."[143] The defeat of the Armada was not, in of itself, decisive, but fortunes in the Netherlands did turn against the Spanish. Parma's advance stalled; soon, the mutinies began. In 1589 Parma proposed a plan to Philip to end the conflict through negotiation. His proposal would allow private Calvinist worship in Holland and Zeeland in return for a restoration of royal authority. Philip refused. In any event, it was too late to expect the United Provinces to accept such limited concessions on the issue of religion. Negotiations in 1591 also came to naught, even though Philip might have been willing to budge a bit further.[144]

Events in France, for Philip, took precedence over the fate of the Netherlands. In 1590 the death of Henry III ended the direct Valois line and left Henry of Navarre as heir-presumptive to the throne. Navarre's ascension represented, for Philip, the worst possible outcome of the French civil

---

[141] Gelderen 1992, 58–59; Kaiser 1990, 37; G. Parker 1977, 218–19, and 1998, 181–88; Rowen 1990, 581

[142] Elliott 2000, 222–24; Lovett 1986, 80–81; G. Parker 1977, 219–21, and 1998, 179–250.

[143] Quoted in Davis 1970, 116.

[144] Kamen 1997, 295–96; G. Parker 1977, 222–23.

wars. Henry was, at least at that time, a Huguenot. The Bourbons and Habsburgs remained staunch dynastic rivals. Philip therefore ordered Parma to turn his forces to armed intervention in France. In August 1590 Parma successfully lifted Henry's siege of Paris, thus prolonging the civil war in France. Parma's forces intervened again in 1592. Both interventions led directly to Dutch gains. Henry's conversion to Catholicism in 1593, however, decisively shifted the balance of power in France in his favor. In 1595 he took the offensive, invading Artois. In 1596, Philip declared bankruptcy for a third time. Although the war with the Dutch would drag on, and the Spanish even hoped, at times, for a victory or negotiated settlement, the northern provinces were now essentially lost.[145]

Religion and the Revolt(s) of the Netherlands

Some of the interpretations of the Dutch Revolt discussed at the outset of this section do not stand up to scrutiny. Dutch nationalism constituted an effect, rather than a cause, of the revolt.[146] The uprisings were not a "revolution of the bourgeoisie," although both the restoration of civic liberties and the conflicts between patricians and ordinary townsfolk did play an important role in the complicated politics of various phases of the revolt.

The Dutch Revolt involved a potent combination of, on the one hand, customary rights and privileges and, on the other, religious dissent.[147] The two inevitably went together: if the Habsburgs wanted to effectively suppress overt religious heterodoxy, they had to strengthen central power at the expense of local privileges. Religious dissent and the quest for local autonomy conjoined in at least two other ways. First, Philip believed, in part because of both the experience of his father in Germany and the breakdown of Valois authority in France, that toleration for religious dissent inevitably undermined dynastic authority. Second, the coalition between militant Calvinists and various disenfranchised townsfolk transformed revolts against magistrates into politico-religious coups.[148]

Dedicated Calvinists operated, however, as a distinct minority in the Netherlands. Protestants and Catholics wound up on both sides of the rebellion, even when religious differences polarized the revolt. Indeed, the attitude of most Netherlanders seems to have been distinctly nonconfessional. Some contemporaries went so far to describe the majority as

---

[145] Israel 1995, 241–54; Kamen 1997, 296–300; Ortíz 1971, 81–83; G. Parker 1977, 225–33, and 1998, 272–77.
[146] Rowen and Harline 1994. Cf. Gorski 2000.
[147] Nierop 2001a; Rowen 1990, 588.
[148] Bercé 1987, 43; Nierop 2001b; te Brake 1998, 79–90; Zagorin 1982a, 104–8.

irreligious and atheistic.[149] The "preconfessional" character of the revolt raises important questions about how to assess the role of religious belief. At least one historian, Joke Spaans, argues that, based upon the pattern of hedge-preaching after the success of the Beggars in moderating Margaret's religious policies. "Calvinism rather seems to have been forged into a weapon for the use of the noble opposition against a centralizing monarchy."[150] Such analysis may hold for many of the moderate nobles, but that should not blind us to the independent impact of the "weapon" of Calvinism, nor to the genuinely felt opinions on tolerance and religion held by many in the Netherlands.

Indeed, as Spaans's analysis suggests, the organizational superiority and strong ideological-theological commitment of the militant Calvinists vis-à-vis Catholics in the Netherlands explains a good deal about the revolt: both its successes *and* failures. Calvinism, as Koenigsberger famously argues, allowed the formation of "revolutionary parties" in France and the Netherlands. The Calvinists in both places gained crucial experience as an underground movement. This experience led to the formation of multiple cells linked through geographically diverse networks. Recall how, in 1554–1557, Calvinists quickly put into place an efficient organization capable of coordinating fiscal-military activity, or how a relatively small group of Calvinists worked to foment iconoclasm. When joined, in effect, to Orange's ability to broker relations with dynastic heads-of-state, Calvinism provided both transregional and "transnational" organizational strength. Catholicism could not, unlike in France, produce anything comparable (see chapter 7).[151]

Calvinism destroyed the unity of the revolt, but it, along with Protestantism in general, helped produce the crises that spurred the rebellion. In conjunction with these crises, cross-class and cross-regional networks worked to ensure that resistance to centralization in the Netherlands would not follow the pattern of the Ghentish uprising against Charles's policies. Moreover, Calvinism provided the backbone of organization and resources for revolt. It made surrender a difficult proposition for those towns, mainly in Holland and Zeeland, where Calvinists had put down significant institutional roots. The question of toleration—on both Catholic and Calvinist sides—prevented the kind of negotiated settlement to the revolt that might have left Habsburg sovereignty intact.

As Antonio Ortíz argues, "But for the indignation of Philip II at the excesses of the Calvinists the established order might have been main-

---

[149] G. Parker 1977, 199–204. On Roman Catholicism in the United Provinces, see Kaplan 1994 and Kooi 1995.
[150] Spaans 1999, 151–53.
[151] Koenigsberger 1971a, 224–52. See also Duke 1999, 125–28; and Smit 1970, 45–46.

tained indefinitely in the Netherlands; it was the Calvinists, albeit a minority, who succeeded in giving coherence to the resistance of those who were initially lukewarm." The conflicts in the Low Countries "were not exclusively religious, but it is unlikely they would have broken out if there had not been religious disaffection. Catholics and Protestants were at one in their indignation at the new taxes and the presence of foreign troops, but it was the Protestants who first resorted to arms."[152]

PHILIP II AND HABSBURG HEGEMONY

At least four of the key events during Philip's reign—the Dutch Revolt, the Morisco Revolt, the intervention in France, and the struggle with England—involved religious networks and identities. But many key developments in the Spanish Habsburg monarchy were, at best, tangentially related to religious considerations. Major changes took place in the New World. The primary period of territorial expansion occurred before Philip became king, but trade and shipping waxed and waned during his reign. In the 1560s the treasure fleet became an institution, bringing regular hauls of silver from the New World. New World silver helped finance Spanish power-projection in Europe—recall that a fresh influx of silver proved critical to the General Settlement of 1577 in which Philip restored his credit. Even after the setbacks caused by English piracy and the defeat of the Armada, Spain's possessions in the Americas played a crucial role in Spanish predominance in Europe, but revenues from Castile itself contributed a consistently greater proportion of wealth to the Spanish treasury.[153]

Expansion: Portugal

In 1580 Philip added Portugal to the Habsburg domains, intervening in a succession crisis there on his own behalf. Philip had a claim to the throne through his mother. His ascension to the throne, however, was "the result of an invasion and military occupation of a temporarily enfeebled kingdom by its more powerful neighbor."[154] Despite this, Philip considered himself the legitimate heir to the Portuguese throne and governed it accordingly—he did not, for example, thoroughly reorganize its government. By adding Portugal to the Spanish Habsburg Empire, Philip gained extensive overseas possessions. Only decades later, during the reign of

[152] Ortíz 1971, 73–74.
[153] Elliott 1989, 3–26; Lovett 1986, 230–35; Lynch 1991, 211–29.
[154] Elliott 1991, 49.

Philip IV, would some of Philip II's policies toward Portugal—themselves related to the Castilianization that was taking place throughout the empire—come back to haunt the Spanish Habsburgs.[155]

Instability in Iberia

Aspects of the composite monarchy in Iberia itself created problems for Philip. Developments in Catalonia during 1568–1569 proved to be little more than a minor annoyance, but a rebellion in Aragon 1591–1592 prevented Philip from mounting military operations against the Huguenots in southern France.

CATALONIA

Catalonia, although loyal to Philip, suffered from chronic socioeconomic problems that, combined with its institutional privileges, prevented it from making much of a contribution to the empire and its wars. At the same time, its geographical position made it an important strategic asset in his struggles against Islam.[156]

Catalonia, like Aragon, retained important aspects of "feudal" organization in its rural regions. This, combined with Catalonia's poverty, led to chronic brigandage and private feuds. The situation was particularly bad along the Catalan-French border, which, like all borders in the sixteenth century, was more a frontier zone of fuzzy jurisdiction and authority. These conditions alarmed Madrid: they raised the specter of Calvinist penetration into Iberia. Reports that Huguenots from France were active among the Catalan brigands prompted Philip to order his representatives in Catalonia to fortify the frontier against purported Huguenot incursions and to step up the activity of the Inquisition.[157]

In 1569, when the Deputies of the *Cortes* asserted their privileges by refusing to pay a tax on parishes demanded by Philip and authorized by the pope, the Inquisition "with characteristic inaccuracy ... confound[ed] a constitutional issue with a religious one" and decided that the Deputies' position was heretical. This confrontation, which led to the arrest of Deputies, had the misfortune of occurring right before a minor invasion by French Huguenots. The local gentry, for their part, "refused to acknowledge any obligation to do so, but voluntarily offered to serve the king in defense of the country."[158]

Philip soon realized his mistake and relented. In 1570 a Catalan army repulsed the invasion, and relations between the Catalans and

---

[155] Elliott 1991; Lynch 1991, 68–70.
[156] Lynch 1991, 301–2.
[157] Ibid., 297–99.
[158] Ibid., 299–300. See also Elliott 1963a, 234–35; and Kamen 1997, 235.

Philip became harmonious once again. Philip left the contractual basis of Catalonia's membership in the composite monarchy, as well as its instittions, intact.[159]

ARAGON

The revolt in Aragon of 1591–1592 proved a far more serious affair. The proximate cause of the uprising involved the flight of Antonio Pérez to Aragon. Pérez was implicated in the murder of Juan de Escobedo, a secretary of Don Juan; more importantly, Pérez held evidence that implicated Philip II in the affair. In 1590 Pérez escaped from prison and sought protection in Aragon. He arrived at an opportune moment. The lesser nobility in Aragon, angry at Philip's attempt to impose his authority on the principality, contemplated secession. Aragon's *fueros* (charter rights) "shielded an archaic social structure" of feudal rights and obligations. The lesser nobility, already chafing at their exclusion from opportunities available to Castilians in the unequal system of the monarchy, took on defense of the *fueros* as a potential route to political power in an independent Aragon.[160]

In 1591 officers of the Inquisition—which had the right to override Aragon's justice system—seized Pérez from protective custody. Their move prompted a riot in Zaragoza under the leadership of a group of lesser nobles. They began plotting to make Aragon an independent republic. Once they seized power in Zaragoza in September 1591, however, they discovered that they lacked support from both the magnates and the general population. Philip sent an invading force. It quickly seized control of the city and executed those rebels who remained behind. Aragon lacked a movement—religious or otherwise—capable of organizing widespread defense of traditional privileges and thus of overcoming within-segment stratifications. Indeed, religion worked against the rebels. Pérez and those co-conspirators who had fled to Béarn sought the protection and support of Henry of Navarre. They even attempted a small invasion with Huguenot forces in February 1592, but the presence of Protestants among the invaders produced a backlash among the Aragonese population.[161]

Philip pursued a moderate course after the rebellion. He opted not to make substantial changes in the *fueros*. Any significant change in the imperial contract with Aragon, in fact, would have required renegotiating the terms of incorporation of the other segments of Aragon-Catalonia, and hence risked greater instability. Moreover, Philip's "adherence to a pluralist conception of monarchy" reflective of the diversity of his hold-

---

[159] Lynch 1991, 300–301.
[160] Ibid., 473–74.
[161] Ibid., 479–80.

ings cautioned against such a move. Nevertheless, the revolt in Aragon had at least one important repercussion: it prevented Philip from launching an intervention in the French civil wars directly from Iberia.[162]

Geopolitics and Empire

Philip died in 1598. His son, Philip III, inherited the pre-eminent power in Europe. But its relative capabilities reflected Philip II's setbacks. War with England and the Dutch continued to drain Spanish Habsburg resources. During the early 1590s Philip poured tremendous resources into France, but opposition to Henry of Navarre virtually collapsed when he abjured Protestantism in July 1593. The new pope, Clement VIII, seeing a resurgent France as a way of diminishing Spanish power, helped confer legitimacy on Henry's conversion. Philip's decision to intervene in France ultimately cost him dearly in the Netherlands by ensuring the survival of the revolt. Henry declared war on Spain in 1595.[163]

The war proved a fluid affair. In April 1596 a Spanish Army seized Calais. A revolt in Ireland against Elizabeth, underway since 1593, drew strength in 1595 from the addition of the Earl of Tyrone to its ranks. The revolt, along with the spectacular failure of an English raid against Panama in 1595–1596 and the threat posed to England by the Spanish seizure of Calais, convinced Elizabeth to enter into alliance with Henry IV, despite her anger at him for having abjured Protestantism. The alliance also brought the Dutch into a united front, and therefore promised a coordinated opposition to Spain.[164]

Spanish forces made gains in France, but Philip's problems mounted due to a raft of bad luck. An English raid against Cadiz in June 1596 was a tremendous blow to Spanish prestige, but two counterexpeditions to support the uprising in Ireland—potentially a far greater threat to England than the attack on Cadiz represented to Spain—ran afoul of bad weather. Meanwhile, the two-pronged war against the Dutch and the French continued to present a dilemma for Philip and his advisors, as any successful operation in one theater required a diversion from the other. Philip opted to try to make peace with Henry. Both monarchs were chronically short of money. Spanish forces suffered repeated mutinies. France, recently emerged from decades of civil conflict, could hardly mount a sustained conflict.[165]

---

[162] Kaiser 1990, 39; Lynch 1991, 480.
[163] Elliott 2000, 242–43.
[164] Ibid., 243.
[165] Elliott 2000, 244–46; Kamen 1997, 306–9; Koenigsberger 1971b, 206–7; G. Parker 1998, 277–78.

Meanwhile, the Huguenots, disgruntled with Henry's change of religion and religious policies, threatened to renew the civil war. They used their religious ties with the English and Dutch to put pressure on Elizabeth, who, in turn, abstained from helping Henry retake Amiens from the Spanish. Henry gave in to both the Huguenots and Philip, signing the Edict of Nantes on 30 April 1596 and the Treaty of Vervins on 2 May 1598.[166]

Philip's wars with the English and Dutch continued after he concluded peace with Henry. Castile, for its part, was exhausted and impoverished. All available silver from the New World immediately went to finance continued military commitment; the Castilian treasury suffered from debilitating interest payments. Bankruptcy in 1596 did little to slow the tremendous demands on Philip's available resources. By the time of Philip II's death, Spain's foreign-policy commitments were enormous—and enormously complicated.[167]

Conclusion: Philip II's Legacy

As Philip III took control, the Spanish monarchy was undergoing important changes. Before his death Philip II and his advisors decided that Spain's situation in northwestern Europe would be simplified by ceding sovereignty of the Netherlands. After he died it became the dowry of his daughter, Isabella, who married (by prior arrangement) its governor, Archduke Albert. Thus, in May 1599 Albert became ruler of the Netherlands, but Spanish troops remained, and it was expected that Albert would follow Madrid's lead when it came to foreign policy. Moreover, the mentality of the court in Madrid in 1598 was decidedly different than it had been at the start of Philip II's reign: the attitude was, as Elliott characterizes it, wary and defensive.[168]

From 1599 onward, the Spanish sought to achieve a "knockout" blow that would resolve the strategic overcommitment created by war with England and the Dutch and the need to guard against potential French intervention, whether in the Netherlands or in Italy. Their attempts to influence the inevitable succession in England—either by placing a pro-Habsburg candidate or Philip himself on the throne—came to naught when on 3 April 1603, King James of Scotland became king of England. A month later, the Spanish discovered that James's ascension was not such

---

[166] Elliott 2000, 244–47.
[167] Elliott 2000, 241–42; Kamen 1997, 309; G. Parker 1998, 279; Stradling 1981, 32–36.
[168] Elliott 2000, 114–15; G. Parker 1977, 233.

a bad thing after all: James issued a unilateral ceasefire. In the ensuing diplomatic maneuvering, however, Albert, pursuing his own agenda, managed to undercut the Spanish position. Moreover, Spanish attempts to arrange tolerance for England's Catholic minority remained an obstacle to peace, as did a number of trade issues. On 30 June 1603 James, Henry, and the United Provinces signed a new alliance. Still, the Spanish continued their policy of rapprochement and, finally, on 29 August 1604, Spain and England made peace—without protection for English Catholics but with some compromises on the issue of trade with the Indies.[169]

War with the Dutch continued. Peace with England did not lead to a great advantage for Spain. After the war appeared to stalemate, Albert and the Dutch agreed to a ten-month ceasefire, which was approved by the States General in April 1606. Philip was not pleased; Albert had exceeded his authority by agreeing to a cease-fire that did not cover Dutch trade in the Indies and hostilities at sea. The Dutch, worried about the potential collapse of the ceasefire, agreed to suspend hostilities at sea but only in the North Sea and English Channel. But another issue interfered with negotiations: the fate of Catholicism. Many in the Spanish court remained concerned that if they could not secure toleration for Catholics in the United Provinces, then the Dutch would use the ceasefire to mount large-scale persecutions against them (just as the English had done in 1604). Philip eventually decided he would offer the Dutch sovereignty in exchange for a guarantee of freedom of Catholic worship. Albert balked, fearing that introducing new elements into the negotiations would be too disruptive. As negotiations continued into 1608, only the issues of trade with the Indies and toleration of Catholicism remained. The Spanish proved willing to make extraordinary concessions.[170]

Nevertheless, the issues of religious tolerance and of trade continued to block any agreement. Toleration of Catholicism presented a particular problem—the Dutch would not consent. They would not accept sovereignty with any conditions, but the idea of abandoning Catholics to potential repression created a backlash in Castile. Yet, eventually, Philip and his advisors concluded a deal. It included neither a formal recognition of Dutch sovereignty nor protection for Catholics in Dutch territory. On 7 July 1609 Philip reluctantly signed the agreement made on 9 April 1609.[171] Indeed, under Philip III, Spanish policy fluctuated from aggressive grand ventures to defensive positioning, and back again. By the time of Philip III's death, Spain was returning to a policy of putting the Catholic cause above all others. The realities of strategic overcommitment even-

---

[169] Allen 2000, 12-14.
[170] Ibid., 156–207.
[171] Ibid., 157–233; G. Parker 1998, 280.

tually clashed with a strong impetus to restore what many perceived as the damaged reputation and reverse the *declinación* (decline) of Spain, an impetus that became an obsession with the triumph of Don Baltasar de Zúñiga and the Count-Duke Olivares at court. Over the course of Philip III's rule, demands for reform in Castile itself grew, as more and more advisors and observers became alarmed at the inequitable tax structure of Castile and the crushing poverty of many of its inhabitants.[172]

I address these developments in chapter 8. For now, I note that, despite all of the factors that worked to determine the fate of Spanish hegemony, we should not lose sight of the clearly important role of the Dutch Revolt in exacerbating or even triggering key processes implicated in Spanish Habsburg decline. In turn, we cannot ignore the tremendous influence of religious divisions upon Habsburg imperial rule in the Netherlands.

It is particularly easy to downplay the role of religion in the increasingly realpolitik environment of the seventeenth century. As we will see, the resumption of the war with the Dutch in 1621 stemmed primarily from concerns about Spanish prestige, as well as Dutch inroads against the Portuguese trading empire. Renewed conflict had little, directly, to do with religion. Yet we have seen that, even after Madrid recognized that Protestantism could not be *eliminated* through military force, the protection and extension of Catholicism remained a major component of Spanish Habsburg policy. Given the ideology that drove Spanish imperial designs, this should not at all be surprising. Even during the Thirty Years' War, when Olivares sent aid to French Huguenots, he only did so after much consideration and a dispensation from a council of Spanish religious advisors. His delay doomed the revolt, and made his compromise of Spanish principles worthless.[173]

Regardless, a series of blunt facts remain. As Henry Kamen remarks of Philip II, "from first to last, his ventures into foreign entanglements were a result of his concern to protect the Netherlands."[174] Under Philip's reign almost all of the factors leading to overextension pivoted on war in the Netherlands: simultaneous conflicts in northwest Europe *and* in the Mediterranean, fighting on multiple fronts in northwest Europe, the Spanish Armada, and so on and so forth. To this we can add the effect of Dutch piracy on Spanish wealth and power, the addition of a powerful and wealthy foe to the Thirty Years' War—Dutch money and diplomacy played an enormous role in supporting the opponents of the Habsburgs—and the direct economic costs of instability in a wealthy

---

[172] Allen 2000; Elliott 1989, 114–21.
[173] Elliott 1984.
[174] Kamen 1997, 257.

province important to the Spanish wool trade. Philip II bequeathed this legacy to his heirs.

Of course, no empire lasts forever. We can only speculate about what configurations of events and processes would have occurred absent the Reformations, let alone the success of the Dutch Revolt. We do know that, under Philip II, Spanish failure was a very near thing on a number of occasions. Geoffrey Parker draws up an impressive list of counterfactuals that I will not repeat here, but suffice it to say that differences in policy toward the Netherlands, changes in timing or strategy vis-à-vis England, alternative outcomes in France, and other contingencies could have made a difference.[175] Spain almost emerged from the great conflicts of the first half of the seventeenth century victorious. The French barely outlasted the Spanish, but because they did, and because of changes in the structure of governance elsewhere in Europe, the dynastic-imperial pathway became significantly less important in the European political system.

In the end, we know what *did* happen to the Spanish Habsburgs: they were done in by a chain of events that began with religious dissent in the Netherlands. There, they pursued unwise policies of imperial management in a context where an increasingly Hispano-Catholic identity undermined multivocal signaling between Castilian rulers and their subjects. Religious heterodoxy, in conjunction with the underlying dynamics of composite states and a number of contingent developments, triggered a sequence of events and mechanisms that, by the onset of the Thirty Years' War, had already primed the Spanish monarchy for devastating overextension.

[175] G. Parker 1998, 292–93.

CHAPTER 7

The French Wars of Religion

THE FRENCH WARS OF RELIGION (1562–1629) provide more evidence for how the spread of heterodox religious movements exacerbated underlying dynamics of resistance and rule in early modern European states. Historians typically divide the French Wars of Religion into nine different conflicts, beginning in 1562 and ending in 1598 with the promulgation of the Edict of Nantes. But the Edict of Nantes did not end religious warfare within the country; Mack P. Holt, therefore, extends the history of the French Wars of Religion until 1629 and the Peace of Alais (June 1629).[1] The political history of overt Protestantism in France continues beyond that, until Louis XIV revoked the Edict of Nantes in 1685.[2]

These conflicts deserve our attention for a number of reasons. First, they profoundly shaped early modern European politics. They destroyed, for decades, the ability of France to operate as a great power. They also intersected in a number of crucial ways, as we have already seen, with the Dutch Revolt and the practice of Spanish hegemony. Thus, the French Wars of Religion provide a stark reminder of the significant political implications of "transnational" religious movements. Second, the conflicts provide additional evidence for the importance of those mechanisms and processes elaborated in this book. Historians have a long tradition of debating the "political" or "religious" character of the civil wars that dominated France in the second half of the sixteenth century. This distinction, which parallels realist and constructivist debates in international-relations theory, no more helps us to understand the French Wars of Religion than it does the Dutch Revolt or the Schmalkaldic War. As Julien Coudy notes, "politics and religion" in the French Wars of Religion "were inextricably intermingled and matched together."[3] This conjunction involved the usual suspects: tensions between localism and centralization; factional struggles between members of the aristocracy; religious aspirations; and the sources of solidarity created by common confessional identities across status, regional, and "national" lines. Foreign intervention, which, until the seventeenth century, almost always took the form of sup-

[1] Holt 1986. See also Turchetti 1991, 24.
[2] The French continued to pursue a policy of relative toleration toward Lutherans in Alsace even after the 1685 Edict of Fontainebleau. See Clark 1998, 1275.
[3] Coudy 1969, vx. See also Thompson 1909, 17–18; and Wood 1996, 4–6.

port for co-confessionals, played a crucial role in shaping the balance of forces at various stages of the multiple conflicts.

I begin with a brief background on the structure of the French state in the sixteenth century, a discussion of the nature of the secession crisis that precipitated the first Wars of Religion, and an overview of the conflicts. I next discuss how international-relations theorists analyze the French Wars of Religion and their aftermath. The bulk of this chapter provides a narrative account of the Wars of Religion that calls our attention to the configurations of mechanisms that shaped the evolution of religious conflict in France. I then conclude with some observations about the implications of the French Wars of Religion for my larger theoretical and historical concerns.

Background and Overview

I have already discussed the structure of the French kingdom in the sixteenth century (see, especially, chapter 3). France was a heterogeneous realm built through dynastic accumulation during the Capetian dynasty, and then rebuilt in the later middle ages by the Valois. Although integrated by the standards of the Spanish monarchy or the Holy Roman Empire, France was not a proto–nation-state (figure 7.1). The French crown expanded its reach and extractive capacities in the fifteenth and first half of the sixteenth centuries by both centralizing power—particularly with respect to the treasury—and proliferating the number of regional authorities. Although "feudal" power relations declined precipitously in France, they were replaced by regional governors and vertical networks of patronage that linked magnates to local clients. Even as the active intervention of the monarchy in local governance increased, the monarchy depended upon noble patron-client networks to govern effectively.[4] As David Kaiser notes, "The history of French politics during the years 1559–1659 testifies more to the persistence of premodern political structures than to the emergence of a prototypical modern state."[5]

Henry II's decision to make peace with Philip in 1559, as we saw in the last chapter, stemmed from three concerns. First, fiscal constraints precluded continued hostilities. The expense of the Valois-Habsburg wars placed the crown in a dreadful financial state. Second, he had already achieved one of his most important aims: the splintering of the Habsburg domains. Third, the rapid expansion of Calvinism deeply alarmed the

[4] Collins 1995, 1–28; Kettering 1986a and b, 1989, 1992; Major 1994, 368–69; D. Parker 1983, 14–27; Swann 2003, 7–25. For a comparative discussion, see Asch 1991.
[5] Kaiser 1990, 49.

Figure 7.1 France at the Middle of the Sixteenth Century

king. Calvinist missionaries operated throughout France. Henry II put aside his dynastic conflicts so that he could turn his attention to the threat posed by heresy within his own domains. The first National Synod of the French Reformed Church, in fact, took place in May 1559.[6] But Henry never carried out his new agenda. On 30 June 1559 he received a mortal wound while participating in a joust during the peace celebrations. He died eleven days later, leaving his fifteen-year-old son, Francis II (who himself died a year later), King of France. The succession crisis precipitated decades of religious civil warfare (table 7.1).

[6] Constant 1999; Knecht 1989, 6–8; Roelker 1996, 214, 226–27.

TABLE 7.1
Chronology of the French Wars of Religion

Years	Conflict	Concluding Agreement	Monarch
1562–1563	First War of Religion	Edict of Amboise	Charles IX
1567–1568	Second War of Religion	Edict of Longjumeau	
1568–1570	Third War of Religion	Edict of St. Germain	
1572–1573	Fourth War of Religion	Peace of La Rochelle	
1575–1576	Fifth War of Religion	Peace of Monsieur	Henry III
1577	Sixth War of Religion	Peace of Bergerac	
1580	Seventh War of Religion	Peace of Fleix	
1584–1598	Eighth War of Religion	Edict of Nantes	Henry III assassinated in 1589; Henry IV claims throne and is formally crowned at Chartres in 1594.
1620–1629	Ninth War of Religion	Peace of Alais	Louis XIII

Source: Holt, 1995, xi–xiv.

Henry II's death ignited intense factional struggles among, ultimately, the great houses of Guise, Montmorency, and Bourbon. The intractability and intensity of religious warfare in France stemmed, in no small measure, from the way these factional struggles intersected with religious disputes. The conflicts quickly took on a general pattern: as "soon as one faction seemed to have established its influence over the monarch, at least one of the others would begin to conspire against it."[7] Any attempt by authorities to steer a moderate course emboldened the Huguenots without assuaging their demands; at the same time, moderation antagonized many Catholics. Thus, each "victory" led to countermobilization and a resumption of military conflict. Despite—or perhaps because of—shifting power configurations and alliances, none of the major parties could achieve a decisive victory. No actor proved capable of brokering a lasting settlement, in no small measure because of the difficulties of legitimating even a compromise position to increasingly polarized religious factions. As the cycle continued, religious polarization increased and popular mobilization became an increasingly important component of the conflicts.

[7] Kaiser 1990, 51–52.

To some extent these processes reached their climax when Henry III's (ruled 1574–1589) brother, Francis, died. This left Henry of Navarre (ruled 1589–1610), a Bourbon and a Huguenot, the presumptive heir to the throne. Although Henry III, under pressure from the Guise, annulled Henry of Navarre's right to succeed him, he subsequently had Henry, Duke of Guise, and Louis, Cardinal of Guise, murdered (23 December 1588) and fled Paris to join with Navarre. A militant Dominican friar assassinated Henry III on 1 August 1589, at which time Henry of Navarre claimed the throne. Henry of Navarre's war with the Guise's Catholic League dominated this last major phase of the conflicts. By converting to Catholicism on 25 July 1593, however, Henry of Navarre managed to isolate his remaining militant opponents. But this move strained his relationship with his erstwhile Huguenot supporters. Nevertheless, his rather unique position as former head of the Huguenot movement allowed him to broker a compromise, the "Edict of Nantes," which kept the confessional peace—with the significant exception of the period from 1620–1629–until its revocation by Louis XIV.

International-Relations Theory and the French Wars of Religion

The previous two chapters dealt with events long assimilated into international-relations theory. Realists, as we have seen, treat the rise and decline of Habsburg hegemony as a straightforward case of, variously, hegemonic overextension, balance-of-power dynamics, or balance-of-threat processes. In doing so, they downplay the crucial significance of religious contention and the specific character of international politics between composite states. In contrast, analysis of the French Wars of Religion in international-relations theory are both sparse and scattered.[8]

A few recent works by ideationalist scholars of political change and state formation do examine the French Wars of Religion. Philpott argues that the Wars of Religion produced a "secularized conception of politics" in France that led it to support "a system of sovereign states." The conflict led, he argues, to the formation of a *politique* party in favor of "domestic toleration" as a means for ending domestic strife. When in power—whether under Henry IV (1589–1610) or in the persons of Cardinals Richelieu (1624–1642) and Mazarin (1642–1661)—those who held *politique* ideas applied them to foreign policy, privileging *raison d'état* above

---

[8] Teschke (2002, 2003) barely mentions the Reformation in his neo-Marxist account of international change in medieval and early modern Europe.

religious considerations. These ideas led them to oppose the Habsburgs and support the sovereign-state system and its instantiation at the Peace of Westphalia.[9]

Philpott correctly stresses the importance of the Reformations in advancing ideas about "reason of state" in France and Europe. But he overplays his hand. Only in the loosest sense can we speak of a *"politique* party" in early modern France. French politicians, moreover, were not alone in their willingness to place security and power above immediate confessional concerns. Even the Spanish Habsburgs sacrificed short-term religious concerns to political necessity; one of their primary objectives during the French Wars of Religion involved ensuring a weak and divided rival. The Count-Duke Olivares supported, albeit with some reluctance, Huguenot insurgents in France during the Thirty Years' War (see chapter 9).[10]

Philpott's sketch of the Wars of Religion captures the basic connection between the structure of the French polity and their dynamics.[11] Because of his focus on how "circumstances of reflection" produce new ideas which, when "socially empowered," cause actors to pursue their associated logics of appropriateness, however, he shows little interest in theorizing this relationship within the broader context of resistance and rule in European composite states.[12]

Hall, similarly, provides an excellent overview of the dynamics of the Wars of Religion; he seeks to explain how France could violate its Catholic "corporate identity" by supporting Protestant powers against the Habsburgs. His answer, like Philpott's: the victory of religious pragmatists, combined with the severity of religious violence in France, meant that France "excised religious identity," at least in a comparative sense, "from its collective identity" and thus "emerged into the thoroughly modern era a bit earlier than the rest of Europe, as indicated by the earlier decoupling of religious identity from French foreign policy."[13]

Heather Rae's study of "pathological homogenization" and state formation reveals another problem with such lines of reasoning. When Louis XIV (1643–1715) revoked the Edict of Nantes and forcibly suppressed the Huguenots, he adopted, from the perspective of European opinion, a *retrograde* policy toward religious minorities.[14] Rae's case study compares the events leading to the Edict of Nantes with Louis XIV's promulgation

---

[9] Philpott 2001, 116–17. I address Philpott's larger arguments about Westphalia in chapters 3 and 8.
[10] Elliott 1984, 127.
[11] Philpott 2001, 129–33.
[12] Ibid., 47–58.
[13] Hall 1999, 57–58.
[14] Rae 2002, 122.

of the Edict of Fontainebleau. She argues that material conditions cannot explain why Louis XIV abandoned religious toleration. The Huguenots proved their loyalty to the Crown during the *Fronde*, they posed no threat to the French state, and their suppression damaged Louis XIV's military, economic, and international position. Rae notes a great many factors that contributed to Louis XIV's decision, but highlights the role of absolutist ideology: "In terms of the ideology of French absolutism, in which the Catholic world view provided the dominant cultural reference points, Huguenots did not fit but should, and could, be 'made to fit,' thereby imposing order and making manifest the completeness of Louis XIV's rule."[15] Rae's account of the French Wars of Religion, like Philpott's, captures some of its essential dynamics.[16] Yet we encounter here some of the same problems with other ideationalist accounts. Rae's own nuanced discussion of the various material and ideological factors that produced the Edicts of Nantes and Fontainebleau undercuts her contention that the consolidation of absolutist ideology explains variation in French religious policy.

As both Rae and Philpott note, the legitimacy of the French monarchy was intimately tied to the "sacral" qualities of the kingship. The French took associated rituals, such as the anointment of new kings, very seriously long after other Europeans discounted them as atavistic. The connection between religion, monarchy, and political community was summed up in the formula "une foi, un loi, un roi" ("one faith, one law, one king"). The major debate between moderates and extremists during the Wars of Religion concerned not whether to tolerate long-term religious heterogeneity, but how to pursue religious homogeneity: should the state suppress heterodoxy by force or embrace a gradual and less violent path? How much should the community accept doctrinal compromises or the toleration of religious dissent to bring about that end? Both the

---

[15] Ibid., 120. Philpott provides no analysis of the revocation of the Edict of Nantes. One could, nevertheless, claim that Philpott's and Rae's (2002, 21) arguments are compatible insofar as once a non-*politique* gained control of French policy, he set about reversing limited toleration for the Huguenots. Yet Louis XIV also formed alliances with Protestant powers, most notably Sweden, and supported the Turks against the Habsburgs. See, for example, Clark 1998, 1276. Even in light of this incongruity between domestic religious ideas and foreign relations, one could still defend Philpott's claims. After all, Louis XIV conducted his policies in a post-Westphalian environment and might therefore be seen as having adopted religious intolerance in the context of settled ideas about state sovereignty. But Louis XIV also put forth a notion of the *Respublica Christiana* as part of his propaganda war justifying Bourbon hegemonic aspirations. Its central claims, and the response of his opponents, echoed the propaganda war surrounding Habsburg hegemony. See also Bosbach 1998.

[16] Rae (2002, 91–110) rightly focuses on how factional and religious contention intermingled to implode the French state.

Huguenots and the Catholics sought a religiously unified polity; they disagreed on whether it should be Reformed or Catholic.[17]

If the ideological pressures for "pathological homogenization" in France were constant, then what, other than developing notions of absolutism, changed between the French Wars of Religion and the Edict of Fontainebleau? The answer can be found in Rae's own analysis: the political context and the constraints faced by the French monarchy. In the period between the outbreak of the French Wars of Religion and the end of the *Fronde*, central authorities in France could not sustain policies of forcible conversion without triggering civil conflict. For most of the Wars of Religion, in fact, they could not even successfully broker sustainable compromises between religious and factional adversaries. The distribution of confessions, their transnational ties, and their connection to noble factions precluded a sustainable peace. The accident of Henry of Navarre's ascension to the throne, his conversion to Catholicism, and shifting military capabilities explain, as we will see, the *relative* success of the Edict of Nantes.

Neither Henry nor his successors, however, broke from the basic goal of one faith, one law, one king. They, and particularly Henry of Navarre's successors, pursued toleration insofar as the threat of domestic insurrection and foreign intervention required them to do so. After reviewing administrative documents concerning the implementation of the Edict of Nantes from 1643 to 1661, Rachel Kleinman reaches the clear conclusion that while the personal dispositions of monarchs toward toleration mattered a great deal,

> there were limits to what a king or minister could do: times of domestic disturbance or danger of Protestant intervention from abroad required a relaxed interpretation of the Edict of Nantes. . . . In times of security and domestic peace the pressure [from clerical and popular opposition to toleration] was difficult to disregard. Whatever differences in outlook may have existed between Louis and Mazarin, the difference in their situation is clear: Mazarin the minister was caretaker of a troubled kingdom; thanks to his efforts Louis the king found himself master of a calmer one. Louis in 1661 was freer to impose his will on the Edict of Nantes because Mazarin had succeeded in pacifying France and removing the threat of foreign intervention on the Huguenots' behalf.[18]

---

[17] Holt 1995, 8–49; Turchetti 1991, 16–20. See also Beame 1966, 251, 265; Philpott 2001, 117; and Rae 2002, 105–8. For prominent exceptions, see Smith 1994.

[18] Kleinman 1978, 571. Indeed, we should also be careful lest we overplay the deleterious consequences of Louis' abandonment of Nantes. For an overview, see Clark 1998, 1276. For a discussion of the numerous methods that seventeenth-century French officials devised to try to bring about the conversion of Calvinists, see Turchetti 1991, 16.

As I have argued at many points in this work, we need not choose between institutionalist analysis and the role of ideas in accounting for state formation in early modern Europe. "Absolutist" strategies of state building may have provided impetus for Louis XIV's revocation of Nantes, but such ideological factors operated through the structural context of early modern states and their dynamics of resistance and rule. Given the domestic and international weakness of the Huguenots' position in 1685 and the relative stability of the French polity, Louis XIV faced a permissive environment for implementing—with the exception of Alsace, where strategic considerations cautioned for continued toleration—long-standing French doctrine concerning religious homogeneity.[19]

Thus, we return to the central problem with ideationalist accounts: we need to theorize the dynamics of the French Wars of Religion rather than treat them as background conditions for the emergence and development of ideas. Doing so helps to answer important questions: why didn't the French composite polity splinter, as did the Habsburg domains, into constituent parts? How do the widely acknowledged aspects of Henry of Navarre's ascension and his abjuration of Protestantism that led to Nantes fit into more general patterns of religious and nonreligious resistance and rule in early modern Europe? It should come as no surprise that the answers to these questions, as I have already suggested, follow from, first, the similarities and differences between French political institutions and those of other composite states in early modern Europe and, second, the specific trajectory of the Reformations in France.

Toward Political-Religious Conflict

The circumstances created by Henry II's death involved, even in the absence of religious contention, many of the ingredients of a crisis for European composite states. France faced severe fiscal overextension as a result of decades of dynastic conflicts. Francis II's age—he was fifteen at the time—created ambiguity concerning the need for a regency government. The court divided between contending aristocratic factions, each with significant military capacity and existing or potential transnational ties.

The crisis that developed in 1559–1560 owed a great deal to factional conflicts among the French nobility. Henry II's reign, according to Francis Knecht, was "largely the story of the rivalry between the two houses of Montmorency and Guise."[20] The Guise were an extremely influential

[19] Clark 1998, 1277.
[20] Knecht 1989, 18.

noble family with dynastic ambitions in their own right. "Through their marriages they were connected with the ruling dynasties of Scotland and Lorraine, and were able to negotiate on an equal footing with the leading princes of Europe."[21] The Guises and the Montmorency faction—headed by Anne de Montmorency, who held the rank of Constable and Grand Master—balanced one another's influence during Henry II's reign. With his premature death in 1559 and the ascension of his young son, Francis II, the Guises took complete control of the government. They soon dismissed Anne de Montmorency.[22]

The Guises' virtual monopoly over the government threatened not only Anne de Montmorency and his clan, but also the Bourbons. Although not powerful at court, the head of the Bourbon family, Antoine de Bourbon, operated as an important dynastic player in European politics. Through his marriage to Jean d'Albert, he succeeded to the right to the throne of Navarre in 1555. As a first prince of the blood, Antoine de Bourbon, not the Guises, had the right to rule while Francis II remained a minor. The ascendancy of the staunchly Catholic Guises threatened the Bourbons for an additional reason: many Bourbons numbered among the Huguenot leadership.[23] The Queen Mother, Catherine de' Medici, for her part, resented Guise domination of the royal government.[24]

The enormous debts accumulated by the monarchy forced the Guises to take a number of highly unpopular measures designed to reduce the kingdom's expenditures and raise additional revenues. At the same time, Calvinism made striking gains in France. Around 1560 the overwhelming majority of the French nobility converted to Calvinism, joining a movement that included burghers, artisans, and other commoners. The Guises intensified Henry II' policy of persecution.[25]

Sometime in 1559, Antoine de Bourbon's younger brother, the prince of Condé, joined a plot to kidnap the young king. The conspirators sought to "liberate" Francis II from the Guises' domination and to expose him to the tenets of the Reformed faith. Many Calvinists believed, rather naïvely, that "if the king and the parlement would only read the Confession of Faith which their first National Synod had adopted, they would see

[21] Elliott 2000, 72–74.
[22] Roelker 1996, 238–39; Salmon 1967, vii—viii.
[23] Wallace 2004, 130. "Huguenot" is a generic term for French Protestants. Huguenots were overwhelmingly Calvinist in orientation, but it is not quite accurate to describe them as "Calvinists." For the sake of simplicity, however, I use the terms more or less interchangeably.
[24] Dunn 1970, 23; Holt 1995, 42–43; Knecht 1989, 18–21; D. Parker 1983, 28; Roelker 1996, 239–44.
[25] Holt 1995, 41–43; Knecht 1989 and 1996c, 366–67; Roelker 1996, 239–40; Rublack 2005, 124–25.

that their doctrine, far from posing a threat to the established order, embodied the truth of the Gospel."[26]

The conspirators traveled around France rounding up support from their fellow Huguenots. Significantly, Calvin himself refused to support the plot; it clashed with his theological understanding of the inviolability of princely rule. Calvin's opposition doomed the endeavor. In the end the conspiracy collapsed. The Guises captured the conspirators and had many of them executed. Condé denied involvement and escaped to plot with his brother.[27]

Catherine de' Medici, however, pursued a policy of moderation. She sought to minimize conflict and, through doing so, enhance the Crown's independence. The Edict of Amboise (2 March 1560), issued before the failure of the plot, granted most heretics a pardon if they returned to the Catholic fold. Shortly after the Edict's proclamation, Francis II—presumably at her urging—freed all religious prisoners and announced his willingness to hear petitions from religious dissenters. This led to a great deal of confusion, since the Huguenots were still expressly forbidden from convening—a necessary step for presenting any petitions to the king. Exploiting the resulting ambiguity, they did more or less what the Calvinists in the Netherlands would soon do: they convened openly and, in some regions, engaged in iconoclasm. The crown responded with the Edict of Romorantin (May 1560), a set of new procedures intended to restore order. The edict proved ineffective.[28]

Francis II called a meeting of his councilors at Fontainebleau on 20 August to deal with the growing crisis. The Bourbons did not attend, but "Montmorency came, accompanied by three of his Châtillon nephews and a large escort." Admiral Coligny—a leading French nobleman and Huguenot—petitioned the king and Catherine on behalf of their Huguenot subjects. After numerous speeches urging religious reform, the council decided to call meetings of the Estates General and of the Gallican Church with the objective of resolving religious differences. But religious unrest continued to grow. On 26 August Condé was implicated in another plot against the court. The Guises moved quickly, mobilizing the royal army and getting a promise of assistance from Philip II. They arrested Condé, but the sudden death of Francis II on 5 December interfered with their plan to execute the prince.[29]

---

[26] Knecht 1996c, 281.
[27] Holt 1995, 43–44; Knecht 1989, 24–25, and 1996c, 329–30; Roelker 1996, 239.
[28] Knecht 1989, 26–27; Roelker 1996, 241.
[29] Holt 1995, 45; Knecht 1989, 27–28.

Francis II's death brought about a radical change in Condé's fortunes. The ambiguity surrounding whether or not Francis's age required a regency government had allowed the Guises to seize power. Charles IX, however, was ten years old and there was no doubt that a regency was in order. Catherine herself became regent. She quickly moved to counter the influence of the Guises by supporting the Bourbons.[30]

Heady days soon followed for the Huguenots. Condé, Coligny, and even Antoine de Bourbon garnered appointments to positions of power in the government. Many Huguenots believed they were on the verge of purifying the Gallican Church—and the whole body politic along with it. Calvin wrote that "if the freedom granted to us by the Edict is maintained, the papacy will fall by itself."[31] Catherine's receptiveness to the Huguenots, however, provoked a backlash among prominent Catholic nobles. Her policy of reconciliation with the Protestant camp even brought the Montmorencies and the Guises together. Along with Jacques d'Albon, they agreed to "defend the Catholic faith with the help of Philip II of Spain."[32]

The years of 1561–1562, in fact, marked a complete failure for Catherine's attempt to steer a middle course. Polyvalent signaling proved impossible. The Huguenots sought complete freedom of action, while the Catholic party refused to accept any substantive toleration of heresy. Yet Catherine recognized that if she adopted a policy of persecution, she would empower the Guises and, in all likelihood, provoke a civil war. A credible commitment to the Huguenots would surely provoke the Catholic party to take up arms. Royal policy, therefore, simultaneously supported the edict while undercutting it through a series of declarations of concord and restrictions on Huguenot worship. Her attempts to achieve a national religious compromise, meanwhile, foundered on the question of the Eucharist—a feature of Reformation politics with which we should now be quite familiar. As instability and violence increased, both sides armed for civil war.[33]

THE FIRST THREE WARS OF RELIGION (1562–1570)

A massacre of Huguenots in the village of Vassy triggered the First War of Religion. The duke of Guise himself played a role in the slaughter; the Huguenots quickly mobilized for war. The rural nobility took the lead,

---

[30] Knecht 1989, 28–29.
[31] Quoted in Turchetti 1991, 20.
[32] Burns 1994, 819–20; Knecht 1989, 30.
[33] Elliott 2000, 72–73; Knecht 1989, 30–42; Turchetti 1991, 21–22.

utilizing "their vast patronage networks to recruit troops for the Protestant cause."[34] In April 1562 the third national synod proclaimed Condé their leader and also "protector and defender of the house and crown of France."[35] Indeed, Catherine's embrace of the house of Bourbon and her attempt to steer a moderate course led many of the leading nobles to believe they could justifiably claim to be the true representatives of the Crown. This helped overcome any opposition tied to Calvin's rejection of a right of violent resistance to authority.[36]

For all the Huguenot talk of protecting the monarchy, however, Condé failed to make good on his pledge to protect the Queen and Charles IX from the Guise, who, in essence, kidnapped Charles from Fountainbleau. Catherine, in consequence, abandoned thoughts of backing the Huguenots and threw her lot in with Montmorency and the Guises. The Huguenots nevertheless made impressive initial gains. Within a short time they took control of many important cities and regions. Meanwhile, spontaneous and semiorganized violence broke out across the kingdom. Antoine de Bourbon, for his part, sided with the Catholic party—who promised him help in regaining Navarre—but was killed at Rouen. Guise himself fell at Orléans in February 1563, killed by an assassin who implicated Coligny in the plot.[37]

But Coligny could not prevail. Elizabeth Tudor agreed to supply the Huguenots with assistance, but she demanded a concession—the cession of Le Havre—that alienated many moderates and even some of Coligny's supporters. The aid brokered by Théodore of Bèze proved more important to the Huguenot cause; Bèze was less committed to Pauline and Augustinian notions about the inviolability of rulers than was Calvin.[38] He made ample use of the pretext that the Huguenots fought for the Crown to arrange for aid from Geneva and the national churches. Geneva "helped to supply arms and munitions for Condé's forces, and played its part in negotiating the loans raised at Lyons, Basle and Strassburg for the financing of his campaigns." Bèze also negotiated with Protestant German princes to form a "mobile Protestant army, ready to accept employment in either the Netherlands or France."[39]

---

[34] Holt 1995, 51.
[35] Quoted in Holt 1995, 52.
[36] Dunn 1970, 25–26; Elliott 2000, 63–74; Holt 1995, 51–52; Knecht 1989, 35–36.
[37] Elliott 2000, 74–75; Holt 1995, 54–55; Kaiser 1990, 55; Knecht 1989, 36–37.
[38] In 1564 Bèze succeeded Calvin as head of the Church in Geneva. Thus, by the time of the Second War of Religion there was no need to claim that the Huguenots were not engaging in resistance to temporal authority.
[39] Elliott 2000, 74–75; See also Kingdon 1967; Koenigsberger 1971a, 224–25; and Sutherland 1967.

Philip II and the papacy matched these efforts with aid to the Catholic party. The war stalemated. Catherine, along with Montmorency and Condé, developed a peace settlement on March 1563–the Edict of Amboise. The edict granted extremely limited toleration for popular Huguenot worship, but gave greater religious rights to the Huguenot nobility. The former constituted a serious flaw in the compromise, since the most significant religious tensions at this point existed among France's urban population. Moreover, the Parlement of Paris and the regional parlements balked at the edict—an act of unlawful defiance against the monarchy. Their eventual, rather grudging, registration of the edict did little to ameliorate the growing religious conflict. The Crown once again tried to placate the Catholic party by imposing restrictions on Huguenot worship. As scholars of contemporary ethnic tensions note, when members of different groups cannot credibly signal that they will abide by agreements in the future, actors are more likely to resort to violence. But the underlying problem stemmed from growing categorical polarization on legitimation claims: many Catholics saw any recognition of the Huguenots as a violation of the king's sacred oath to defend the kingdom from heresy.[40]

Two events sparked the Second War of Religion. Catherine and Charles met with the Duke of Alva in Bayonne in June 1565 while, ironically, on a tour of France that they hoped would promote the settlement. During 1567 Alva led his army along the French border on their way to the Netherlands (see chapter 6). Fearing possible Spanish intervention on behalf of the Catholic cause, Catherine mobilized the French Army to reinforce key defensive positions. The Huguenots, remembering the meeting in Bayonne and concerned about continued Guise dominance at court, misinterpreted the military preparations as the start of a Franco-Spanish plot to destroy Protestantism. Condé and Coligny massed an army with the aim of capturing Catherine and the king. They failed, but soon took a number of important towns. The Cardinal of Lorraine, one of the remaining Guise brothers, invited Alva to intervene.[41]

The Huguenots, even with foreign support from John Casimir of the Palatine, still could not achieve military victory. Most importantly, they failed to take Paris. Anne de Montmorency died defending a Paris suburb from Huguenot forces. Without additional foreign support—which they could not secure—the Huguenots entered into peace negotiations. The Edict of Longjumeau (March 1568) essentially reinstated the Edict of Amboise.[42]

---

[40] Holt 1995, 57–59; Knecht 1989, 38–39; Turchetti 1991, 22. On credible commitments and the onset of conflict, see Fearon and Laitin 1996. See also Fearon 1998.

[41] Holt 1995, 64–65; Knecht 1989, 40.

[42] Ibid.; Roelker 1996, 315.

The Cardinal of Lorraine and the Catholic party's leaders rejected this new compromise. They also wanted revenge for the assassination of the Cardinal's brother, and they saw Alva's success against the rebels in the Netherlands as a sign of their own chances for victory. The Guises and their supporters developed a plot to capture key Huguenot towns and to take Condé and Coligny into custody. In August 1568 Condé and Coligny signed a treaty with William of Orange, thereby officially linking the struggle in the Netherlands to the factional and religious conflicts in France. The Guises themselves had, earlier in the year, entered into a plot to place the Cardinal's niece, Mary Queen of Scots, on the English throne. All of these factors, combined with Alva's intervention, made the Third War of Religion an even more international affair than the previous outbreaks of organized violence in France.[43] In September the Crown buckled to Catholic pressure and promulgated the Edict of Saint-Maureles-Faussés, which revoked toleration and imposed "one confession—Roman Catholic apostolic—on all the subjects of the realm."[44]

The Third War of Religion also saw the growth of nonstate co-confessional networks. The emergence of Catholic confraternities created a network of organized ultra-Catholics that, in many instances, "designed to provide arms and men for the church militant in a holy crusade against French Protestantism."[45] The French Wars of Religion stand out, in this respect, from many other confessional conflicts in that *both* Protestants and Catholics developed cross-regional and cross-class ties independent of central authorities.

The third war broke out when Condé and Coligny got wind of the Cardinal's plot. The military conflict lasted until 1570. As we might expect, the growth of cross-regional and cross-state networks, as well as increasing polarization among the combatants, account for its longer duration. German Protestants and an army under Louis of Nassau both intervened in the war, as did Spanish troops. Condé fell at the battle of Jarnac on 12 March 1569; Coligny assumed de facto command of the Huguenot forces, and despite a string of reversals pulled off a stunning victory by marching on Paris and forcing the Crown to make peace. The Edict of St. Germain (29 July 1570) was a major victory for the Huguenots. They gained the right of open worship in specified towns and the right to occupy four fortified towns. Three of these—La Rochelle, Cognac, and Montauban—gave them control over the southwest of France. The fourth, La Charité, "gave them a bridgehead on the Loire."[46]

---

[43] Holt 1995, 65–67; Knecht 1989, 40–41.
[44] Turchetti 1991, 22.
[45] Holt 1995, 67.
[46] Ibid., 69–70. See also Knecht 1989, 41–42; and Roelker 1996, 316.

Yet the Crown once again sought to balance between the two poles by banning Huguenot schools, which undercut the practical effect of the edict.[47]

THE FOURTH THROUGH SEVENTH WARS OF RELIGION (1572–1580)

The Edict of St. Germain led to another major shift at court. The Guises were out, the Bourbons back in. Catherine de' Medici sought two marriages that she hoped would seal the peace, one between her daughter, Marguerite of Valois, and Henry of Navarre—Antoine's son, who, with the death of Condé, became the nominal Huguenot leader—and one between Henry of Anjou and Elizabeth of England. Henry of Anjou torpedoed his proposed marriage when he refused to marry a heretic. Catherine decided to promote her youngest son, Francis (whom we met in chapter 6) in his place. But his ties to the Guises, his age, and his unattractiveness all worked against the match. The Huguenot faction itself was less than enthusiastic about the possible marriage between Henry of Navarre and Marguerite.[48]

Developments in the Netherlands, as they had in the previous conflict, provided the proximate cause of the Fourth War of Religion. Many of the Dutch rebels sought refuge in France and remained there. The Sea Beggars conducted raids from the port of La Rochelle, making France a base for Calvinist insurrection. The Huguenot leadership, particularly Coligny, wanted to honor their alliance with Orange and to promote their co-confessionalists' cause by aiding in their planned invasion of the Netherlands. Charles IX eventually agreed, but Catherine, fearful of the consequences for relations with Spain and with her Catholic subjects, blocked the decision. Orange and the rebels acted on their own, capturing Brill and moving inland in the northern Netherlands. Coligny continued to seek authorization to come to their aid. When royal sanction failed to materialize, he set about preparing an army of his own—which participated in the failed rebellion of 1572. The Guises, infuriated by the prospect of French support for the Dutch rebels and sensing that Coligny might fall from favor, decided the time had come to take their revenge.[49]

These events occurred against a backdrop of increasing Catholic-Huguenot hostility across France. Tensions in Paris grew steadily worse. Mutual harassment led to low-level violence between ordinary members

---

[47] Turchetti 1991, 22.
[48] Holt 1995, 77; Knecht 1989, 43; Sutherland 1967, 121–60, 222–46, 290–311.
[49] Holt 1995, 81; Knecht 1989, 43–47; Sutherland 1967, 161–83.

of both faiths. The presence of "Protestant cells ... within the overwhelmingly Catholic capital" worsened "the normal socioeconomic tensions" of the period.[50] The Edict of St. Germain's mandate that they remove monuments celebrating the persecution of Huguenots outraged Catholics in Paris. The propaganda war between the two sides intensified.[51] It was in this environment that prominent Huguenots descended on Paris for the 18 August 1572 wedding between Henry of Navarre and Marguerite of Valois.

The wedding festivities lasted six weeks, more than enough time for popular anger to mount against the marriage of the princess to a heretic, and for the Guises to plot their strike against Coligny and his Huguenot allies. On 22 August Coligny survived an assassination attempt. On 23 August it became clear that Henry, Duke of Guise, was involved. The crown arranged for an armed escort to protect Coligny, but a Catholic militant headed the detachment. That same day, Catherine and her advisors decided that it would be safer to eliminate Coligny than to risk greater violence by attempting to bring him to justice. Indeed, she herself may have been involved in the plot to kill Coligny. Regardless, the king believed that she was, and that in consequence he had no choice but to authorize a second assassination attempt. The king, Catherine, and their counselors also decided to use the opportunity not just to kill Coligny (and some of his associates), but to wipe out the Huguenot leadership. In the early morning of 24 August—St. Bartholomew's Day—royal agents murdered Coligny and over a dozen prominent Huguenots in their beds. Henry, Duke of Guise, got his revenge, killing Coligny with his own hands.[52]

News of the murders led to an explosion of popular violence against the Huguenots in Paris. For the next three days, grisly scenes played out all over the city, as Catholics slaughtered the Calvinists in their midst. Reports that Henry, Duke of Guise, had uttered the words "it is the king's command" while murdering Coligny implied royal authorization for the massacre, as did Charles's statement to the Parlement of Paris on 26 August that "everything that has occurred was done by his express commandment." Nevertheless, although the king and his compatriots did nothing to prevent the massacre, all evidence suggests that they did not order it. The massacre spread outwards from Paris. Over the next six weeks, the slaughter of Huguenots claimed as many as 8,000 lives in the provinces, in addition to the estimated 3,000 killed in Paris.[53]

[50] Holt 1993, 539.
[51] Diefendorf 1985, 1086–88; Holt 1993, 539.
[52] Elliott 2000, 146–48; Holt 1995, 81–85; Knecht 1989, 48–49; Roelker 1996, 317.
[53] Holt 1995, 88–90; te Brake 1998, 80.

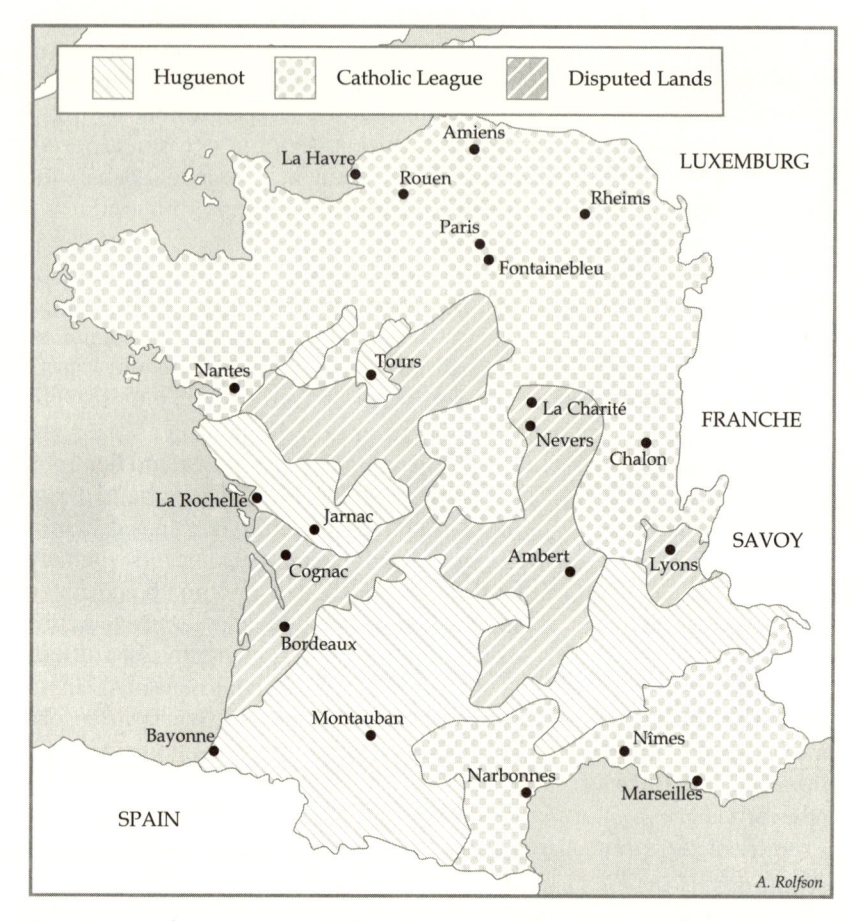

Figure 7.2 Religious Divisions after the St. Bartholomew's Day Massacre

Of the Huguenot leadership, only Henry of Navarre, held captive in Paris and forced to abjure Protestantism, and Henry of Condé, the late Condé's young son, who escaped to Germany, survived. Thousands of Huguenots responded to the violence by rejoining the Catholic Church, while others fled abroad. Many considered the massacre to be God's punishment. Those that were left now turned to open revolt (figure 7.2).[54]

Between 1572 and 1573 the remaining Huguenot strongholds in the southwest of France broke from royal administration. Huguenot assemblies established an independent "state within a state," with a constitution

[54] Holt 1995, 94–98; Knecht 1996c, 429–32.

that essentially created a federal republic. The Huguenots took over the collection of royal taxes to fund their activities. In this they presaged the Union of Utrecht, but without the same degree of unity or expertise in funding warfare. The confederation neither included all of the major Huguenot enclaves nor formed a territorially contiguous unit.[55]

For all this, the Fourth War of Religion proved surprisingly brief. Royal and Catholic forces could not capture La Rochelle. Financial pressures, as they did throughout the conflicts, precluded long-term military operations. Poland elected Henry of Anjou—Charles IX's younger brother, later Henry III, king of France—king of Poland. Henry decided to call off the siege.[56] The Peace of La Rochelle ended the war, but with concessions far short of what the Huguenots wanted. They were only granted the right to practice their faith in public in La Rochelle, Montauban, and Nîmes. Between 1574 and 1576 the intrigues of the youngest Valois prince, Francis; the death of Charles IX on 30 May 1574; Henry III's leisurely trip home to claim the crown; Condé's intriguing in Germany; and the escape of Henry of Navarre from captivity in Paris all exacerbated the underlying instability of the settlement.[57]

In the Fifth War of Religion, Henry III faced a large combined force including Condé and John Casimir of Palatine's German soldiers, a new Protestant army raised by Henry of Navarre, the new Montmorency, and Francis. With no finances to raise an army and their enemies converging on Paris, Henry III and Catherine negotiated for peace and issued the Edict of Beaulieu (6 May 1576). Protestants gained full religious rights, including public practice and the construction of churches, everywhere in France except Paris. Neutral courts would oversee religious cases. The edict also called for the Estates General to meet in six months—as Protestant resistance theory had called for. This last was a mistake for the Huguenots, since the Estates General, when it did meet, was composed almost entirely of Catholics. All three estates called for overturning the edict and taking up arms, if necessary. Even before then, the Parlement of Paris refused to register the edict, and some of the towns that were supposed to be turned over to the Huguenots refused to comply. The Estates General, however, was unwilling to take steps to finance the new war, which, in view of the growing national debt, would have required a new source of revenue.[58]

---

[55] Elliott 2000, 149; Holt 1995, 81–85; Knecht 1989, 51–53, and 1996c, 436–38; Nierop 1995, 47–48.

[56] Achieving a religious peace was imperative if he was to take up the throne of Poland, which embraced religious tolerance. See Elliott 2000, 157.

[57] Knecht 1989, 70–71; Wood 1996, 5–7.

[58] Holt 1986, 45–69, and 1995, 103–8; Roelker 1996, 323–25.

The meeting of the Estates General involved two other important developments. First, an increasing number of voices among Catholic nobles and councilors urged moderation and peace. Their opponents branded them as *"politiques"*: those who would place political expediency before the faith. Many historians and some political scientists treat the *politiques* as an organized movement, but the term covers a number of influential, and often very different, actors who came to believe that the best way to ensure "une foi, un loi, un roi" was through peaceful efforts of conversion and persuasion in the context of loyalty to the monarchy.[59] Nancy Lyman Roelker notes that the *politiques* believed that "in the circumstances of civil war, it was preferable to make *temporary* concessions on confessional uniformity rather than to suffer the destruction of the national community."[60] Mack P. Holt argues that "it is claimed that these so-called *politiques* were the birth of the modern view that political considerations should always take precedence over religious considerations: in other words, the decline of confessional politics. Nothing could be more misleading."[61]

Second, France saw the emergence of a "Catholic League." After the edict the Guise party and other militant Catholics lobbied heavily for war; they simultaneously intrigued to form a new defensive league of like-minded ultra-Catholics. Henry III recognized the threat to his authority and placed himself at the head of the League, but his assumption of titular control over the movement had little practical impact. At the Estates General, in Paris, and elsewhere in the country, the edict met with an overwhelmingly hostile response. Henry III, convinced that he could not sustain his attempt to forge a compromise, agreed to renew the war in 1577. The highly polarized religious environment once again undermined the ability of the Crown to broker a solution, while the growth of co-confessional networks precluded Henry from dividing and ruling the different factions.[62]

The Sixth War of Religion proved a tepid affair. The royal army lacked adequate financing and, in consequence, failed to mount an effective campaign. Two Huguenot towns fell in May and June 1577, but continuing the offensive any further was beyond royal resources. The Peace of Bergerac (17 September 1577) and the Edict of Poitiers rolled back some of the liberties granted to the Huguenots in the Edict of Beaulieu and banned

---

[59] For discussions, see Beame 1993; Bettinson 1989; Holt 1986, 76–85; Holt 1995, 108–9, 168–69; and Roelker 1996, 326–28. For the standard view of the *politiques*, see Philpott 2000 and 2001.
[60] Roelker 1996, 238.
[61] Holt 1995, 109.
[62] Ibid., 109–10; Knecht 1989, 56–57.

the formation of any league and association in the kingdom; otherwise, they mirrored Beaulieu.[63]

The Seventh War of Religion, which lasted from November 1579–November 1580, also proved inconclusive. It was the culmination of several small-scale conflicts, and took place against the backdrop of a series of peasant uprisings. This time, a number of Huguenot towns of the Midi opposed the resumption of hostilities, and Francis of Anjou's (to whom had been given the duchy that once belonged to Henry III) ambitions in the Netherlands prompted him to work hard to negotiate a peace. The Peace of Fleix reinstated Poitiers with minor modifications.[64]

Ideological Developments: Legitimating Rule and Resistance

A small explosion of literature developing theories of resistance followed upon the outbreak of the Fourth War of Religion. Calvinists, like Lutherans, initially rejected challenges to political authority. But just as Luther proved adaptable, so did Calvin's successor, Théodore de Bèze. Faced with a military struggle that involved Calvinists, Bèze formulated a theory of armed resistance in *The Right of Magistrates* (1574), which joined Francis Hotman's *Francogallia* (1573) and the *Vindiciae contra tyrannos* (1579), probably by Phillipe Du Plessis-Mornay, as three of the most notable among the many texts of Huguenot political theory written during the wars. Both Bèze and Hotman argued that the right of resistance was limited to those officers and institutions "endowed with part of that government's authority." Hotman pointed to the Estates General, but Bèze extended that right to the inferior magistrates of the realm: that is, "high-ranking nobles holding hereditary offices in national or provincial government, and the elected magistrates who administered many French cities." Mornay also vested inferior magistrates with the right to resist tyrannical policies, but went even further, arguing that the state operated through two contracts: between God and king and God and the people. Moreover, the sovereignty of the people, Mornay argued, stood above that of the king. In consequence, "If the king fails to do his duty to uphold the church and the law of God, the 'inferior magistrates' must not only resist him, but also remove him."[65]

As Kathleen Parrow notes, none of these theories of resistance was particularly novel; the key claims resonated with long-standing (and familiar) arguments in European political thought.[66] Nevertheless, the articulation

---

[63] Holt 1995, 110–11; Knecht 1989, 56–57.
[64] Holt 1995, 116–17; Knecht 1989, 57–59; Wood 1996, 282–83.
[65] Knecht 1989, 70–71. See also Holt 1995, 100–101; and Linder 1966.
[66] Parrow 1993, 3.

of these theories in the context of the French political-religious struggle mattered a great deal. They provided justifications for first Huguenot and then ultra-Catholic resistance to the Crown. They also provoked alternative formulations of sovereignty and resistance. In 1576 Jean Bodin published his famous *Six Books of the Commonwealth*, in which he argued, contra theories of resistance, that sovereignty was indivisible and absolute. What mattered was where it lay: with the people (democracy), an elite (aristocracy), or the prince (monarchy). Since France, by its laws, customs, and traditions was a monarchy, there was no right of resistance. Bodin's work became incredibly influential in the development of the theory of sovereignty, particularly in the seventeenth century. It even inspired an enormous debate in the seventeenth century—primarily after the Peace of Westphalia—about what kind of sovereignty existed in the Holy Roman Empire, a debate that Samuel Pufendorf justly mocked in his *On the Present State of Germany*.[67]

The Problem of Succession and the Eighth War of Religion (1580–1598)

Henry III's decision to place himself at the head of the Catholic League may not have helped his cause at the Estates General, but it did undermine the strength of the League considerably—which was, after all, one his objectives. From 1580–1584 France enjoyed a period of relative religious peace. In June 1584, however, Francis of Anjou, brother of Henry III, died of chronic disseminated tuberculosis. The militant French Catholics viewed Anjou's activities in the Netherlands and intrigues with the Huguenots with apprehension, but his death posed an even greater threat to their position. Henry III was clearly never going to produce offspring; the likely extinction of the Valois line left Henry of Navarre as the next heir to the throne.[68]

The Guises and other militant Catholics moved quickly. They formed a new Catholic League (The "Holy Union") devoted to preventing the " 'Most Christian King' from falling into the hands of a heretic."[69] They put forth the Cardinal of Bourbon, Henry of Navarre's uncle, as their own candidate to succeed Henry III. The Guises signed a treaty with Spain on December 1584, in which Philip agreed to subsidize the Catholic League's war against the Huguenots. The Guises agreed to some territorial concessions and to promulgate the Council of Trent in France (that

[67] Pufendorf 1690; Schmit 1998, 452–53.
[68] Holt 1995, 208–12; Knecht 1989, 120.
[69] Holt 1995, 121. See also Parrow 1993, 51.

is, to implement the Counter-Reformation in the kingdom). The League was composed of prominent hard-line Catholic nobles who in turn were linked to a network of "urban notables and magistrates who would eventually organize League cells in city halls throughout the kingdom."[70] This gave the League an organizational structure on par with that of the Huguenots and enhanced its strength further, though not necessarily its cohesion. In 1585 Catholic hard-liners in Paris created the "Sixteen"—an independent revolutionary organization devoted to the Catholic cause and widely embraced by Parisians of different social standings.[71]

Outmaneuvered by the Guises, Henry III signed the Treaty of Nemours in July 1585. Nemours wiped out all toleration for the Huguenots and ordered them to cede control of their fortified towns. It banned heretics from holding royal offices. It also triggered a new phase of organized conflict. The Guises took the initiative; with their superior strength and financing they operated outside of Henry III's control. Soon, another army of German Protestants intervened on the Huguenots' behalf. The Germans were defeated, but Henry of Navarre's forces met with some success on the battlefield.[72]

The period of 1587–1588 witnessed a series of complicated political developments. Henry of Navarre found allies among some moderate Catholics, particularly his own relatives. Henry III raised an army to fight Henry of Navarre, but he scored his most important victories by convincing the Swiss and German mercenaries supporting the Huguenots to disband. Moreover, Henry III appointed one of his own favorites, Jean-Louis of Nogaret, Duke of Épernon, to a number of positions coveted by the Guises. Henry, Duke of Guise, set out to topple Épernon. At the same time, the Guises worried about the succession of the French monarchy. The Cardinal of Bourbon's advanced age precluded him from reigning for long—if he even survived until Henry III's death. In the ensuing maneuvering, Henry III forbade Henry of Guise from entering Paris—a wise precaution, since that would have allowed him to link up with the militant Catholics there—but Henry of Guise still managed to take effective control of Paris in May 1588. A few months later, Henry III orchestrated the murders of Henry of Guise and the Cardinal of Guise. He also had many of their supporters imprisoned.[73]

Henry III's treachery inflamed pro-League passions. League cells took control of cities and towns throughout France. The League and its allies now embraced the very resistance theories first promulgated by the Hu-

---

[70] Holt 1995, 122–23. See also Harding 1981, 379–90.
[71] Holt 1995, 122–23; Knecht 1989, 60–61.
[72] Holt 1995, 125–26.
[73] Ibid., 127–30; Knecht 1989, 60, 162–64, and 2000, 230–34.

guenots. Henry III turned to Henry of Navarre and the Huguenots for support. They formalized their new alliance on 3 April 1589. Many ultra-Catholics now openly claimed that Henry III's actions deprived him of the right to rule. By the summer Henry III and the forces of his Huguenot allies threatened to retake the capital, but on 1 August 1589 a Catholic monk assassinated Henry III. One of Henry's last acts was to declare Henry of Navarre (Henry IV) his successor and to recommend that he abjure Protestantism.[74]

With Henry III dead, moderate nobles shifted their support to Henry IV. By the spring of 1590 Henry IV's forces encircled Paris. Parma's interventions in 1590 and 1592, and the presence of a Spanish garrison in the city, kept Paris in militant Catholic hands. But the League and the rule of the Sixteen began to fracture along traditional class and status divisions. Support for the ultra-Catholic position, meanwhile, eroded throughout much of France. Many notables and ordinary people grew tired of continued internal strife and repeated foreign interventions. By mid-1593, fewer and fewer people had the stomach—in Paris, literally, which repeatedly ran short of food—for continued fighting. Henry IV's abjuration, when it finally came on 25 July 1593, completely isolated the most militant Catholics. His largesse also helped rally magistrates and nobles throughout France to their new king. The Gallican Church sanctioned his conversion.[75]

But Henry IV could not secure his kingship while Paris held out. With his abjuration and the continued siege of the capital, opinion within Paris shifted in his favor. On 22 March 1594 the new Governor of Paris betrayed the Sixteen and opened the gates to Henry IV's forces. The Spanish troops left. Pope Clement VIII, anxious to find a counterweight to the Spanish, accepted his conversion in 1595. With support falling into place, it was now time to expel the Spanish from the rest of France, and Henry IV promptly declared war on Spain.[76] Parrow nicely summarizes the impact of Henry IV's abjuration on the ability of ultra-Catholics to legitimize continued resistance: "Support for the Catholic League now clearly carried the stigma of *lièse-majesté*. Since Henry IV had converted, been absolved by the pope, and crowned King of France, the League's close ties to Spain meant it was supporting a foreign power against a legitimate Catholic French king. That was treason."[77]

[74] Elliott 2000, 226–27; Holt 1995, 132–33; Knecht 1989, 64–65; Parrow 1993, 54–55; Sutherland 1967, 33–34; Tracy 1999, 151.
[75] Finley-Croswhite 1999, 17–18; Holt 1995, 133–59; Knecht 1989, 77–79; Tracy 1999, 152.
[76] Ascoli 1974; Holt 1995, 159–60; Knecht 1989, 79–80.
[77] Parrow 1993, 63.

Henry IV's abjuration gave him control of Paris and most of France, but it alienated his base of support among the Huguenots. The war with Spain created a superficial unity in the realm, but the growing militancy of the Huguenot demands carried with them real risks for the new regime. Huguenot communities stopped contributing royal taxes. Others threatened armed insurrection. In April 1598 the two sides reached an agreement, the famous Edict of Nantes. As with the previous compromises, the edict satisfied neither Huguenots nor former members of the Catholic League. Modeled after the Edicts of Beaulieu and Poitiers, that of Nantes provided for limited toleration, complete freedom of conscience, equal political rights, and a number of other concessions including a temporary right to hold some two hundred fortified towns and keep arms. The edict also restored Catholic worship in Huguenot towns and regions, and mandated that the Huguenot population refrain from work on Catholic religious holidays.[78] According to Holt,

> It is often claimed that the edict was a victory of modern *raison d'état* over religious dogmatism, that Henry IV and his "politique" supporters clearly viewed the salvation of the state as more important than religious unity. In other words, religious piety and zealous faith were forced to take a backseat to modern secular politics. This view is not only anachronistic—there was no such thing as secular politics in the sixteenth century—but it also completely overlooks Henry's goals of religious concord and unity as well as his own understanding of confessional politics. The Edict of Nantes was, to be sure, a forced settlement like most of the earlier edicts of pacification. It resulted from the particular circumstances of the 1590s: Henry's abjuration, the submission of the League, and his politics of appeasement. But the edict was also a product of Henry's commitment to the Gallican monarchy of his predecessors. Rather than religious toleration or modern reason of state, the underlying principles of the Edict of Nantes was the restoration of "one king, one faith, one law."[79]

THE LAST WAR OF RELIGION (1626–1629) AND THE
FATE OF THE HUGUENOTS

Despite the growing antagonism between Henry IV and the Huguenots that marked the period before the promulgation of the Edict of Nantes, Henry had one major advantage over his predecessors in bringing about religious peace. As a former Protestant, Henry maintained strong ties with

---
[78] Holt 1995, 164–66; Knecht 1989, 80–82; Tracy 1999, 152–53.
[79] Holt 1995, 163.

the Huguenots. At the same time, his total victory over the militant members of the League, the growing number of Catholic moderates, and the sanction of his abjuration allowed him to speak to most Catholics as one of their own. His own positioning, and the changing relationship between Catholic identity and expectations of appropriate behavior, allowed him to project more effective polyvalent signals than the Valois kings were ever able to do.

The last military conflict between the Huguenots and the Crown provides compelling evidence for this interpretation. A Catholic militant assassinated Henry IV in May 1610. His son, Louis XIII, was only eight years old. Henry IV's wife, Marie de' Medici, became regent. Marie was an Italian and a staunch Catholic. After the Duke of Sully resigned from the royal council, the regency government became completely dominated by Catholics and took on a pro-papal orientation. The Huguenots had good reason not to trust the disposition of the Crown, or its willingness to defend the integrity of the Edict of Nantes. At an assembly held at Saumur in 1611, Henri, Duke of Rohan, a member of the more militant Huguenot faction, assumed the political leadership of the French Protestants. Developments at court prompted a princely rebellion in 1614, and many Huguenot princes joined in the attempt to limit Italian influence at court. They did so to halt the developing momentum to end religious tolerations: a 1614 meeting of the Estates General involved a concerted effort by many of the delegates to rescind the Edict of Nantes.[80]

In April 1617 Louis XIII, who had reached his majority in 1614, asserted more authority over royal affairs. Louis XIII, however, soon moved to end the independence of the Bourbon principality of Béarn. As Béarn was not subject to the Edict of Nantes, this allowed him to restore Church property there. He could not enforce his decision, however, without recourse to military force. The campaign of 1620 turned into a pretext for rooting out "those few Huguenot militants who might be able to rouse significant opposition to the crown." Béarn capitulated, but Louis' actions prompted the Huguenots to countermobilize, particularly in La Rochelle. The uprising of Huguenot militants in the city did not extend to the bulk of the community. The two sides reached a compromise in 1626, but a new uprising broke out—supported by English aid—in 1627. The final war of religion in France ended with the Peace of Alais in 16 June 1629. The edict reaffirmed the toleration clauses of the Edict of Nantes, but the Huguenots were forced to abandon their military and political guarantees. In 1685 the whole process ended when Louis XIV revoked the Edict of Nantes.[81]

---

[80] Ibid., 172–76.
[81] Desplat 1991, 68–83; Holt 1995, 176–87.

CONCLUSIONS

The dynamics of the French Wars of Religion caution against placing too much emphasis on "ideas" and logics of appropriateness in their own right. First, norms of appropriate conduct, particularly with respect to rule and resistance, proved quite adaptable to circumstances. The Huguenots only adopted strong norms of resistance when they felt strongly threatened by royal authorities. As Henry III shifted his support toward the Bourbon and Huguenot cause, the Huguenots downplayed these claims while the ultra-Catholic faction appropriated them for their own purposes. After Henry III's assassination prominent Huguenots adopted the arguments and logics of Catholic moderates as they sought to isolate their ultra-Catholic rivals. Second, not a few actors proved quite flexible in adjudicating between their religious interests and power-political goals. Henry IV stands out in this regard, but, as we have seen, many sought to reconcile conflicting interests in the light of shifting circumstance.[82]

The French Wars of Religion provide, instead, compelling evidence for how the spread of religious heterogeneity intersected with the dynamics of composite states. Religious identities and ties provided a basis for cross-regional, cross-class, and inter-state collective mobilization capable of challenging the limited autonomous resources of the French state.[83] As James Wood argues, "What presented problems for the state . . . offered opportunities for the Protestant minority in France, since all that was needed to exploit" its fiscal, administrative, and military vulnerabilities "was a cause capable of mobilizing widespread support. . . . When religion fused with rebellion, the Huguenots were able with their own resources or the aid of foreign powers to sustain military resistance long enough to exhaust both the royal army and the royal treasury."[84]

The composite structure of the French state and the significant autonomy enjoyed by key intermediaries—particularly as coercion-wielders—both limited the ability of the Crown to enforce religious ordinances and rendered it vulnerable to the formation of opposing cross-class and cross-regional religious ties. But this was more than a matter of a weak state unable to capitalize on new military-technical developments. Religious differences exacerbated factional conflicts at the French court by raising the stakes of victory and defeat—not only for great nobles but also for ordinary people who might otherwise be relatively indifferent to which noble house dominated the government. Religion provided a categorical

---

[82] For an example, see Joan Davies's study (1990) of the Duke of Montmorency's attempt to maintain his position as governor of Languedoc during Henry III's reign.
[83] Parrow 1993, 9.
[84] Wood 1996, 5.

difference through which actors yoked together a variety of groups and interests into relatively well-bounded sites for collective mobilization, whether Huguenot or ultra-Catholic in orientation. This process not only allowed sustained, cross-regional resistance to central authorities, but also deprived the royal government of revenue and manpower for use against internal and external threats.

The consistent failure of central authorities—or their agents—to broker between opposing confessions and factions also played a key role in the French Wars of Religion. One might argue that these failures were overdetermined: given the weakness of the monarchy, it could not have successfully kept factional conflicts in check even without the added problem of religious differences. But religious cleavages not only made these conflicts much more intractable, they also escalated them beyond a "simple" power struggle at court. The Crown repeatedly proved incapable of making religious concessions that could satisfy Catholics and Huguenots alike. Even Henry IV, who enjoyed a unique position as a bridge between the Huguenots and mainstream Catholics, faced difficulties in his attempts to reconcile the Huguenots to his authority. Violent struggles between the Crown and its Huguenot subjects continued into the Thirty Years' War.

The Wars of Religion and State Formation

We can best understand the impact of the French Wars of Religion on France's pathway of state formation by considering two features of the civil strife. First, unlike in the Netherlands, France saw a significant Catholic countermobilization against Calvinism. Second, the Huguenot minority in France never made a sustained bid for outright secession. The reasons behind these two aspects of the French Wars of Religion account for how the Reformations accelerated France's movement along the sovereign-territorial pathway and why religious contestation ultimately favored that pathway in Europe as a whole.

To begin with, why was there a significant Catholic countermobilization in France; why did a subset of Catholics form an effective "revolutionary party" there but not in the Netherlands? Historians offer a number of answers. First, they point to the greater strength of popular piety in France than in the Netherlands. Recall that, in the Low Countries, large segments of the population were either hostile or indifferent to the Catholic Church. The connection between religion and legitimacy, moreover, held particular force in France: the French king was the "Most Christian King" and was oath-bound to defend the country against heresy. While many Europeans considered rituals of sacral kingship rather quaint, the French took them very seriously. Finally, the weakness of the Crown, and then doubts about its allegiances, forced Catholics to resort to "self-help" to preserve their religion far more than they did in the Netherlands.[85]

Second, why didn't the Huguenots mount a major secession effort in the sixteenth century? After all, they established a functional "state within a state" during the Wars of Religion. One reason might stem from the structure of the French composite state. The French Wars of Religion did not involve an absentee and "foreign" king. Control over the center in France meant control over the government of the entire composite polity, as opposed to control over a segment—albeit a composite one itself—of the larger Spanish monarchy. In France the continued *political* weakness of the Crown kept the various noble factions focused upon the long-term goal of controlling it. For both the religious parties and the factions with which they intertwined, control over the center provided crucial rewards of wealth, status, and prestige. Secession meant forgoing these attractive prospects. Thus, the *comparative* centralization and "modernization" of the French state rendered outright secession a relatively unattractive prospect to most participants in the conflict. We should also remember that secession was, for most of the Dutch rebels, a last resort. They only embraced it when they saw no other means of sustaining their struggle.[86]

If we follow this line of reasoning, we come to an important, if somewhat unsurprising, conclusion: as a general matter, religious contention in early modern Europe most threatened the long-term integrity of political communities where, first, segmentation of constituent political units was most advanced, and, second, where religious differences aligned in some way with those fault lines. Such circumstances favor patrimonial-style secessions that detach a particular node, as opposed to struggles for control over the entire polity.[87] But this explanation strikes me as somewhat unsatisfying, as the Huguenots could have detached—as they did in practice at various stages of the conflict—constituent segments of the French polity. Such reasoning raises an important counterfactual: we know that a military solution to the conflicts proved impossible before Henry IV's ascension and abjuration. In 1621 the Huguenot assembly at La Rochelle did, in fact, decide to develop an independent military structure and many of their opponents raised the specter of the Dutch Revolt.[88] If, during the sixteenth-century wars of religion, the Huguenots had lost hope of accommodation with the Crown—if, for example, the

---

[85] For discussions, see Holt 1995, 8–49; Koenigsberger 1971a, 242–43; Nierop 1995, 38–44; and Venard 1999, 133–80.

[86] Benedict 1999, 3–10; Nierop 1995, 47–50.

[87] Compare Cooley's arguments (2005, 96–99) about the path-dependant effects of integrated (U-Form) hierarchies and territorially segmented (M-Form) hierarchies.

[88] Bonney 1991, 227; Lestringant and Blair 1995, 288; D. Parker 1971, 75.

Guise had secured their candidate—might the Huguenots have decided to go the way of the Dutch?

I have no persuasive answer to this question. But spinning out such counterfactuals—whatever their plausibility—should remind us of the fundamental contingencies that led to the resolution of the sixteenth-century French Wars of Religion. It took Henry IV, as a former Huguenot leader and a Catholic king, to isolate and overcome ultra-Catholic opposition while retaining, however precariously, Huguenot support for the Crown. In restoring royal authority and, through the terms of the Edict of Nantes, building a constituency among Huguenots for accommodation with the monarchy, he created the conditions that eventually allowed his successors to impose religious unity on the country by force.

All of this suggests a tension with some of my earlier arguments, but one involving an interesting possibility with respect to mechanisms of multivocal signaling. For most of the sixteenth-century wars of religion, the Crown and its agents could not simultaneously establish inclusive identities with both the Huguenot and ultra-Catholic factions. They oscillated between the two religious groups but failed to establish a stable middle ground. This specific failure accounts for important dynamics in the French Wars of Religion. But resulting uncertainty over the *ultimate* orientation of the center encouraged the Huguenots to continue to struggle for its control. Contrast these conditions with the Dutch Revolt, where Philip II's actions removed any doubt concerning where his religious loyalties lay. The institutional ambiguity of the French monarchy thus combined with the specific failure of the Valois to bridge religious identities to shape the fate of France.

These factors help make sense of one of the ironies of the French Wars of Religion: the fragmentation and weakening of royal authority created by the Wars of Religion ultimately strengthened sovereign-territorial impulses in France. They gave expanded meaning to the ideology of "one faith, one law, one king." Moreover, the effort to avoid a repeat of the cataclysm by creating new institutions, and reinvigorating old ones, helped lay the ideological and institutional groundwork for at least the resumption of a pathway of state formation with sovereign-territorial attributes. But France remained, despite the ideological trappings of central control and absolutism, a composite state; the *Fronde* may have been one of the last serious rebellions in France against centralization, but that in no way meant that France became a "nation-state" in early modern Europe.[89]

---

[89] See Holt 1995, 210–16; Major 1994, 370; D. Parker 1983, 46–59; and Smith 1993.

CHAPTER 8

Westphalia Reframed

THE PRECEDING THREE CHAPTERS provide strong evidence for a central claim of this study: the Protestant Reformations led to a crisis in European politics because they triggered specific mechanisms and processes embedded in the structure of early modern European composite states. I examine, in this chapter, these dynamics in the context of the Thirty Years' War and its aftermath. Religious contention in this period shaped political relations in very similar ways as it had in the preceding century: by influencing dynamics of resistance and rule, producing opportunities for foreign intervention, and by linking otherwise discrete conflicts over local concerns. But we also find additional evidence for my fundamental argument that religious contention provided one, among many, pathways to significant collective resistance to dynastic authority.

In this chapter I take up the broader issue of international change in early modern Europe. I both amplify and qualify the finding of a growing number of historians and international-relations scholars: the 1648 Peace of Westphalia played some role in the development of the European sovereign-territorial state system, but not as a "watershed" or "revolutionary" moment in this processes. Nor did the Protestant Reformations themselves play *the* decisive role in the emergence of sovereign-territorial states in Europe.[1] These claims lead directly to an important question: in what way is this book a study in international-political change? I answer this question in two distinct ways.

First, the Protestant Reformations—and the Peace of Westphalia—did contribute to the conditions of possibility for the emergence of modern state sovereignty. They did so, in part, through a process historians term "confessionalization": the mapping of religious sites of difference, at least among some elites, within Latin Christendom to the boundaries of polities. Theories of sovereignty and political necessity, both of which received significant elaboration as a result of religious conflicts, also played an important role in providing resources for the later development of relations that looked more like an ideal-typical sovereign-territorial state system. The Protestant Reformations also undermined—but far from eliminated— the viability of dynastic-agglomerative pathways of state formation.

[1] Krasner 1993, Osiander 2001, Teschke 2003.

Second, the debate about sovereignty obscures the true significance of the Protestant Reformations as a "case" of international continuity and change. The most important implication of this study, from a contemporary perspective, lies in the basic fact that "transnational" religious movements and religious contention significantly altered the terms of power and political competition in Europe for over a century. This amounts to an important finding for both international-relations theory and contemporary geopolitical concerns.

I begin with an overview of the conflicts that conjoined in the Thirty Years' War and its immediate aftermath. I discuss how the dynamics of its interrelated conflicts reflect broader political processes and mechanisms, both within and among composite states. In many ways the ultimate fate of the conflict hinged on a race between Bourbon France and Habsburg Spain to see which polity would implode first. Habsburg Spain won that race and, in consequence, lost its position of pre-eminence to France. I next turn to a closer analysis of the Peace of Westphalia and its significance in the evolution of the European states system. I then discuss the ways in which the Protestant Reformations reconfigured states and interstate practices. I conclude with an evaluation of the significance of the Protestant Reformations for international change. This sets the stage for the final chapter, where I discuss how the substance of this study, my specific theory of composite-state dynamics, and the general approach I outline for the study of continuity and change matter beyond the confines of early modern Europe.

The Thirty Years' War

The Thirty Years' War originated in a 23 May 1618 revolt in Prague: a Protestant uprising against Emperor Matthias's (1612–1619) decision to aggressively pursue counterreformation in the Austrian Habsburg domains. Matthias soon faced a military alliance composed of his many Protestant nobles. Religion, once again, provided motivation and opportunity for cross-cutting collective mobilization.

Matthias died in 1619, not long after the death of the archduke Maximilian of Tyrol, leaving all of the Habsburg lands under the control of the Archduke Ferdinand (Emperor Ferdinand II, 1619–1637). Ferdinand, in his position as archduke, had aggressively and successfully pursued a policy of counterreformation within his domains. The Bohemian rebels, aware of the danger Ferdinand's rule posed to Protestantism, offered their kingdom to the Calvinist Elector Frederick V of the Palatine. They crowned him king of Bohemia on 4 November 1619.[2]

---

[2] Ingrao 2000, 30–31; Wallace 2004, 155–56; Wedgwood 1961, 69–92.

Some sort of crisis was probably inevitable.[3] The 1555 Peace of Augsburg began to founder soon after its inception as a result of disputes over principalities, ambiguities in its construction, and the growth of Calvinism. In 1608 the German Protestant princes formed an Evangelical Union. In 1609 the elector of Bavaria followed suit by creating the Catholic League. A succession crisis in Jülich-Cleves led to limited hostilities, but the death of Henry IV of France in May 1610, and the uncertainties it created, prevented the onset of a full-blown confessional war in Germany. The parties nearly came to blows again over the Duchy in 1613–1614, but the Dutch and Spanish resolved the conflict by dividing the Duchy between a Calvinist and Catholic claimant.[4]

Calvinism, as we have seen, emerged as a disciplined, militant, and international movement in the second half of the sixteenth century. These factors made it attractive to some German princes, who formed the bulk of the group around Elector Frederick V. Calvinist militancy exacerbated the developing crisis in Bohemia; Frederick's own extremism contributed to his provocative decision to accept the Bohemian offer. In fact, the Elector of Saxony, a more moderate Protestant, judiciously declined the same offer when the Bohemian rebels first went shopping for a new ruler.[5]

The efforts of external powers doomed the anti-Habsburg rebellion. King Sigismund of Poland, Maximilian of Bavaria and the German Catholic League, Philip III of Spain, and Pope Paul V all intervened on behalf of the Catholic cause, as did the Protestant John George of Saxony, who sought to prevent a Calvinist from gaining the throne of Bohemia. The kings of England and France persuaded the Evangelical League not to support a revolt against a rightful sovereign. Catholic forces crushed the Protestant army, and with it the hopes of Bohemian Calvinists, at the Battle of White Mountain on 8 November 1620.[6]

The main theater of the German conflict turned toward the Palatine. As Catholic forces sought to oust the Elector Frederick from his dynastic stronghold, the Twelve Years' Truce between the Spanish Habsburgs and the Dutch Republic expired. The war resumed in April 1621, as the Dutch would not concede to Madrid's demands, including not only "maritime and commercial concessions" linked to Dutch penetration into Spanish and Portuguese overseas domains but also "toleration of public practice

---

[3] Sutherland (1992) rejects the designation of something called "The Thirty Years' War." He argues that the conflicts comprised specific eruptions of a generalized struggle over Habsburg power. For a rejoinder—that contemporaries did see the conflict as a discrete war—see Mortimer 2001.

[4] Wallace 2004, 147–48.

[5] In addition to earlier discussions, see Kingdon 1998.

[6] Bonney 1991, 190, and 2002, 16–17; Ingrao 2000, 32–33; Koenigsberger 1971b, 225–26; Wallace 2004, 156–57; Wedgwood 1961, 101–26.

of the Catholic religion in the 'rebel' provinces."[7] Internal divisions and frayed foreign alliances placed the Dutch at a serious disadvantage. Intensifying political and religious conflicts, in fact, plagued the republic since the conclusion of the Twelve Years' Truce. By 1619 the Orthodox Calvinist party—the Counter-Remonstrants, who supported the doctrine of Predestination—controlled the republic. Indeed, they provided the main vector for financial and military support of extremist Protestants in Germany.[8]

As Spanish pressure on the republic intensified, Catholic forces defeated the Elector Frederick in 1623. By deposing Frederick V and giving his electorship to Maximilian of Bavaria, the Catholic allies unintentionally prompted a new Protestant alliance, this time between Christian IV—the Lutheran prince of Denmark, and a prince of the empire by virtue of holding the Duchy of Holstein—the Netherlands, England, and Frederick V. This directly linked the Spanish-Dutch war to the growing conflict in Germany. The Spanish, unable to finance all their commitments, shifted their resources away from the Netherlands—where the reinvigorated Dutch, aided by French subsidies and their capture of a Spanish treasure fleet in the Caribbean, made important military gains. Imperial troops under the command of Albrecht von Wallenstein, however, decisively defeated Christian's forces in 1627. In May 1629 Christian made peace, but not before Wallenstein's stunning military successes swept Germany virtually free of any opposition to the Habsburgs and their allies.[9]

That same year saw the outbreak of a limited war between France and Spain over the fate of the Duchy of Mantua. The death of Duke Vincent II without a direct heir allowed his cousin, the French Duke of Nevers, to claim his territories. The Count-Duke Olivares, chief advisor to Philip IV, decided on pre-emptive intervention on behalf of the right of the emperor to invest a new ruler of Mantua. The Spanish Army, however, became bogged down in a prolonged siege of Casale. Meanwhile, La Rochelle fell to royal forces on 28 October 1628, putting an effective end to the Ninth French War of Religion and freeing France, under the direction of Cardinal Richelieu, to take action. In February 1629 French forces defeated Savoy, a Spanish ally, and forced the Spanish to lift their siege of Casale. The conflict continued, with "horrifying" costs for both sides—including, for the Spanish, a diversion of resources and attention from the war with the Dutch.[10]

[7] Israel 1995, 473.
[8] Ibid., 421–80; C. Parker 1997, 57–58.
[9] Bonney 1991, 192–95; Israel 1995, 497–99; Koenigsberger 1971b, 227–39.
[10] Elliott 1984, 95–112; Stradling 1986. Stradling provides a nice overview of the debate about the significance of the Mantuan Conflict—whether it contributed to the eventual defeat of Spain by France or proved a minor detour in the history of their rivalry.

A few months after the French intervention in Italy, Ferdinand made a crucial mistake in Germany: he dictated severe terms against the German protestants in the "Edict of Restitution" (May 1629), which overturned all secularization of Church land since 1552 and proscribed Calvinism. The issuing of the edict not only inflamed Protestant opinion, but also angered Ferdinand's Catholic allies because he had not submitted it for consideration to the Imperial Diet[11] The Catholic princes also held Wallenstein, a commoner, in contempt, and they resented Habsburg control over the restored Catholic bishoprics. In general the German princes feared that "Ferdinand wanted to destroy German Protestantism or to transform the Empire into an absolute monarchy." Among other acts of retaliation, they forced the dismissal of Wallenstein.[12]

Richelieu convinced the Swedish king, Gustavus Adolphus, to intervene in Germany on behalf of the Protestant cause. He did so in June 1630, achieving a series of startling and spectacular successes. On 30 May 1631 the French split the Catholic alliance in Germany by concluding an alliance with Maximilian of Bavaria. Although the French did poorly in the field, their diplomatic successes and the Swedish rout of their foes in Germany forced Spain to conclude a treaty with France on 19 June 1631. In October 1632 imperial forces—now under the command of Wallenstein again—began to check Swedish advances. In November 1632 Gustavus fell in battle, and the Swedish position in Germany slowly disintegrated. Ferdinand II arranged for Wallenstein to be murdered in February 1634, but a combined Austrian-Spanish army soundly defeated the Swedes in September 1634.[13]

Habsburg power once again stood on the brink of victory in Germany. Nearly all the Protestant German princes agreed to the 1635 Peace of Prague. As part of the Peace, Ferdinand II made many crucial concessions, but did not go far enough to cement his relations with the Protestants.[14] Richelieu decided he had no choice but to intervene, if only to keep the Swedes in the war. Without pressure on the Habsburgs in Germany, Spain would have a free hand. With France firmly committed to war, the Thirty Years' War turned into a truly pan-European affair, one which stretched on for another thirteen years. Swedish and French forces marched back and forth across Germany. The conflict led to catastrophic civilian casual-

---

[11] The Spanish themselves were "furious." See Osiander 2001, 257.

[12] Bonney 1991, 194–95; See also Bireley 1976b, 35; Dunn 1970, 73; Koenigsberger 1971b, 240–41; and Wallace 2004, 158.

[13] Bonney 1991, 195–98; Ingrao 2000, 45–47; Koenigsberger 1971b, 241–45. Wallenstein, a former Protestant whose officer corps included both Catholics and Protestants, engaged in a variety of negotiations with Ferdinand's enemies. Vienna came to believe that he was about to abandon the Habsburg cause.

[14] Bireley 1976a, 60.

ties and displacement. Historians once estimated that as many as 30 percent of the German population died from the direct and indirect effects of the war, but many now believe that precise figures are impossible to ascertain.[15]

Whether the Spanish Habsburgs and their allies or the French coalition would emerge victorious was far from clear. As Elliott argues of Habsburg Spain and Bourbon France:

> In both countries . . . similar processes were at work. The demands of war provoked an intensive fiscalism, which itself . . . extended taxation, whether direct or indirect, to regions and social groups which had hitherto been shielded by customary privileges. In the process it set up intense resentments, which in France in particular led year after year to major tax results. . . . By the late 1630s it was an open question as to which country, France or Spain, would be the first to break. In the event, it was Spain. After major successes in the opening years of the war with France, the enormous military effort involved in fighting simultaneously against the French and the Dutch began to tell. The pressures of defeat . . . increased still further the strain on Spanish resources, and forced Olivares into ever more desperate measures.[16]

In 1648, in the two treaties of Westphalia, the Austrian Habsburgs made peace with their foes; Spain formally recognized and made peace with the Dutch, but continued the war, now on its own, with France. From 1648 to 1653 France itself sunk into the chaos of the *Fronde*, and the Spanish achieved some degree of domestic stability, but Philip IV made the mistake of continuing the war. In 1656 England joined the conflict against Spain. In 1659 Philip IV was forced to make peace with France (the Peace of the Pyrenees).[17]

In 1660 Philip's son, Charles II, succeeded to the throne. Soon France, under Louis XIV, threatened to establish hegemonic dominance in Europe. Spain found itself one among a number of potential counterbalancers to French power. In 1700 Charles II died without a direct heir; in his will and testament, he named Louis XIV's grandson, Philip, as his successor—thus upsetting the balance of power in Europe (we can now speak of one without risk of anachronism) and ushering in the War of Spanish Succession (1701–1714). In the end, Louis' grandson became Philip V, king of Spain. The non-Iberian possessions split apart, with the

---

[15] Ibid., 60–61; Bonney 1991, 198–200, and 2002, 72–75; Ingrao 2000, 46–49.
[16] Elliott 1984, 141.
[17] Bonney 1991, 219–24, 232–41; Collins 1995, 61–78; Elliott 1963a, 341–60; Koenigsberger 1971b, 239–78; Stoye 1969, 107–30.

bulk of them going to a newly enlarged Austria. The Spanish Habsburg Empire had, in the oft-quoted phrase of Hegel, been relegated to the dustbin of history.[18]

This may strike international-relations scholars as a rather familiar story, one involving a hegemonic war between a pre-eminent Spain and a rising France. The hegemonic power, suffering from strategic overextension and internal decline, failed to reconcile its strategic imperatives and found itself on the short end of classic power-transition dynamics. Such an account captures important parallels between the seventeenth-century struggle for European dominance and many other hegemonic struggles, but it misses some very important features of the conflict.

First, two of the major epicenters of the conflict, Germany and the Netherlands, involved religious concerns. The Habsburgs repeatedly snatched defeat from the jaws of victory by, in no small measure, overplaying their hand on the matter of a religious settlement in Germany. These decisions involved something other than purely realpolitik considerations—although, as I shall discuss below, the actions of even the Spanish Habsburgs cannot be reduced to religious logics of appropriateness. It is difficult to make sense of the emergence, development, or dénouement of the conflicts without sustained attention to the dynamics of religious contention.[19]

Second, the Thirty Years' War was not a conflict involving modern states, but rather composite political communities linked together by a variety of religious ties and vectors of authoritative claims. The brief triumph of hard-line Calvinists in the Dutch Republic provided crucial support to anti-Habsburg forces in Germany. The English supported the Huguenot uprising, centered in La Rochelle, against France, despite the questionable prudence of such a decision in light of Habsburg ambitions. The weakness of the two contenders for dominance in Europe—Bourbon France and Habsburg Spain—stemmed from their composite-state structures and their consequent problems in extracting and mobilizing resources for warfare.[20] In order to finance their struggle they sought to abrogate the customary rights of their constituent segments and, in doing so, triggered local resistance.

Indeed, the Count-Duke Olivares fatally undermined the Spanish position by reviving his 1625 proposal for a "Union of Arms": an attempt to

---

[18] Ingrao 2000, 107–19; Lynn 1999, chap. 7; Munck 1990, 376; Tracy 1999, 166.

[19] Paul Kennedy (1987, 31–72) makes precisely this point in his classic statement of great-power rise and decline.

[20] Hui (2004, 2005) effectively contrasts the collective-mobilization capacity of early modern European states with the much "stronger" state infrastructures found in Warring States China.

subject all of the Iberian holdings to a uniform imperial bargain based upon the terms of Habsburg control over Castile. Elliott remarks that it "is obvious that, in attempting to involve Catalonia and Portugal more fully in the Castilian war effort, Olivares was playing with fire. Richelieu, on the other hand, was notably cautious about attempting to turn *pays d'états* into *pays d'élections.*"[21] Olivares's bid to override the contractual bargains of the other Iberian segments of the Habsburg monarchy, combined with policies that appeared to many to disadvantage the kingdoms, produced near-simultaneous rebellions in 1640 in Catalonia and Portugal. These rebellions—followed by military setbacks as well as uprisings in Naples and Palermo (1647)—decisively shifted the overall terms of the conflict against Spain.[22]

The Catalans rose first. In his attempt to suppress a rural rebellion, the Habsburg viceroy "transformed a localized resistance into a more general uprising." A group of Catalan nobles soon turned against Habsburg authority, "tap[ping] their extensive networks of family and political clientage to sustain an elite resistance to Madrid in the summer and fall."[23] On 16 January 1641 the rebels formed a Catalan Republic, but then decided to secure French support by declaring Louis XIV their sovereign. The French intervened and appointed a viceroy for Catalonia. The Catalans soured rather quickly on their new French masters, opening the door for the Habsburgs to reassert control by 1652.[24]

In December 1640 a group of Portuguese nobles capitalized upon Spanish distraction with the Catalan revolt and mounted a coup d'état against the Habsburg government, declaring the Portuguese duke of Bragança as their king. The Union of Arms, from their perspective, marked the latest stage in a long string of unreasonable demands on the part of Madrid. When Madrid ordered the Portuguese aristocracy to fight against the Catalans, they decided they would rather risk their lives and livelihood for Portuguese independence than for Castilian interests. As Elliot argues, "By 1640, when incorporation threatened to turn into integration, an alternative future" of independence "was once again a realizable possibility, thanks to a perhaps unrepeatable combination of favourable geographical and international circumstances."[25] The overextended Spanish monarchy finally responded with force in 1643, but the Portuguese repulsed the invasion. With external support from Spain's rivals, the Portu-

---

[21] Elliott 1984, 141.
[22] Bonney 1991, 219–24, 232–41; Elliott 1963a, 341–60; Stoye 1969, 107–30. On Naples, and Palmero in particular, see Koenigsberger 1971b, 253–77; and te Brake 1998, 129–36.
[23] te Brake 1998, 123, 124.
[24] See Elliott 1963b and 1970; Munck 1990, 208–12; te Brake 1998, 121–26.
[25] Elliott 1991, 65.

guese fought on until 1668, when Madrid capitulated to the new reality of an independent Portugal.[26]

An astute reader may notice the large number of events that I have referred to in broad terms as "fatally weakening" or "undermining" Spanish Habsburg hegemony: the Dutch Revolt, mistakes in Germany, and the rebellions in Portugal and Catalonia, to name but a few. But this is the heart of the matter. If we remove any of these occurrences, the fate of Spanish Habsburg power looks rather different. The same could be said of a number of other events and developments, including different weather patterns in the North Atlantic in 1588, the choices of many actors—such as Philip II's decision not to go to the Netherlands and Olivares's decision to integrate Iberia— economic downturns, or even the highly contingent fate of specific battles.

We gain a great deal of analytic leverage over many of these factors, however, when we examine how they intersect with the relational dynamics of dynastic agglomerations. Indeed, we can trace a chain of events all the way back to the reign of Charles of Habsburg, during which the spread of religious heterodoxy, general patterns of resistance and rule, and the choices made by actors located in key structural locations at the intersection of long-standing and emerging social relations conjoined to produce the 1648 Peace of Westphalia and its aftermath (figures 8.1a and b).

Unpacking the "Westphalian Moment"

Did the Protestant Reformations decisively influence the development of the European sovereign-territorial state system? Any answer to this question requires an investigation of a number of different arenas: the 1648 Peace of Westphalia itself, legal and theoretical ideas about sovereignty, practices of power-political competition, and shifting institutional patterns in European political communities. Those scholars who argue for some variant of the "Westphalian hypothesis" often point to developments in each of these arenas in order to assemble their case for the significance of the Protestant Reformations in the development of the modern state system. They argue that alterations in ideas, practices, and international law provide evidence for an overall gestalt shift in the nature of the European political system toward a sovereign-territorial order.[27]

---

[26] For accounts of the revolt, see Bonney 1991, 221–22; Elliott 1991, 58–66; te Brake 1998, 127–29.

[27] See, for example, Gross 1948, Philpott 2000 and 2001, Ruggie 1993.

Figure 8.1a The 1648 Peace of Westphalia: Europe

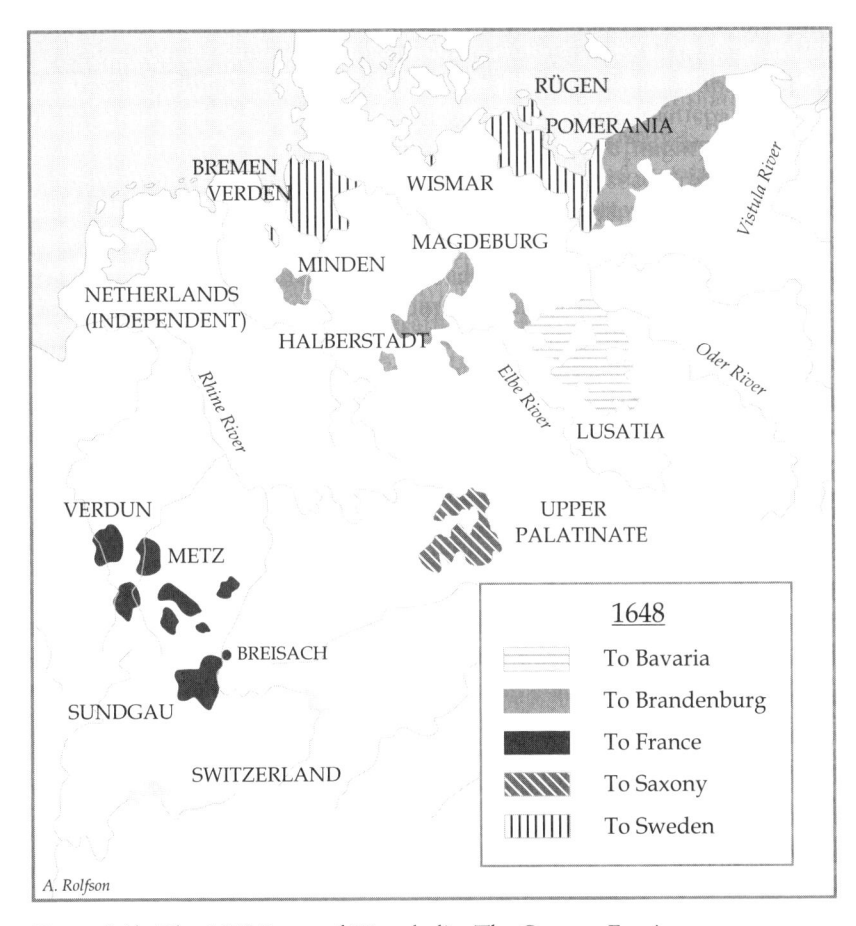

Figure 8.1b The 1648 Peace of Westphalia: The German Empire

But this line of reasoning generates two major problems. First, it confuses the emergence of a number of *elements* of the configuration we associate with the sovereign-territorial states system with the actual instantiation of such a system. Second, it fails to make a convincing counterfactual case that, in the absence of the Reformations, military-technical, economic, and ideational change would not have resulted in international structures with broadly similar attributes. While the Protestant Reformations clearly mattered a great deal in the evolution of the European state system, the "Westphalian hypothesis" cannot be sustained in the face of mounting countervailing evidence.

The Case for a "Westphalian Moment"

Some of the case for the Peace of Westphalia as a watershed moment in the development of the European state system depends on a set of before-and-after claims, while other arguments hinge on the content of the treaties themselves. As its proponents contend, Westphalia marked an end to major interstate religious conflicts in Europe. "In general," Daniel Philpott argues, "religion ceased to be a casus belli. Whereas before Westphalia, religion was a constant cause of war ... religion caused only three wars, all between Europeans and Muslims" after Westphalia.[28] Richard S. Dunn describes the transformation in stark terms: "Statesmen of the late seventeenth and eighteenth centuries looked back on [the Thirty Years' War] as a model of how *not* to conduct warfare. In their view, the Thirty Years' War demonstrated the dangers of religious passion, and of amateur armies led by soldiers of fortune."[29]

Westphalia, the argument goes, also extended to German princes the key perquisites of sovereignty, including the right to make alliances and prosecute wars. Philpott stresses that "Article 65" of the Treaty of Münster, "incorporates into these rights [that is, the liberties of German princes and states] another fundamental characteristic of sovereignty—the right to ally outside the empire, a vital perquisite that princes long enjoyed, but which the empire had contested during the Thirty Years' War."[30]

As Thomas Munck writes, Westphalia created the "legal basis" for "unchallenged princely or territorial absolutism (*Landeshoheit*) even over foreign policy, although this was not to be used against the emperor."[31] Princes pursued, in practice, often independent foreign policies from future kings of the Romans. Philpott quotes John Gagliardo's contention that: "The empire after 1648 was never again to function to any significant extent as a real superterritorial government."[32]

Advocates of this position also stress the side-by-side quality of the Westphalian negotiations, in which the representatives of sovereign states enjoyed formal equality with one another.[33] Westphalia, the argument goes, gave expression to, as Volker Gerhardt argues, a "new concept of statehood" based on legal principles rather than, for example, territorial power.[34] It was a "meeting of independent territorial and political

---

[28] Philpott 2001, 89.
[29] Dunn 1970, 78. See also Bonney 1991, 531.
[30] Philpott 2001, 85.
[31] Munck 1990, 23.
[32] Philpott 2001, 87.
[33] Ibid., 88.
[34] Gerhardt 1998, 487.

entities, where, for the first time, relevant alliances were taken into account. The Holy See was present only as an observer." Westphalia therefore represented an "exemplary case of conflict resolution *among states*" [my emphasis].[35]

Proponents of the significance of Westphalia also point to the ways in which religion became increasingly territorialized over the course of the sixteenth and seventeenth centuries. By reaffirming aspects of Augsburg 1555, Westphalia "established and delimited confessional spheres of influence and . . . it also brought the Churches together politically."[36] John Ruggie repeats a venerable claim when he argues that Westphalia marked the creation of an independent, secular sphere that was distinct from sectarian concerns.[37]

Finally, dynasticism, some maintain, lost its salience as a vector of "transnational" influence. Philpott argues that "the monarchies of Europe remained richly connected by marriage and family ties, which often governed succession within their realm, shaped their alliance commitments, and even acted as a cause of war, though never a sufficient one, as Holsti points out." But, after Westphalia, "no monarch, by virtue of his dynastic affiliation, exercised legal, constitutional authority within the territorial affairs of another monarch. Dynasties might have defined the holders of sovereignty within states, but they did not compromise sovereignty."[38]

Defining Westphalia Down

These claims have much to recommend them, but we need to tread carefully. Philpott's impressive case for the importance of the Peace of Westphalia, for example, often conflates the various reasons for the *importance* of the treaties with its significance as an originating point of the sovereign-territorial state system.[39] Westphalia was, by any account, a significant treaty in the history of European politics. Its importance might be compared to other major peace agreements, such as the Treaty of Utrecht (1713). Such treaties exercised a significant influence over subsequent developments in European political relations without necessarily amounting to a revolution in the basic texture of international politics. Westphalia, for example, provided a model for future treaties, reorganized the constitution of the empire, led to territorial readjustments, and recognized the

---

[35] Ibid., 485. See also Colegrove 1919, 478–80.
[36] Gerhardt 1998, 485.
[37] Ruggie 1983, 163.
[38] Philpott 2001, 91.
[39] See, in particular, ibid., 84.

278 • Chapter 8

independence, albeit in a highly specific form, of the Swiss Confederation. The Spanish, as part of a related agreement, finally accepted the sovereignty of the Dutch Republic.[40]

Let me consider each of the major arguments advanced in favor of the Westphalian hypothesis. Proponents of this hypothesis correctly note that, after Westphalia, religion diminished in importance as a source of intra-European warfare. We find fewer obvious instances of inter-state conflict justified primarily on religious grounds after 1648 than during the reign of Philip II of Spain (1556–1598) or during the Thirty Years' War (1608–1648). Yet religion played important roles in William of Orange's invasion of England in 1688, his campaigns in Ireland, the various attempts at Jacobite restorations in Britain, and in the English struggles with France in the seventeenth and eighteenth centuries.[41]

Many of the factors that produced this transformation, moreover, operated independently of Westphalia itself. If the war had ended in 1629 or 1635, religion might have continued to be a crucial issue in intra-German politics: the carnage and exhaustion much of Europe experienced—and Germany in particular—between 1635 and 1648 clearly turned many against the pursuit of confessional objectives through military conflict. But imagine that the Thirty Years' War had ended on Habsburg terms. Under these circumstances, Europe might also have seen a diminishment of the significance of religious considerations as a casus belli among Latin Christian polities—but in the context of a very different confessional balance of power.

Another wrench in this analysis stems from trends in Europe prior to the sixteenth century. Immediately before the Protestant Reformations we do not find a great many examples of conflicts between Christian rulers justified primarily on religious grounds. We might consider the Protestant Reformations, in this sense, as producing an *interruption* in general trends toward the "secularization" of intra-European war. The diminished importance of religious causes of war among European Christians looks very significant in the aftermath of over one hundred years of confessional conflict, but only because of the political consequences of the Reformations in the first place.

What of the reorganization of the empire accomplished at Westphalia? Andreas Osiander persuasively argues that, although the rights and privileges accorded to German princes and territories bear some resemblance to sovereign prerogatives, "what makes the *landershoheit* interesting from an [international-relations] point of view is precisely what makes them different from sovereignty":

---

[40] See, for example, Gerhardt 1998, Osiander 2001, Repgen 1998, and Schmit 1998.
[41] Israel 1995, Lenman 2000 and 2001.

The autonomy of the estates was limited in two ways: externally through the laws of the empire and internally through the constitutional arrangements with the various territories. The estates were not free to shake off either kind of restraint unilaterally. Changing the laws of the empire required the consent of the majority of at least two of the three Reichstag councils and of the emperor. Likewise, the constitutional changes within the various territories of the empire could not be imposed by the government without the consent of existing representative bodies in those territories.[42]

Westphalia, in fact, specifically rejected the formula of 1555 Augsburg by freezing in place the confessions of individual German territories and granting subjects limited rights of private religious dissent. "The *jus reformandi* (right of reform) was modified so that each prince would retain power to control public . . . church life in his own territory as it had been in 1624, and not necessarily as his own beliefs dictated."[43] Only Calvinism gained official sanction at Westphalia: other non-Augsburg confessionals (that is, non-Catholic and non-Lutheran) "were excluded from recognition: Anabaptists, Unitarians, Bohemian and Moravian Brethren, and others." All disputes pertaining to these matters became subject to adjudication through imperial courts. The system worked rather effectively until the abolition of the Holy Roman Empire, even if it did not preclude warfare between members of the empire. And recall that the empire often suffered from internal military conflict prior to Westphalia.[44]

Westphalia, in the words of Georg Schmidt, "did not destroy the more tightly articulated Empire but reconfirmed its federal unity." The negotiators at Westphalia specifically avoided granting the princes, estates, and knights "sovereignty," instead opting for the confirmation of existing rights and privileges—including a qualified right to make external alliances on the condition that those alliances did not oppose the empire. This merely affirmed existing practice.[45] A comparison of France's rights over Alsace reinforces the problems with interpreting these developments as grants of sovereignty. Imperial law continued to lack an equivalent to the concept of *souveraineté*. France, therefore, only received de facto sovereignty over Alsace through a combination of such terms as "*superioritas, sublime territorii ius*" as well as the formulation "*ius supreme dominii*."[46]

---

[42] Osiander 2001, 272.

[43] Munck 1990, 23.

[44] Ibid., 24. See also Jahn 1998; Krasner 2001, 37; Osiander 2001, 272–73; Schmit 1998, 447–52; Teschke 2003, 240–41.

[45] Osiander 2001, 273; Schmidt 1998, 477.

[46] Repgen 1998, 367, 372n85. See also Osiander 1994, 77–82. Osiander correctly notes that relative autonomy, not sovereignty, was the key issue with respect to the German

Thus, the Peace of Westphalia did not extend sovereignty throughout Europe.[47] If anything, it reaffirmed the confederative character of the empire and thereby *precluded* the Habsburgs from imposing greater administrative unity on the empire; that is, from transforming it into something more like a unified state (which the Habsburgs might have accomplished had the 1635 Peace of Prague lasted).[48] This accounts for why early modern theorists of sovereignty found the empire so troublesome, and why Samuel Pufendorf argued that the empire adopted an "irregular" form: it conjoined elements of central authority, federative decision making, and significant autonomy rights that extended even into the realm of foreign policy.[49]

Similar problems caution against overplaying the side-by-side qualities of the Westphalian negotiations. Delegations from the imperial estates, for example, participated in the negotiations at Münster and Osnabrück along with representatives of states.[50] Many of the practices associated with equality resulted from maneuvering for diplomatic advantage rather than any broad ideational shift associated with, for example, religious beliefs. As Osiander argues, the Spanish Habsburgs treated the Dutch "with complete equality" as "part of Spain's strategy to decouple the Dutch from the French." Ferdinand "instructed his delegates to treat the electors' delegates with the same honours afforded" the ambassadors of sovereign states for similar reasons. Indeed, the French, not the Habsburgs, dragged their feet on the question of diplomatic equality—not only for the electors and the Dutch, but also for France's Swedish allies.[51] European dynasts remained at least somewhat concerned with juridical priority well into the eighteenth century; the politics of these claims factored, for example, into Louis XIV's diplomatic practices.[52] Westphalia certainly helped establish an important precedent, but we should be wary about concluding that its side-by-side character marked the emergence of modern sovereign-territoriality.

What of confessionalization and the territorial delimitation of confessional differences? The Protestant Reformations played, in this context, an important role. In te Brake's words, the Thirty Years' War "revived and expanded the truly 'confessional' era in European history during which

---

princes. Regarding Alsace, it is interesting that the French negotiators considered simply holding Alsace as a fief of the empire, which would have allowed the Bourbons to have direct legal influence in the empire. They ultimately decided not to pursue this formula. For additional discussion, see Krasner 2001, 36

[47] Teschke 2003, 238–39.
[48] Rowen 1961, 55; Tracy 1999, 162.
[49] Pufendorf 1690; Schroeder 1999. See also Osiander 2001, 269.
[50] See Gerhardt 1998; Osiander 1994, 17–18; and Repgen 1998.
[51] Osiander 1994, 82–87.
[52] See, in general, Lynn 1999.

an uncompromising princely claim to cultural and religious sovereignty became the hallmark of what is often called absolutism." This did not amount to a secularization of politics, but to a domestication of religious conflict.[53] This process proved important to the erosion of the dynastic-imperial pathway, but Westphalia largely ratified shifts in political and social relations already underway. We also should consider a difficult counterfactual question: would something similar have occurred regardless of the specifics of the Protestant Reformations? The period before Luther witnesses a general trend of aggressive dynasts expanding their control, although not without reversals, over their local Churches.[54]

I find claims that Westphalia marked an effective end to the centrality of dynastic practices of war and peace confusing. While inter-European struggles after Westphalia involved more than simply dynastic claims, the same holds for the great dynastic struggles of the preceding centuries. Dynastic norms continued to shape territorial and geostrategic conflict into the eighteenth century, and played an important role in territorial claims after Napoleon's defeat in the nineteenth century. The Wars of Spanish Succession (1701–1714) and Austrian Succession (1740–1748) demonstrate the continued vitality of dynasticism in the post-Westphalian era. As Benno Teschke notes, in this period "international relations were decisively structured by inter-dynastic family relations."[55] Both Mlada Bukovansky and Rodney Hall convincingly argue that the Enlightenment and the emergence of popular and national sovereignty mark the major transition away from dynasticism as the fundamental currency of European war and peace.[56]

The Protestant Reformations, as I argue below, supplied important social and ideational resources for all of these transitions; but neither they, nor Westphalia, marked *the* key turning point in the development of the European sovereign-territorial state and state system. Westphalia was an important treaty that ratified political-institutional and power-political developments on the ground, both prior to the Thirty Years' War and during the actual dénouement of the conflict. The notion that it had a greater significance remains a thorny proposition. The fact that it became emblematic of these changes, and that theorists have reconstructed Westphalia as the origin of the sovereign state system, demonstrates that it mattered a great deal. But it does not vindicate the Westphalian hypothesis.[57]

---

[53] te Brake 1998, 115. See also Gorski 1993 and 1999, Hsia 1989, and Schilling 1992.
[54] Elton 1964, chap. 10.
[55] Teschke 2003, 226–27.
[56] Bukovansky 2002, Hall 1999.
[57] On the nineteenth-century reconstruction of Westphalia, see Osiander 2001, and Schmit 1998, 448–49.

Conceptual "Innovations"

I need only briefly remark on the significance of the Reformations period for the development of *ideas* about sovereignty. We have already seen how the French Wars of Religion prompted the elaboration of older theories of resistance and sovereign authority; such arguments also marked the German confessional struggles.[58] Such seminal figures as Jean Bodin, Hugo Grotius, Thomas Hobbes, and Samuel Pufendorf formulated theories of sovereignty in the context of religious civil wars and their aftermath. Bodin and Hobbes, for example, both forwarded the notion that in the absence of clearly located sovereign authority, polities would be doomed to the bloody consequences of religious strife. Another major strand in the elaboration of sovereignty, however, stemmed from the European discovery of the Americas and debates over by what right, if any, the Spanish and Portuguese Crown might claim title to extra-European possessions.[59]

We should, at the end of the day, accord the Reformations an important role in provoking renewed interest in, and elaboration of, the concept of sovereignty. But we should be careful about overplaying correlations between Protestant thought—particularly Luther's "Two Kingdoms Doctrine"—and aspects of sovereignty discourse.[60] As we have seen, Catholics and Protestants alike proved quite flexible in their willingness to deploy claims about the nature of sovereignty, where it resided, and what kinds of justifiable resistance followed. Many of the most important theories of sovereignty were hardly isolated from questions of theology and doctrine, but the main impulse for their elaboration stemmed from the *experience* of confessional conflict; in other words, from the ways in which the spread of religious heterodoxies triggered crises in European political relations.

Other developments in statecraft also contributed to the emergence of more "modern" international practices. During the Reformations period, decision makers often confronted situations in which confessional politics—the support of co-religionists—clashed with dynastic struggles. They responded by articulating ideas about "necessity" and "reason of state" that, while still far from later notions of realpolitik, implied a divergence between proximate religious concerns and the necessities of power-political struggles.[61] We should not view these developments in purely ideational terms and associate doctrines of necessity exclusively with, for example, a French *politique* tradition.[62]

[58] See, for example, Shoenberger 1977 and 1979.
[59] See Bodin 1992, Hobbes 1951 [1651], and Tuck 1999.
[60] Cf. Philpott 2001, 107.
[61] Elliott 1984, 44–45, 121, 125, 136–37, 142, 148. See also Mackenney 1993, 64.
[62] Cf. Philpott 2001, 117.

French *devouts*, of course, often opposed Richelieu's anti-Habsburg policies on the grounds that they undermined the Catholic cause. In doing so, they accused him of adopting *politique* and Machivellian principles of statecraft. But Richelieu, in turn, justified them by asserting that that they would best serve the long-term interests of the Catholic cause. Richelieu's Castilian counterpart, the Count-Duke Olivares, himself authorized support for French Protestant rebels in order to weaken the Bourbon cause. True, he convened a junta of theologians to justify his actions, but the rationales they provided were strikingly similar to those embraced by Richelieu.[63] As Elliott remarks, "It seems necessary ... to discard any straightforward picture of a Spanish foreign policy dictated by purely confessional considerations and a French foreign policy operating in conformity with the unvarnished requirements of *raison d'état*." The fact that the French crossed confessional lines far more systematically than the Spanish, he concludes, was because they had more opportunities to do so in support of their strategic goals.[64]

Here again, though, we need to consider counterfactual questions. These notions received their fullest articulation by Italian diplomats whose concerns had little to do, at least directly, with confessional conflict.[65] Guicciardini's and Machiavelli's ideas provided a ready template for decision makers confronting difficult choices between reason of dynasty, state security, and religious goals, but rulers and their advisors faced such tradeoffs even without the added pressure created by the spread of religious heterodoxy. I think it is fair to say that the Reformations contributed to their elaboration—and to the specific conditions of possibility for *raison d'état*—and that we should be careful about overstating the centrality of confessional conflicts to the later production of sovereign-territorial inter-state practices.

Confessionalization

I have already raised the issue of "confessionalization," both in earlier chapters and in the context of the 1648 Peace of Westphalia. The notion of confessionalization, formulated by German historians, posits a processes whereby the boundaries between major confessions became reified and elaborated through political, ideological, and theological developments. As Susan Boettcher writes:

> Confessionalization describes the ways an alliance of church and state mediated through confessional statements and church ordinances facili-

---

[63] Elliott 1984, 125–27. See also Le Roy Ladurie 1996, 37, 42–47.
[64] Elliott 1984, 127.
[65] See Guicciardini 1972 and 1984, Machiavelli 1994, and Mackenney 1993.

tated and accelerated the political centralization underway after the fifteenth century—including the elimination of local privileges, the growth of state apparatuses and bureaucracies, the acceptance of Roman legal traditions, and the origins of absolutist territorial states. Formal political and administrative elements accompanied parallel tendencies in cultural, intellectual, and social life. The changes also meant an increased level of social discipline in the lives of subjects. Originally, authors ended the confessional age with the Thirty Years' War, but it is now clear that the processes described with the short-hand "confessionalization" often persisted into the eighteenth century.[66]

Confessionalization resonates with a variety of impulses in the study of state formation, particularly for those interested in finding a connection between the Reformations and the development of the modern state. Not only do the advocates of the "strong" version of confessionalization explicitly develop such a connection, but they do so in ways that move us beyond claims about often abstract ideas put forth by theologians and legal theorists. Philip Gorski's synthesis of Weberian and Foucauldian accounts of state formation and the "disciplinary revolution," for example, leans heavily upon the confessionalization hypothesis.[67]

Indeed, to the extent that confessionalization processes operated in early modern Europe, it follows that the Reformations produced a greater homology between political-religious identities and territorial boundaries of the kinds presupposed in the states-under-anarchy model. Numerous microlevel studies, however, cast doubt on key aspects of the argument. Confessionalization processes operated in local communities and not always in the top-down manner posited in some variants of the argument. The salience of such processes varied tremendously across time and space. Large segments of the population remained indifferent or even hostile to confessionalization, let alone state-led religious discipline.[68] Ulinka Rublack dismisses the argument entirely. "The concept of a 'confessionalized' Europe, marked by . . . joint efforts of state and church to create a subservient population is, even for the Reformed tradition, of little relevance."[69]

Yet the development of territorial Churches did exercise some influence on state formation. It heightened, at least at the elite level, a sense of

---

[66] Boettcher 2004, 1–2. For an important English-language statement of this thesis, see Schilling 1992.

[67] Gorski 1993, 1999, and 2003. See also Hsia 1989.

[68] Boettcher 2004, 3–5; Lotz-Heumann and Pohlig 2007, 38–45; Wallace 2004, 191–94. For an example, see Dixon 2007.

[69] Rublack 2005, 145.

distinctive religious identity associated with territorial boundaries. In some places, such as France, state-building processes became increasingly intertwined with questions of religious space and identity. Such processes—however incomplete, varied in their sources and directions, and heterogeneous in their content—provided resources for yoking together political identities and state boundaries. They accelerated societal differentiation and enhanced the leverage of centralizing state authorities.[70]

The institutionalization of religious heterodoxy, as I noted in chapter 3, also limited the possibilities for dynastic-empire building. Although England, for example, did not legally prohibit its monarchs from being Catholic until the eighteenth century, the fact is that Catholic-Protestant marriages became rare and almost invariably involved one of the parties converting to the other confession. After the spread of the Reformations and Counter-Reformation, polities, whether Protestant- or Catholic-dominated, grew increasingly unwilling to accept rule by a member of a different confession.[71] While dynastic empire building remained possible—consider the transfer of the southern Low Countries to the Austrian Habsburgs after the War of Spanish Succession—its significance as a pathway of state formation declined.

Some of the developments, as I have already argued, were already underway prior to Luther's agitation for reformation. Some others would have manifested, albeit in different forms, even in the absence of the Protestant Reformations. But the spread of religious heterodoxy in early modern Europe, through its intersection with ongoing processes of resistance and rule, created conditions of possibility for tighter connections between political identity, territory, and state than might otherwise have emerged.[72]

THE REFORMATIONS AND INTERNATIONAL-POLITICAL CHANGE

The debate over the Protestant Reformations and international-political change tends to pivot on the question of whether or not the Reformations played a key role in the emergence of a European sovereign-territorial state system. Participants in this debate elaborate some ideal-typical conception of what sovereign-territoriality and a sovereign-territorial state system looks like. They then evaluate the degree to which European political arrangements departed from or approached this ideal type before and

---

[70] See Bendix 1978, 267–68; Gorski 2000 and 2003; and Schilling 1992.

[71] Flemming 1973; Kann 1973, 388–89. For examples of seventeenth-century marriage negotiations across confessional lines, see Hayden 1973, 17–19.

[72] On the role of religious conflict in the development of national identities, see Marx 2005.

after the Reformations era. My own analysis in the preceding sections follows, more or less, this kind of reasoning. But, as we have seen, we find only qualified evidence in support of the Westphalian hypothesis and its related arguments.

The Protestant Reformations provide an attractive case for such an approach to international change. They present us with an origin point, a series of major shocks and reverberations on the European landscape, and a plausible dénouement in the Thirty Years' War and the Peace of Westphalia. No wonder that, almost from the moment the Reformations era seemed to come to a close, theorists and scholars have sought to establish the significance of the Reformations in creating a new order for the European state system.[73] The status of the Reformations era as a watershed moment also owes something to Protestant triumphalism; in what Stephen Davies aptly calls the "folk memory of the educated in most of the historically Protestant nations," the Protestant Reformations become conflated with the later European Enlightenment movements: "The Reformation is thus connected with freethought, individualism, and the decline of religious authority in the secular sphere."[74]

We have already seen, in fact, how many of the arguments in favor of the Westphalian hypothesis depend on developments in eighteenth- and nineteenth-century European political practices. The very tendency of some European thinkers to retrospectively identify Westphalia as a founding moment for sovereignty norms, religious toleration, and secularization, one might argue, gives superficial plausibility to readings of the Protestant Reformations and Westphalia as crucial to these developments.

In his brilliant account, Philpott notes that he "cannot deny that had the Reformation not intervened in history," military-technical and economic change "might still have brought about the states system. But the Reformation," he continues, "did intervene in history, and because it did, the state system came far sooner, and in a different manner, and with far different historical consequences, than it might otherwise have come."[75] Philpott gets some very important things right here, even if his claims beg many important counterfactual questions.[76] We should not, of course,

---

[73] But many looked to that "new order" for something different than state sovereignty. William Penn (1983 [1693]), for example, treated Westphalia as a model for European unity. Penn's use of Westphalia illustrates nicely Ian Clark's recent claim (2007, 51–70) that Westphalia's importance lies in its affirmation of a European "international society" with both criteria of membership and collective goals, including peace among its members.

[74] Davies 2005. For the underlying problem with this argument, see Toulmin 1990. Although, I should note, forms of religious toleration did emerge in some times and places, as a result of the Reformations, prior to the eighteenth century.

[75] Philpott 2001, 99.

[76] Nexon 2005, 715–16.

overlook the Reformations' contributory effects on state and system formation in Europe. Many of the arguments considered in this chapter, once sufficiently qualified, also suggest that the Reformations played some role in the development of practices, ideas, and institutional arrangements associated with sovereign-territorial states and state systems.

But I want to suggest a different perspective on the Protestant Reformations and political change. A focus on the question of sovereign-territoriality, in particular, skews our assessment of the importance of the era as a case of international-political change. I begin with a major theme of the next chapter: human history has never seen a sovereign-territorial state system of the kind that international-relations theorists take as a baseline for their debates. The kind of system described, for example, in structural-realist theory is an *ideal type*, not an exhaustive description of real political relations in international politics. Even the Cold War international order, with its well-developed conceptions of sovereignty and national self-determination, involved composite polities, routine violations of sovereignty, formal and informal empires, and other arrangements that departed markedly from this baseline.[77]

If we conceive of change in terms of shifting relational contexts of collective action, however, the Reformations period takes on a very different significance. The era witnessed *significant changes in the texture of international politics* through the emergence of trans-state and trans-regional nonstate actors centered around religious identities and ideas. Many of these movements, as we have seen, became violence-wielding players in the power-political struggles within and among European polities. In other words, they significantly shaped the texture of early modern politics. Even if we decide to code the Reformations period as an *interruption* in longer-term processes of state and system formation, then, the very fact that it amounted largely to an interruption, rather than a radical reconfiguration, is itself significant for theories of international change.

The study of the Reformations era, moreover, demonstrates how translocal and trans-state movements constituted by common ideas and identities may alter the balance of power among and within political communities. The Reformations, as I have repeatedly stressed, fatally weakened Habsburg hegemony, imploded Valois France, and led to the emergence of the Dutch Republic as a new European power. The Dutch disrupted the Spanish and Portuguese overseas empires and carved out their own extra-European possessions. Religious differences shaped alliance patterns, including that of Tudor and Stuart England. The Reformations led to a significant international peace treaty that reorganized the

---

[77] See Goddard and Nexon 2005, Hobson and Sharman 2005, and Krasner 1999.

constitutional structure of the Holy Roman Empire—one of the most important political communities in medieval and early modern Europe. Only if we hold to an anemic conception of the "texture of international politics" as nothing more than the "pursuit of power by actors in the absence of a central government" can we dismiss early modern Europe as a case of international-political change.

CHAPTER 9

Looking Forward, Looking Back

THE PROTESTANT REFORMATIONS intersected with patterns of resistance and rule in early modern composite polities such that they increased the likelihood of devastating challenges to central authority. They did so when they overcame firewalls against the spread of resistance to central authorities; undermined the ability of central authorities to engage in multivocal signaling; enhanced the ability of local intermediaries to enhance their own autonomy vis-à-vis their rulers; exacerbated—both directly and indirectly—the endemic cross pressures faced by central authorities; and created new vectors for the "internationalization" of "domestic" conflicts and the "domestication" of "international" conflicts. A relational-institutionalist approach allows us to theorize these effects in terms of general processes and mechanisms associated with the structure of composite states.

But these challenges did not lead to a radical transformation in logics of European political organization. Their long-term effects on European state formation and the European international order proved more subtle than proponents of the "Westphalian Hypothesis" contend, but they were still more consequential than most of its opponents recognize. In this context, relational institutionalism provides an alternative way of understanding the relationship between the Reformations and international change. The Reformations themselves are a case of international-political change. They shifted patterns of collective mobilization at both the "international" and "domestic" levels, introduced new actors into early modern Europe, and altered the balance of power in the period.

These findings hold intrinsic importance for the study of international relations. The content of this study, however, also sheds some light on important international-relations debates and contemporary concerns, including international change, the significance of religion and religious movements for international relations, the conceptualization of the texture of world politics, and the fate of the state under conditions of globalization.

GENERALIZATION AND THE LESSONS OF HISTORY

Many scholars conclude their studies of historical examples of international change by attempting to extend their specific theories to contemporary political change. They might argue, at a minimum, that since economic factors, warfare, or ideational developments drove past change in the texture of world politics, we should expect that the same factors will drive future alterations in the character of international relations. We lack, however, obvious reasons to believe that political change follows invariant or quasi-invariant laws. Actors in, for example, pre-Columbian Mesoamerica, Warring States China, the Roman Empire, the Xiongnu Steppe confederation, the Carolingian era, Mughal India, ancient Mesopotamia, the globe after World War II, and myriad other times and places faced distinctive political, social, economic, and environmental conditions. Thus, change in one period may occur for very different reasons than change in another.

It should come as no surprise, therefore, that social scientists have a miserable track record when it comes to predicting future international change, such as the end of the Cold War and the subsequent collapse of the Soviet Union.[1] These limitations need not incline us to forgo attempts to make sense of, or even point to salient dynamics in, contemporary change. They certainly supply no warrant for abandoning comparative-historical analysis in favor of a relentless presentism.

International-relations scholars, as I argued in the introduction, should seek to understand and explain developments in world politics—both in the past and the present. At a minimum, historical studies serve an important purpose. They allow us to confirm, qualify, or reject analogies put forth by scholars, pundits, and policymakers between past events and those of the present. This study, I hope, dispels claims that current upheavals in the Islamic world stem from the lack of something comparable to the Protestant Reformations. If this kind of analogy makes any sense, then it points in the opposite direction: a parallel between contemporary radical Islamicism and a number of early modern Reformation movements. They share a desire to restore their religious communities to their putative original states by conjoining "correct" theology to political practice.[2]

This study also calls into question the ways in which international-relations scholars, most notably those of a realist persuasion, treat the Spanish Habsburgs as an archetypal case of hegemonic overextension. The Spanish Habsburgs confronted counterbalancing coalitions and suffered from strategic overextension. Many of the most important mecha-

---

[1] See Bennett and Ikenberry 2006, Elman and Elman 1997, Hechter 1995. While some point to a few scattered examples of predictive accuracy, we should be wary about concluding too much from these isolated prophetic pronouncements. If we surveyed a thousand astrologers, we might very well find disturbingly correct predictions scattered among proclamations of astounding inaccuracy or hopeless ambiguity, but we would not put our faith, therefore, in either those particular astrologers or the pseudoscience of astrology.

[2] Davies 2005.

nisms that created these conditions, however, bear only a superficial resemblance to the theoretical accounts discussed in previous chapters. When we observe hegemonic and imperial powers that rule through star-shaped political systems, this study suggests, we need to pay attention to a number of dynamics that international-relations scholars tend to ignore, downplay, or relegate to the "domestic level of analysis."

I will return to this point later. For now, it takes us to the heart of how we should think about historical analysis and comparative-historical reasoning. An increasing number of social scientists argue for mechanism- and process-based generalization.[3] The relational-institutionalist synthesis developed provides one way to approach such generalizations: through identifying tendencies and regularities associated with social and political forms that recur, at various levels of analysis, across time and space. The specific implications of these mechanisms and processes depend, of course, on how such forms embed in other relational contexts, their specific ideational content, and the strategies and choices of relevant actors. But we can generalize about those dispositional tendencies and thereby find, however provisional and humble in character, "lessons" for explaining past outcomes and informing present policies.

Religion and International Relations

The field of international relations appears on the brink of its own religious reformation. A growing number of scholars urge the field to, in effect, "bring religion into international relations."[4] Elizabeth Shakman Hurd claims, along these lines, that international-relations theory remains marred by "secularist epistemological and ontological foundations" that take for granted the separation between religion and politics and thus "has not been able to account for religion because it has not come to terms with the politics involved in defining and enforcing particular concepts and practices of the secular."[5] My colleague Joshua Mitchell, a political theorist, argues that religion has an irreducible otherworldly component: religious experience cannot, therefore, be reduced to a "value," "interest" or "identity."[6] Jonathan Fox and Shmuel Sandler, in contrast, agree that the secularist foundations of international-relations theory explain its neglect of religion, but see fewer barriers to the integration of

---

[3] See, for example, George and Bennett 2005, Jackson and Nexon 2002, and Tilly 1995 and 1997b.

[4] Fox and Sandler 2006, 1. See also Byrnes and Katzenstein 2006, Hurd 2008, and Philpott 2002.

[5] Hurd 2008, 152–53. See also Hurd 2004.

[6] Mitchell 2007.

religion into the study of world politics. "The key," they write, "is not to focus on what religion is, but what religion does." For them, religion is a source of identity and legitimacy, and is associated with "formal institutions" such as "the Catholic Church."[7]

These claims capture important dimensions of the challenge international-relations theory faces from its religious awakening. Particular religious frameworks do operate, as Hurd suggests, as discursive contexts that imply various styles of reasoning and argument. They inflect features of the natural and social worlds with different meanings and therefore require some form of translation across different discursive configurations, including various forms of secularism. And we should recognize the socially constructed nature of secularist ideologies and how those ideologies—particularly in terms of their views of the separation of religion and politics—inform international-relations theory.[8]

My analysis of the impact of the Protestant Reformations on European political relations, however, cautions against a view of religion as sui generis. We can, as I hope my study demonstrates, construct fruitful theories by focusing on how religion operates to produce identities, interests, social ties, and conditions of possibility for the legitimation of authority and resistance. Indeed, fetishizing religion undercuts our ability to make sense of the dynamics of the Reformations era. Doing so leads us to ignore the important continuities in patterns of resistance and rule between struggles in which religious heterodoxy played little role and those in which it did.

In this respect religion need not be seen as categorically different from discursive frameworks of the kinds associated with Marxism, secular nationalism, or other ideologies. The *content* of claims associated with various belief systems—such as the kinds of categories they bring with them—matters a great deal for understanding the particular dynamics of routine and contentious interaction among actors. But we can still generalize about the social forms produced and impacted by belief systems: how they make particular forms more likely to obtain, how they trigger trajectories of collective mobilization while interfering with others, and so forth. We can also generalize about the formal characteristics of ideological frameworks—including religious ones—such as their relative inclusiveness or exclusiveness with respect to other identities and social boundaries.

To this extent, what we found in early modern Europe tracks rather well with studies of more contemporary religious conflict. Monica Toft, for example, seeks to make sense of the finding that Islamic states appear more prone to religious civil wars than other contemporary political com-

[7] Fox and Sandler 2006, 176–77.
[8] Hurd 2008.

munities. She argues that, because of the transnational character of Islam and its specific ideological content, appeals to Islam provide an attractive way for embattled elites to secure external support from co-religionists of disparate "races and nationalities," such as

> Afghan mujahadeen appeals for cash and Muslim fighters from Iran, Pakistan, and Saudi Arabia during the Soviet intervention from 1979 to 1989; Shiite calls for cash and fighters from Iran during the first and second wars with Iraq (1990–1991 and 2003); and Chechen calls for support from Muslims during Chechnya's two most recent wars with Russia (1994–1996 and 1999–present).[9]

Toft also notes that "the more central religion is to a violent conflict, the less likely that conflict will be resolved through negotiation."[10] The "indivisibility of religious doctrine" makes it more difficult for actors to negotiate a compromise than if they merely faced profane questions involving the distribution of resources, rights, and obligations. Religious issues, she argues, "have an uncompromising character such that even rational actors may find it difficult to arrive at a nonviolent resolution."[11] Toft draws explicit parallels to the early modern European experience, but the kind of sustained study I have offered not only provides support for her claims, but also makes some important amendments.

First, the "secular bias" in international-relations theory often manifests itself by artificially separating so-called "religious passions" from "strategic interests."[12] Toft emphasizes processes whereby elites frame their conflicts in religious terms to enhance their strategic position by, for example, garnering external support from co-religionists. This reasoning tracks with the existing divide between rationalist and constructivist interpretations of identity politics, in which the former emphasize the strategic logic of elite appeals to identity while the latter focus on the normative dimensions of such appeals.

The evidence from early modern Europe casts doubt on the utility of this distinction. We found rather inconsistent evidence concerning whether actors advanced religious claims out of instrumental or substantive motivations. Some pursued religious goals in a very calculating manner, while others sought power-political advantage with passions that might strike us as irrational. They often muddled through, trying to reconcile their various interests or developing justifications for privileging some over others. From my perspective, the question of which logics

---

[9] Toft 2007, 105.
[10] Ibid., 107.
[11] Ibid., 100, 106.
[12] Cf. Hirschman 1997.

predominanted, and with respect to what ends, should be treated as an empirical one.

Second, when religious disputes take center stage in conflict, they *often* increase the stakes of the struggle. But so, too, do disputes centering on the cosmological dimensions of secular ideologies, or even on more mundane considerations. The presence of cosmological disputes need not, moreover, render negotiation and contention irrational.

Consider the "indivisible" character of some religious disagreements. Such conflicts often involve, at a theological or existential level, indivisible concerns. But the degree to which those concerns manifest as barriers to successful negotiations depends on a number of factors. One of these factors, at least in the early modern European experience, involved the ability of brokers to engage in multivocal signaling. The case studies I have analyzed suggest that such forms of brokerage will often prove incredibly difficult, but not necessarily impossible. Brokers may, in fact, engage in polyvalent performances that render negotiations possible across apparently irreconcilable differences—religious or otherwise.[13]

The politics of the Reformations also caution against extrapolating from the irreconcilable claims of theologians to the orientations of other elites and ordinary people. Confessional differences, in many ways, mattered more as identity markers than for their doctrinal content. Religious identities in early modern Europe were often rather fluid, while religious norms demonstrated adaptability to changing circumstances. They also lost their salience, or otherwise became submerged, through the activation of other relational and categorical identities.

Common threats and profane interests, in fact, sometimes overcome apparently indivisible religious differences, as they did in the formation of the League of Schmalkald, the Spanish support of Huguenot rebels in France, or the Valois and Bourbon assistance to Protestants against the Habsburgs. Religious disputes, particularly when they took on indivisible characteristics, rendered negotiations more difficult, yet actors found other ways of compensating for the inability to divide a specific issue.[14]

I see no reason why such caveats apply only to the Reformations era. But, whatever their merits, we cannot ignore some of the striking continuities between contemporary and early modern religious conflicts. Developments over the past few decades suggest that these dynamics may intensify.

---

[13] Goddard 2006. In this respect aspects of the process of "secularization" both reflect the construction of political spaces for such claims *and* the increasingly successful deployment of multivocal signaling across religious boundaries.

[14] Fearon 1995, Goddard and Nexon 2005.

Islamic groups represent only one class of actors mobilizing in support of co-religionists in the contemporary era.[15] A number of Christian groups in the United States, for example, have engaged in support, albeit mostly nonviolent in character, for co-religionists in other areas of the globe. Christian conservatives joined with liberal evangelicals and human rights groups to exert pressure on the American government to resolve the decades-long war in southern Sudan. They agitate for protection for Christians in Africa, the Middle East, and China. Christian conservatives, for theological reasons, have emerged as an important force for continued strong American support of Israel. Some organized religious movements, in fact, actively seek to cast current geopolitics in terms of religious struggles; to the extent that they succeed, they reconfigure existing conflicts in terms that have profound implications for international relations. They activate boundaries that cut across existing political boundaries, provide vectors for transregional and transnational collective mobilization, and shift the terms of conflict and cooperation in world politics.[16]

In this respect, the challenge presented by bringing religion back into international-relations theory reflects the overarching problem of how to incorporate nonstate actors into our accounts of international structure. Nonstate actors, in fact, compose only one dimension of the analytic necessity of linking variation in the kinds of actors that operate in world politics to differences in the texture of international relations.

Composite Political Structures

I find it noteworthy that many of the examples Toft uses in her discussion of religious civil wars involve composite political structures. The civil wars in the former Yugoslavia arose out of modular secessions from a federative polity in the context of a bid for dominance by its Serbian segment.[17] The Russian Federation, as Charles King argues, at present displays important structural similarities with imperial composite states. The Chechen wars are the most explosive example of how Russia's push for centralization, no matter how limited, triggers broadly similar dynamics—including tensions between local and central control—of the kind found in other imperial composites. There, transnational religious ties have escalated and prolonged the conflict.[18]

---

[15] Juergensmeyer 1993.
[16] See, for example, Flibbert 2006, Martin 1999.
[17] Cooley 2005, 127–36.
[18] King 2003, 138–39.

Religious identities and networks also emerged as key factors in the American-led occupations of Iraq and Afghanistan, as well as the Soviet intervention in Afghanistan. Some international-relations scholars, of course, distinguish between imperial control and occupations. David Edelstein argues, for example, that "occupation is the temporary control of a territory by another state that claims no right to permanent sovereign control over that territory." Thus, it differs from "annexation" and "colonialism."[19] But even temporary "occupations" create relational structures akin to those found in imperial composite polities: indirect rule through an occupying authority or local regime, coupled with a bargain specific to that territory.[20]

Each of these cases involves the intersection of, at the inter-state level, indirect rule and heterogeneous contracting interfacing with, at the substate level, violence-wielding patron-client networks. Paul MacDonald, in an important study, isolates failures by American authorities to come to grips with the fundamental issues that result from such instances of imperial control. American difficulties in Iraq, he argues, resulted from its lack of "extensive relations with local collaborators. Prior to the war, the U.S. relied too heavily on exile parties who were unreliable, had alternative sources of patronage, and lacked sizeable domestic constituencies in Iraq."[21] By dissolving the Iraqi Army, the United States greatly undermined its ability to harness local institutions to effectuate control. Through its reliance on non-Iraqi private contractors, the United States further failed to "bind" significant local interests to the occupation and to the American-sponsored government.[22] Indeed, as Alexander Cooley notes, indirect rule, once layered on top of private contracting, produced severe principal-agent problems. Resulting opportunistic corruption greatly hampered American efforts to provide public goods in the form of economic and political reconstruction. These failures overwhelmed whatever benefits the United States gained from the plausible deniability inherent in the arrangement.[23]

In Iraq and Afghanistan, as I have already noted, the United States confronts religiously based brokerage, boundary activation, and polarization resulting in patterns of collective mobilization that, at least at this time, undermine its policy objectives. In both cases, co-religious networks and identities provide vectors for foreign support, with consequences that

[19] Edelstein 2000, 52.
[20] MacDonald 2006, Nexon and Wright 2007, Zisk 1984. Edelstein's own analysis (2000, 67–69) makes this fact clear, as he discusses the costs and benefits of the use of different kinds of intermediaries and other problems inherent in imperial composite rule.
[21] MacDonald 2006, 4.
[22] Ibid., 24–25, 30–31.
[23] Cooley 2005, 144–56. For an overview of these and other issues, see Diamond 2005.

should, by now, be all too familiar.[24] We need not declare the United States an "empire" to note how transnational religious ties and identities erode firewalls to resistance within and between "sovereign" states such as, on the one hand, Iraq, Syria, and Iran and, on the other hand, Afghanistan and Pakistan.[25]

Informal imperial arrangements involve embedded hub-and-spoke relations between putatively sovereign states.[26] The European Union reflects a territorially expansive, uneven, and incomplete process of composite political formation.[27] But composite states, both formal or informal, persist in the supposed era of the nation-state. The Russian Federation provides one example, but there are many others. Pakistan serves as a base for Taliban activities, in part, because Pakistani central authorities exercise extremely weak forms of indirect rule over the country's western provinces. The government engages in contracting with local clans and other patron-client networks of governance.[28] A great many "developing" states involve such composite forms of rule.

Scott Radnitz's analysis of political mobilization in Kyrgyzstan demonstrates how informal structures of patronage and rule created composite-state dynamics even in the absence of well-developed formal segmentation and heterogeneous contracting. The Kyrgyz "revolution" of 2005, he argues, resulted when state officials challenged the position of elites with extensive vertical patron-client ties. They utilized their own cross-cutting networks to coordinate mobilization of their patron-client networks. The most important mechanism of successful resistance in this case, he notes, involved brokerage dynamics: "Embedded elites linked by networks that transcend geographical boundaries . . . mobilize[d] their respective supporters to broker between them to form a single movement."[29] Radnitz draws insightful parallels with processes of collective resistance in early modern England and France, as well as competitive brokerage attempts and social mobilization in Iraq's Shiite community.[30]

Of course, very few contemporary states—composite or otherwise—involve the same cultural content as early modern Europe. Dynastic norms, at least in their traditional form, have largely given way to variations on the theme of popular sovereignty. Economic relations, forms of warfare, technologies for the dissemination of information, and a whole host of other contextual factors also differentiate the contemporary pe-

---

[24] See, for example, Riedel 2007.
[25] See, for example, Khan 2007, Lieven 2002, and Zahab and Roy 2006.
[26] Barkawi and Laffey 1999 and 2002, Cha 2004, Cox 2004.
[27] Some even find traces of imperial, or postmodern imperial, logics in the European Union. See Behr 2007.
[28] See, for example, Khan 2007.
[29] Radnitz 2006a, 16
[30] Ibid., 191–212. See also Radnitz 2006b.

riod from early modern Europe. These intersect with the mechanisms associated with imperial and empire-like composite polities to produce different conditions of possibility than those that existed in early modern Europe. But we can still identify structural tendencies, processes, and tradeoffs associated with composite political structures that, no matter how they are embedded in other relational structures and adjacent processes, will matter for international politics for some time to come.

Indeed, a great deal of evidence points to the continued salience of composite political communities in world politics. Pressures within Spain, Britain, Italy, and other European polities for the devolution of political authority continue, in part because such states never erased their origins as composite polities.[31] Many states, whether in Central Asia or Africa, remain essentially composite polities where much governance is carried out through highly autonomous intermediaries—such as regional governors, clan networks, and other forms of patron-client relations—and processes of "globalization" create ever increasing connections between their fates and those of the citizens of other states. Regional organizations, if they achieve similar levels of institutional authority as those in Europe, also generate composite entities of tremendous heterogeneity. Informal imperial relations, whether in the form of great-power spheres of dominance or multilateral "neotrusteeship" relations, show no signs of exiting the world stage.

And here we come back to an important set of empirical and theoretical claims advanced in this book. The states-under-anarchy framework is a theoretical construct. International-relations scholars associate it with at least two conditions: the principle of sovereign-territoriality and the institutional structure associated with nation-states as relatively nonsegmented, direct forms of rule. These two conditions are distinct: one may obtain without the other. They also, as I have noted, fail to conjoin across the entire domain of international politics in nearly every historical period.

This seems to cast doubt on the appropriateness of the states-under-anarchy framework. But if we treat "anarchy" as a relational context in which high-category and high-network social sites interact in a low-category and low-network environment, then it follows that the collective-action dynamics associated with the states-under-anarchy framework do provide explanatory leverage in some settings. Those settings need not, however, involve the conjunction of sovereign-territorial logics with nation-state institutional forms. Thus, we should reconsider attempts to locate a particular historical period as *the* period in which the states-under-anarchy framework obtains.

[31] Nexon 2006, 280. For a global perspective on this point, see Roeder 2007.

Rather, we have good reasons to think of international politics as a realm of authority structures that nest within one another to produce a variety of composite political arrangements. But we should avoid turning the notion of "composite states" into an empty metaphor.[32] Not all composite political structures display the same organizational properties. They differ in terms of the number, function, and domain of intermediaries, the heterogeneous and uniform character of their bargains, their vectors of political authority, and their degree of hierarchical control. On the other hand, I believe that treating composite polities—of various forms—as ideal types will probably prove more productive than using the "nation-state" as the most important benchmark against which to judge contemporary political communities.[33] A relational-institutionalist approach allows us, I believe, to operationalize this shift in perspective.

Globalization and the Fate of the "State"

Attention to the continuing salience of composite political forms matters a great deal in the context of debates about globalization and the fate of the state. When scholars and pundits debate about the putative decline of the nation-state, they consider, in essence, whether or not states are losing their asymmetric advantages as sites through which actors collectively mobilize resources for the provision of public goods. Those who answer in the affirmative argue that current trends—in communications, transportation, military technology, economic production, and collective identification, for example—are leading to new focal points for collective action. New social sites, such as international institutions, transnational movements, and multinational corporations, now operate as significant channels for some combination of collective violence, governance, and economic activity and states must confront them, if not on an equal footing, then at least as serious rivals in specific arenas.[34]

Many observers push this logic quite far. "The state," writes Martin Van Creveld, "is in decline. . . . Many existing states are either combining together into larger communities or falling apart." Even where the current states persist, "Already many of their functions are being taken over by a variety of organizations which . . . are not states."[35] This view is far from atypical. Peter Taylor argues that "in contemporary globalization

---

[32] Ferguson and Mansbach 1996.
[33] Paul 1999, 227. For a similar point in the context of ethnic conflict, see King 2001.
[34] For discussions, see Guidry, Kennedy et al. 2000; Keohane 2001; Risse-Kappen 1995a, 7–19; and Tarrow 2005, 2–12, 201–19.
[35] Van Crevald 1999, vii.

territories can no longer preserve their distinctiveness behind political boundaries.... Cities are replacing states in the construction of social identities."[36] But when should we locate the heyday of the modern nation-state? In the nineteenth century, during the high point of European colonial empires? After World War II, when much of the world was divided between two, although very different, informal empires? In the contemporary period, when observers routinely prognosticate about the end of the "state"?

The key questions of the present era, I contend, concern less the decline of the state than how changing opportunities for, and constraints upon, collective action will intersect with *evolving* relational contexts of authority. If we want to find overarching lessons from the early modern European experience, however, let me suggest one. Recall Timothy Garton Ash's concern that the future threatens a multipolar rivalry among great powers in the context of myriad nonstate actors, some armed with the capacity to inflict very destructive violence.

In this respect we might be headed "back to the future": early modern Europe saw a not entirely dissimilar concatenation of power-political struggles in the context of expanded economic and communication flows.[37] In terms of state-society relations, collective-mobilization capacity, and violence-wielding ability, however, early modern European states were far weaker than many contemporary states—and certainly far weaker than contemporary advanced industrialized states of the kind found in Europe, East Asia, and North America.

Yet early modern polities survived, more or less, the challenge of the Protestant Reformations. Many emerged from the conflagration as stronger political entities. They formed tacit agreements to limit the influence of nonstate religious movements on their great-power rivalries. They enforced a peace agreement designed to prevent a resumption of conflict in Germany—one that failed at this task but did maintain the empire for over a century. While we should conclude that nonstate transnational actors may determine the fate of great-power struggles, the early modern European experience cautions against declaring the premature death of the "state" as a significant corporate actor in world politics.

---

[36] Taylor 1995, 38.

[37] In 1990 John J. Mearsheimer published an article in *International Security* entitled "Back to the Future: Instability in Europe after the Cold War." He argued that the transition to multipolarity would trigger time-honored patterns of geopolitical competition. In this light I suppose an alternative title for this chapter might have been "*Further* Back to the Future." But as I am loathe to overdraw the parallels identified here, such a title struck me as inappropriate.

References

Abbott, Andrew (2001). *Time Matters: On Theory and Method.* Chicago: University of Chicago Press.
Abdelal, Rawi, Yoshiko M. Herrara et al. (2006). "Identity as a Variable." *Perspectives on Politics* 4(4): 695–711.
Adamson, Fiona B. (2005a). "Global Liberalism Versus Political Islam: Competing Ideological Frameworks in International Politics." *International Studies Review* 7(4): 547–69.
———. (2005b). "Globalization, Transnational Political Mobilization, and Networks of Violence." *Cambridge Review of Internatioanl Affairs* 18(1): 21–49.
Adler, Emanuel (1997). "Seizing the Middle Ground: Constructivism in World Politics." *European Journal of International Relations* 3(3): 316–63.
Adler, Emanuel, and Michael Barnett, eds. (1998a). *Security Communities.* Cambridge: Cambridge University Press.
———. (1998b). "A Framework for the Study of Security Communities." In *Security Communities*, ed. Emanuel Adler and Michael Barnett. Cambridge: Cambridge University Press, 29–65.
Alexander, Jeffrey (1988). *Action and its Environments.* New York: Columbia University Press.
Allen, Paul C. (2000). *Phillip III and the Pax Hispanica.* New Haven: Yale University Press.
Allsen, Thomas T. (1987). *Mongol Imperialism: The Policies of the Grand Qan Möngke in China, Russia, and the Islamic Lands, 1251–1259.* Berkeley: University of California Press.
———. (1991). "Changing Forms of Legitimation in Mongol Iran." In *Rulers from the Steppes: State Formation in the Eurasian Periphery*, ed. G. Seaman and D. Marks. Los Angeles: Ethnographic Press/Center for Visual Anthropology, University of Southern California, 223–54.
Anderson, Perry (1974). *Lineages of the Absolutist State.* London: Verso.
Armitage, David (1998a). "Introduction." In *Theories of Empire, 1450–1800*, ed. David Armitage. Brookfield, Vt: Ashgate, xv–xxxiii.
———, ed. (1998b). *Theories of Empire, 1450–1800.* Brookfield, Vt: Ashgate.
———. (2004). "The Fifty Years' Rift: Intellectual History and International Relations." *Modern Jounal of History* 1(1): 97–109.
Arquilla, John, Paul Ronfeldt et al. (1999). "Countering the New Terrorism." In *Conquering the New Terrorism*, ed. I. O. Lesser, B. Hoffman, John Arquilla et al. Washington, D.C.: RAND, 39–84.
Asch, Ronald G. (1991). "Introduction." In *Princes, Patronage, and the Nobility: The Court at the Beginning of the Modern Age, c. 1450–1650*, ed. Ronald G. Asch and A. M. Birke. Oxford: Oxford University Press, 1–40.

Ascoli, Peter M. (1974). "A Radical Pamphlet of Late Sixteenth Century France: La Dialogue D'Entre Le Mahuestre Et Le Manant." *Sixteenth Century Journal* 5(2): 3–22.

Axelrod, Robert (1984). *The Evolution of Cooperation*. New York: Basic.

Axelrod, Robert, and Robert O. Keohane (1993). "Achieving Cooperation Under Anarchy: Strategies and Institutions." In *Neorealism and Neoliberalism: The Contemporary Debate*, ed. D. A. Baldwin. New York: Columbia University Press, 85–115.

Baker, J. Wayne (1993). "The Convenantal Basis for the Development of Swiss Political Federalism: 1291–1848." *Publius* 23(2): 19–41.

Barfield, Thomas J. (1989). *The Perilous Frontier: Nomadic Empires and China, 221 BC to AD 1757*. Cambridge: Mass.: Blackwell.

Barkawi, Tarak, and Mark Laffey (1999). "The Imperial Peace: Democracy, Force and Globalization." *European Journal of International Relations* 5(4): 403–34.

———. (2002). "Retrieving the Imperial: Empire and International Relations." *Milennium: Journal of International Studies* 31(1): 109–27.

Barkey, Karen (1991). "Rebellious Alliances: The State and Peasant Unrest in Early Seventeenth-Century France and the Ottoman Empire." *American Sociological Review* 56(6): 699–715.

———. (1994). *Bandits and Bureaucrats: The Ottoman Route to State Centralization*. Ithaca: Cornell University Press.

Barnett, Michael (1999). "Culture, Strategy, and Foreign Policy Change: Israel's Road to Oslo." *European Journal of International Relations* 5(1): 5–36.

Baron, Hans (1939). "Imperial Reform and the Habsburgs, 1486–1504." *American Historical Review* 44(2): 293–303.

Barraclough, Geoffrey (1968). *The Medieval Papacy*. New York: W. W. Norton.

Barrett, Thomas M. (1995). "Lines of Uncertainty: The Frontiers of the North Caucasus." *Slavic Review* 54(3): 578–601.

Bates, Robert H., Avner Greif et al. (1998). "Introduction." In *Analytic Narratives*, ed. Robert H. Bates, Avner Greif, J.-L. Rosenthal and B. Weingast. Princeton: Princeton University Press, 3–22.

Baumgartner, Frederic J. (1988). *Henry II: King of France 1547–1559*. Durham, N.C.: Duke University Press.

Baumgartner, T., W. Buckley et al. (1975). "Relational Control: The Human Structuring of Cooperation and Conflict." *Journal of Conflict Resolution* 19(3): 414–40.

Beame, Edmond M. (1966). "The Limits of Toleration in Sixteenth-Century France." *Studies in the Renaissance* 13: 250–65.

———. (1993). "The Politiques and the Historians." *Journal of the History of Ideas* 54(3): 355–79.

Bean, Richard (1973). "War and the Birth of the Nation State." *Journal of Economic History* 33(1): 203–21.

Bearman, Peter S. (1993). North Carolina Lectures on Networks. Chapel Hill, N.C.

Behr, Harmut (2007). "The European Union in the Legacies of Imperial Rule? EU Accession Politics Viewed from a Historical Comparative Perspective." *European Journal of International Relations* 13(2): 239–62.

Beissinger, Mark R. (2002). *Nationalist Mobilization and the Collapse of the Soviet State*. Cambridge: Cambridge University Press.

Bendix, Reinhardt (1978). *Kings or People*. Berkeley: University of California Press.

Benedict, Philip (1999). "Introduction." In *Reformation, Revolt and Civil War in France and the Netherlands*, ed. Philip Benedict, G. Marnef, H. v. Nierop and M. Venard. Amsterdam: Royal Netherlands Academy of Arts and Sciences, 1–22.

Bennett, Andrew, and G. John Ikenberry (2006). "The *Review*'s Evolving Relevance for U.S. Foreign Policy 1906–2006." *American Political Science Review* 100(4): 651–58.

Bercé, Yves-Marie (1987). *Revolt and Revolution in Early Modern Europe*. Manchester: Manchester University Press.

Berger, Peter L., and Thomas Luckmann (1966). *The Social Construction of Reality: A Treatise in the Sociology of Knowledge*. New York: Anchor.

Bettinson, Christopher (1989). "The Politiques and the Politique Part: A Reappraisal." In *From Valois to Bourbon: Dynasty, State and Society in Early Modern France*, ed. K. Cameron. Exeter: University of Exeter Press, 35–50.

Bhaskar, Roy (1989). *Reclaiming Reality*. London: Verso.

Biersteker, Thomas, and Cynthia Weber, eds. (1996). *State Sovereignty as Social Construct*. Cambridge: Cambridge University Press.

Bireley, Robert (1976a). "The Peace of Prague (1635) and the Counterreformation in Germany." *Journal of Modern History* 48(1; On Demand Supplement): 31–70.

———. (1976b). "The Peace of Prague (1635) and the Counterreformation in Germany." *Journal of Modern History* 48(1): 31–70.

Blanford, Nicholas (2007a). "Region's Strife Tears at Lebanon's Fragile Seams." *Christian Science Monitor*, February 14, p. 1

———. (2007b). "Syria Seeks to Gain From Regional Tumult." *Christian Science Monitor*, March 7, p. 7.

Blickle, Peter (1984). "Social Protest and Reformation Theology." In *Religion, Politics and Social Protest*, ed. K. von Greyerz. London: George Allen and Unwin, 1–23.

———. (1985). *The Revolution of 1525: The German Peasant's War from a New Perspective*. Baltimore: The Johns Hopkins University Press.

Blockmans, Wim P. (2002). *Emperor Charles V, 1500–1558*. London: Arnold.

Blockmans, Wim P., and Charles Tilly, eds. (1989). *Cities and the Rise of States in Europe, A.D. 1000 to 1800*. Boulder: Westview.

Bodin, Jean (1992). *On Sovereignty: Four Chapters from the Six Books of the Commonwealth*. Cambridge: Cambridge University Press.

Boettcher, Susan R. (2004). "Confessionalization: Reformation, Religion, Absolutism, and Modernity." *History Compass* 2(1): 1–10.

Bonney, Richard (1991). *The European Dynastic States: 1494–1660*. Oxford: Oxford University Press.

Bonney, Richard (2002). *The Thirty Years' War, 1618–1648*. Oxford: Osprey.
Bosbach, Franz (1998). "The European Debate on Universal Monarchy." In *Theories of Empire, 1450–1800*, ed. D. Armitage. Brookfield, Vt.: Ashgate, 81–98.
Bourdieu, Pierre, and Loïc J. Wacquant (1992). *An Invitation to Reflexive Sociology*. Chicago: University of Chicago Press.
Bowen, H. V. (2002). "Perceptions from the Periphery: Colonial American Views of Brtain's Asiatic Empire, 1756–1783." In *Negotiated Empires: Centers and Peripheries in the Americas, 1500–1820*, ed. C. Daniels and M. D. Kennedy. New York: Routledge, 283–300.
Braddick, M. J. (2000). *State Formation in Early Modern England*. Cambridge: Cambridge University Press.
Bradford, William (1971 [1850]). *Correspondence of the Emperor Charles V and His Ambassadors at the Courts of England and France, from the Original Letters in the Imperial Family Archives at Vienna; with a Connecting Narrative and Biographical Notices of the Emperor, and of Some of the Most Distinguished Officers of His Army and Household; Together with the Emperor's Itinerary from 1519–1551*. New York: AMS Press.
Brady, Thomas A., Jr. (1994). "Jacob Sturm and the Seizure of Brunswick-Wolfenbüttel by the Schmalkaldic League, 1542–1545." *Politics, Religion and Diplomacy in Early Modern Europe: Essays in Honor of De Lamar Jensen*, ed. M. R. Thorp and A. J. Slavin. Kirksville, Mo.: Sixteenth Century Journal Publishers, 33–52.
Brenner, William J. (2006). "In Search of Monsters: Realism and Progress in International Relations Theory After September 11." *Security Studies* 153(3): 496–528.
Brewer, John (1990). *The Sinews of Power: War, Money and the English State, 1688–1783*. Cambridge, Mass.: Harvard University Press.
Brittain, Clay V. (1963). "Adolescent Choices and Parent-Peer Cross pressures." *American Sociological Review* 28(3): 385–91.
Brodek, Theodor V. (1971). "Socio-Political Realities in the Holy Roman Empire." *Journal of Interdisciplinary History* 1(3): 395–405.
Brubaker, Rogers, and Frederick Cooper (2000). "Beyond "Identity"." *Theory and Society* 29(1): 1–47.
Brunt, P. A. (1965). "Reflections on British and Roman Imperialism." *Comparative Studies in Society and History* 7(3): 267–88.
Bukovansky, Mlada (2002). *Legitimacy and Power Politics: The American and French Revolutions in International-political Culture*. Princeton: Princeton University Press.
Bull, Hedley (1977). *The Anarchical Society: A Study of Order in World Politics*. London: Macmillan.
Bull, Hedley, and Adam Watson, eds. (1984). *The Expansion of International Society*. Oxford: Oxford University Press.
Burke, Jason, and Ed Vuliamy. (2002, November 12). "How a Suitcase Full of Dollars Finished off the Taliban." Retrieved April 17, 2007, from http://observer.guardian.co.uk/afghanistan/story/0,841901,00.html.

Burns, Loretta T. Johnson (1994). "The Politics of Conversion: John Calvin and the Bishop of Troyes." *Sixteenth Century Journal* 25(4): 809–22.
Burt, Ronald S. (1992). *Structural Holes: The Social Structure of Competition.* Cambridge, Mass.: Harvard University Press.
Busby, Joshua (2007). "Bono Made Jesse Helms Cry: Jubilee 2000, Debt Relief, and Moral Action in International Politics." *International Studies Quarterly* 51(2): 247–75.
Buzan, Barry (1993). "From International System to International Society: Structural Realism and Regime Theory Meet the English School." *International Organization* 47(3): 327–52.
———. (1996). "The Timeless Wisdom of Realism?" In *International Theory: Positivism and Beyond*, ed. S. Smith, K. Booth, and Z. Marvsia. Cambridge: Cambridge University Press, 47–55.
———. (2004). *From International to World Society? English School Theory and the Social Structure of Globalisation.* Cambridge: Cambridge University Press.
Buzan, Barry, Charles Jones et al. (1993). *The Logic of Anarchy.* New York: Columbia University Press.
Buzan, Barry, and Richard Little (2000). *International Systems in World History.* Oxford: Oxford University Press.
Byrnes, Timothy A., and Peter J. Katzenstein, eds. (2006). *Religion in an Expanding Europe.* Cambridge: Cambridge University Press.
Carpenter, R. Charli (2007). "Setting the Advocacy Agenda: Theorizing Issue Emergence and Nonemergence in Transnational Advocacy Networks." *International Organization* 51(1): 99–120.
Carr, E. H. (1946). *The Twenty Years' Crisis, 1919–1939.* London: Macmillan.
Cederman, Lars-Erik, and Christopher Daase (2003). "Endogenizing Corporate Identities: The Next Step in Constructivist IR Theory." *European Journal of International Relations* 9(1): 5–36.
Cerny, Philip G. (1995). "Globalization and the Changing Logic of Collective Action." *International Organization* 49(4): 595–625.
Cha, Victor D. (2004). "Power Play: Origins of the American Alliance System in Asia," Unpublished Manuscript, Georgetown University.
Chase, Ivan D. (1980). "Social Processes and Hierarchy Formation in Small Groups: A Comparative Perspective." *American Sociological Review* 45(6): 905–24.
Checkel, Jeffrey T. (1999). "Norms, Institutions, and National Identity in Contemporary Europe." *International Studies Quarterly* 43(1): 83–114.
Christensen, Carl C. (1984). "John of Saxony's Diplomacy, 1529–1530: Reformation or Realpolitik?" *Sixteenth Century Journal* 15(4): 419–30.
Chudoba, Bohdan (1969). *Spain and the Empire, 1519–1643.* New York: Octagon.
Clark, Ian (2007). *Legitimacy in International Society.* Oxford: Oxford University Press.
Clark, Samuel (1998). "International Competition and the Treatment of Minorities: Seventeenth-Century Cases and General Propositions." *American Journal of Sociology* 103(5): 1267–1308.

Cohen, Eliot A. (2004). "History and the Hyperpower." *Foreign Affairs* 83(4): 49–63.

Cohn, Henry J. (1971). "Introduction." In *Government in Reformation Europe*. ed. Henry J. Cohn. London: Macmillan, 9–42.

Colegrove, Kenneth (1919). "Diplomatic Procedure Preliminary to the Congress of Westphalia." *American Journal of International Law* 13(3): 450–82.

Collins, James B. (1995). *The State in Early Modern France*. Cambridge: Cambridge University Press.

Constant, Jean Marie (1999). "The Protestant Nobility in France during the Wars of Religion: A Leaven of Innovation in a Traditional World." In *Reformation, Revolt and Civil War in France and the Netherlands 1555–1585*, ed. P. Benedict, G. Marnef, H. v. Nierop and M. Venard. Amsterdam: Royal Netherlands Academy of Arts and Sciences, 69–82.

Cooley, Alexander (2000/2001). "Imperial Wreckage: Property Rights, Sovereignty, and Security in the Post-Soviet Space." *International Security* 25(3): 100–127.

———. (2005). *Logics of Hierarchy: The Organization of Empires, States, and Nations in Transit*. Ithaca: Cornell University Press.

Cooley, Alexander, and James Ron (2002). "The NGO Scramble: Organizational Insecurity and the Political Economy of Transnational Action." *International Security* 27(1): 5–39.

Cooper, J. P. (1971). "General Introduction." In *The Decline of Spain and the Thirty Years' War, 1609–48/49*, ed. J. P. Cooper. Cambridge: Cambridge University Press, 1–66.

Copeland, Dale C. (2000). "The Constructivist Challenge to Structural Realism: A Review Essay." *International Security* 25(2): 187–212.

Coudy, Julien, ed. (1969). *The Huguenot Wars*. Philadelphia: Chilton.

Covington, Cary R. (1988). "Building Presidential Coalitions among Cross-Pressured Members of Congress." *Western Political Quarterly* 41(1): 47–62.

Cox, Michael (2004). "Empire, Imperialism and the Bush Doctrine." *Review of International Studies* 30(4): 585–608.

Craven, Paul, and Barry Wellman (1973). "The Network City." *Sociological Inquiry* 43: 57–88.

Darby, Graham (2001a). "Introduction." *The Origins and Development of the Dutch Revolt*, ed. G. Darby. New York: Routledge, 1–7.

———. (2001b). "Narrative of Events." *The Origins and Development of the Dutch Revolt*, ed. G. Darby. New York: Routledge, 8–28.

David, Steven R. (1991a). *Choosing Sides: Alignment and Realignment in the Third World*. Baltimore: The Johns Hopkins University Press.

———. (1991b). "Explaining Third World Alignment." *World Politics* 43(2): 233–56.

Davies, Joan M. (1990). "The Duc de Montmorency, Philip II and the House of Savoy: A Neglected Aspect of the Sixteenth-Century French Civil Wars." *English Historical Review* 105(417): 870–92.

Davies, Stephen (2005, September 6). "The Reformation and Islam." *Liberty and Power: Group Blog*. Retrieved May 5, 2007, from http://hnn.us/blogs/entries/15372.html.

References • 307

Davis, James C., ed. (1970). *Pursuit of Power: Venetian Ambassadors' Reports on Spain, Turkey, and France in the Age of Philip II, 1560–1600*. New York: Harper and Row.

Desplat, Christian (1991). "Louis XIII and the Union of Béarn and France." In *Conquest and Coalescence: The Shaping of the State in Early Modern Europe*, ed. M. Greengrass. New York: Edward Arnold, 68–83.

Dessler, David (1989). "What's at Stake in the Agent-Structure Debate." *International Organization* 43(3): 441–73.

Diamond, Larry (2005). *Squandered Victory: The American Occupation and the Bungled Attempt to Bring Democracy to Iraq*. New York: Times.

Diani, Mario (2003). " 'Leaders' or Brokers? Positions and Influence." In *Social Movements and Networks: Relational Approaches to Collective Action*, ed. Mario Diani and D. McAdam. Oxford: Oxford University Press, 105–22.

Diefendorf, Barbara (1985). "Prologue to a Massacre: Popular Unrest in Paris, 1557–1572." *American Historical Review* 90(5): 1067–91.

Dixon, C. Scott (2007). "Urban Order and Religious Coexistance in the German Imperial City: Augsburg and Donauwörth, 1548–1608." *Central European History* 40(1): 1–33.

Doty, Roxanne Lynn (1999). "A Reply to Colin Wight." *European Journal of International Relations* 5(3): 387–90.

Downing, Brian (1989). "Medieval Origins of Constitutional Government in the West." *Theory and Society* 18(2): 213–47.

Downing, Brian M. (1992). *The Military Revolution and Political Change: Origins of Democracy and Autocracy in Early Modern Europe*. Princeton: Princeton University Press.

Dueck, Abe J. (1982). "Religion and Temporal Authority in the Reformation: The Controversy Among the Protestants Prior to the Peace of Nuremberg, 1532." *Sixteenth Century Journal* 12(2): 55–74.

Duke, Alistair (1999). "Dissident Propaganda and Political Organization at the Outbreak of the Revolt of the Netherlands." In *Reformation, Revolt and Civil War in France and the Netherlands 1555–1585*, ed. P. Benedict, G. Marnef, H. v. Nierop and M. Venard. Amsterdam: Royal Netherlands Academy of Arts and Sciences, 115–32.

Dunn, Richard S. (1970). *The Age of Religious Wars 1559–1689*. New York: W. W. Norton.

Edelstein, David M. (2000). "Occupational Hazards: Why Military Occupations Succeed or Fail." *International Security* 29(1): 49–91.

Eisenstadt, S. N. (1963). *The Political Systems of Empires*. Glencoe, Ill.: Free Press.

Elias, Norbert (1978). *What Is Sociology?* New York: Columbia University Press.
———. (1989). *The Society of Individuals*. Oxford: Blackwell.
———. (1994). *The Civilizing Process*. Oxford: Blackwell.

Elliott, J. H. (1963a). *Imperial Spain, 1469–1716*. London: Penguin.
———. (1963b). *The Revolt of the Catalans: A Study in the Decline of Spain (1598–1640)*. Cambridge: Cambridge University Press.

Elliott, J. H. (1970). "Revolts in the Spanish Monarchy." In *Preconditions of Revolution in Early Modern Europe*, ed. R. Forster and J. P. Greene. Baltimore: The Johns Hopkins University Press, 109–30.

———. (1984). *Richelieu and Olivares*. Cambridge: Cambridge University Press.

———. (1989). *Spain and its World, 1500–1700*. New Haven: Yale University Press.

———. (1991). "The Spanish Monarchy and the Kingdom of Portugal, 1580–1640." *Conquest and Coalescence: The Shaping of the State in Early Modern Europe*, ed. M. Greengrass. London: Edward Arnold, 48–67.

———. (1992). "A Europe of Composite Monarchies." *Past and Present* (137): 48–71.

———. (2000). *Europe Divided, 1559–1598*. Oxford: Blackwell.

Elman, Colin, and Miriam Fendius Elman (1997). "Diplomatic History and International Relations Theory: Respecting Differences and Crossing Boundaries." *International Security* 22(1): 5–21.

Eltis, David (1995). *The Military Revolution in Sixteenth-Century Europe*. New York: St. Martin's Press.

Elton, G. R. (1964). *Reformation Europe: 1517–1559*. Cleveland: World.

Emirbayer, Mustafa (1997). "Manifesto for a Relational Sociology." *American Journal of Sociology* 103(2): 281–317.

Emirbayer, Mustafa, and Jeffrey Goodwin (1994). "Network Analysis, Culture, and the Problem of Agency." *American Journal of Sociology* 99(6): 1141–54.

Ertman, Thomas (1997). *The Birth of Leviathan: Building States and Regimes in Medieval and Early Modern Europe*. Cambridge: Cambridge University Press.

Esteban, Emilia Salvador (2001). *Carlos V. Emperador de Imperios*. Pamplona: EUNSA.

Evans, R.J.W. (1979). *The Making of the Habsburg Monarchy 1550–1700: An Interpretation*. Oxford: Oxford University Press.

Fearon, James D. (1995). "Rationalist Explanations for War." *International Organization* 49(3): 379–414.

———. (1998). "Bargaining, Enforcement, and International Cooperation." *International Organization* 52(2): 269–305.

Fearon, James D., and David D. Laitin (1996). "Explaining Interethnic Cooperation." *American Political Science Review* 90(4): 715–35.

———. (2000). "Review: Violence and the Social Construction of Ethnic Identity." *International Organization* 54(4): 845–77.

Ferguson, Yale, and Richard Mansbach (1996). *Polities: Authority, Identities, and Change*. Columbia: University of South Carolina Press.

Fernández-Armesto, Felipe, and Derek Wilson (1996). *Reformations: A Radical Interpretation of Christianity and the World (1500–2000)*. New York: Scribner.

Fichtner, Paula Sutter (1980). "The Disobedience of the Obedient: Ferdinand I and the Papacy, 1555–1562." *Sixteenth Century Journal* 11(2; Catholic Reformation): 25–34.

Fierke, Karen M., and Knud Erik Jørgensen, eds. (2001). *Constructing International Relations: The Next Generation*. International Relations in a Constructed World. Armonk, N.Y.: M. E. Sharpe.

Finley-Croswhite, S. Annette (1999). *Henry IV and the Towns: The Pursuit of Legitimacy in French Urban Society, 1589–1610*. Cambridge: Cambridge University Press.

Finnemore, Martha (2004). *The Purpose Of Intervention: Changing Beliefs About The Use Of Force*. Ithaca: Cornell University Press.

Finnemore, Martha, and Katheryn Sikkink (1998). "International Norm Dynamics and Political Change." *International Organization* 52(4): 887–917.

Fischer-Galati, Stephen A. (1954). "Ottoman Imperialism and the Lutheran Struggle for Recognition in Germany, 1520–1529." *Church History* 23(1): 46–67.

Flemming, Patricia H. (1973). "The Politics of Marriage Among Non-Catholic European Royalty." *Current Anthropology* 14(3): 231–49.

Flibbert, Andrew (2006). "The Road to Baghdad: Ideas and Intellectuals in Explanations of the Iraq War." *Security Studies* 15(2): 310–52.

Flynn, Dennis O. (1982). "Fiscal Crisis and the Decline of Spain (Castile)." *Journal of Economic History* 42(1): 139–47.

Forster, Robert, and Jack P. Greene, Eds. (1970). *Preconditions of Revolution in Early Modern Europe*. Baltimore: The Johns Hopkins University Press.

Fox, Jonathan, and Schmuel Sandler (2006). *Bringing Religion into International Relations*. New York: Palgrave.

Francois, Martha Ellis (1974). "Revolts in Late Medieval and Early Modern Europe: A Spiral Model." *Journal of Interdisciplinary History* 5(1): 19–43.

Freeman, Linton C. (1977). "A Set of Measures of Centrality Based on Betweenness." *Sociometry* 40(1): 35–41.

Frost, Robert I. (2000). *The Northern Wars, 1558–1721*. London: Longman.

Fubini, Riccardo (1995). "The Italian League and the Policy of Balance of Power at the Accession of Lorenzo de' Medici." *Journal of Modern History* 67 (Supplement: The Origins of the State in Italy, 1300–1600): S166–99.

Fuhrmann, Horst (1986). *Germany in the High Middle Ages c. 1050–1200*. Cambridge: Cambridge University Press.

Gagnon, V. P. (1994/1995). "Ethnic Nationalism and International Conflict: The Case of Serbia." *International Security* 19(3): 130–66.

Galtung, Johan (1971). "A Structural Theory of Imperialism." *Journal of Peace Research* 8(2): 81–117.

Garrisson, Janine (1991). *A History of Sixteenth-Century France, 1483–1598: Renaissance, Reformation and Rebellion*. London: Macmillan.

Garton Ash, Timothy (2006, July 20). "Lebanon, North Korea, Russia . . . : Here is the world's new multipolar disorder." Retrieved December 11, 2006, from http://www.guardian.co.uk/comment/story/0,1824420,00.html.

Gelderen, Martin van (1992). *The Political Thought of the Dutch Revolt 1555–1590*. Cambridge: Cambridge University Press.

Gentile, Ian (1994). *The New Model Army: In England, Ireland and Scotland, 1645–1653*. Cambridge: Blackwell.

George, Alexander L., and Andrew Bennett (2005). *Case Studies and Theory Development in the Social Sciences*. Cambridge, Mass.: The MIT Press.

Gerhardt, Volker (1998). "On the Historical Significance of the Peace of Westphalia: Twelve Theses." In *1648: War and Peace in Europe*, ed. K. Bussman and H. Schilling. Münster: Westfälisches Landesmuseum, 485–89.

Geyl, Pieter (1958). *The Revolt of the Netherlands (1555–1609)*. New York: Barnes and Noble.

Giddens, Anthony (1984). *The Constitution of Society*. Berkeley: University of California Press.

———. (1995). *A Contemporary Critique of Historical Materialism*. Stanford: Stanford University Press.

Gilpin, Robert (1981). *War and Change in World Politics*. New York: Cambridge University Press.

———. (1986). "The Richness of the Tradition of Political Realism." In *Neorealism and Its Critics*, ed. R. O. Keohane. New York: Columbia University Press, 301–21.

Given, James (1990). *State and Society in Medieval Europe: Gwynedd and Languedoc under Outside Rule*. Ithaca: Cornell University Press.

Glaser, Charles L. (2003). "Structural Realism in a More Complex World." *Review of International Studies* 29(3): 403–14.

Glete, Jan (2002). *War and the State in Early Modern Europe: Spain, the Dutch Republic and Sweden as Fiscal-Military States, 1500–1600*. London: Routledge.

Goddard, Stacie E. (2006). "Uncommon Ground: Indivisible Territory and the Politics of Legitimation." *International Organization* 60(1): 35–68.

Goddard, Stacie E., and Daniel Nexon (2005). "Paradigm Lost? Reassessing *Theory of International Politics*." *European Journal of International Relations* 11(1): 9–61.

Gorski, Philip S. (1993). "The Protestant Ethic Revisited: Disciplinary Revolution in Holland and Prussia." *American Journal of Sociology* 99(2): 255–316.

———. (1999). "Calvinism and State-Formation in Early Modern Europe." In *State/Culture: State-Formation After the Cultural Turn*, ed. G. Steinmetz. Ithaca: Cornell University Press, 147–81.

———. (2000). "The Mosaic Moment: An Early Modernist Critique of Modernist Theories of Nationalism." *American Journal of Sociology* 105(5): 1428–68.

———. (2003). *The Disciplinary Revolution: Calvinism and the Rise of the State in Early Modern Europe*. Chicago: University of Chicago Press.

Gould, Roger V. (1993). "Collective Action and Network Structure." *American Sociological Review* 58(2): 182–96.

Gould, Roger V., and Roberto M. Fernandez (1989). "Structures of Mediation: A Formal Approach to Brokerage in Transaction Networks." *Sociological Methodology* 19: 89–126.

Granovetter, Mark (1973). "The Strength of Weak Ties." *American Journal of Sociology* 78(6): 1360–80.

———. (1983). "The Strength of Weak Ties: A Network Theory Revisited." *Sociological Theory* 1: 201–33.

Graus, Frantisek (1976). "From Resistance to Revolt: The Late Medieval Peasant Wars in the Context of Social Crisis." In *The German Peasant War of 1525*, ed. J. M. Bak. London: Frank Cass, 1–9.

Greengrass, Mark (1991). "Conquest and Coalescence: The Shaping of the State in Early Modern Europe." In *Conflict and Coalescence*, ed. Mark Greengrass. London: Edward Arnold, 1–24.

Grieco, Joseph (1993). "Anarchy and the Limits of Cooperation: A Realist Critique of the Newest Liberal Institutionalism." In *Neorealism and Neoliberalism: The Contemporary Debate*, ed. D. A. Baldwin. New York: Columbia University Press, 116–42.

Griffiths, Gordon (1960). "The Revolutionary Character of the Revolt of the Netherlands." *Comparative Studies in Society and History* 2(4): 452–72.

Grimm, Harold J. (1965). *The Reformation Era, 1500–1658*. New York: Macmillan.

Gross, Leo (1948). "The Peace of Westphalia, 1648–1948." *American Journal of International Law* 42(1): 20–41.

Grunberg, Isabelle. (1990). "Exploring the 'Myth' of Hegemonic Stability." *International Organization* 44(4): 431–77.

Guarini, Elena Fasano (1995). "Center and Periphery." *Journal of Modern History* 67(Supplement: The Origins of the State in Italy, 1300–1600): S74–96.

Guicciardini, Francesco (1972). *Maxims and Reflections*. Philadelphia: University of Pennsylvania Press.

———. (1984). *The History of Italy*. Princeton: Princeton University Press.

Guidry, John A., Michael D. Kennedy et al. (2000). "Globalization and Social Movements." In *Globalization and Social Movements: Culture, Power, and the Transnational Sphere*, ed. John A. Guidry, Michael D. Kennedy, and M. N. Zald. Ann Arbor: University of Michigan Press, 1–32.

Haas, Richard N. (2006). "The New Middle East." *Foreign Affairs* 85(6): 2–11.

Habsburg, Otto von (1967). *Charles V*. London: Weidenfeld and Nicolson.

Hacker, Jacob S., and Paul Pierson (2005). *Off Center: The Republican Revolution and the Erosion of American Democracy*. New Haven: Yale University Press.

Hacking, Ian (1999). *The Social Construction of What?* Cambridge, Mass.: Harvard University Press.

Hafner-Burton, Emilie, and Alexander H. Montgomery (2006). "Power Positions: International Organizations, Social Networks, and Conflict." *Journal of Conflict Resolution* 50(1): 3–27.

Hale, J. R. (1985). *War and Society in Renaissance Europe, 1450–1620*. Baltimore: The Johns Hopkins University Press.

Haliczer, Stephen (1981). *The Comuneros of Castile: The Forging of a Revolution, 1475–1521*. Madison: University of Wisconsin Press.

Hall, Rodney Bruce (1999). *National Collective Identity: Social Constructs and International Systems*. New York: Columbia University Press.

———. (2002). "The Socially Constructed Contexts of Comparative Politics." In *Constructivism and Comparative Politics*, ed. D. M. Green. Armonk, N.Y.: M. E. Sharpe, 121–50.

Hammarström, Mats, and Heldt Birger (2002). "The Diffusion of Military Intervention: Testing a Network Position Approach." *International Interactions* 28: 335–77.

Harding, Robert (1981). "Revolution and Reform in the Holy League: Anger, Rennes, Nantes." *Journal of Modern History* 53(3): 379–416.

Hardy, Roger. (2006). "The Lebanese Crisis Explained." Retrieved January 5, 2007, from http://news.bbc.co.uk/1/hi/world/middle_east/6173322.stm.

Hasenclever, Andreas, and Volker Rittberger (2000). "Does Religion Make a Difference? Theoretical Approaches to the Impact of Faith on Political Conflict." *Milennium: Journal of International Studies* 29(3): 641–74.

Hayden, J. Michael (1973). "Continuity in the France of Henry IV and Louis XIII: French Foreign Policy." *Journal of Modern History* 45(1): 1–23.

Head, Randolph C. (1995). "William Tell and His Comrades: Association and Fraternity in the Propaganda of Fifteenth- and Sixteenth-Century Switzerland." *Journal of Modern History* 67(3): 527–57.

Hechter, Michael (1995). "Introduction: Reflections on Historical Prophecy in the Social Sciences." *American Journal of Sociology* 100(6): 1520–27.

Hechter, Michael, and William Brustein (1980). "Regional Modes of Production and Patterns of State Formation in Western Europe." *American Journal of Sociology* 85(5): 1061–94.

Hendrix, Scott H. (1994). "Loyalty, Piety, or Opportunism: German Princes and the Reformation." *Journal of Interdisciplinary History* 25(2): 211–24.

Hintze, Otto (1975). *The Historical Essays of Otto Hintze*. New York: Oxford University Press.

Hirschman, Albert O. (1997). *The Passions and the Interests: Political Arguments for Capitalism Before Its Triumph*. Princeton: Princeton University Press.

Hitchcock, William R. (1958). *The Background of the Knights' Revolt*. Berkeley and Los Angeles: University of California Press.

Hobbes, Thomas (1951 [1651]). *Leviathan*. New York: Penguin.

Hobden, Stephen, and John M. Hobson, eds. (2002). *Historical Sociology of International Relations*. Cambridge: Cambridge University Press.

Hobson, John M. (2002). "What's at Stake?" *Historical Sociology of International Relations*, ed. Stephen Hobden and John M. Hobson. Cambridge: Cambridge University Press, 3–41.

Hobson, John M., and J. C. Sharman (2005). "The Enduring Place of Hierarchy in World Politics: Tracing the Social Logics of Hierarchy and Political Change." *European Journal of International Relations* 11(1): 63–98.

Holborn, Hajo (1959). *A History of Modern Germany: The Reformation*. Princeton: Princeton University Press.

Holsti, Kalevi J. (2004). *Taming the Sovereigns: Institutional Change in International Politics*. Cambridge: Cambridge University Press.

Holt, Mack P. (1986). *The Duke of Anjou and the Politique Struggle During the Wars of Religion*. Cambridge: Cambridge University Press.

———. (1993). "Review Article: Putting Religion Back in the Wars of Religion." *French Historical Studies* 18(2): 524–51.

———. (1995). *The French Wars of Religion, 1562–1629*. Cambridge: Cambridge University Press.

Howard, Michael (1976). *War in European History*. Oxford: Oxford University Press.

Howe, Stephen (2002). *Empire, A Very Short Introduction*. Oxford: Oxford University Press.

Hsia, R. Po-Chia (1989). *Social Discipline in the Reformation, Central Europe 1550–1750*. London and New York: Routledge.

Hubatsch, Walther (1971). "Albert of Brandenburg-Ansbach, Grand Master of the Order of the Teutonic Knights and Duke in Prussia, 1490–1568." In *Government in Reformation Europe, 1520–1560*, ed. H. J. Cohn. London: Macmillan, 169–202.
Hui, Victoria Tin-bor (2004). "Towards a Dynamic Theory of International Politics: Insights from Comparing Ancient China and Early Modern Europe." *International Organization* 58(1): 175–205.
———. (2005). *War and State Formation in Ancient China and Early Modern Europe*. Cambridge: Cambridge University Press.
Hulsman, John C., and Alexis Y. Debat (2006). "In Praise of Warlords." *National Interest* (84): 51–58.
Hurd, Elizabeth Shakman (2004). "The Political Authority of Secularism in International Relations." *European Journal of International Relations* 10(2): 235–62.
———. (2008). *The Politics of Secularism in International Relations*. Princeton: Princeton University Press.
Ikenberry, G. John (2001). *After Victory: Institutions, Strategic Restraint, and the Rebuilding of Order After Major War*. Princeton: Princeton University Press.
Ingram, Paul, Jeffrey Robinson et al. (2005). "The Intergovernmental Network of World Trade: IGO Connectedness, Governance, and Embeddedness." *American Journal of Sociology* 11(3): 824–58.
Ingrao, Charles W. (2000). *The Habsburg Monarchy, 1618–1815*. Cambridge: Cambridge University Press.
Isaac, Benjamin (1992). *The Limits of Empire: The Roman Army in the East*. Oxford: Clarendon.
Israel, Jonathan (1995). *The Dutch Republic: Its Rise, Greatness, and Fall, 1477–1806*. Oxford: Oxford University Press.
Jackson, Patrick, and Daniel Nexon (1999). "Relations Before States: Substance, Process, and the Study of World Politics." *European Journal of International Relations* 5(3): 291–332.
———. (2001). "Whence Causal Mechanisms? A Comment on Legro." *Dialogue-IO* 1(1): 1–21.
———. (2002). "Globalization, the Comparative Method, and Comparing Constructions." *Constructivism and Comparative Politics*, ed. D. Green. Armonk, N.Y.: M. E. Sharpe, 88–120.
———. (2004). "Realist Constructivism or Constructivist Realism?" *International Studies Review* 2(6): 337–41.
Jackson, Patrick Thaddeus (2003). "Defending the West: Occidentalism and the Formation of NATO." *Journal of Political Philosophy* 11(3): 223–52.
———. (2004). "Hegel's House, or 'People are States too.' " *Review of International Studies* 30(2): 281–87.
———. (2006a). *Civilizing the Enemy: German Reconstruction and the Invention of the West*. Ann Arbor: University of Michigan Press.
———. (2006b). "Making Sense of Making Sense: Configurational Analysis and the Double Hermeneutic." In *Interpretation and Method: Empirical Research Methods and the Interpretive Turn*, ed. D. Yanow and P. Schwartz-Shea. Armonk: M. E. Sharpe, 264–81.

Jackson, Robert H. (1990). *Quasi-states: Sovereignty, International Relations, and the Third World*. Cambridge: Cambridge University Press.

Jahn, Sigrid (1998). "The Imperial Justice System as Mirror of the Imperial and Religious Constitution." In *1648: War and Peace in Europe*, ed. K. Bussman and H. Schilling. Münster: Westfälisches Landesmuseum, 455–63.

Jervis, Robert (1976). *Perception and Misperception in International Politics*. Princeton: Princeton University Press.

———. (1978). "Cooperation Under the Security Dilemma." *World Politics* 30(2): 167–214.

Joachim, Jutta (2003). "Framing Issues and Seizing Opportunities: The UN, NGOs, and Women's Rights." *International Studies Quarterly* 47(2): 247–74.

Juergensmeyer, Mark (1993). *The New Cold War? Religious Nationalism Confronts the Secular State*. Berkeley: University of California Press.

Kaiser, David (1990). *Politics and War: European Conflict from Philip II to Hitler*. Cambridge, Mass.: Harvard University Press.

Kamen, Henry (1997). *Philip of Spain*. New Haven: Yale University Press.

———. (2003). *Empire: How Spain Became a World Power, 1492–1763*. New York: HarperCollins.

Kann, Robert A. (1973). "Dynasic Relations and European Power Politics (1848–1918)." *Journal of Modern History* 45(3): 387–410.

———. (1974). *A History of the Habsburg Empire, 1526–1918*. Berkeley: University of California Press.

Kaplan, Benjamin J. (1994). " 'Remnants of the Papal Yoke': Apathy and Opposition in the Dutch Reformation." *Sixteenth Century Journal* 25(3): 653–69.

Karsh, Efraim, and Inari Karsh (1999). *Empires of the Sand: The Struggle for Mastery in the Middle East, 1789–1923*. Cambridge, Mass.: Harvard University Press.

Katzenstein, Peter J. (1996). "Introduction: Alternative Perspectives on National Security." In *The Culture of National Security: Norms and Identity in World Politics*, ed. P. J. Katzenstein. New York: Columbia University Press, 1–32.

Katznelson, Ira (1997). "Structure and Configuration in Comparative Politics." In *Comparative Politics: Rationality, Culture, and Structure*, ed. M. I. Lichbach and A. S. Zuckerman. Cambridge: Cambridge University Press, 81–112.

Kaufman, Stuart J. (1996). "Spiraling to Ethnic War: Elites, Masses, and Moscow in Moldova's Civil War." *International Security* 21(2): 108–38.

Keck, Margaret E., and Katheryn Sikkink (1998). *Activists Beyond Borders: Advocacy Networks in International Politics*. Ithaca: Cornell University Press.

Keen, Maurice H. (1991). *The Penguin History of Medieval Europe*. New York: Penguin.

Kennedy, Paul (1987). *The Rise and Fall of the Great Powers: Economic Change and Military Conflict from 1500 to 2000*. New York: Random House.

Keohane, Robert O. (1984). *After Hegemony: Cooperation and Discord in the World Political Economy*. Princeton: Princeton University Press.

———. (2001). "Governance in a Partially Globalized World." *American Political Science Review* 91(1): 1–14.

Keohane, Robert O., and Joseph S. Nye, Jr. (1989). *Power and Interdependence*. 2d ed. New York: HarperCollins.

Kettering, Sharon (1986a). "Patronage and Kinship in Early Modern France." *French Historical Studies* 16(2): 408–35.
———. (1986b). *Patrons, Brokers, and Clients in Seventeenth-Century France*. Oxford: Oxford University Press.
———. (1989). "Clientage during the French Wars of Religion." *Sixteenth Century Journal* 20(2): 221–39.
———. (1992). "Patronage in Early Modern France." *French Historical Studies* 17(4): 839–62.
Khan, M. Ilya (2007) "Taleban spread wings in Pakistan." *BBC News*, March 5. Retrieved May 14, 2007 from http://news.bbc.co.uk/1/hi/world/south_asia/6409089.stm.
Kiernan, V. G. (1980). *State and Society in Europe 1550–1650*. Oxford: Blackwell.
Kim, Hyojoung, and Peter S. Bearman (1997). "The Structure and Dynamics of Movement Participation." *American Sociological Review* 62: 70–93.
King, Charles (2001). "The Benefits of Ethnic War: Understanding Eurasia's Unrecognized States." *World Politics* 53(4): 524–52.
———. (2003). "Crisis in the Caucasus: A New Look at Russia's Chechen Impasse." *Foreign Affairs* 82(2): 134–39.
Kingdon, Robert M. (1967). "Calvinist Religious Aggression." In *The French Wars of Religion: How Important Were Religious Factors?*, ed. J.H.M. Salmon. Boston: D. C. Heath, 6–10.
———. (1998). "International Calvinism and the Thirty Years' War." In *1648: War and Peace in Europe*, ed. K. Bussman and H. Schilling. Münster: Westfälisches Landesmuseum, 229–35.
Kirshner, Julius (1995). "Introduction: The State Is 'Back in.' " *Journal of Modern History* 67(Supplement: The Origins of the State in Italy, 1300-1600): S1–10.
Kiser, Edgar, and April Linton (2001). "Determinants of the Growth of the State: War and Taxation in Early Modern France." *Social Forces* 80(2): 411–48.
———. (2002). "The Hinges of History: State-Making and Revolt in Early Modern France." *American Sociological Review* 67(6): 889–910.
Kittelson, James M. (1986). "Renaissance and Reformation in Germany: An Agenda for Research." *Journal of Modern History* 58(Supplement: Politics and Society in the Holy Roman Empire, 1500–1806): S124–40.
Kleinman, Ruth (1978). "Changing Interpretations of the Edict of Nantes: The Administrative Aspects, 1643–1661." *French Historical Studies* 10(4): 541–71.
Knecht, R. J. (1982). *Francis I*. Cambridge: Cambridge University Press.
———. (1989). *The French Wars of Religion, 1559–1598*. New York: Longman.
———. (1996a). *French Renaissance Monarchy: Francis I and Henry II*. London: Longman.
———. (1996b). *Renaissance Warrior and Patron: The Reign of Francis I*. Cambridge: Cambridge University Press.
———. (1996c). *The Rise and Fall of Renaissance France*. London: Fontana.
———. (2000). *The French Civil Wars, 1562–1598*. Harlow: Longman.
Koenigsberger, H. G. (1955). "The Organization of Revolutionary Parties in France and the Netherlands During the Sixteenth Century." *Journal of Modern History* 27(4): 333–51.

Koenigsberger, H. G. (1971a). *Estates and Revolutions: Essays in Early Modern European History.* Ithaca: Cornell University Press.

———. (1971b). *The Habsburgs and Europe, 1516–1660.* Ithaca: Cornell University Press.

———. (1986). *Politicians and Virtuosi: Essays in Early Modern History.* London: Hambledon.

———. (1987). *Early Modern Europe: 1500–1789.* New York: Longman.

———. (1994a). "Politics of Philip II." In *Politics, Religion and Diplomacy in Early Modern Europe: Essays in Honor of De Lamar Jensen,* ed. M. R. Thorp and A. J. Slavin: Sixteenth Century Journal Publishers, 171–90.

———. (1994b). "Prince and States General: Charles V and the Netherlands (1506–1555): The Prothero Lecture." *Transactions of the Royal Historical Society, 6th Series* 4: 127–51.

Koenigsberger, H. G., and George L. Mosse (1968). *Europe in the Sixteenth Century.* London: Longman.

Kollock, Peter (1994). "The Emergence of Exchange Structures: An Experimental Study of Uncertainty, Commitment, and Trust." *American Journal of Sociology* 100(2): 313–45.

Kooi, Christina (1995). "Popish Impudence: The Perseverance of the Roman Catholic Faithful in Calvinist Holland, 1572–1620." *Sixteenth Century Journal* 26(1): 75–85.

Kossman, E. H., and A. F. Mellink, eds. (1974). *Texts Concerning the Revolt of the Netherlands.* Cambridge: Cambridge University Press.

Krasner, Stephen D. (1993). "Westphalia and All That." In *Ideas and Foreign Policy: Beliefs. Institutions, and Political Change,* ed. J. Goldstein and R. O. Keohane. Ithaca: Cornell University Press, 235–64.

———. (1999). *Sovereignty: Organized Hypocrisy.* Princeton: Princeton University Press.

———. (2001). "Rethinking the Sovereign State Model." *Review of International Studies* 27(5): 17–42.

Krebs, Ronald R., and Patrick Thaddeus Jackson (2007). "Twisting Tongues and Twisting Arms: The Power of Political Rhetoric." *European Journal of International Relations* 13(1): 35–66.

Krodel, Gottfried G. (1982). "Law, Order, and the Almighty Taler: The Empire in Action at the 1530 Diet of Augsburg." *Sixteenth Century Journal* 13(2): 75–106.

Kupchan, Charles (1996). *The Vulnerability of Empire.* Ithaca: Cornell University Press.

Lake, David A. (1993). "Leadership, Hegemony, and the International Economy: Naked Emperor or Tattered Monarch?" *International Studies Quarterly* 37(4): 459–89.

———. (1996). "Anarchy, Hierarchy and the Variety of International Relations." *International Organization* 50(1): 1–33.

———. (1999). *Entangling Relations: American Foreign Policy in Its Century.* Princeton: Princeton University Press.

———. (2001). "Beyond Anarchy: The Importance of Security Institutions." *International Security* 26(1): 129–60.

Lake, David A. (2003). "The New Sovereignty in International Relations." *International Studies Review* 5(3): 303–24.
Lal, Deepak (2004). *In Praise of Empires: Globalization and Order*. New York: Palgrave.
Lambert, Michael (1977). *Medieval Heresy: Popular Movements from the Gregorian Reform to the Reformation*. London: Blackwell.
Lange, Matthew (2003). "Structural Holes and Structural Synergies: A Comparative-Historical Analysis of State-Society Relations and Development in Colonial Sierra Leone and Mauritius." *International Journal of Comparative Sociology* 44(4): 372–407.
Lapid, Joseph, and Friedrich Kratochwil (1996). "Revisiting the 'National': Towards an Identity Agenda in Neorealism?" In *The Return of Culture and Identity in IR Theory*, ed. Joseph Lapid and Friedrich Kratochwil. Boulder: Lynne Reinner, 105–28.
Le Roy Ladurie, Emmanuel (1996). *The Ancien Régime: A History of France, 1610–1774*. Oxford: Blackwell.
Legro, Jeffrey W. (1997). "Which Norms Matter? Revisiting the 'Failure' of Internationalism." *International Organization* 51(1): 31–63.
Lemann, Nicholas (2003). "The Controller: Karl Rove is Working to get George Bush Reelected, but He Has Bigger Plans." *New Yorker*, May 12. Retrieved on July 2, 2008, from http://www.newyorker.com/archive/2003/05/12/030512factlemann?currentPage=all.
Lemke, Douglas (2002). *Regions of War and Peace*. Cambridge: Cambridge University Press.
Lemke, Douglas, and Suzanne Werner (1996). "Power Parity, Commitment to Change, and War." *International Studies Quarterly* 40(2): 235–60.
Lendon, J. E. (1997). *Empire of Honour: The Art of Government in the Roman World*. Oxford: Oxford University Press.
Lenman, Bruce (2000). *Britain's Colonial Wars, 1550–1688*. London: Longman.
———. (2001). *Britain's Colonial Wars, 1688–1783*. London: Longman.
de León, Fernando González, and Geoffrey Parker (2001). "The Grand Strategy of Philip II and the Revolt of the Netherlands." In *The Origins and Development of the Dutch Revolt*, ed. G. Darby. New York: Routledge, 107–32.
Lestringant, Frank, and Ann Blair (1995). "Geneva and America in the Renaissance: The Dream of the Huguenot Refuge 1555–1600." *Sixteenth Century Journal* 26(2): 285–95.
Lewis, Martin, and Karen Wïgen (1997). *The Myth of Continents: A Critique of Metageography*. Berkeley: University of California Press.
Lieven, Anatol (2002). "The Pressures on Pakistan." *Foreign Affairs* 81(1): 106–10.
Linder, Robert D. (1966). "Pierre Viret and the Sixteenth-Century French Protestant Revolutionary Tradition." *Journal of Modern History* 38(2): 125–37.
Liu, Henry C. K. (2005, April 28). "Militarism and Failed States: Part 8." Retrieved June 27, 2006, from http://www.atimes.com/atimes/Front_Page/GD28Aa02.html.
Lotz-Heumann, Ute, and Matthias Pohlig (2007). "Confessionalization and Literature in the Empire, 1555–1700." *Central European History* 40(1): 35–61.

Lovett, A. W. (1986). *Early Habsburg Spain, 1517–1598*. Oxford: Oxford University Press.

———. (1982). "The General Settlement of 1577: An Aspect of Spanish Finance in the Early Modern Period." *Historical Journal* 25(1): 1–22.

Luttwak, Edward N. (1976). *The Grand Strategy of the Roman Empire: From the First Century A.D. to the Third*. Baltimore: The Johns Hopkins University Press.

Lynch, John (1991). *Spain 1516–1598: From Nation-State to World Empire*. Oxford: Blackwell.

Lynn, John A. (1999). *The Wars of Louis XIV, 1667–1714*. Essex: Addison Wesley/Longman.

MacDonald, Paul K. (2004). *Peripheral Pulls: Great Power Expansion and Lessons for the "American Empire."* Paper Presented at the Annual Meeting of the International Studies Association, Montreal, Canada.

———. (2006). "Occuption or Empire? Explaining America's Failure in Iraq." Unpublished Mansucript. Belfer Center for Science and International Affairs, Harvard University.

Machiavelli, Niccòlo (1994). *Selected Political Writings*. Cambridge: Hackett.

Mackenney, Richard (1993). *Sixteenth-Century Europe: Expansion and Conflict*. Basingstoke: Macmillan.

Macy, Michael W. (1991). "Learning to Cooperate: Stochastic and Tacit Collusion in Social Exchange." *American Journal of Sociology* 97(3): 808–48.

Major, J. Russell (1971). "The French Renaissance Monarchy as Seen Through the Estates General." In *Government in Reformation Europe: 1520–1560*, ed. H. J. Cohn. London: Macmillan, 43–57.

———. (1994). *From Renaissance Monarchy to Absolute Monarchy: French Kings, Nobels, & Estates*. Baltimore: The Johns Hopkins University Press.

Malowist, M. (1966). "The Problem of Inequality of Economic Development in Europe in the Later Middle Ages." *Economic History Review, New Series* 19(1): 15–28.

Mann, Michael (1993). *The Sources of Social Power*. Cambridge: Cambridge University Press.

Maravall, J. A. (1983). *Las Comunidades de Castila: Una Primera Revolución Moderna*. Madrid: Revista de Occidente.

March, James G., and Johan P. Olsen (1998). "The Institutional Dynamics of International-political Orders." *International Organization* 52(4): 943–69.

Mardsen, Peter V. (1990). "Network Data and Measurement." *Annual Review of Sociology* 16: 435–63.

Marnef, Guido (1999). "The Dynamics of Reformed Religious Militancy: The Netherlands, 1566–1585." In *Reformation, Revolt and Civil War in France and the Netherlands, 1555–1585*, ed. P. Benedict, Guido Marnef, H. v. Nierop, and M. Venard. Amsterdam: Royal Netherlands Academy of Arts and Sciences, 51–68.

Martin, William (1999). "The Christian Right and American Foreign Policy." *Foreign Policy* 114: 66–80.

Marx, Anthony W. (2005). *Faith in Nation : Exclusionary Origins of Nationalism*. Oxford: Oxford University Press.

Mastanduno, Michael (2005). "Hegemonic Order, September 11, and the Consequences of the Bush Revolution." *International Relations of the Asia-Pacific* 5(2): 177–96.

Matheson, Peter (1998). *The Rhetoric of Reformation*. Edinburgh: T and T Clark.

Mattern, Janice Bially (2004). *Ordering International Politics; Identity, Crisis and Representational Force*. New York: Routledge.

Mattingly, Garrett (1988). *Renaissance Diplomacy*. New York: Dover.

McAdam, Doug (2003). "Beyond Structural Analysis: Towads a More Dynamic Understanding of Social Movements." In *Social Movements and Networks: Relational Approaches to Collective Action*, ed. M. Diani and Doug McAdam. Oxford: Oxford University Press, 281–98.

McAdam, Doug, Sidney Tarrow et al. (2001). *Dynamics of Contention*. Cambridge: Cambridge University Press.

McElwee, William Lloyd (1936). *The Reign of Charles V, 1516–1558*. London: Macmillan.

McGrath, Alister E. (2004). *The Intellectual Origins of the European Reformation*. London: Blackwell.

McNeil, John T. (1966). *The History and Character of Calvinism*. Oxford: Oxford University Press.

Mearsheimer, John (1990). "Back to the Future: Instability in Europe after the Cold War." *International Security* 15(1): 5–56.

———. (2001). *The Tragedy of Great Power Politics*. New York: W. W. Norton.

———. (2002). "Through the Realist Lens: Conversation with John Mearsheimer." *Conversations with History* Retrieved December 14, 2006, from http://globetrotter.berkeley.edu/people2/Mearsheimer/mearsheimer-con0.html.

Mercer, John (1995). "Anarchy and Identity." *International Organization* 49(2): 299–352.

Miles, Jack (2003). "Religious Freedom and Foreign Policy." *New Perspectives Quarterly* 20(4). Retrieved July 2, 2008, from http://www.digitalnpq.org/archive/2003_fall/miles.html.

Milner, Helen (1997). *Interests, Institutions, and Information: Domestic Politics and International Relations*. Princeton: Princeton University Press.

Mische, Ann (2003). "Cross-talk in Movements: Reconceiving the Culture-Network Link." In *Social Movements and Networks: Relational Approaches to Collective Action*, ed. M. Diani and D. McAdam. Oxford: Oxford University Press, 258–80.

Mitchell, Joshua (2007). "Religion is Not a Preference." *Journal of Politics* 69(2): 349–60.

Mitzen, Jennifer (2005). "Reading Habermas in Anarchy: Multilateral Diplomacy and Global Public Spheres." *American Political Science Review* 99(3): 401–17.

Moeller, Bernd (1982). *Imperial Cities and the Reformation: Three Essays*. Durham, N.C.: Labyrinth.

Mommsen, Wolfgang J. (1984). "Introduction." In *Religion, Politics and Social Protest*, ed. K. von Greyerz. London: George Allen and Unwin, ix–xii.

———. (1989). *The Political and Social Theory of Max Weber*. Chicago: University of Chicago Press.

Montgomery, Alexander H. (2005). "Proliferation Determinism or Pragmatism? How to Dismantle an Atomic Bomb Network." *International Security* 30(2), 153–87.

Moravcsik, Andrew (1997). "Taking Preferences Seriously: A Liberal Theory of International Politics." *International Organization* 51(4): 513–54.

Mortimer, G. (2001). "Did Contemporaries Recognize a 'Thirty Years' War?' " *English Historical Review* 116(465): 124–36.

Motyl, Alexander J. (1997). "Thinking About Empire." In *After Empire: Multiethnic Societies and Nation-Building*, ed. K. Barkey and M. v. Hagen. Boulder: Westview, 19–29.

———. (1999). *Revolutions, Nations, Empires: Conceptual Limits and Theoretical Possibilities*. New York: Columbia University Press.

———. (2001). *Imperial Ends: The Decay, Collapse, and Revival of Empires*. New York: Columbia University Press.

Mukerji, Chandra (1997). *Territorial Ambitions and the Gardens of Versailles*. Cambridge: Cambridge University Press.

Muldoon, James (1999). *Empire and Order: The Concept of Empire, 800–1800*. New York: St. Martin's.

Müller, Gerhard (1977). "Alliance and Confession: The Theological-Historical Development and Ecclesiastical-Political Significance of Reformation Confessions." *Sixteenth Century Journal* 8(4): 123–40.

Munck, Thomas (1990). *Seventeenth Century Europe, 1598–1700*. London: Macmillan.

Nathan, Laurie (2006). "Domestic Instability and Security Communities." *European Journal of International Relations* 12(2): 275–99.

Nexon, Daniel (2005). "Zeitgeist? Neo-Idealism in the Study of International Change." *Review of International-political Economy* 12(4): 700–719.

———. (2006). "Religion, European Identity, and Political Contention in Historical Perspective." In *Religion in an Expanding Europe*, ed. T. A. Byrnes and P. J. Katzenstein. Cambridge: Cambridge University Press, 256–82.

Nexon, Daniel, and Thomas Wright (2007). "What's at Stake in the American Empire Debate." *American Political Science Review* 101(2): 253–71.

Nierop, Henk van (1995). "Similar Problems, Different Outcomes: The Revolt of the Netherlands and the Wars of Religion in France." In *A Miracle Mirrored: The Dutch Republic in European Perspective*, ed. K. Davids and J. Lucassen. Cambridge: Cambridge University Press, 26–56.

———. (1999). "The Nobility and the Revolt of the Netherlands: Between Church and King, and Protestantism and Privileges." In *Reformation, Revolt and Civil War in France and the Netherlands, 1555–1585*, ed. P. Benedict, G. Marnef, Hen van Nierop, and M. Venard. Amsterdam: Royal Netherlands Academy of Arts and Sciences, 83–98.

———. (2001a). "Alva's Throne: Making Sense of the Revolt of the Netherlands." In *The Origins and Development of the Dutch Revolt*, ed. G. Darby. New York: Routledge, 29–47.

———. (2001b). "The Nobles and the Revolt." In *The Origins and Development of the Dutch Revolt*, ed. G. Darby. New York: Routledge, 48–66.

North, Douglas (1990). *Institutions, Institutional Change and Economic Performance*. Cambridge: Cambridge University Press.
North, Douglas, and Robert Thomas (1973). *The Rise of the Western World*. Cambridge: Cambridge University Press.
Nye, Joseph (2002). *The Paradox of American Power: Why the World's Only Superpower Can't Go It Alone*. Oxford: Oxford University Press.
Onuf, Nicholas (1989). *World of Our Making: Rules and Rule in Social Theory and International Relations*. Columbia: University of South Carolina Press.
Oresko, Robert, G. C. Gibbs et al. (1997). "Introduction." In *Royal and Republican Sovereignty in Early Modern Europe*, ed. Robert Oresko, G. C. Gibbs, and H. M. Scott. Cambridge: Cambridge University Press, 1–42.
Organski, A.F.K. (1958). *World Politics*. New York: Alfred A. Knopf.
Ortíz, Antonio Domínguez (1971). *The Golden Age of Spain, 1516–1659*. New York: Basic.
Osiander, Andreas (1994). *The States System of Europe, 1640–1990: Peacemaking and the Conditions of International Stability*. Oxford: Clarendon.
———. (2001). "Sovereignty, International Relations, and the Westphalian Myth." *International Organization* 55(2): 251–88.
Ostrogorski, George (1969). *History of the Byzantine State*. New Brunswick, N.J.: Rutgers University Press.
Owen, John M. (2005). "When Do Ideologies Produce Alliances? The Holy Roman Empire, 1517–1555." *International Studies Quarterly* 49(1): 73–99.
Ozment, Steven E. (1975). *The Reformation in the Cities: The Appeal of Protestantism to Sixteenth-Century Germany and Switzerland*. New Haven: Yale University Press.
Padgett, John F., and Christopher K. Ansell (1993). "Robust Action and the Rise of the Medici, 1400–1434." *American Journal of Sociology* 98(6): 1259–1319.
Pagden, Anthony (1995). *Lords of All the World: Ideologies of Empire in Spain, Britain and France, c. 1500–c. 1800*. New Haven: Yale University Press.
———. (2001). *Peoples and Empires: A Short History of European Migration, Exploration, and Conquest, from Greece to the Present*. New York: Modern Library.
Parker, Charles H. (1997). "To the Attentive, Nonpartisan Reader: The Appeal to History and National Identity in the Religious Disputes of the Seventeenth-Century Netherlands." *Sixteenth Century Journal* 28(1): 57–78.
Parker, David (1971). "The Social Foundations of French Absolutism." *Past and Present* (53): 67–89.
———. (1983). *The Making of French Absolutism*. London: Edward Arnold.
Parker, Geoffrey (1972). *The Army of Flanders and the Spanish Road, 1567–1659*. Cambridge: Cambridge University Press.
———. (1976). "The 'Military Revolution,' 1560–1660--A Myth?" *Journal of Modern History* 48(2): 195–214.
———. (1977). *The Dutch Revolt*. Ithaca: Cornell University Press.
———. (1988). *The Military Revolution: Military Innovation and the Rise of the West, 1500–1800*. Cambridge: Cambridge University Press.
———. (1998). *The Grand Strategy of Phillip II*. New Haven: Yale University Press.

Parker, Geoffrey (2004). "What If . . . Philip Had Gone to the Netherlands?" *History Today* 54(8): 40–46.

Parrot, David (1997). "A Prince Sovereign and the French Crown: Charles de Nevers, 1580–1637." In *Royal and Republican Sovereignty in Early Modern Europe : Essays in Memory of Ragnhild Hatton*, ed. R. Oresko, H. M. Scott, and G. C. Gibbs. Cambridge: Cambridge University Press, 149–87.

Parrow, Kathleen A. (1993). "From Defense to Resistance: Justification for Violence During the French Wars of Religion." *Transactions of the American Philosophical Society* 83(6): i–v, 1–79.

Paul, Darel E. (1999). "Sovereignty, Survival and the Westphalian Blind Alley in International Relations." *Review of International Studies* 25(2): 217–31.

Peattie, Mark R. (1984). "The Nan'yo: Japan in the South Pacific, 1885–1945." In *The Japanese Colonial Empire, 1895–1945*, ed. R. H. Myers and Mark R. Peattie. Princeton: Princeton University Press, 172–212.

Penn, William ([1693] 1983). *An Essay Towards the Present and Future Peace of Europe by the Establishment of an European Dyet, Parliament or Estates*. New York: Hildesheim.

Pérez, Joseph (1970). *La revolution des "Comunidades" de Castille, 1520–1521*. Bordeaux: Bibliothéque de l'École des Hautes Études Hispaniques.

———. (1989). *Los Comuneros*. Madrid: Historia 16.

Pettegree, Andrew (2001). "Religion and the Revolt." In *The Origins and Development of the Dutch Revolt*, ed. G. Darby. London: Routledge, 67–83.

Phillips, William D., Jr., and Carla Rahn Phillips (1977). "Spanish Wool and Dutch Rebels: The Middelburg Incident of 1574." *American Historical Review* 81(2): 312–30.

Philpott, Daniel (2000). "The Religious Roots of Modern International Relations." *World Politics* 52: 206–45.

———. (2001). *Revolutions in Sovereignty: How Ideas Shaped Modern International Relations*. Princeton: Princeton University Press.

———. (2001/2002). "Liberalism, Power, and Authority in International Relations: On the Orgins of Colonial Independence and Internationally Sanctioned Intervention." *Security Studies* 11(2): 117–63.

———. (2002). "The Challenges of September 11 to Secularism in International Relations." *World Politics* 55: 66–95.

Pollis, Admantia (1973). "Intergroup Conflict and British Colonial Policy: The Case of Cyprus." *Comparative Politics* 39(3): 289–95.

Potter, D. L. (1977). "Foreign Policy in the Age of the Reformation: French Involvement in the Schmalkaldic War, 1544–1547." *Historical Journal* 20(3): 525–44.

Pouliot, Vincent (2004). "The Essence of Constructivism." *Journal of International Relations and Development* 7: 319–36.

———. (2006). "The Alive and Well Transatlantic Security Community: A Theoretical Reply to Michael Cox." *European Journal of International Relations* 12(1): 119–27.

Powell, Robert (2006). "War as a Commitment Problem." *International Organization* 60(1): 169–203.

Pratt, John W., and Richard Zeckhauser, eds. (1991). *Principals and Agents: The Structure of Business*. Cambridge, Mass.: Harvard Business School Press.

Price, Richard (1995). "A Genealogy of the Chemical Weapons Taboo." *International Organization* 49(1): 73–103.

———. (1998). "Reversing the Gun Sights: Transnational Civil Society Targets Land Mines." *International Organization* 52(3): 613–44.

Pufendorf, Samuel (1690). *The Present State of Germany*. London: Printed for Richard Chiswell, at the Rose and Crown in St. Paul's Church-Yard.

Radnitz, Scott (2006a). "It Takes More than a Village: Mobilization, Networks, and the State in Central Asia." Ph.D. Diss., Massachusetts Institute of Technology.

———. (2006b). "What Really Happened in Kyrgyzstan?" *Journal of Democracy* 17(2): 133–46.

Rae, Heather (2002). *State Identities and the Homogenisation of Peoples*. Cambridge: Cambridge University Press.

Rector, Chad (2004). "Self-Restraint and Second-Image Theories of Hierarchy." Paper Presented at the Annual Convention of the American Political Science Association, Chicago, Illinois.

Repgen, Konrad (1987). "What is a 'Religious War?'" In *Politics and Society in Reformation Europe*, ed. E. I. Kouri and T. Scott. London: Macmillan, 311–28.

———. (1998). "Negotiating the Peace of Westphalia: A Survey with an Examination of the Major Problems." In *1648: War and Peace in Europe*, ed. K. Bussman and H. Schilling. Münster: Westfälisches Landesmuseum, 355–72.

Riedel, Bruce (2007). "Al Qaeda Strikes Back." *Foreign Affairs* 86(3): 24–40.

Ringer, Fritz (1997). *Max Weber's Methodology: the Unification of the Cultural and Social Sciences*. Cambridge, Mass.: Harvard University Press.

Ringmar, Erik (1996). *Identity, Interest and Action: A Cultural Explanation of Sweden's Intervention in the Thirty Years' War*. Cambridge: Cambridge University Press.

Risse, Thomas (2000). "Let's Argue!": Communicative Action in World Politics." *International Organization* 54(1): 1–39.

Risse-Kappen, Thomas (1995a). "Bringing Transnational Relations Back In: Introduction." In *Bringing Transnational Relations Back In: Nonstate Actors, Domestic Structures and International Institutions*, ed. Thomas Risse-Kappen. Cambridge: Cambridge University Press, 3–36.

———, ed. (1995b). *Bringing Transnational Relations Back In: Nonstate Actors, Domestic Structures and International Institutions*. Cambridge: Cambridge University Press.

Roberts, Michael (1967). *Essays in Swedish History*. Minneapolis: University of Minnesota Press.

Robinson, James Harvey (1894). "Review Essay: Staatenbund und Bundesstaat." *Annals of the American Academy of Political and Social Science* 4: 145–49.

Roeder, Philip G. (2007). *Where Nation-States Come From*. Princeton: Princeton University Press.

Roelker, Nancy Lyman (1996). *One King, One Faith: The Parlement of Paris and the Religious Reformations of the Sixteenth Century.* Berkeley: University of California Press.

Rosen, Stephen Peter (2003). "An Empire, If You Can Keep It." *National Interest* (71): 51–62.

Rosenfeld, Paul (1971). "The Provincial Governor of the Netherlands from the Minority of Charles V to the Revolt." In *Government in Reformation Europe, 1520–1560*, ed. H. J. Cohn. London: Macmillan, 257–64.

Rowen, Herbert H. (1961). "The Peace of Westphalia Revisited." *Journal of Modern History* 33(1): 53–56.

———, ed. (1972). *The Low Countries in Early Modern Times.* New York: Harper and Row.

———. (1988). *The Princes of Orange.* Cambridge: Cambridge University Press.

———. (1990). "The Dutch Revolt: What Kind of Revolution?" *Renaissance Quarterly* 43(3): 570–90.

Rowen, Herbert H., and Craig Harline (1994). "The Birth of the Dutch Nation." In *Politics, Religion and Diplomacy in Early Modern Europe: Essays in Honor of De Lamar Jensen*, ed. M. R. Thorp and A. J. Slavin. Kirksville, Mo: Sixteenth Century Journal Publishers, 67–81.

Rublack, Ulinka (2005). *Reformation Europe.* Cambridge: Cambridge University Press.

Ruggie, John Gerard (1983). "Continuity and Transformation in the World Polity: Towards a Neorealist Synthesis." *World Politics* 35(2): 261–85.

———. (1993). "Territoriality and Beyond: Problematizing Modernity in International Relations." *International Organization* 47(1): 139–74.

———. (1998). *Constructing the World Polity.* New York: Routledge.

Russell, Joycelyne G. (1986). *Peacemaking in the Renaissance.* London: Gerald Duckworth.

Safire, William (2005). "On Language." *New York Times Magazine*, April 24. Retrieved on July 8, 2008, from http://www.nytimes.com/2005/04/24/magazine/24ONLANGUAGE.html.

Salem, Paul (2006). "The Future of Lebanon." *Foreign Affairs* 85(6): 13–22.

Salmon, J.H.M. (1967). "Introduction." In *The French Wars of Religion: How Important Were Religious Factors?*, ed. J.H.M. Salmon. Boston: Heath, 1–5.

Schilling, Heinz (1983). "The Reformation in the Hanseatic Cities." *Sixteenth Century Journal* 14(4): 443–56.

———. (1992). *Religion, Political Culture and the Emergence of Early Modern Society: Essays in German and Dutch History.* Leiden: E. J. Brill.

Schmidt, Georg (1998). "The Peace of Westphalia as the Fundamental Law of the Complementary Empire-State." In *1648: War and Peace in Europe*, ed. K. Bussman and H. Schilling. Münster: Westfälisches Landesmuseum, 447–54.

Schroeder, Peter (1999). "The Constitution of the Holy Roman Empire after 1648: Samuel Pufendorf's Assessment in His Monzambano." *Historical Journal* 42(4): 961–83.

Schulze, Winfried (1986). "Majority Decision in the Imperial Diets of the Sixteenth and Seventeenth Centuries." *Journal of Modern History* 58(Supplement: Politics and Society in the Holy Roman Empire, 1500–1806): S46–S63.

Schweller, Randall L. (1994). "Bandwagoning for Profit: Bringing the Revisionist State Back In." *International Security* 19(1): 72–107.

———. (2001). "The Problem of International Order Revisited: A Review Essay." *International Security* 26(1): 161–86.

———. (2004). "Unanswered Threats: A Neoclassical Realist Theory of Underbalancing." *International Security* 29(2): 159–201.

———. (2006). *Unanswered Threats: Political Constraints on the Balance of Power*. Princeton: Princeton University Press.

Schweller, Randall L., and William C. Wohlforth (2000). "Power Test: Evaluating Realism in Response to the End of the Cold War." *Security Studies* 9(3): 60–107.

Scott, Jonathan (2000). *England's Troubles: Seventeenth-Century English Political Instability in a European Context*. Cambridge: Cambridge University Press.

Scribner, R. W. (1994). "Communalism: Universal Category or Ideological Construct? A Debate in the Historiography of Early Modern Germany and Switzerland." *Historical Journal* 37(1): 199–207.

Sea, Thomas F. (2007). "The German Princes' Responses to the Peasants' Revolt of 1525." *Central European History* 40(2): 219–40.

Seshia, Shalia (1998). "Divide-and-rule in Indian Party Politics: The Rise of the Bharatiya Janata Party." *Asian Survey* 38(11): 1036–50.

Sessions, Kyle C. (1972). "The War over Luther and the Peasants: Old Campaigns and New Strategies." *Sixteenth Century Journal* 3(2): 25–44.

Sharma, Vivek (2005). "The Impact of Institutions on Conflict and Cooperation in Early Modern Europe." Ph.D. Diss., New York University.

Shennan, J. H. (1974). *The Origins of the Modern European State, 1450–1725*. London: Hutchinson.

Sherman, Michael A. (1977). "Political Propaganda and Renaissance Culture: French Reactions to the League of Cambrai, 1509–10." *Sixteenth Century Journal* 8: 97–128.

Shoenberger, Cynthia Grant (1977). "The Development of the Lutheran Theory of Resistance: 1523–1530." *Sixteenth Century Journal* 8(1): 61–76.

———. (1979). "Luther and the Justifiability of Resistance to Legitimate Authority." *Journal of the History of Ideas* 40(1): 3–20.

Sikkink, Katheryn (1999). *The Power of Human Rights: International Norms and Domestic Change*. Cambridge: Cambridge University Press.

Simmel, Georg (1971). *On Individuality and Social Forms*. Chicago: University of Chicago Press.

Slaughter, Anne-Marie (2004). *A New World Order*. Princeton: Princeton University Press.

Smit, J. W. (1970). "The Netherlands Revolt." In *Preconditions of Revolution in Early Modern Europe*, ed. R. Forster and J. P. Greene. Baltimore: The Johns Hopkins University Press, 19–54.

Smith, George H. (1895). "The Theory of the State." *Proceedings of the American Philosophical Society* 34(148): 181, 183, 185–334.

Smith, Jay M. (1993). " 'Our Sovereign's Gaze': Kings, Nobles, and State Formation in Seventeenth-Century France." *French Historical Studies* 18(2): 396–415.

Smith, Malcolm C. (1994). "Early French Advocates of Religious Freedom." *Sixteenth Century Journal* 25(1): 29–51.
Snyder, Jack (1991). *Myths of Empire: Domestic Politics and International Ambition*. Ithaca: Cornell University Press.
———. (2003). "Imperial Temptation." *National Interest* (71): 29–40.
Sommers, Margaret R. (1998). " 'We're No Angels': Realism, Rational Choice, and Relationality in Social Science." *American Journal of Sociology* 104(3): 722–84.
Sørensen, Georg (1998). "States are Not Like Units": Types of State and Forms of Anarchy in the Present International System." *Journal of Political Philosophy* 6(1): 79–98.
Spaans, Joke (1999). "Catholicism and Resistance to the Reformation in the Northern Netherlands." In *Reformation, Revolt and Civil War in France and the Netherlands 1555–1585*, ed. P. Benedict, G. Marnef, H. v. Nierop, and M. Venard. Amsterdam: Royal Netherlands Academy of Arts and Sciences, 149–64.
Spitz, Lewis (1980). "The Augsburg Confession: 450 Years of History." *Sixteenth Century Journal* 11(3): 3–9.
Spruyt, Hendrik (1994). *The Sovereign State and Its Competitors: An Analysis of Systems Change*. Princeton: Princeton University Press.
Stalnaker, John C. (1979). *Towards a Social Interpretation of the German Peasant War*. London: George Allen and Unwin.
Stayer, James M. (1991). *The German Peasants' War and Anabaptist Community of Goods*. Montreal and Kingston: McGill-Queen's University Press.
Sterling-Folker, Jennifer (2002a). "Realism and the Constructivist Challenge: Rejecting, Reconstructing, or Rereading." *International Studies Review* 4(1): 73–97.
———. (2002b). *Theories of International Cooperation and the Primacy of Anarchy: Explaining U.S. International Monetary Policy-Making After Bretton Woods*. New York: State University of New York Press.
Stevenson, William B., and Dana Greenberg (2000). "Agency and Social Networks: Strategies of Action in a Social Structure of Position, Opposition, and Opportunity." *Administrative Science Quarterly* 45(4): 651–78.
Stoye, John (1969). *Europe Unfolding, 1648–1688*. New York: Harper and Row.
Stradling, R. A. (1981). *Europe and the Decline of Spain: A Study of the Spanish System, 1580–1720*. London: George Allen and Unwin.
———. (1986). "Olivares and the Origins of the Franco-Spanish War, 1627–1635." *English Historical Review* 101(398): 68–94.
———. (1994). *Spain's Struggle for Europe 1598–1668*. London: Hambledon.
Sutherland, N. M. (1967). "Calvin's Idealism and Indecision." In *The French Wars of Religion: How Important Were Religious Factors?*, ed. J.H.M. Salmon. Boston: D. C. Heath, 14–23.
———. (1992). "The Origins of the Thirty Years' War and the Structure of European Politics." *English Historical Review* 107(424): 587–625.
Swann, Julian (2003). *Provincial Power and Absolute Monarchy: The Estates General of Burgundy, 1661–1790*. Cambridge: Cambridge University Press.

Symcox, Geoffrey (1997). "From Commune to Capital: The Transformation of Turn, Sixteenth to Eighteenth Centuries." In *Royal and Republican Sovereignty in Early Modern Europe: Essays in Memory of Ragnhild Hatton*, ed. R. Oresko, G. C. Gibbs, and H. M. Scott. Cambridge: Cambridge University Press, 242–71.

Tajfel, Henri (1978). *Differentiation Between Social Groups: Studies in the Social Psychology of Intergroup Relations*. New York: Academic.

———. (1981). *Human Groups and Social Categories: Studies in Social Psychology*. Cambridge: Cambridge University Press.

Tannenwald, Nina (2005). "Stigmatizing the Bomb: Origins of the Nuclear Taboo." *International Security* 29(4): 5–49.

Tarrow, Sidney (2005). *The New Transnational Activism*. Cambridge: Cambridge University Press.

Taylor, Peter J. (1995). "World Cities and Territorial States: The Rise and Fall of Their Mutuality." In *World Cities in a World-System*, ed. P. L. Knox and Peter J. Taylor. Cambridge: Cambridge University Press, 48–62.

te Brake, Wayne (1988). "Violence in the Dutch Patriot Revolution." *Comparative Studies in Society and History* 30(1): 143–63.

———. (1998). *Shaping History: Ordinary People in European Politics, 1500–1700*. Berkeley: University of California Press.

Teschke, Benno (1998). "Geopolitical Relations in the European Middle Ages: History and Theory." *International Organization* 52(2): 325–58.

———. (2002). "Theorizing the Westphalian System of States: International Relations from Absolutism to Capitalism." *European Journal of International Relations* 8(1): 5–48.

———. (2003). *The Myth of 1648: Class, Geopolitics and the Making of Modern International Relations*. London: Verso.

Thielen, Kathleen (1999). "Historical Institutionalism in Comparative Politics." *Annual Review of Political Science* 2(1): 369–404.

Thompson, James Westfall (1909). *The Wars of Religion in France, 1559–1576: The Huguenots, Catharine de' Medici and Philip II*. Chicago: University of Chicago Press.

Thomson, John A. (1998). *The Western Church in the Middle Ages*. London: Arnold.

Tierney, Brian (1988). *The Crisis of Church and State, 1050–1300*. Toronto: University of Toronto Press.

Tilly, Charles (1975). "Reflections on the History of European State-Making." In *The Formation of National States in Western Europe*, ed. Charles Tilly. Princeton: Princeton University Press, 3–84.

———. (1978). *From Mobilization to Revolution*. New York: Addison-Wesley.

———. (1992). *Coercion, Capital, and European States, AD 990–1992*. Cambridge: Blackwell.

———. (1995). "To Explain Political Processes." *American Journal of Sociology* 100(6): 1594–1610.

———. (1997a). "How Empires End." In *After Empire: Multiethnic Societies and Nation-Building*, ed. K. Barkey and M. von Hagen. Boulder: Westview, 1–11.

Tilly, Charles (1997b). "Means and Ends of Comparison in Macrosociology." *Comparative Social Research* 16: 43–53.

———. (1998). "International Communities, Secure or Otherwise." In *Security Communities*, ed. E. Adler and M. Barnett. Cambridge: Cambridge University Press, 397–412.

———. (1999). "Epilogue: Now Where?" In *State/Culture: State Formation after the Cultural Turn*, ed. G. Steinmetz. Ithaca: Cornell University Press, 407–20.

———. (2002). *Stories, Identities, and Political Change*. Lanham, Md.: Rowman and Littlefield.

———. (2003). *The Politics of Collective Violence*. Cambridge: Cambridge University Press.

———. (2005). *Identities, Boundaries, and Social Ties*. Boulder: Paradigm.

Toft, Monica Duffy (2007). "Getting Religion? The Puzzling Case of Islam and Civil War." *International Security* 31(4): 97–131.

Togan, Îsenbike (1998). *Flexibility and Limitations in Steppe Formation*. New York: Brill.

Toulmin, Stephen (1990). *Cosmopolis: The Hidden Agenda of Modernity*. Chicago: University of Chicago Press.

Tracy, James D. (1990). *Holland under Habsburg Rule, 1506–1566: The Formation of a Body Politic*. Berkeley: University of California Press.

———. (1999). *Europe's Reformations, 1450–1650*. Lanham, Md.: Rowman and Littlefield.

Tüchle, Hermann (1971). "The Peace of Augsburg: New Order or Lull in the Fighting?" In *Government in Reformation Europe, 1520–1560*, ed. H. J. Cohn. London: Macmillan, 145–68.

Tuck, Richard (1999). *The Rights of War and Peace*. Oxford: Oxford University Press.

Turchetti, Mario (1991). "Religious Concord and Political Tolerance in Sixteenth- and Seventeenth-Century France." *Sixteenth Century Journal* 22(1): 15–25.

Van Crevald, Martin L. (1999). *The Rise and Decline of the State*. Cambridge: Cambridge University Press.

Van Evera, Stephen (1994). "Hypotheses on Nationalism and War." *International Security* 18(4): 5–39.

———. (1998). "Offense, Defense, and the Causes of War." *International Security* 22(4): 5–43.

Vann, James A. (1986). "New Directions for the Study of the Old Reich." *Journal of Modern History* 58 (Supplement): S3–22.

Venard, Marc (1999). "Catholicism and Resistance to the Reformation in France, 1555–1585." In *Reformation, Revolt and Civil War in France and the Netherlands 1555–1585*, ed. P. Benedict, G. Marnef, H. v. Nierop and Marc Venard. Amsterdam: Royal Netherlands Academy of Arts and Sciences, 133–48.

Waite, Gary (1992). "The Dutch Nobility and Anabaptism, 1535–1545." *Sixteenth Century Journal* 23(3): 458–85.

Wallace, Peter G. (2004). *The Long European Reformation*. New York: Palgrave.

Walston, James (1988). *The Mafia and Clientelism: Roads to Rome in Post-War Calabria*. New York: Routledge.

Walt, Stephen M. (1985). "Alliance Formation and the Balance of Power." *International Security* 9(4): 2–43.
———. (1987). *The Origins of Alliances*. Ithaca: Cornell University Press.
———. (1997). *Revolution and War*. Ithaca: Cornell University Press.
Waltz, Kenneth (1979). *Theory of International Politics*. New York: Addison-Wesley.
———. (1986). "Reflections on Theory of International Politics: A Response to My Critics." In *Neorealism and Its Critics*, ed. R. O. Keohane. New York: Columbia University Press, 322–46.
Ward, Hugh (2006). "International Linkages and Environmental Sustainability: The Effectiveness of the Regime Network." *Journal of Peace Research* 43(2): 149–66.
Ward-Perkins, Bryan (2005). *The Fall of Rome and the End of Civilization*. Oxford: Oxford University Press.
Wasserman, Stanley, and Katherine Faust (1994). *Social Network Analysis: Methods and Applications*. Cambridge: Cambridge University Press.
Watson, Adam (1992). *The Evolution of International Society*. New York: Routledge.
Weart, Spencer R. (1994). "Peace among Democratic and Oligarchic Republics." *Journal of Peace Research* 31(3): 299–316.
Weber, Katja (1997). "Hierarchy amidst Anarchy: A Transaction Costs Approach to International Security Cooperation." *International Studies Quarterly* 41(2): 321–40.
Weber, Max (1946). "Science as a Vocation." In *From Max Weber: Essays in Sociology*, ed. H. H. Gerth and C. W. Mills. New York: Oxford University Press, 77–179.
———. (1949). " 'Objectivity' in Social Science and Social Policy." In *Max Weber on the Methodology of the Social Sciences*, ed. E. A. Shils and H. A. Finch. New York: Free Press, 49–112.
———. (1978). *Economy and Society: An Outline of Interpretative Sociology*. Berkeley: University of California Press.
———. (1999). "Die 'Objektivität' Sozialwissenschaftlicher und Sozialpolitischer Erkenntnis." In *Gesammelte Aufsätze zur Wissenschaftslehre*, ed. E. Flitner. Potsdam: Internet-Ausgabe, 146–214. Retrieved August 9, 2007, from Mhttp://www.uni-potsdam.de/u/paed/Flitner/Weber/.
Wedgwood, C. V. (1961). *The Thirty Years' War*. Garden City, N.Y.: Doubleday.
Wellman, Barry (1983). "Network Analysis: Some Basic Principles." *Sociological Theory* 1: 155–200.
Wellman, Barry, and Stephen Berkowitz, Eds. (1998). *Social Structures: A Network Approach*. Cambridge: Cambridge University Press.
Wendt, Alexander (1987). "The Agent-Structure Problem in International Relations Theory." *International Organization* 41(3): 335–70.
———. (1992). "Anarchy Is What States Make of It." *International Organization* 46(2): 391–425.
———. (1994). "Collective Identity Formation and the International State." *American Political Science Review* 88(2): 384–97.

Wendt, Alexander (1996). "Identity and Structural Change in International Politics." In *The Return of Culture and Identity in International Relations Theory*, ed. J. Lapid and F. Kratochwil. Boulder: Lynne Reinner, 47–64.

———. (1999). *Social Theory of International Politics*. Cambridge: Cambridge University Press.

Westergaard, Waldemar (1953). "Review: Die Hanse, Kurt Pagel." *American Historical Review* 59(1): 90–93.

White, Harrison C. (1972). "Do Networks Matter? Notes for Camden." Unpublished Manuscript, Cambridge, Mass.: 26.

———. (1992). *Identity and Control: A Structural Theory of Social Action*. Princeton: Princeton University Press.

White, Harrison C., and Scott A. Boorman (1976). "Social Structure from Multiple Networks, II. Role Structures." *American Journal of Sociology* 81(6): 1384–1446.

White, Harrison C., Scott A. Boorman et al. (1976). "Social Structure from Multiple Networks, I. Blockmodels of Roles and Positions." *American Journal of Sociology* 81(4): 730–80.

Wight, Colin (1999). "They Shoot Dead Horses Don't They? Locating Agency in the Agent-Structure Problematique." *European Journal of International Relations* 5(1): 109–42.

———. (2006). *Agents, Structures and International Relations: Politics as Ontology*. Cambridge: Cambridge University Press.

Wilson, James Q. (2002). "The Reform Islam Needs." *City Journal* 12(4). Retrieved July 2, 2008, from http://www.city-journal.org/html/12_4_the_reform_islam.html .

Wilson, Peter H. (1999). *The Holy Roman Empire, 1495–1806*. London: Macmillan.

Winter, William L. (1948). "Netherland Regionalism and the Decline of the Hansa." *American Historical Review* 53(2): 279–87.

Wohlforth, William C. (1999). "The Stability of a Unipolar World." *International Security* 24(1): 5–41.

Wohlforth, William C., Richard Little et al. (2007). "Testing Balance-of-Power Theory In World History." *European Journal of International Relations* 13(2): 155–85.

Wolfart, Johannes C. (2002). *Religion, Government and Political Culture in Early Modern Germany: Lindau, 1520–1628*. New York: Palgrave.

Woltjer, Juliaan (1999). "Political Moderates and Religious Moderates in the Revolt of the Netherlands." In *Reformation, Revolt and Civil War in France and the Netherlands, 1555–1585*, ed. P. Benedict, G. Marnef, H. v. Nierop, and M. Venard. Amsterdam: Royal Netherlands Academy of Arts and Sciences, 185–200.

Wong, Bin R. (1997). *China Transformed: Historical Change and the Limits of the European Experience*. Ithaca: Cornell University Press.

Wood, James B. (1996). *The King's Army: Warfare, Soldiers, and Society During the Wars of Religion in France, 1562–1576*. Cambridge: Cambridge University Press.

Wyntjes, Sherrin Marshall (1981). "Family Allegiance and Religious Persuasion: The Lesser Nobility and the Revolt of the Netherlands." *Sixteenth Century Journal* 12(2): 43–60.

Zacher, Mark (1992). "The Decaying Pillars of the Westphalian Temple: Implications for International Order and Governance." In *Governance without Government: Order and Change in World Politics*, ed. J. N. Rouseanau and E.-O. Czempiel. Cambridge: Cambridge University Press, 58–101.

Zagorin, Perez (1982a). *Rulers and Rebels, 1500–1600. Volume II: Provincial Rebellion, Revolutionary Civil Wars, 1560–1660*. Cambridge: Cambridge University Press.

———. (1982b). *Rulers and Rebels, 1500–1660. Volume I: Society, States, and Early Modern Revolution--Agrarian and Urban Rebellions*. Cambridge: Cambridge University Press.

Zahab, Mariam Abou, and Olivier Roy (2006). *Islamist Networks: The Afghan-Pakistan Connection*. New York: Columbia University Press.

Zisk, Kimberly Marten (1984). *Enforcing The Peace: Learning From The Imperial Past*. New York: Columbia University Press.

Index

Abbott, Andrew, 46
absolutism, 281
Accord (for freedom of worship), 204
Act of Abjuration (1581), 222
Adamson, Fiona, 22n7
Adrian of Utrecht, 140, 144–46
Aerschot, duke of, 198, 216, 218
Afghanistan, 17; patron-client networks and, 41–2; US military presence as example of imperial dynamics and, 296–97
Africa: composite states and, 298; quasi-state and, 58; transnational religious movements and, 295
agent-structure co-constitution, 14; relationalism and, 40, 43
aggregate imperial structure, 103, 105–8, 111–12; cross-pressures and, 112–16
Alais, Peace of (1629), 235, 260
Albert (Archduke of Netherlands), 231–34
Albrecht of Mainz, 167, 173
Alexander IV, Pope, 86
alliances: anarchy and, 30; federations and, 75–77; Marxist accounts of state formation and, 63n172; international structure and, 57–58, 61; Luther's condemnation of, 164; marriages and, 94, 97; relationalism and, 26, 57–58; religion and, 9, 55, 241n17; social-network analysis and, 22n7, 27; Westphalian Hypothesis and, 276–77, 279. *See also* balance of power; divide-and-rule; federative alliances; *specific alliances*
Alsace, 243, 279; Bourbons and, 279–80n46
Alva, duke of, 193, 206, 248–49; regime of, 207–11; Second Dutch Revolt and, 212–14
Amboise, Edict of (1560), 245, 248
Ambrosian Republic, 86
Amsterdam, 218–19
Anabaptism, 166–67, 197, 202–3, 279; German Peasants Movement and, 157
anarchy: as defined in structural-realist theory 29–30; alliances and, 29–30, 77n42; balance of power and, 29–30, 105–6;

constructivism and, 11, 34–35, 38, 57; collective mobilization and, 16, 23, 48–49, 52; cooperation and, 48–49, 52; Holy Roman Empire and, 55;, 82 international structures and, 24, 26–27, 55; neoliberal institutionalism and, 50, 52; as relational structure, 14–16, 26–27, 40, 49–50, 54n144, 61–62, 298; relationalism and, 26–27, 40, 57; structural-realism and, 33n54. *See also* states-under-anarchy framework
Andalusia, 107, 144–45
Angevin empire, 83
Anna of Saxony, 199
Ansell, Christopher F., 112n31, 114
antiheresy laws: Anabaptism and, 197; Dutch Revolt and, 200, 202–3, 206
Antwerp, 204, 206, 219, 223; "Spanish Fury" and, 215–16
appropriateness, logic of: *see* logics of social action
Aragon, 60, 135, 150, 189; *Comuneros* revolt and, 144; composite polities and, 82, 86, 94, 100; Charles's ascension and, 140, 150; Charles's strategic priorities and, 149; rebellion (1591–1592) and, 228, 229–30
Aragon-Catalonia. *See* Aragon
aristocracy: Aragon and, 229; Catalan Revolt (1640–1652) and, 272; *Comuneros* revolt and, 137, 144–48, 182–83; dynamics of composite states and, 8, 68, 101, 119, 125–26, 131; dynasticism and, 127–28; Dutch Revolt and, 191, 194, 198–201, 203–4, 207, 209, 216, 218, 226; French Wars of Religion and, 42, 131–32, 236, 242–48, 254, 255, 257–58, 261–63 ; Holy Roman Empire and, 80–81; Hungarian succession and, 162; Netherlands and, 196–98, patron-client networks and, 42, 132, 236; Poland and, 91; Portugal and, 272; religious conversion and, 42, 132, 157, 197; right of resistance and, 255; state formation and, 63n172, 75, 86, 88, 119, 197, 263;

aristocracy, (cont'd)
theories of government and, 256; Thirty Years' War and, 266. See also class
Arras, 219
Arras, Treaty of (1579), 220–21. See also Union of Arras
Asia, 58, 298, 300
Asia Times Online, 2
Augsburg, 175
Augsburg, Diet of (1530), 165–67; League of Schmalkald and, 167
Augsburg, Diet of (1547–1548), 176. See also Augsburg, Interim of (1548)
Augsburg, Interim of (1548), 1, 176–77
Augsburg, Peace of (1555), 2, 55, 137, 178–79, 181–82, 184, 185, 215, 267; *cuius regio eius religio* and, 178, 181–82; Pacification of Ghent and, 215; state formation and, 179–80, 181–82; Westphalian Hypothesis and, 277, 279
Augsburg, Recess of (1530), 167. See also Augsburg, Diet of (1530)
Augsburg Confession, 167–68, 171, 178; alliance politics and, 168
Austria, 7, 180–81; confessionalization and, 285; counterreformation and, 266; Thirty Years' War and, 269, 271. See also Habsburgs; *specific monarchs*
Austrian Habsburgs. See Habsburgs
Austrian Succession, War of, 281
Authority: anarchy and, 15; hegemonic-order theory and, 30–31; international change and, 13, 30–31
Axelrod, Robert, 56

"Back to the Future: Instability in Europe after the Cold War" (Mearsheimer), 300n37
balance of power, 9, 19–20; anarchy and, 29–30, 33n54; Charles V and, 135–36, 138; constructivism and, 39; dynastic-imperialism and, 67; early modern period and, 12; German Reformations and, 152; nested relational configurations and, 51; realism and, 32; Reformations and, 3; Thirty Years' War and, 270
Battle of White Mountain, 267
Baumgartner, Frederic J., 185
Bearman, Peter, 48n125
Béarn, France, 260–61
Beaulieu, Edict of (1576), 253–54, 255
Beggars, 202–7, 226. See also Sea Beggars

Beissinger, Mark, 111
Belgium, 7. See also Low Countries
belief systems: religion and, 292
bellocentrists: defined, 69; realism and, 69–70; dynastic-imperial pathway and, 84; military-technical change and, 87; rise of urban centers and, 77. See also military-technical change
Bergerac, Peace of (1577), 254
Bèze, Théodore de, 247, 255
bipolar systems, 14
Blockmans, Wim, 136, 173, 177, 184
Bodin, Jean, 127n71, 256, 282
Boettcher, Susan, 283
Bohemia, 79, 175, 266–67; and Hussites, 156
Bohemian Brethren, 279
Boissevain, Jeremy, 41
Bonney, Richard, 94
Borgias, 86
Borge, Caeser, 116
Boulogne, 94
Bourbon, Antoine de, 244–47
Bourbon, Cardinal of, 256–57
Bourbons: Alsace and, 279–80n46; Béarn and, 260; dynastic agglomerations and, 82, 271; dynastic rivalry with Habsburgs and, 88–89, 225, 271; Dutch Revolt and, 225; French Wars of Religion and, 238–39, 244–47, 250, 261; Italy and, 88–89; Thirty Years' War and, 266, 270–71, 283; Westphalian Hypothesis and, 241n15. See also *specific monarchs*
bourgeoise. See burghers
Bowen, H. V., 113
Brabant, Netherlands: anti-Granvelle campaign and, 201; political centralization and, 196; Second Dutch Revolt and, 213; revolt against Maximilian of Habsburg and, 123; Third Dutch Revolt and, 215–16, 218–19; Union of Utrecht and, 220–22
Brederode, Hendrik, 204, 207, 210. See also Beggars
Brenner, William, 33
Brill, Netherlands, 212–13; English intervention in the Dutch Revolt and, 223n140; French Wars of Religion and, 250
broker. See brokerage
brokerage 42, 44; Afghanistan and, 296; centrality and, 103–4; central authorities and, 104; composite polities and, 296–

97; corporate actors and, 45–6, 47–8; cross-pressures and, 111–12; dynastic agglomeration and, 84, 86, 104; Dutch Revolt and, 205; Holy Roman Empire and, 55; international structures and, 59; international change and, 63; local intermediaries and, 105; multivocal signaling and, 294; as network position, 44; patron-client networks and, 42; relationalism and, 59, 65; relational-institutionalism and, 63; religious conflict and, 294; state formation and, 64n172; Tulip Revolution (Kyrgyzstan) and, 297; United States occupation of Iraq and, 48n124, 296
Brunswick, duke of. See Brunswick-Wolfenbüttel, Duchy of
Brunswick-Wolfenbüttel, Duchy of, 1, 171, 174
Bukovansky, Mlada, 281
burghers, 63n172, 102, 119, 216, 244. See also city-empires; city-leagues; city-states; class; Simpson, Homer
Burgundian "Circle," 196
Burgundian composite state, 76, 83, 109; Dutch Revolt and, 193; rump, 122–24, 150, 171, 179, 190, 196
Burgundy, Duchy of: French conquest of, 122–23; court culture and, 139; dynastic claims and, 94; Holy Roman Empire and, 79–80; Treaty of Madrid (1526), and 159–60

Calais, 83, 230
Calvin, John, 245–47
Calvinism: Alva's regime and, 209–10; Beggars and, 203–4; Castile and, 184; Catalona and, 228; cell structure and, 132; confessionalization and, 284; Counter-Remonstrants and, 268; Dutch Revolt and, 21, 194, 206–7, 212, 216, 218–19, 220–23, 224, 225–27; Edict of Nantes and, 240–43; Edict of Restitution and, 269; French Wars of Religion and, 236–37, 246, 250–51, 262; growth of, 202–4, 244, 267; Habsburg hegemony and, 228; Islam and, 192–93; legitimacy and, 255; Morisco uprisings and, 193; Netherlands and, 202; "pathological homogenization" and, 240–43; patron-client networks and conversion to, 42; Peace of Augsburg (1555) and, 182; plot to kidnap Francis II, and 244–45; right of resistance and, 245, 247, 255–56; St. Bartholomew's Day Massacre and, 251–52; Sea Beggars and, 212–13; Thirty Years' War and, 182, 267–69, 271; as transnational movement, 109, 132, 226, 271; Treaty of Cateau-Cambrésis and, 237–38; Union of Utrecht and, 220–21; yoking and, 47n121. See also Huguenots
Cambrai, League of, 95n121
Cambrai, Peace of (1529), 160
Capetians, 67–68; dynastic agglomeration and, 82, 236; Wars of Religion and, 236
capitalism, 87, 122
Caribbean, 268
Don Carlos (son of Philip II), 208
Carolingian Empire, 79, 209
Carr, E. H., 29
Casale, 268
Casimir, John, 219, 220, 248, 253
Cateau-Cambrésis, Treaty of, 186, 236–37
Castile: Castilianization and, 148–49, 180–81, 183, 189, 190–91; Catholicism and, 190–93; Charles V and, 135, 137, 138–39, 140–44, 147–49, 180; collective identification and, 94; composite polities and, 9, 73, 100, 125; *Comuneros* revolt and, 107, 144–47; empire and, 231; Diet of Worms (1521) and, 153; federative alliances and, 77; Habsburg hegemony and, 135, 185, 188, 227; Iberia and, 138, 140–44, 147; Islam and, 192–93; negotiations with the Dutch and popular opinion in, 232; Philip II and, 184, 233; Philip II's legacy and, 232; strategic overextension and, 186, 186n6, 190, 231, 233; Union of Arms and, 271–72; wool trade with Flanders, 188
Catalonia: Charles V and, 140; dynastic agglomeration and, 82, 135; Iberia and, 140; revolt (1640–1659), 9, 125, 129; 271–72, 273; Philip II's reign and, 228–29; Thirty Years' War and, 272–73
Cateau-Cambrésis, Treaty of (1559), 186, 189
Categories: defined, 25, 40; collective mobilization and, 44–48, 57; international structures and, 53, 55–56; nested relational configurations and, 48–52; religion and, 294. See also catness; collective identification; identity; relational configurations

336 • Index

Catholic Church, 7, 97, 292; Charles V and, 151–52, 175; dynastic empires and, 85–86, 97; Gregorian Reforms and, 80; Holy Roman Empire and, 80, 152, 161, 176–77; Investiture Conflict and, 80; Netherlands and, 200, 268; Philip II and, 191; Reformations and, 154–55, 166, 168. *See also* Counter-Reformation; *specific popes*

Catholicism: Castile and, 183, 189, 190–92, 234; Charles V, and 138, 143, 183, 184; confessionalization and, 181; Dutch Revolt and, 130–31, 194, 204, 213, 214, 216, 218–23, 225–27, 232; England and, 179, 223n140, 232; Ferdinand I (K. of the Romans) and, 180n168; France and, 240–43; French Wars of Religion and, 132, 238, 242–43, 246, 248–49, 256–64; Holy Roman Empire and, 130, 150; Netherlands and, 197; Philip II and, 189, 191; Pilgrimage of Grace and, 109–10, 155; Reformations and, 7, 130, 154n39, 160, 166, 168, 171, 173; Swiss Confederation and, 76, 168; Thirty Years' War and, 269n13; Westphalian Hypothesis and, 3. *See also* Counter-Reformation

Catholic League (France), 239, 252, 254–55, 256–59, 260

Catholic League (Germany), 267–68

catness: defined 48; collective-mobilization dynamics and, 48–52; constructivism and, 57. *See also* categories

centrality: defined, 43–44; brokerage and, 103–4; local intermediaries and, 104, 117. *See also* brokerage

centralization: advances in technologies of governance and, 90–91; Aragon and, 229; composite polities and, 295; confessionalization and, 284–85; divide-and-rule and, 105; dynastic agglomeration and, 69, 91; Catalan Revolt and, 271–72; Catalonia (1569–1570) and, 228–29; Dutch Revolt and, 193–96, 197–98, 200–201, 225; federative alliances and, 76; French Wars of Religion and, 235, 236, 263–64; Holy Roman Empire and, 80–82; networks and, 42; Portuguese Revolt and, 272–73; Moriscos and, 192; Reformations and, 288–89; religious contention and, 99, 100; resistance and, 8, 105,122; states-under-anarchy framework and, 33; Weber's definition of the state and, 71; Westphalian Hypothesis and, 280. *See also* core-periphery relations.

Charles, Duke of Orléans, 172

Charles II, 270

Charles IX, 246–48, 250, 253

Charles the Bold (duke of Burgundy), 76, 87, 122, 194

Charles V (King of the Romans; Charles I, King of Spain), 7, chapter 5; anti-Habsburg alliance and, 163–65; ascension of, 74; Augsburg and, 181–82; binding strategy (use of), 119; Castile and, 115, 119, 138–40; 141–49; 189; *Comuneros* revolt and, 107–8, 119, 144–47; dynamics of resistance and rule and, 107–8, 123–24; 137–38; division of Habsburg lands and, 180–81; Dutch Revolt and, 196–97, 226; dynastic agglomeration and, 7, 82, 91; Germany and, 158–62; German Peasants Movement and, 155–58; Ghent and, 123–24, 170; international-relations theory and, 135–36; Netherlands' governance and, 190, 194, 196–97, 199; political failures of, 176–80; realism and, 32, 135–36; Reform of Holy Roman Empire and, 79; Reformations and, 1–2, 132–33, 149–79; Schmalkaldic League's expansion and, 169–72; Schmalkaldic League's formation and, 165–69; Schmalkaldic War and, 1–2, 172–76; sovereign-territorial state and, 91; Thirty Years' War and, 273. *See also* Castilianization; Habsburgs

Chechnya, 293, 295

China, 55n146, 108, 290; contrast with early modern Europe, 271n20; contemporary religious activism and, 295

Christensen, Carl C., 162

Christian II (king of Denmark), 75

Christian IV (prince of Denmark), 268

Christianity, 3, 7, 58, 295

Christian Reconquest, 145

Cisneros, Cardinal, 138

city-empires, 77–79, 88; decline of, 88; dynastic-imperial pathway and, 85–86. *See also* city-states

city-leagues, 68, 75. *See also* federative alliances

city-states, 68, 77, 85; federative alliances and, 75. *See also* city-empires

Clark, Ian, 286n73
class: decline of nobility and, 81n62; dynamics of composite polities and, 4, 6, 8–9, 83, 101–2, 119–20, 124–25, 130–32; *Comuneros* revolt and, 139, 144–45, 146–47, 148, 183; Dutch Revolt and, 194, 202, 205, 207, 212, 215–16, 226; economic change and altering composition of, 122; French Wars of Religion and, 131–32, 249, 258, 261; German Reformation and, 153, 159; *Germanias* revolt and, 144; Ghent uprising (1539–1540); Marxist theories and, 63n172; state forms and, 73. *See also* aristocracy; burghers; German Peasant's Movement; guilds; Wat Tyler rebellion
Clement VII, Pope, 165
Clement VIII, Pope, 160, 230, 258
clientele networks. *See* patron-client relations
clients. *See* patron-client relations
co-constitutive relationships, 14–15, 40, 43, 52–53
Coercion, Capital and European States, AD 990–1990 (Tilly), 68
Cognac, League of, 160
Cold War, 287, 290
Coligny, Gaspard de, 245, 247–49; French Wars of Religion and, 246, 250–51
collective action. *See* collective mobilization
collective identification: anarchy and, 15, 35, 57; categories and, 25; collective mobilization and, 35, 50, 57; constructivism and, 24; credible commitments and, 35; definition of collective mobilization and, 2; Dutch Revolt and, 212; dynamics of rule and resistance in composite polities and, 106, 108; early modern European "nationalism," and 69; international structure and, 35, 40; multivocal signaling and, 114; relationalism and, 40, 45; relative gains and, 114n35. *See also* categories, catness, identity
collective mobilization: defined, 23; actors and, 48; Afghanistan and, 296; agency and, 27; alliances and, 58; anarchy and, 40, 49; "collective-action problem" and, 48–49; *Comuneros* revolt and, 137; complex-interdependence theory and, 56; constructivism and, 24, 35–39, 56–57; domestic structures and, 26, 30n46, 51, 59–61, 271n20; Dutch Revolt and, 205, 213, 215–16; dynamics of rule and resistance in early modern Europe and, 109, 121, 159; Estates General and, 109n24; form/content distinction and, 38, 64; French Wars of Religion and, 261–62; globalization and, 19, 36, 299–300; German Peasant's Movement and, 155–56; German Reformations and, 137; hegemonic-order theory and, 23–24, 30–31; historical institutionalism and, 40, 63; identity and, 35, 45, 50, 56–57; international change and, 22–23, 28, 36, 63, 287, 289, 300; international-relations theory debates and, 23–24, 28; international structures and, 38, 48, 53–54, 56; Iraq and, 48, 296, 297; Israel-Hezbollah conflict, and 58; levels of analysis and, 26, 40; liberalism and, 24, 56; norms and, 24, 35; patron-client networks and, 41; peripheral segmentation and, 104, 105; Prisoner's Dilemma and, 49–50, 56; realism and, 29–31, 33–34, 40, 50, 51, 53, 54n144; relational-institutionalism and, 28; relational configurations and, 40, 48–52, 63; relationalism and, 26, 40, 58–60, 66; religion and, 3, 99, 121, 137, 159, 205, 213, 261–62, 289, 292, 295; September 11, 2001, and, 51; social ties and, 41, 48–52, 52n136, 53–61; states-under-anarchy framework and, 53–55; "state mobilization capacity" and, 30n46; structure and, 23; structure of early modern European international relations and, 16, 60–61; technology and, 36; Thirty Years' War and, 266; transnational actors and, 36; Tulip Revolution (Kyrgyzstan), and 297. *See also* catness; netness
colonialism, 38, 108, 111, 113, 127, 300
complex-interdependence theory, 56
composite polities: defined 6–7, 70–73; Aragon and, 229–30; Castile and, 144, 146–47; Catalonia and, 228–29; change processes and, 88; Charles V and, 136–37, 150, 183; city-empires and, 77–79, 88–90; Cold War and, 287; contemporary period and, 13, 19, 287, 295–99; Dutch Revolt and, 205, 212; dynastic agglomerations and, 82–84; dynasticism and, 8–9, 67, 84–86, 90–94, 98; dynamics of, 98–129; early modern period and,

338 • Index

composite polities, (cont'd)
12; economic change and, 86–87; econocentrists and, 87; empires and, 16, 18, 72–73, 101, 108, 110; federative alliances and, 75–77, 88–90; French Wars of Religion and, 243, 261, 263; generalization and, 27; German Peasants' Movement and, 155; globalization and, 299; Holy Roman Empire and, 79–82, 153, 159, 175; ideal types and, 16, 100–4, 110–14, 120–21; international structure and, 15, 59–60; medieval-to-modern transition and, 97; military-technical change and, 87–88; Netherlands and, 201; overextension and, 120–21; Philip II and, 201; realism and, 13, 34, 239; Reformations and, 3–4, 10, 16, 130–34; 179, 183, 289; sovereign-territorial state and, 18, 67, 69; state formation and, 66, 67–74, 88–92, 264; Thirty Years' War and, 266, 271; theory and, 13, 15–16; Westphalia and, 3–4; within-segment structure and, 104–5. *See also* dynastic agglomerations; dynastic-imperial pathways; empire; federations (heterogeneity, 35, 135, 261; composite polities and, 72–73, 96, 296–99)

Comuneros revolt, 18, 144–47, 183; binding strategy and, 119, 137; Castilianization and, 148–49, 180, 189; Charles V and, 136–38, 149; class divisions and, 124–25, 137, 147, 148, 182–83; cross-pressures and, 159; firewalls and, 107, 144, 145; German Reformations and, 153; identity and, 115, 137, 143, 145, 148, 182–83; multivocal signaling and, 137, 138; radicalization of, 146–47

Condé, prince of. *See* Henry I of Bourbon; Louis I of Bourbon

Confession of Augsburg. *See* Augsburg Confession

Confessionalization, 98, 182, 265, 280, 283–85

configurational analysis: 17n35, 48–52, 61–63 66n77; applications and, 88–92, 127–29, 170, 188–89, 234, 236, 287, 276, 295 *See also* relational-institutionalism; relationalism; relational structures

Confutatio, 166

consequences, logic of. *See* logics of social action

constructivism, 34–37; anarchy and, 11, 34–35; Charles V and, 136; collective mobilization and, 23–24, 28, 35–37, 45, 56–57; constitutive norms, and 5; early modern Europe and, 14–15, 37–39; French Wars of Religion and, 235, 239–43; ideationalists and, 69; international change and, 11, 13, 24, 28; generalization and, 14, 38, 62; relationalism and, 43, 62; residual variation and, 39; secularism and, 292; "secular bias" and, 293; social facts and, 34; transnational actors and, 36; unit variation and, 36–37, 54

Contarini, Gasparo, 171

contracts, 6, 8; composite polities and, 72–73, 97, 296–97; dynastic agglomeration and, 68, 83

contrition. *See* marginalization by footnote

Cooley, Alexander, 296

core-periphery relations, 114; Castilianization and, 180; early modern state formation and, 71–72, 77, 83n69, 101; empires and, 72, 103–4, 113–16, 116–18; Netherlands and, 117, 180, 191. *See also* centralization; cross-pressures

cortes (of Castile), 140–44, 148, 183; activities during *Comuneros* revolt, 145–46

cortes (of Catalonia), 228

Coudy, Julien, 235

Council of State, 201, 215, 223; Beggars and, 202–3

Council of Trent, 172–73,176; Dutch Revolt and, 209; French Wars of Religion and, 256–57; Schmalkaldic War and, 173, 176. *See also* Counter-Reformation

Council of Troubles, 208–9

Counter-Reformation, 173; confessionalization and, 283–85; dynamics of composite states and, 109; dynastic-imperial pathway and, 285; French Wars of Religion and, 257; Schmalkaldic War and, 173; Thirty Years' War and, 266; *See also* Council of Trent; Jesuits

Crépy, Peace of, 172

cross-pressures: defined,111; Charles V and, 137, 151, 159, 163, 169–70; complex-interdependence theory and, 56; dynamics of composite states and, 99–100, 111–16; multivocal signaling and, 114–16; Philip II and, 189; Reforma-

tions and, 4, 134, 289; strategic overextension and, 120–21
Crusade, anti-Turkish (abortive), 149
customary rights, 5, 127–28, 129; dynastic identity and, 115; Netherlands and, 116, 198, 225, 207, 211, 222n135; Philip II and, 191; Reformations and, 130; Thirty Years' War and, 271
Cyprus, 192

d'Albert, Henri, 150
d'Albert, Jean, 244
d'Albon, Jacques, 246
Davies, Stephen, 286
de la Mack, Robert, 150
Denmark, 75, 90, 268
density. *See* network density
Diani, Mario, 44
direct rule: composite polities and, 73; in early modern European polities, 68; ideal types and, 72n127; nation-states and, 72n127, 73. *See also* indirect rule
divide-and-rule strategies, 105–8; brokerage and, 47; *Comuneros* Revolt and, 147; composite states and, 99, 125; Dutch Revolt, and 201; factors undermining, 108–11; Holy Roman Empire and, 55; local intermediaries and, 118–20; multivocal signaling and, 115; religious contention and, 99, 131–33; Schmalkaldic War and, 1, 132
Dueck, Abe J., 167
Dunn, Richard S., 276
Du Plessis-Mornay, Phillipe, 255
Dutch Republic, 89, 194, 287; Jürich-Cleves and, 264; Thirty Years' War and, 267–68, 271; Westphalia and, 270, 277–78, 280. *See also* Netherlands
Dutch Revolt, 9, 193–94, 205–27; Anabaptism and, 197; Castile and, 137, 189, 191, 211, 231; causes of (debate over), 193–94; ecclesiastical reorganization plan and, 200–202, 209; French Wars of Religion and, 224–25; 263–64; dynasticism and, 129; geography and, 89; Habsburg hegemony and, 184, 188, 234, 227–31, 273; intermediary autonomy and, 116–17; Mexico and, 191; multivocal signaling and, 130–31, 189; Netherlands' governance and, 109, 197–99; Philip II's absence and, 206; Philip II's legacy and, 233–34; relationalism and,

59–60; religion and, 19, 131, 214–17, 225–27; second revolt and, 212–15; Spanish Armada and, 224–25; strategic overextension and, 184, 188, 230, 233–34; third revolt and, 215–25; Tudor intervention in, 233n140, 223–24. *See also* Council of State, Council of Troubles, Treaty of Arras, Union of Arras, Union of Utrecht, *specific personages*
dynastic agglomeration: 6–8, 67–68, 82–84; Burgundy and, 76; Charles V and, 7, 135; city-empires as, 85–86; composite polities and, 93–97; confessionalization and, 265, 285; constructivism and, 37–38; contemporary relevance of, 16, 66, 300; dynastic-imperial pathway and, 18, 67–68, 84–88, 90–92; empire and, 71–74; federative alliances and, 75–77; Holy Roman Empire and, 79–82; ideal-typical structure of, 100–105; international structure and, 15, 93–97; legitimacy and, 126–28; realism and, 93–97; Reformations and, 9–10, 97–98, 129–34, 285–88; relationalism and, 66; state-formation literature and, 68–70; variation in, 82–84; 15–16; Westphalian Hypothesis and, 277, 281. *See also* composite polities; dynasticism
dynasticism, 6–8, 84–86; constructivism and, 38; dynastic-imperial pathway and, 18, 84–86, 88n88; Hanseatic League and, 89; international political practices and, 92–97, 127–28; international-relations theory and, 6n15, 13; realism and, 32; religion and, 10, 29, 169–70, 186n3; sovereign-territoriality and, 15–16, 90, 92; succession and, 127–28; Vivek Sharma and, 6n15, 88n88; William of Orange and, 198, 226; Westphalian Hypothesis and, 277, 281. *See also* composite polities; dynastic agglomerations; norms

econocentrists, 69–70, 84; city-empires and, 77; federative alliances and, 75–76; dynastic-imperial pathway and, 86–87
economics: complex interdepedence and, 56; constructivism and, 34–36; changes in during early modern period, 86–87, 89; dynastic-imperial pathway and, 81–84, 88n88, 90–94, 121–22; federative alliances and, 76, 89; form/content distinction and, 64; globalization and, 299;

economics, (cont'd)
  Hanseatic League and, 86–87, 108; hegemonic-order theory and, 30–32; historical institutionalism and, 62–63; Holy Roman Empire and, 81; imperial dynamics and, 101, 109, 111, 113; realism and, 29; Reformations and, 286, 290; relationalism and, 58; social ties and, 40–42; warfare and, 132. See also econocentrists; specific personages and places; strategic overextension
Edelstein, David, 296
Edward VI, 94
Egmond, duke of, 198–99, 207; anti-Granvelle campaign, 200–201; Beggars and, 202–4; execution of, 209
Elias, Norbert, 23, 86
elites: composite-state dynamics and, 101–3, 105–7, 109–12, 118–20, 124–26, 129–30, 131. See also aristocracy, class
Elizabeth I: alliance with Henry IV, 230–31; ascension of, 185–86; Dutch Revolt and, 191, 211–12, 219, 223n140, 223–24; French Wars of Religion and, 247, 250; as ruler of composite state, 94, 230
Elliott, J. H.: on Castilian decline, 186n6; on Castilian identity in Habsburg monarchy, 149; on composite polities, 68; on Philip III's court, 231; political ideas and, 283; on rule and resistance, 124; state formation and, 9, 68; on strategic overextension, 270; on Thirty Years' War and, 270, 272
Elman, Colin and Miriam Fendius, 10, 12
Elton, G. R., 165, 169n123, 177, 178n162
empire: defined 72–73; Castile and, 143, 149, 180, 184, 190; city-empires and, 77–79; composite polities and, 16, 18, 72, 101, 295–98; confessionalization and, 285; constructivism and, 38–39; contemporary period and, 19, 296–97, 298, 300; dynasticism and, 84–88, 94–97; federations and, 72–73; federative alliances and, 75–77; globalization and, 300; Habsburg hegemony and, 230–31; hegemonic-order theory and, 30; Holy Roman Empire and, 79–82; modular secession in, 111; prevalence of, 116; Reformations and, 152–55, 287; relationalism and, 25, 59, 66; religion and, 291; strategic overextension and, 120; United States and, 296–97; within-segment structure and, 104–5. See also composite polities; dynastic-imperial pathway; specific polities; strategic overextension
England: composite polities and, 9, 73, 84, 297; confessionalization and, 285; dynastic agglomeration and, 82, 84; dynasticism and, 94, 127–28; German Protestants and, 47, 168; Habsburg hegemony and, 121, 179, 227, 230–34; Pilgrimage of Grace and, 154–55n59; Schmalkaldic League and, 47, 170; Spanish Armada and, 21; Thirty Years' War and, 268, 270–71; Westphalian Hypothesis and, 278, 285. See also specific monarchs
English-school theorists, 11, 13; constructivism and, 39
Enlightenment era, 281; Reformations and, 286
Épernon, duke of, 257
Ertman, Thomas, 91
Escobedo, Juan de, 229
Estates General, 140; early modern rebellions and, 109n24; French Wars of Religion and, 253–54, 260; legitimacy and, 255–56
Eternal Edict (1577), 216
ethnic cleansing, 47, 55. See also "pathological homogenization"
Eucharist, 164, 246
European Union, 19, 297; empire and, 297n27
Evangelical Union, 267

failed states, 59
Farnese, Alexander (prince of Parma), 117, 216, 219–21
federations, 75–77, 84–85, 90; composite polities and, 72, 96, 295; empire and, 72–73; Holy Roman Empire and, 81; Westphalian Hypothesis and, 280. See also composite polities
Ferdinand II, King of Aragon, 138
Ferdinand I, King of the Romans, 2, 140, 142; Bavarian Dukes, and 173; Diet of Speyer and, 165; German Peasants' War and, 158; Kingdom of Hungary and, 160, 162, 169–70; Peace of Augsburg and, 2, 178; Peace of Crépy and, 172; Reformations and, 161, 163; Imperial Succession and, 165–66, 167, 177, 180; War of Schmalkald and, 175

Ferdinand II, King of the Romans, 266, 269; Peace of Westphalia and, 280
Ferguson, Yale, 48n126
feudalism, 37, 87–88; early modern states and, 92, 122, 228, 229, 236
firearms, 87–88. *See also* technology
Fischer-Galati, Stephen A., 162
Flanders, 123, 170, 190, 222; Beggars and, 202, 204; Castile and, 188, 191; duke of Anjou and, 222; Third Dutch Revolt and, 218–19; Union of Arras and, 220. *See also* Walloons
Fleix, Peace of (1580), 255
Florence, 77, 85–86
form/content distinction, 27, 65–66; social networks and, 43
Fountainebleau, Edict of (1685), 241–42
Fox, Jonathan, 291
France, 149, 285; Carolingian Empire and, 79; Catalonia and, 129, 228, 272; colonialism and, 111; composite polities and, 72–73, 82, 84, 93–94, 96, 297; Diet of Speyer and, 161–62; Dutch Revolt and, 188, 191, 201, 202, 211, 212, 213, 216, 219, 222–23, 224–25, 226–27; dynamics of resistance and rule and, 106, 109n24, 117; dynastic agglomeration and, 82–84, 92–93, 96; dynastic-imperial pathway and, 67–68, 85, 93–96; *gabelle* revolt and, 106; England and, 171, 216, 278; German Protestants and, 161–62, 177, 267; Habsburg hegemony and, 32, 135, 138, 141, 149, 150, 160, 169, 170–72, 176, 177, 185–86, 188, 201, 227–28, 230; international structure and, 60; Kyrgyzstan and, 297; patron-client networks and, 42, 92, 117, 125, 130–33; League of Cognac and, 160; Mantua and, 268; realism and, 32; sovereignty and, 67, 279, 282–83; Thirty Years' War and, 266, 268–71, 272; Venetian Republic and, 84, 95n121; Westphalian Hypothesis and, 278–80, 285. *See also* French Wars of Religion; Huguenots; *specific monarchs*; *specific personages*
Franche-Compté, 135, 172, 199
Francis, Duke of Anjou, 219, 220, 250, 253, 255–56
Francis I: Charles V's capture of, 159–60; *Comuneros* revolt and, 149; Diet of Speyer and, 159–60; Diet of Worms and, 153; election of King of the Romans and, 141, 141n12; *gabelle* revolt and, 106; Ghent and, 170; Habsburg hegemony and, 135, 150, 153 160; 170–72, 176; League of Cognac and, 160; Schmalkaldic League and, 169–70, 175
Francis II, 237, 243–46
Francogalla (Hotman), 255
Frederick II (Emperor), 123
Frederick III (Emperor), 80
Frederick III ("The Wise," Elector of Saxony), 152, 158
Frederick V, 266–68
French Wars of Religion, 9, 18–19, 235–39, 245–49, 261–64; Alva's regime and, 211; international structure and, 59–60, last war of, 259–61; middle wars of, 250–54; sovereignty and, 255–56, 282; Thirty Years' War and, 268; Westphalian Hypothesis and, 280. *See also* Huguenots; *politiques*; *specific monarchs*; *specific personages*
Friesland, 196, 218, 220
Fronde, 9, 84n76, 126, 264; Huguenots and, 241–42; Thirty Years' War and, 270
Frost, Robert I., 90
fueros (charter rights), 229
Fugger, Jacob, 141

Gagliardo, John, 276
Gallican Church, 245–46, 258
Garton Ash, Timothy, 20, 300
Gelderland, 123, 218, 220
General Settlement of 1577, 218n116, 227
Geneva, 76, 109, 247
Genoa, 77
Gerhardt, Volcker, 276
Germanías, rebellion of, 107, 140–41, 144
German Peasants Movement, 124 155–58, 158
Germany: Augsburg (Peace of) and, 181–82; Castile and, 138, 141, 149; Charles V and, 135, 137, 149, 158–62; Charles V's political failures and, 176–80, 182–84; city-empires and, 77n45, 78; as composite state, 100; "communal" Reformation and, 157n73; confessionalization and, 170, 181–82, 197, 283; Dutch Revolt and, 200, 206–7; 210, 219, 222, 225; dynamics of resistance and rule and, 109, 118; dynastic-imperial path-

Germany, (cont'd)
way and, 85, 92; economy and, 81; French Wars of Religion and, 247, 249, 252–53, 256–57; globalization and, 300; Habsburg hegemony and, 32, 135; Hanseatic League and, 75, 85; international structures and, 55, 82; Ottoman Empire and, 151, 160, 162, 165, 167, 172, 178, 180; Reformations and, 1, 7, 46, 55, 130, 132, 135, 137–38, 150–84, 267; Schmalkaldic League and, 165–69, 169–72, 172–76; state formation and, 79, 91; sovereignty and, 179–82, 276, 279, 279–80n46, 282; Thirty Years' War and, 91, 267–71, 273; Westphalia and, 275; Westphalian Hypothesis and, 91, 276, 278–79, 300. *See also* Hanseatic League; Holy Roman Empire; Peace of Augsburg; Peace of Westphalia; *specific monarchs*; *specific personages*; Thirty Years' War

Ghent, 122, 123, 123–24, 125, 170, 194, 197, 215–16, 218–19, 226
Gilpin, Robert, 33, 54
globalization, 19, 289, 298–300
Golden Bull of 1356, 80
Gonzaga, Ludovico, 96
Gorski, Philip, 284
Gould, Roger V., 52
Granada, 144–45, 192
Granvelle, Cardinal Amtoine Perrenot de, 117, 117n41, 190, 198–202, 207, 221
Greengrass, Mark, 92, 96
Gregory VII, Pope, 80
Groningen, 196, 218, 221
Grotius, Hugo, 282
Guicciardini, Francesco, 283
guilds, 124, 170, 194
Guise, house of, 243–44; French Wars of Religion and, 238–39, 246–51, 254, 256–57, 264
Gustava Vasa, 75
Gustavus Adolphus, 269

Haarlem, Netherlands, 214, 218–19
Habsburgs, 7; Augsburg (Peace of) and, 181–82; Austrian Branch of, 179, 181, 210, 221, 266, 270–71, 285; Charles V and, 135–39, 180; composite polities and, 68, 93–94, 96, 125, 130, 271; dynastic agglomeration and, 7, 82, 91, 98, 130, 179; dynastic division of, 180–81; dynastic-imperial pathway and, 68, 85; dynastic rivals and, 88–89, 93–94, 158, 161, 168–69, 171, 172–73, 176, 241n35, 271; dynasticism and, 93–94, 96; hegemony and, 2, 9,12, 32–33, 98, 133, 135, 227–31, 233–34, 287, 290; Holy Roman Empire and, 79–80, 91, 163, 165, 280; Netherlands and, 123–24, 132; plausible deniability (routine use of), 116–17; Portugal and, 227–28, 271–73; realism and, 32–33, 290; Reformations and, 2, 9, 12, 98, 130, 133, 233–34, 287, 290; Swabian League and, 76; Swiss and, 76, 85; Thirty Years' War and, 266–67, 269–73; Westphalian Hypothesis and, 278, 280. *See also* Charles V; Maximilian II; Philip II; *specific domains*; *specific personages*; *specific rulers*

Hainaut, 219, 220
Haliczer, Stephen, 145
Hall, Rodney Bruce, 38, 240, 281; constructivism and, 35
Hanseatic League, 75, 85, 89–90, 212; formation of, 75, 108; Reformations and, 175, 181–82
Hegel, G.W.F., 271
hegemonic-order theory, 23–24, 30–32, 135 hegemony, 18–19; anarchy and, 33n54; Charles V and, 136; constructivism and, 39; dynastic agglomeration and, 98; dynastic-imperialism and, 67; Reformations and, 287, 290; religion and, 291; strategic overextension and, 12, 31, 39, 130, 121, 135–36, 186, 239, 290; Thirty Years' War and, 273. *See also* Habsburgs
Henry, Duke of Rohan, 260
Henrietta of Kleve, 96
Henry, Duke of Guise, 239, 251, 257
Henry I of Bourbon (Prince of Condé), 252–53
Henry II, 236–37; Charles V and, 2, 135, 172, 176–78; captivity of, 172; *gabelle* and, 106; Philip II and, 185–86; Schmalkaldic League and, 172
Henry III: assassination of, 258; Catholic League and, 254, 256–57; Dutch Revolt and, 223–24; French Wars of Religion and, 238, 239, 253–55, 256–58, 261; Poland and, 93, 253; proposed marriage to Elizabeth I, 250

Henry IV (of Navarre), 80, 239, 243; abjuration of, 258–60; Aragon and, 229; assassination of, 267; Dutch Revolt and, 216, 224–25; Edict of Nantes and, 239, 242, 259; French Wars of Religion and, 238, 239, 250–54, 256–59, 262–64; Habsburg hegemony and, 229–32

Henry VIII (king of England), 47, 94, 127, 148, 159, 170–71; Pilgrimage of Grace and, 109, 154–55n59

heredity. *See* succession

heterodoxy (religious), 2,15–16, 18, 46, 100, 121, 193, 202, 225, 234, 241, 273, 283, 285, 292

Hezbollah, 17, 20–21, 42, 58

Hierarchy: composite polities and, 299; divide-and-rule and, 106; imperial structures and, 103; international structure and, 15, 82

high-category environments, 53, 59, 298; nested relational configurations and, 50–51

high-network environments, 53, 298; nested relational configurations and, 50–51

historical-institutionalism, 5, 14, 22, 23n12, 25, 40, 61–65

historicism, 11

Hobbes, Thomas, 282

Hohenstaufens, 80

Hohenzollern, Albrecht von, 158

Holland, 123, 190, 196, 212–16, 218, 220–22, 224, 226

Holstein, Duchy of, 75, 268

Holsti, K. J., 277

Holt, Mack P., 235, 254, 259

Holy Junta, 145–47

Holy Roman Empire, 7, 79–82, 135, 165; Charles V's election and, 140–42; city-empires (city-states) and, 78; composite polities and, 72–73, 96, 236; dynastic-imperial pathway and, 85, 92, 96; federative alliances and, 76–77; legitimacy and, 256; Reformations and, 1, 130, 132–33, 138, 149–82,183, 288; self-help and, 81; Swiss Confederation and, 76; Westphalian Hypothesis and, 274–77, 278–79. *See also* Germany; Thirty Years' War

Hornes, duke of, 201, 209

Hotman, Francis, 255

Hubatsch, Walter, 91

Huguenots, 18, chapter 7; defined, 244n23; Aragon and, 228, 229; anti-Granvelle campaign, 201; Bourbon policy toward, 240–43, 260; Catalonia and, 228; conversion patterns and, 42, 132; Dutch Revolt and, 206, 210, 211, 212, 225; expulsion from France, 240–41, 242; Henry IV and, 231, 239, 259–60, 262; political ideas and, 255–56; secession (general lack of) from France, 263–64; Spanish support for, 233; Thirty Years' War and, 233, 271; Transnational Calvinism and, 109. *See also* Calvinism; French Wars of Religion

Hui, Victoria Tin-Bor, 26n25, 52n166, 135

Hundred Years War, 94

Hungary, 83, 151, 159–60, 162, 169–70

Hurd, Elizabeth Shakman, 291–92

Hussite Movement, 156, 175

Iberia, 136, 138–39, 147–49; resistance and, 140–44; Thirty Years' War and, 271–72, 273. *See also* Aragon; Castile, Catalonia; Portugal; Valencia

ideal types, 64–65, 65n176; anarchy and, 40, 58–59, 93, 287; composite polities and, 16, 71–2, 99–121, 299; empires and, 35; form/content distinction and, 64–65;Holy Roman Empire and, 81; international structure and, 40, 51, 59, 93, 287; modern state and, 71; nation-states and, 25, 72n27, 58–59, 299; networks and, 16, 40, 42, 50, 64; patron-client relations and, 42; Reformations and, 285, 287; relational structures and, 48; relationalism and, 65–66; sovereign-territorial state system and, 265, 285

ideationalists, 19, 69–70; Charles V and, 137; Dutch Revolt and, 205; dynastic-imperial pathway and, 84; French Wars of Religion and, 239–43; Reformations and, 290; Westphalian Hypothesis and, 275, 280

identity, 1; categories and, 44–48; Castile and, 149; Charles V and, 140, 143, 182; city-empires and, 78; composite polities and, 8, 67, 72, 104, 296; constructivism and, 34–35, 38; divide-and-rule and, 119; Dutch Revolt and, 205, 213; dynasticism and, 115, 127–28; dynastic-imperial pathway and, 67; Henry IV and, 260–61; international structures and, 55;

identity, (cont'd)
  Moriscos and, 193; multivocal signaling and, 114–15, 140, 260–61; nested relational configurations and, 48–52; nationalism and, 71, 94n119; networks and, 64; Philip II and, 184, 191; realism and, 13; Reformations and, 1, 240; relationalism and, 25, 57; religion and, 292–93; religion and, 291–94; state formation and, 69. See also categories
Ikenberry, G. John, 31
Imperial Knights, 155–58
indirect rule: defined, 71; American primacy and, 296; composite polities and, 7, 71–72, 72n27, 99, 101; contemporary sates and, 297; divide-and-rule and, 106; Dutch Revolt, 205; dynastic agglomeration and, 68, 83; Holy Roman Empire and, 82; religious contention and, 4, 99; tradeoffs associated with, 116–18; Westphalia and, 4. See also centralization; direct rule
instrumentalists, 1n3
intersubjective norms, 27, 34–35, 38–39, 54–55
Investiture Conflict, 80
Iran, 20–21, 58, 293, 297
Iraq, 48, 61, 293; US military presence as example of imperial dynamics and, 296–97
Ireland, 83, 278
Isabella of Castile, 138, 146
Isabella (Isabel) of Portugal, 148
Isabella Clara Eugenia, 224, 231
Islam, 292–93, 295; Castilian identity and, 149; Catalonia and, 228; Charles V and, 150; Reformation and, 2–3, 290; Spanish hegemony and, 192–93; Westphalian Hypothesis and, 2–3, 276. See also Moriscos; Ottoman Empire
isomorphism, 64
Israel, 17, 20–21, 26; war with Hezbollah (2006) and, 20–22, 58
Israel, Jonathan, 122, 188
Italian League, 78
Italy, 7, 176, 298; Catholic Church and, 97; Charles V and, 138, 148–49, 150, 159–60, 162; city-empires and, 77–79, 88; dynastic-imperial pathway and, 85–86; Dutch Revolt and, 198, 208; federative alliances and, 75; French Wars of Religion and, 260; Holy Roman Empire and, 79–80, 85; Investiture Conflict and, 80; Islam and, 192–93; Ottoman Empire and, 193; Philip II and, 179, 185, 186, 193; realpolitik and, 283; republicanism and, 128; social ties and, 42; Spanish overextension and, 231; Thirty Years' War and, 268–69; unified monarchy and, 150; Valois dynasty and, 82n65; Valois-Habsburg conflict over, 93–94, 93–94n113, 95n121, 150, 159–60, 162, 185, 186. See also *specific city-states*

Jackson, Robert, 58
Jacobitism, 278
James I, 231–32
Japan, 108
Jean-Louis of Nogaret, 257
Jesuits (Society of Jesus), 132
John Frederick of Saxony, 1, 173–76
John George of Saxony, 267
John of Saxony ("The Steadfast"), 158, 162–64, 168; League of Torgau and, 158
joint-action. See collective mobilization
Juana (Joanna) of Castile, 138, 141, 145
Don Juan of Austria, 216, 218–19, 229
Jülich-Cleves, Duchy of, 171, 267
jus reformandi (right of reform), 279

Kaiser, David, 236
Kamen, Henry, 191, 233
Kennedy, Paul, 186, 271n19
Kettering, Sharon, 41
King, Charles, 295
Kittelson, James, 179
Kleinman, Rachel, 242
Kleve, house of, 96
Knecht, R. J., 106, 243
Koenigsberger, H. G., 87–88, 125, 148, 191, 201; city-empires and, 77; "composite states" and, 71n20; religious networks and, 131; dynastic agglomeration and, 83; "revolutionary parties" and, 226
Kollack, Peter, 56
Kyrgyzstan, 297

Lake, David A., 72
Landeshoheit (territorial absolutism), 276, 278–79
La Rochelle, France, 133, 238, 249–50, 253, 260, 263, 268, 271
League of Compromise, 202–4

League of Schmalkald, 1, 47, 196; expansion of, 169–72; formation of, 165–69
League of Torgau, 158–59
Lebanon, 20–21, 26, 58–59
legitimacy, 4, 13, 17, 292; abjuration of Henry IV and, 230, 258; anarchy and, 15; centralization and, 105; *Comuneros* revolt and, 135, 142, 145, 148; constructivist accounts of change and, 37–38; dynasticism and, 7, 125; Dutch Revolt and, 205, 211, 213, 222n135; early modern European resistance and, 127–29; French Wars of Religion and, 238, 248, 255–59; Habsburg monarchy and, 150; Holy Roman Empire and, 80; intermediary autonomy and, 116–17, 117n41; multivocal (polyvalent) signaling and, 100, 114, 130–31, 134, 137, 150; relationalism and, 45, 62; religion and, 292; religion, the French Monarchy and, 241–42, 262; Reformations and, 129–31, 156
Leicester, earl of, 223–24
Lepanto, Battle of 193
liberal evangelicals, 295
liberalism (international-relations theory), 17, 23–24, 28, 56; state formation and, 69. *See also* complex-interdependence theory, neoliberal institutionalism
linguistics, 22n7
Liu, Henry C. K., 2
local intermediaries, 6, 8–9; autonomy and, 116–18; composite polities and, 298; divide and rule strategies and, 118–20; Reformations and, 289; religious contention and, 101, 103. *See also* indirect rule
logics of social action, 29, 41–42, 62n168; religion and, 186n3, 205, 240, 271, 293–94
Longjumeau, Edict of (1568), 238, 248
Lorraine, 79, 178, 244
Lorraine, Cardinal of, 248–49
loss-of-strength gradient, 31
Louis, Cardinal of Guise, 239
Louis I of Bourbon (Prince of Condé), 244–49, 250
Louis II of Hungary, 160, 162
Louis of Nassau, 207, 213, 249
Louis of the Palatine, 167
Louis XIII, 129, 238, 260

Louis XIV: absolutism and, 241, 243; Catalonia and, 129, 272; diplomatic practices of, 280; Edict of Nantes (revocation of) and, 235, 239, 240–43, 260; French hegemony and, 270–71; War of Spanish Succession and, 270–71
low-category environments, 53, 298; nested relational configurations and, 49–51; relationalism and, 59
Low Countries. *See* Dutch Republic; Dutch Revolt; Netherlands
low-network environments, 53, 298; nested relational configurations and, 49–51; relationalism and, 59
Lübeck, 75, 77
Luther, Martin, 7; Charles V, and 152–53; confessionalization and, 285; Dutch Revolt and, 196; early princely supporters of, 158; Eucharist and, 164; German Peasants' Movement and, 156–57; opposition to religious compromise and, 171;Two Kingdoms Doctrine of, 255, 282; views on Protestant military alliance, 164, 164n103, 168; Westphalian Hypothesis and, 281
Lutheranism, 47, 131–32, 164, 171; Augsburg Confession and, 166; Augsburg (Peace of) and, 179, 182; Dutch Revolt and, 208, 218, 221–22; France and, 235n2; Netherlands and, 196–97; Schmalkaldic League's formation and, 165–69; Westphalia and, 297
Luxembourg, 150
Lynch, John, 139

Macdonald, Paul, 296
Machiavelli, Niccolò, 11, 116, 117, 138, 283; republicanism and, 78n48
MacKenney, Richard: dynasticism and, 6, 95; composite polities and, 95; religious contention and, 100
Macy, Michael W., 52n136
Mafia, 42
Magyars, 79
Malta, 192
Mansbach, Richard, 48n126
Mantua, 96, 268
Margaret of Parma, 117,189–90; Alva and, 208–9; anti-Granvelle campaign, 201; Beggars and, 202–4; Dutch Revolt and, 206–7, 219, 226
marginalization by footnote. *See* contrition

Marguerite of Valois, 250–51
Marxism: dynasticism and, 6n15; German Peasants' Movement and, 157n73; Spruyt, Hendrik and, 37n78; religion and, 292; state formation and, 63n172, 70
Mary of Burgundy, 122–23, 126
Mary of Hungary (aka of Austria), 1, 124, 173
Mary Stuart, 185, 249
Mary Tudor, 148, 179–80, 185
Mathias, Archduke, 218
Matthias (Habsburg emperor), 266
Mattingly, Garrett, 93
Maurice of Saxony, 177–78, 178n162, 199; Schmalkaldic War and, 175–76
Maximilian I, 80, 140, 17; Netherlands, 123–24, 126, 170, 194
Maximilian II, 210, 218
Maximilian of Bavaria, 267–69
Maximilian of Tyrol (Archduke), 266
Mazarin, Jules (Cardinal), 239, 242
Mearsheimer, John J., 33, 33n54; "Back to the Future: Instability in Europe after the Cold War" and, 300n37
Mechelen, Netherlands, 196, 200
Medici, Catherine de', 244–51, 253
Medici, Cosmo de', 114
Medici, Marie de', 260
Medieval era, 7, 37, 67–69, 71, 73, 75, 82–84, 86–88, 91–92, 95, 97, 106, 119, 127–28, 179, 182, 239, 288
Melanchthon, Philip, 164, 166
Mexico, 191, 212
Milan, 85–86, 94, 160, 170, 172; Holy Roman Empire and, 82
military; city-empires and, 77; composite polities and, 297; constructivism and, 34–35; dynastic agglomerations and, 83, 86, 92; federative alliances and, 75; realism and, 13, 29–30, 30–32
military-technical change, 66, 76, 77, 81; bellocentric accounts of change and, 63n172, 69–70, 87–88, 88n88; Charles V and, 182; dynastic-imperial pathway and, 63, 84; French Wars of Religion and 261; Hanseatic League and, 89–90; Holy Roman Empire and, 81; realism and, 11; institutions and, 63; Swiss Confederation and, 76; Westphalian Hypothesis and, 275, 286
Mitchell, Joshua, 291

mmmm. *See* burghers
monetarization, 86
Montigny, duke of, 201
Montmorency, Anne de, 244, 248
Montmorency, house of, 238, 243–45, 253
Moravian Brethren, 279
Morgan, J. P., 90
Moriscos, 192–93, 208, 227; *Comuneros* revolt and, 145
Mosse, George L., 77
Mota, Bishop of Badajoz, 142–43, 148, 183
Motyl, Alexander J., 108
multipolarity, 14, 20
multivocal signaling, 99–100, 264, 289, 294. *See also* polyvalent signaling
Munck, Thomas, 276
Münster, 157, 197, 276

Nantes, Edict of (1596), 231, 235, 238, 259, 260; revocation of, 240–42, 264
Naples, 85–86, 94, 125, 135, 160, 180; Thirty Years' War and, 272
Napoleon Bonaparte, 281
Nassau, Johann von, 218
Nationalism 1: constructivism and, 35; dynastic agglomeration and, 98; Dutch Revolt and, 225; early modern Europe and, 93–95, 95n123; empire and, 111; religion and, 292; state formation and, 69
nation-states, 10, 73, 90, 93, 297–99; dynastic agglomeration and, 98; international structures and, 54; state formation and, 68–70
necessity, doctrine of, 10, 98. See also *realpolitik*
Nemours, Treaty of (1585), 257
neoliberal-institutionalism, 50, 52–53, 56–57. *See also* liberalism (international-relations theory)
Netherlands, 7, 60, 89, 245, 285; Anabaptism and, 197; Burgundy and, 109; Calvinism and, 131–32; Castile and, 137, 180, 190–91; Charles V and, 139, 152, 153, 159, 172, 173, 178, 179, 196; colonial empire and, 111; dynastic agglomerations and, 100, 109, 132; French Wars of Religion and, 132, 247–50, 255, 262; Habsburg governance, 194–97; Hanseatic League and, 89; intermediary autonomy and, 116–17; Lutheranism and, 197; Philip II and, 65, 178n162, 190,

193; resistance and, 122–26; Schmalkaldic War and, 177; Spanish Armada and, 21; Spanish hegemony and, 121, 186, 188–89, 193–97; Thirty Years' War and, 267–68, 270–71, 273; Valois-Habsburg conflicts and, 94; Westphalian Hypothesis and, 280. *See also* Dutch Republic; Dutch Revolt; Thirty Years' War

netness: defined, 48; collective-mobilization dynamics and, 48–52; constructivism and, 57. *See also* density; networks; social ties

network density: defined, 43–44; anarchy and, 15, 53–54; city-empires and, 78; composite state structure and, 103; divide-and-rule and, 108, 137, 105, 119; form/content distinction and, 64; nested relational configurations and, 48–52; relationalism and, 25, 57. *See also* collective mobilization; netness; networks; social ties

networks: defined, 25, 42; anarchy and, 15, 26; brokerage and, 42, 47–48; centrality and, 44; collective mobilization and, 48–52; corporate actors and, 45–46; generalization and, 16–17; international-relations scholarship and, 22n7; institutions and, 28n33; international structure and, 26–27, 39–40, 48, 52–61; patron-client relations and, 41–42, 122, 128; relational institutionalism and, 14; relationalism and, 25; social ties and, 40–44; structures and, 14, 40, 42; transnational, 36; yoking and, 46–47. *See also* netness; network density; relationalism; social ties; structural holes

Nevers, Duchy of, 96
Nevers, duke of, 268
New World (America), 1, 7, 135, 183, 188, 227, 231, 282
Nine Years' Aid, 198
nobility. *See* artistocracy
nonstate actors, 13, 20–21, 300; constructivism and, 36; international change and, 287; international structure and, 59; military-technical revolution and, 88n86; realism and, 33, 55; religion and, 295; states and, 300
Nonsuch, Treaty of (1585), 223
Normans, 80, 107
norms: constitutive, 5, 62; collective mobilization and, 35, 52, 57; constructivism and, 34, 35, 36, 37–38, 39, 57, 62; dynastic, 6, 29, 32, 84, 94, 96–97, 281, 297; English-School theory and, 39; form/content distinction and, 17; French Wars of Religion and, 261; historical institutionalism and 62n167; ideationalist accounts of change, and 69; international change and, 13–14, 24; international structure and, 24, 27, 34, 38–39; realism and, 10–11, 14, 29, 32–33; in relationalism, 25, 45; religion and, 294; sovereignty and, 30n48, 38, 281, 286, 297; states-under-anarchy framework and, 54–55; systemic, 62; *See also* co-constitutive relationships; constructivism; logics of social action; identity

norms-oriented frameworks, 62n167
North Korea, 20

occupations (military), 296
offense/defense balance theory, 70n16
Olivares, Count Duke, 233, 268, 270–73; Catholicism and, 240; necessity and, 283; Spanish hegemony and, 186
On the Present State of Germany (Pufendorf), 256
Orange, house of, 129. *See also* William of Orange
ordinary people, 6, 92, 102–3, 105, 109, 118–19; 120, 124–25, 126, 128–29, 140, 155–57, 200, 225, 258, 261, 294
Ortíz, Antonio, 226
Osiander, Andreas, 278, 279n46, 280
Ottoman Empire: British Empire and, 110; Charles V and, 135–36, 149, 151, 159, 160, 162–63, 165, 169, 172, 178; French alliance with, 132; dynastic agglomeration and, 91; Dutch Revolt and, 218; Holy Roman Empire and, 151, 160, 162–63, 165; Hungary and, 151, 160, 162; Iberia and, 143, 192–93; patrimonial secession and, 118n44; Philip II and, 189, 190, 192–93; Schmalkaldic League and, 165, 169; Schmalkaldic War and, 172
Otto the Great (Saxon king), 79
overextension. *See* strategic overextension
Owen, John, 55, 158

Padgett, John F., 114
Pakistan, 293, 297
Palermo, 272

papacy. *See* Catholic Church; *specific popes*
Papal States, 85
Paris, France, 253, 258; French Wars of Religion and, 225, 248, 249, 250–54, 257–59
Parker, Geoffrey, 83, 191, 206, 209, 234; anti-Granvelle campaign, 201; Beggars and, 204; Spanish hegemony and, 188
Parma, 222–25, 258
Parrow, Kathleen, 255
partible inheritance, 81
Passau, Treaty of (1552), 178
"pathological homogenization," 240, 242
patronage, 41; *Comuneros* revolt and, 138–39; dynasticism and, 94–95, 128; French Wars of Religion and, 246–47; intermediary autonomy and, 117; Kyrgyzstan and, 297; Netherlands and, 196, 198–99, 200; state formation and, 71, 78, 83, 86, 122; US occupation of Iraq and, 296. *See also* patron-client relations
patterns of interaction. *See* transactional patterns
Paul III, Pope, 171, 176
Paul V, Pope, 267
pays d'élections, 72–73, 272
pays d'état, 72, 272
Penn, William, 286n73
Pérez, Antonio, 229
Pérez, Joseph, 138
Philip II, 2, 135, 179; anti-Granvelle campaign, 201; Aragon and, 229–30; Beggars and, 202–4; Castile and, 149, 184, 189–92; Catalonia and, 228–20; Catholicism and, 191–92; Dutch Revolt and, 65, 116–17, 121, 189, 193–97, 204–7, 207–8; 210–11, 212, 214–15, 218, 221–22, 224–26; ecclesiatical reorganization and, 200–202; Elizabeth I and, 185–86, 212, 223n142; England and, 121, 179, 185–86, 212, 231; French Wars of Religion and, 224–25, 236, 245–46, 248, 264; Habsburg-Valois conflict and, 185; Holy Roman Empire and, 149, 177; identity and, 115–16, 149, 189, 205; Iberia and, 148; Islam and, 192–93; Mary Tudor and, 179, 180, 185; Netherlands' governance and, 198–99; Ottoman Empire and, 189, 192–93, 218; Portugal and, 227–28; Protestantism and, 185, 191–92, 224, 225, 226; Schmalkaldic War and, 173; Spanish Armada and, 224; Spanish hegemony and, 180, 184, 185–89, 230–31; Thirty Years' War and, 273; Westphalian Hypothesis and, 278.
Philip III, 187, 189, 230, 232–33, 267; Dutch Revolt and, 121; England and, 121
Philip IV, 129, 187, 227–28, 268, 270
Philip V (Bourbon king of Spain), 270
Philip of Hesse, 1, 158, 162–63, 165, 168–70 173–74, 176; bigamy and, 171n134
Philpott, Daniel, 67, 154, 239–41; composite polities and, 68; constructivism and, 38 Edict of Nantes and, 241n15; state system and, 3n8; Westphalian Hypothesis and, 4, 276, 277, 286–87
pike squares, 76, 87
Poitiers, Edict of (1577), 254–55, 259
Poland-Lithuania, 83, 89, 91–92, 253; composite polities and, 73
politiques, 239–40, 241n15, 254, 259, 282–83
polyvalent signaling, 100, 130–31, 294. *See also* multivocal signaling
Portugal, 189, 223n148, 227–28, 233, 267, 287; *Comuneros* revolt and, 146, 148; rebellion and, 9, 271–73; sovereignty and, 282
poststructuralism, 22n7. *See also* marginalization by footnote
power-political competition, 1, 11; anarchy and, 30; complex-interdependence theory and, 56; constructivism and, 39; econocentrists and, 86–87; historical institutionalism and, 61; international change and, 4, 283; international structures and, 21, 56; nonstate actors and, 13, 86, 96, 283; realism and, 29, 32, 39, religion and, 183, 186n3, 261, 293; Westphalian Hypothesis and, 273, 281. *See also* necessity, doctrine of; *raison d'état*; realism; *realpolitik*
practices, 40, 43; confessionalization and, 47n121; customary rights and, 127, 199; dynastic, 66, 85, 88, 94–96, 97, 121, 134, 281; divide-and-rule and, 134, 148; early modern European international structure and, 96; form/content distinction and, 42; dynastic-imperial pathway and, 85, 88, 121; Japanese Empire and, 108; realism and, 10–11; religion and, 181, 291; sovereignty and, 97, 273,

282–83; systems theories and, 62; theorizing religion and, 291; Westphalian Hypothesis and, 273, 280–81, 282–83, 286–87. *See also* norms
Prague, Austria, 266
Prague, Peace of (1635), 269, 280
predestination, doctrine of, 268
price revolution, 86
primogeniture, 81n61, 85
Prisoner's Dilemma, 49, 56
property rights, 87
Protestant League, 177
Protestant Reformations, 2–3, 47n121; Charles V and, 136, 137, 149–84; class and, 134, 156–57, 167–68, 174; "communal," 157n73; composite polities and, 3–9, 16, 121, 129–34, 183; constructivism and, 37–39; contemporary developments and, 2–3, 290, 294–95, 300; globalization and, 300; international change and, 9–10, 12, 63, 66, 69, 266, 285–88, 289; Islam and, 2–3, 290, 295; Netherlands and, 196–97, patron-client relations and, 42; *raison d'état* and, 239–40; realism and, 38–39; sovereign-territorial state and, 3, 97–98, 239–40, 262–64, 265, 278, 280–81, 282–83; state formation and, 91, 182, 262–64, 273–75, 280–81, 283–85; theories of state formation and, 70, 97–98, 179–80. *See also* confessionalization; Dutch Revolt; French Wars of Religion; Thirty Years' War; Westphalia; *specific events*; *specific movements*; *specific personages*
Pufendorf, Samuel, 280, 282; *On the Present State of Germany*, 256
Pyrenees, Treaty of (1659), 186, 270

quasi-states, 58

Radnitz, Scott, 297
Rae, Heather, 240–42
raison d'état, 9, 98, 239, 259, 283
rational-choice theory, 62n168. *See also* logics of social action
rational-institutionalism, 62n168
rationalism, 52, 56, 293
realism, 11–12, 29–32, 67; anarchy and, 29–30; city-empires and, 78; collective mobilization and, 23–24; composite polities and, 93; constructivism and, 11, 24, 34–39; early modern Europe and, 32–

34, 39, 67, 135; international change and, 10–12, 13–16, 21; international structures and, 53–55; relational-institutionalism and, 16, 28; relationalism and, 27, 39–40; state formation and, 69–70. *See also* hegemonic-order theory; nonstate actors; power-political competition; *realpolitik*; states-under-anarchy framework; structural realism
realpolitik, 282. *See also* necessity, doctrine of; *raison d'état*; realism; structural realism
Reconquista. *See* Christian Reconquest
Reformations: explanation for plural form and, 2n4. *See also* Protestant Reformations; *specific movements*; *specific personages*
Reformed Church. *See* Calvinism; Huguenots
Regensberg, Diet of (1527–1528), 162
relational-contracting theory, 57, 72
relational-institutionalism, 5, 14–17, 28, chapter 2, chapter 4; contemporary political structures and, 299; generalization and, 289, 291; ideal-typification and, 101; Reformations and, 289; strategic overextension and, 121. *See also* relationalism
relationalism, 14, 22, 24–28, 39–61, 64–66; globalization and, 300; historical institutionalism and, 61–63; international structures and, 15, 52–56; nested configurations and, 48–52; religion and, 294. *See also* networks; social ties; *specific concepts*
relational structures, 15, 93, 298; historical institutionalism and, 63; nested relational configurations and, 48–52
Renaissance, 78
republicanism, 128–29
Requeséns, Luis de, 214–15
Restitution, Edict of (1629), 269
Richelieu, Cardinal, 239, 268–69, 272, 283
Rights of Magistrates, The (Bèze), 255
Roelker, Nancy Lyman, 254
Rome, 42, 79, 108, 149, 160, 284
Romorantin, Edict of (1560), 245
Rublack, Ulinka, 284
Ruggie, John, 37, 67, 277
Russia, 20, 58, 158, 293, 295, 297. *See also* Soviet Union

St. Bartholomew's Day Massacre (1572), 213–14, 251–52
Saint-Maureles-Faussés, Edict of (1568), 249
Salamanca, 142
Salian dynasty, 79–80
salience, 56, 294, 298–99; nested relational configurations and, 50–52
Sandler, Shmuel, 291
Saudi Arabia, 293
Sauvage, Jean de, 140
Savoy, 268
Saxony, 79, 267
Scandinavia, 47, 83
Schilling, Heinz, 158
Schmalkaldic League. *See* League of Schmalkald
Schmalkaldic War, 1, 9, 18, 91, 138, 172–76
Schmidt, Georg, 279
Schweller, Randall L., 29, 51
Scotland, 231, 244, 249
Sea, Thomas F., 155
Sea Beggars, 211–13, 250
secularism, 291–92, 293–94
security communities, 57
Segovia, 144–45
self-determination, 39
self-help, 30, 35–36; French Wars of Religion and, 263; Holy Roman Empire and, 81
September 11, 2001, 51
servicio (grant), 140–41, 143–44, 147
Seville, 7
Sforza, Francesco, 170
Sforzas, 86
Sharma, Vivek, 6, 85, 88n88
Shebaa Farms, Israel, 20
Shennan, J. H., 95
Shiites, 20, 58, 297; religion and, 293
siege artillery, 87–88
Sigismund (king of Poland), 267
Sigismund Vasa (king of Sweden), 91
Simmel, George, 64
Simpson, Homer. *See* mmmm; burghers
Six Books of the Commonwealth (Bodin), 256
social-network analysis, 28, 42; historical institutionalism and, 62n167; structural determinism and, 45.
social ties, 40–45; categories and, 45–46; identities and, 45–46; nested relational configurations and, 48, 52; relationalism and, 25, 40. *See also* density; netness; networks; structure
sociological-institutionalism, 62n167
sociological-relational analysis, 5
sovereign territoriality, 9–10, 19, 183; bellocentrists and, 87–88; city-empires and, 78; composite polities and, 93, 95–96, 298; confessionalization and, 265; constructivism and, 38; dynastic agglomeration and, 90–92, 97–98; dynastic-imperialism and, 67, 84; federative alliances and, 75; international structures and, 54–55; political ideas and, 283; Reformations and, 2, 285, 287; state formation and, 69–70; Westphalia and, 5, 275; Westphalian Hypothesis and, 276–77, 280–81
sovereignty, 5, 9, 18, 121–34; Charles V and, 136, 138–39; city-empires and, 79; composite polities and, 93, 95, 297; confessionalization and, 285; constructivism and, 39; divide-and-rule strategies and, 108–11; early modern period and, 12; Iberia and, 140–44; legitimacy and, 255–59; Penn (William) and, 286n73; political ideas and, 282; Reformations and, 3, 289; relationalism and, 66; religion and, 292; religious contention and, 99–100; social ties and, 40; state formation and, 70; theory and, 13, 16; Thirty Years' War and, 266; Westphalia and, 3–4; Westphalian Hypothesis and, 276, 278–81
Soviet Union, 58, 290, 293, 296. *See also* Russia
Spaans, Joke, 226
Spain, 7, 18, 20, 135–39; anti-Habsburg alliance and, 163–65; Augsburg and, 181–82; bellocentrists and, 88; Catholicism and, 240; Charles V and, 149, 180; Dutch Revolt and, 196–97, 215–19, 226; dynastic agglomeration and, 82, 91; early modern period and, 12; firewalls and, 107; French Wars of Religion and, 248–49, 263; Germany and, 158–62; Habsburgs and, 195–99, 210–14, 225–29; hegemony of, 185–89, 185–234; Holy Roman Empire and, 79; Islam and, 192–93; Netherlands' governance and, 199; Philip II and, 190–94, 205–9, 220–24; realism and, 32; Reformations and,

1–2, 287, 290; religious contention and, 115; resistance and, 123; Schmalkaldic League and, 165–72; Schmalkaldic War and, 172–76; sovereignty and, 282–83; Thirty Years' War and, 266–68, 270–73; Westphalian Hypothesis and, 278, 280. *See also* Aragon; Castile; Catalonia

Spanish Armada, 65, 216, 224, 227, 233; parallels with contemporary period, 20–21

Spanish Succession, War of, 270, 281, 285

Speyer, Diet of, 164; Schmalkaldic League's formation and, 165

Spruyt, Hendrik: city-states and, 78n49; decline of Hansa (account of) 89–90; divide-and-rule strategies and, 119; federative alliances and, 75; international structure and, 37; sovereignty (account of) and, 67, 68; Westphalian Hypothesis and, 150

St. Germain, Edict of (1562), 249: Catholic backlash and, 251; factional struggles at French court and, 250

star-shaped systems: contemporary period and, 291; composite polities and, 99, 103; cross-pressures and, 113, 115, 120; divide-and-rule and, 108–9; local intermediares in, 118; multivocal signaling and, 114–15

states, 6–7, 9–10, 18–19; Catholicism and, 240; city-empires and, 77–79; composite polities and, 70–74; confessionalization and, 265, 284–85; constructivism and, 34, 36–37; dynastic agglomeration and, 82–84, 92; dynastic-imperialism and, 67; dynastic-imperial pathway and, 84–88; early modern period and, 11–12; federative alliances and, 75–77; formation of, 99–103, 109–13, 119–23, 129–33; French Wars of Religion and, 262–64; globalization and, 299–300; historical institutionalism and, 63; Holy Roman Empire and, 79–82; international structures and, 56; nation-states and, 68–70; nested relational configurations and, 51; Reformations and, 286–87, 289; relationalism and, 57; religious contention and, 104–8, 114–18, 124–28; theory and, 15–17; Thirty Years' War and, 266; Westphalia and, 4. *See also* sovereignty; states-under-anarchy framework

States General, 123, 215–23, 232; Beggars and, 203; Dutch Independence and, 194

states-under-anarchy framework: collective mobilization and, 16, 23; composite polities and, 298; confessionalization and, 284; constructivism and, 36; early modern Europe and, 13–14, 16, 33, 67; dynastic-imperialism and, 67; Israel-Hezbollah War and, 21–22, 58; international structures and, 53–54; realism and, 13, 33; as relational configuration, 15, 50, 53–55, 93; sovereignty and, 93; as theoretical construct, 298; transnational actors and, 36; variation in units and, 58–61. *See also* anarchy; realism; structural realism

Sterling-Folker, Jennifer, 54n144

Strategic overextension, 12, 120–21, 290; Charles V and, 136; constructivism and, 39; Spanish Habsburgs and, 186, 188, 239, 270, 290. *See also* composite polities; empire; hegemonic-order theory; hegemony

structural holes: defined, 43; collective mobilization and, 104, 106; Cosimo de' Medici and, 114; divide-and-rule and, 104; dynastic agglomerations and, 104; firewalls and, 106; multivocal signaling and, 114; "robust action" and, 114

structural-functionalism, 62

structural realism, 23, 30, 37; different variants, and 33n54; ideal types and, 287; relationalism and, 40, 54–58. See also *Theory of International Politics* (Waltz); Waltz, Kenneth

structure (concepts and theory): defined, 23–24, 24–25, 40; categories and, 44–45; constructivism and, 14, 34–35, 38–39, 62; English-School theory and, 11, 39; form/content distinction and, 64–65, 66; ideal-typification and, 64–65; meso-level and, 61–62; patron-client relations and, 41–43; political change and, 11, 13–17, 23–24, 28; relationalism and, 14–17, 24–27, 39–40; as networks, 40, 42–48; as relational configuration, 48–52, 52–61; state forms and, 36–37. *See also* agent-structure co-constitution; anarchy; catnets; collective mobilization; composite polities; empires; historical institutionalism; networks; relational-institutionalism; relational structures

Stuarts, 82; Reformations and, 287. *See also* James I

substate actors, 33–34; constructivism and, 36; international structures and, 56. *See also* transnational actors

succession: abortive German war of 1610 and, 267; composite polities and, 73, 94–95; *Comuneros* revolt and, 138–39, 142; conflict between England and Spain and, 231–32, 270; dynastic-imperial pathway and, 6–9, 85, 95; French Wars of Religion and, 9, 237, 256–59; Holy Roman Empire and, 81; legitimacy and, 128; as source of instability, 7–8, 127–28; Portugal and, 237; Westphalian Hypothesis and, 277, 281. *See also* Austrian Succession, War of; dynastic agglomeration; Spanish Succession, War of

Sunnis, 58

Sussex School. *See* marginalization by footnote

Swabian League, 46, 124, 183; as federative alliance, 75–76; Charles's election as king of the Romans and, 141n12; German Peasants Movement and, 124, 155, 157; organization of the Holy Roman Empire and, 81; religious polarization and, 170, 183; Schmalkaldic League's expansion and, 169–70; Swiss Confederation and, 76

Sweden: 280; Denmark (Union of Kalmar) and, 75; Hanseatic League and, 75; Reformations and, 131; relations with Poland and, 91–92; Spanish Habsburg overextension and, 186; Thirty Years' War and, 241n15, 269; Westphalian Hypothesis and, 280

Swiss Confederation, 73, 76, 85, 89, 167–68, 278; Dutch Revolt and, 129, 220; French Wars of Religion and, 109, 247, 257; Holy Roman Empire and, 82, 85; military-technical change and, 76, 87–88

Switzerland, 76, 90

Syria, 21, 26, 58, 297

systemic norms. *See* norms

Taliban, 41, 297

taxation, 4, 5–6, 8–9, 122–23, 141, 148, 211, 270. *See also* servicios; Tenth Penny

Taylor, Peter, 299

te Brake, Wayne, 7, 124, 154–56, 280

technology, 87, 90, 297, 299; hegemonic-order theory and, 31; realism and, 11; relationalism and, 66. *See also* military-technical change

Tenth Penny, 211–12, 213–14

terrorism, 3, 33; networks and, 42n99

Teschke, Benno, 281

Teutonic Order, 89, 158

Théodore of Bèze, 247, 255

Theory of International Politics (Waltz), 11

Thirty Years' War, 18–19, 265–69, 271–73; Augsburg (Peace of) and, 182; balance of power and, 270; Catholicism and, 240; composite polities and, 271; confessionalization and, 280–81, 284; dynastic agglomeration and, 91; Huguenots and, 262; necessity (doctrine of) and, 240; Philip II's legacy and, 233–34; Reformations and, 2, 286; strategic overextension and, 270; Westphalian Hypothesis and, 2, 276, 278, 280. *See also* Union of Arms; Westphalia, Peace of (1648)

Tilly, Charles, 47, 49n128, 68, 116

Toft, Monica, 292–93, 295

Toledo, 141–42; *Comuneros* revolt and, 144, 145, 147

Tracy, James D., 135, 157, 161

transactional patterns, 22n7, 24–25, 45, 53, 64; anarchy and, 14–15; nested relational configurations and, 52; Prisoners' Dilemma and, 56; social ties and, 43; structure as, 24–25. *See also* networks

transnational actors; complex-interdependence theory and, 56; contemporary religious movements as, 295; composite polities and, 297; constructivism and, 36; divide-and-rule and, 109, 153; dynastic agglomeration and, 92, 98; dynasticism and, 96–97; French Wars of Religion and, 243; globalization and, 9, 21–22, 299–300; international change and, 287, 289; Islam and, 293; levels of analysis and, 22, 59–60; networks and, 42n99; papacy as, 97; realism and, 33–34; Reformations and, 3, 153, 287; relationalism and, 22n7, 25, 40, 59–60; religion and, 293, 295; Westphalia and, 3–4

trans-state movements. *See* transnational actors

treasure fleet, 218, 227, 268
Tripoli, 192
Tudors, 100, 110, 125, 127, 202, 287. See also *specific monarchs and personages*
Turks. *See* Ottoman Empire
Twelve Years' Truce (1609), 188, 194, 267–68
Two Kingdoms Doctrine, 282
Tyrone, earl of, 230

Ulrich, Duke of Württemberg, 169, 175
uniform contracting: state forms and, 72–73
Union of Arms, 271–72
Union of Arras, 220
Union of Utrecht, 220–24, 221; Huguenot activity compared with, 253
Unitarians, 279
United Nations, 38
United Provinces, 90, 98, 232
United States, 21, 48, 61; empire and, 296–97; nested relational configurations and, 51; religion and, 2, 295; social ties and, 41; Westphalia and, 3
unit type, 37–38
utopia, 65n176
Utrecht, 190, 219; Union of, 220–24
Utrecht, Treaty of, 277

Valencia, 60, 82, 100, 140, 148; *Comuneros* revolt and, 107, 144
Valois, house of, 86, 190; change processes and, 89; Charles V and, 135, 180; composite polities and, 93–94; Dutch Revolt and, 224–25; dynastic agglomeration and, 82; French Wars of Religion and, 236, 260, 264; Holy Roman Empire and, 80; Iberia and, 141; legitimacy and, 256; Reformations and, 287; resistance and, 122, 124; Schmalkaldic League's expansion and, 170, 172; Spanish hegemony and, 185–89, 186. See also *specific monarchs*
van Aytta, Vigilius, 190
Van Creveld, Martin, 299
van Stralen, Antoon, 209
Venetian Republic, 71, 82, 85, 88–89, 160; city-empires and, 77–78; Islam and, 192–93.
Venice. *See* Venetian Republic
Vervins, Treaty of (1598), 231

Vincent II, Duke of Mantua, 268
Vindiciae contran tyrannos (Du Plessis-Mornay), 255
Visconti, 86

Waite, Gary, 197
Wales, 83; Pilgrimage of Grace and, 154–55n59
Wallenstein, Albrecht von, 268–69
Walloons, 219, 200
Walt, Steven, 188
Waltz, Kenneth, 29, 53–54; generationalization and, 38; international change and, 11, 32–33; contrast with Mearsheimer and, 33n54
Wat Tyler rebellion, 156
weak states, 17, 59
Weber, Max, 65, 65n176, 71; Gorski, Philip, and, 284
Wendt, Alexander, 11, 34; collective identification and, 49, 53, 57
West Indies, 7, 223, 232
Westphalia, Peace of (1648), 1–5, 18–19, 275–79; Catholicism and, 240; Charles V's political failures and, 179; confessionalization and, 265, 283–85; constructivism and, 38; dynastic-imperialism and, 67; legitimacy and, 256; Reformations and, 2–3; relationalism and, 57; state formation and, 70; Thirty Years' War and, 266, 273–74
Westphalian Hypothesis, 273–75, 278, 281; Reformations and, 286, 289
"Westphalian Moment." *See* Westphalian Hypothesis
William of Orange, 190, 210, 221–22, 278; anti-Granvelle campaign, 200–201; assassination of, 223; Beggars and, 202–4; Dutch Revolt and, 207, 212–13, 216, 218–19, 226; dynastic practices and, 198; French Wars of Religion and, 249; Netherlands' governance and, 198
William V of Jülich-Cleves, 171
Wohlforth, William C., 29, 57
Wood, James, 133, 261
World War I, 58
World War II, 300
Worms, Edict of (1521), 152–53, 160, 162, 166; *Comuneros* revolt and, 153n52

yoking, 46–48, 55; confessionalization and, 284
Yugoslavia, 295

Zagorin, Perez, 107, 124
Zápolyai, John, 162

Zeeland, 123, 190, 214, 215, 216, 220–21, 222, 224, 226; Elizabeth and, 223n140
Zúñiga, Don Baltasar de, 233
Zwingli, Huldrych, 164, 167
Zwinglians, 47n121, 164, 166–68